MEAL

BLUE DELLIQUANTI
WITH SOLEIL HO

inquiry@ironcircus.com   www.ironcircus.com

IRON
CIRCUS
COMICS

strange and amazing

Publisher's Cataloging-In-Publication Data
(Prepared by The Donohue Group, Inc.)

Names: Delliquanti, Blue. | Ho, Soleil.
Title: Meal / Blue Delliquanti, with Soleil Ho.
Description: [Chicago, Illinois] : Iron Circus Comics, [2018]
Identifiers: ISBN 9781945820304
Subjects: LCSH: Cooking (Insects)--Comic books, strips, etc. | Entomophagy--Comic
    books, strips, etc. | Women cooks--Comic books, strips, etc. | LCGFT: Graphic
    novels.
Classification: LCC PN6727.D45 M43 2018 | DDC 741.5973 [Fic]--dc23

FEB 0 5 2019

first printing: October 2018   printed in China   ISBN: 978-1-945820-30-4

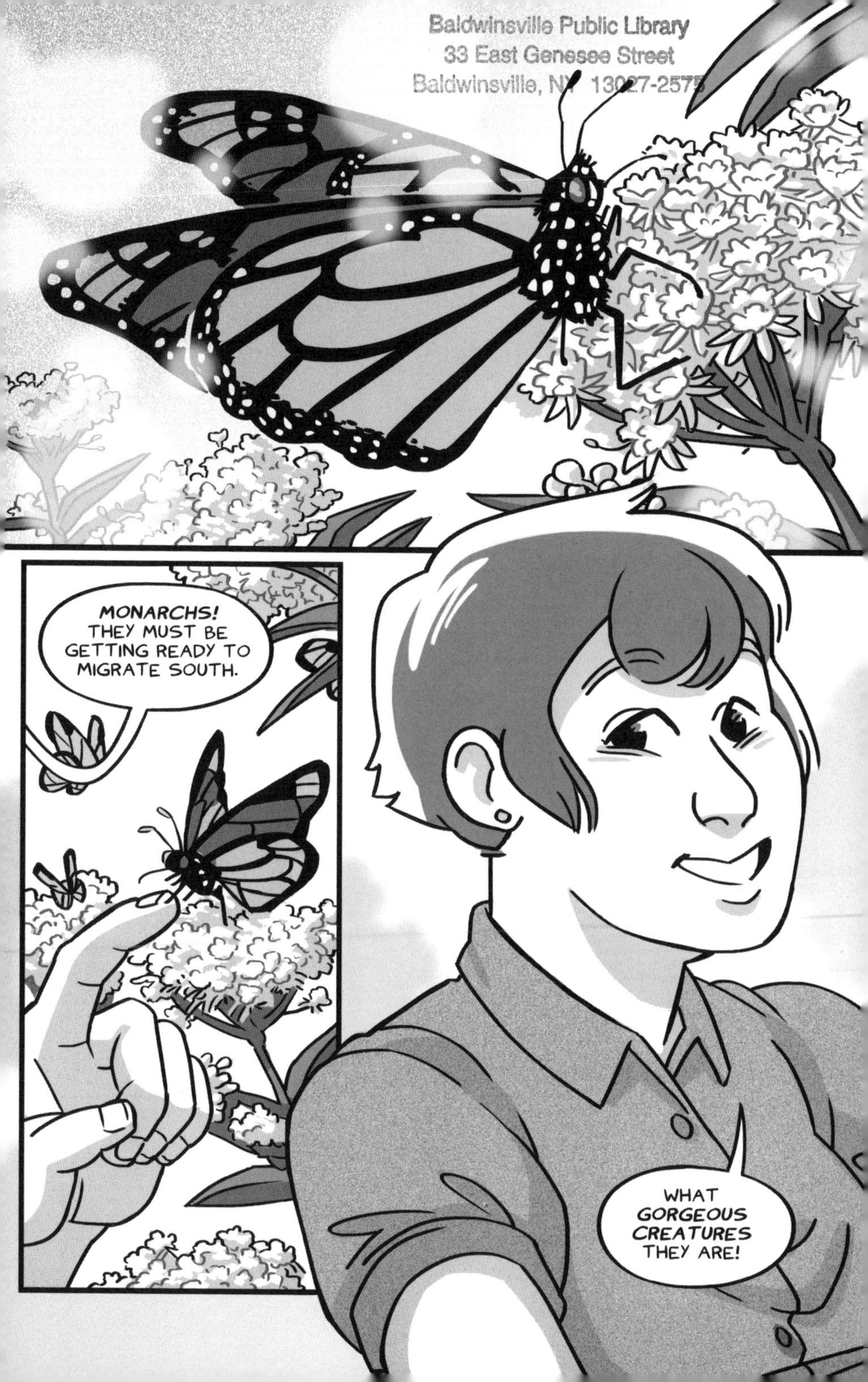
MONARCHS! THEY MUST BE GETTING READY TO MIGRATE SOUTH.
WHAT GORGEOUS CREATURES THEY ARE!

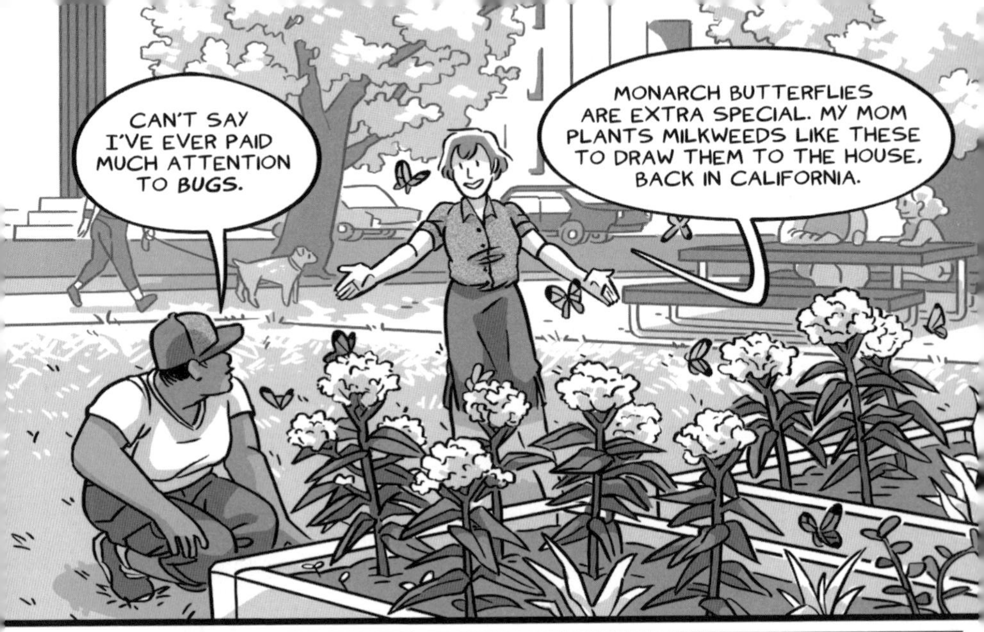
CAN'T SAY I'VE EVER PAID MUCH ATTENTION TO **BUGS**.
MONARCH BUTTERFLIES ARE EXTRA SPECIAL. MY MOM PLANTS MILKWEEDS LIKE THESE TO DRAW THEM TO THE HOUSE, BACK IN CALIFORNIA.

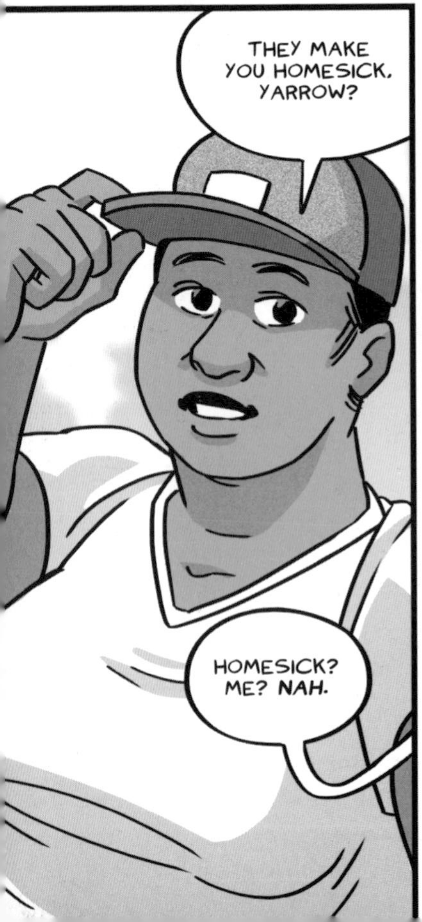
THEY MAKE YOU HOMESICK, YARROW?
HOMESICK? ME? **NAH**.

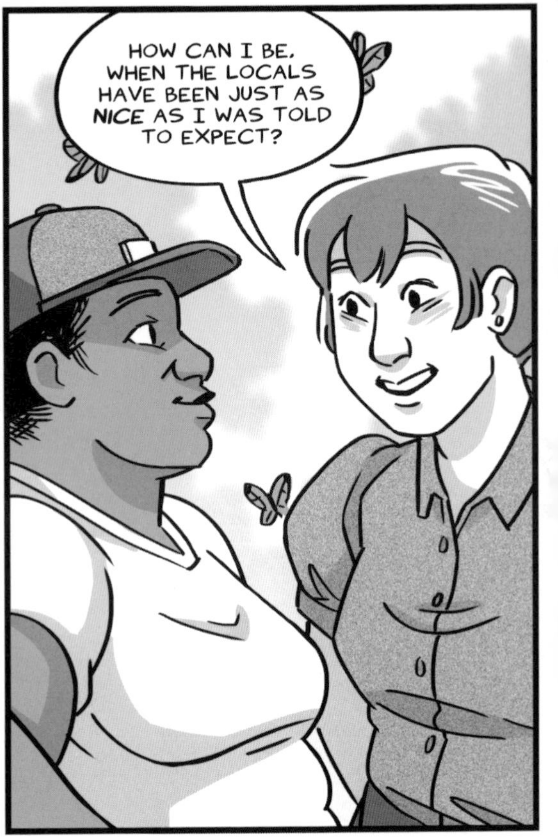
HOW CAN I BE, WHEN THE LOCALS HAVE BEEN JUST AS **NICE** AS I WAS TOLD TO EXPECT?

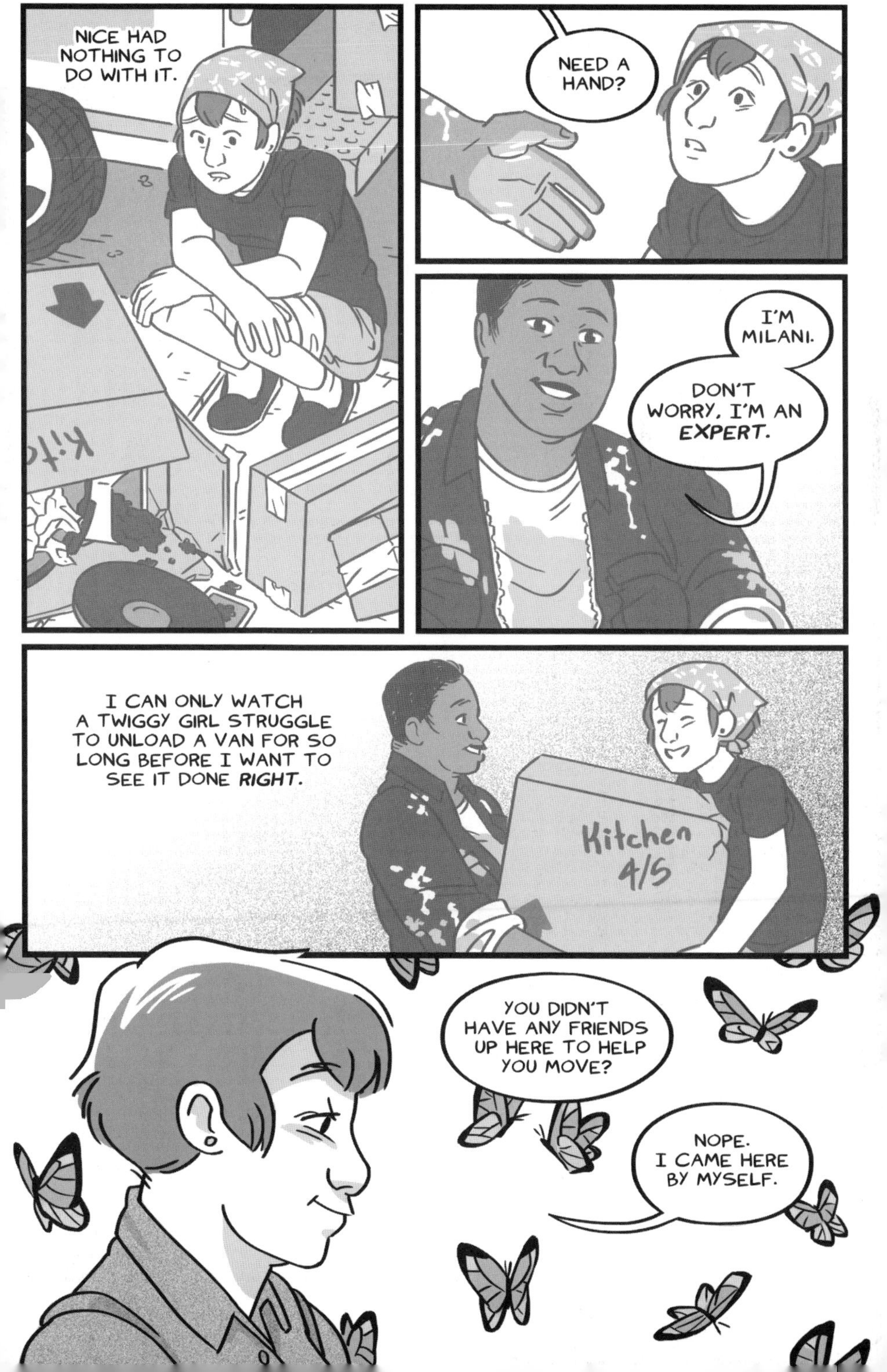

NICE HAD NOTHING TO DO WITH IT.
NEED A HAND?
I'M MILANI.
DON'T WORRY, I'M AN *EXPERT*.
I CAN ONLY WATCH A TWIGGY GIRL STRUGGLE TO UNLOAD A VAN FOR SO LONG BEFORE I WANT TO SEE IT DONE *RIGHT*.
Kitchen 4/5
YOU DIDN'T HAVE ANY FRIENDS UP HERE TO HELP YOU MOVE?
NOPE. I CAME HERE BY MYSELF.

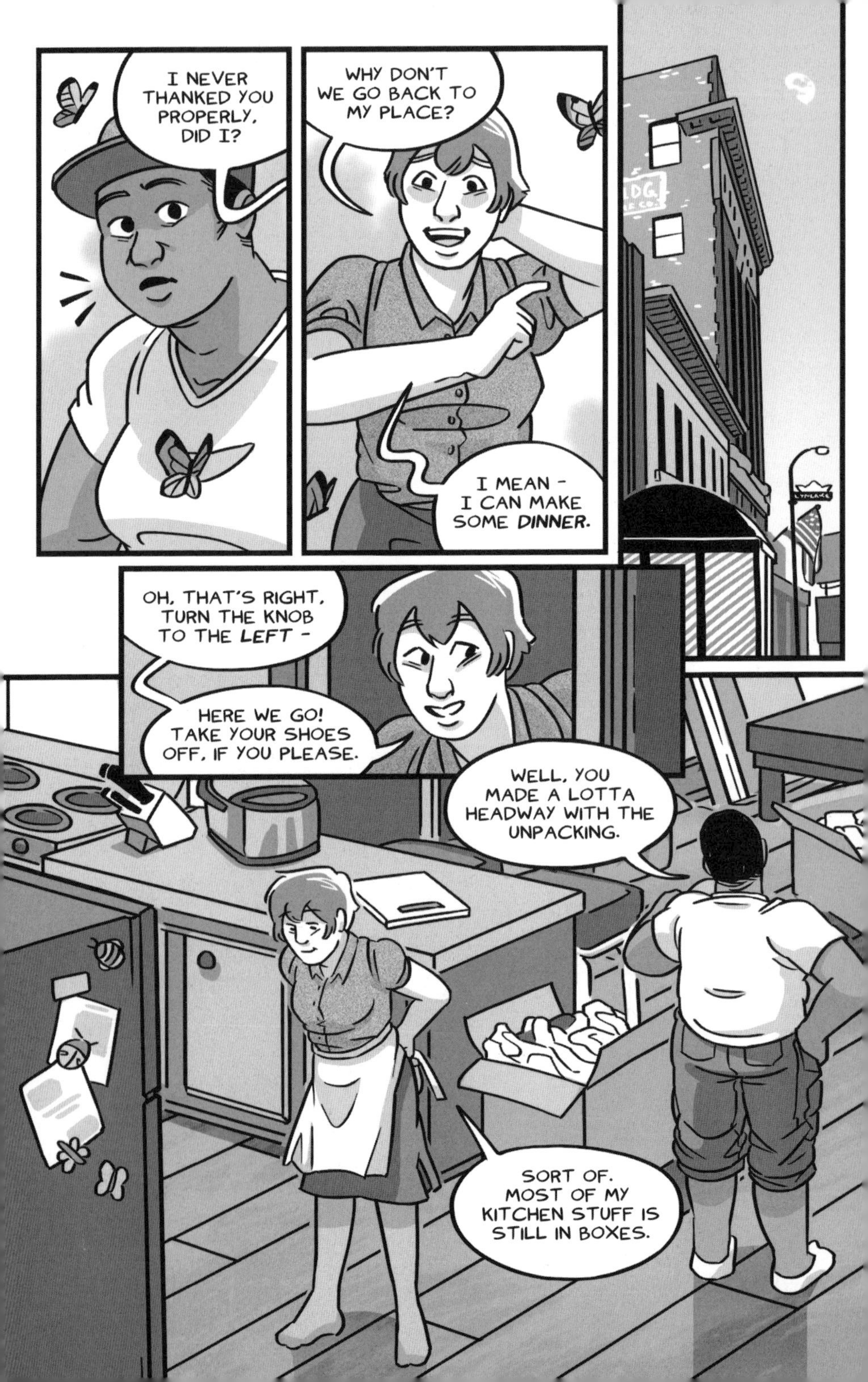
I NEVER THANKED YOU PROPERLY, DID I?
WHY DON'T WE GO BACK TO MY PLACE?
I MEAN - I CAN MAKE SOME **DINNER**.
OH, THAT'S RIGHT, TURN THE KNOB TO THE **LEFT** -
HERE WE GO! TAKE YOUR SHOES OFF, IF YOU PLEASE.
WELL, YOU MADE A LOTTA HEADWAY WITH THE UNPACKING.
SORT OF. MOST OF MY KITCHEN STUFF IS STILL IN BOXES.

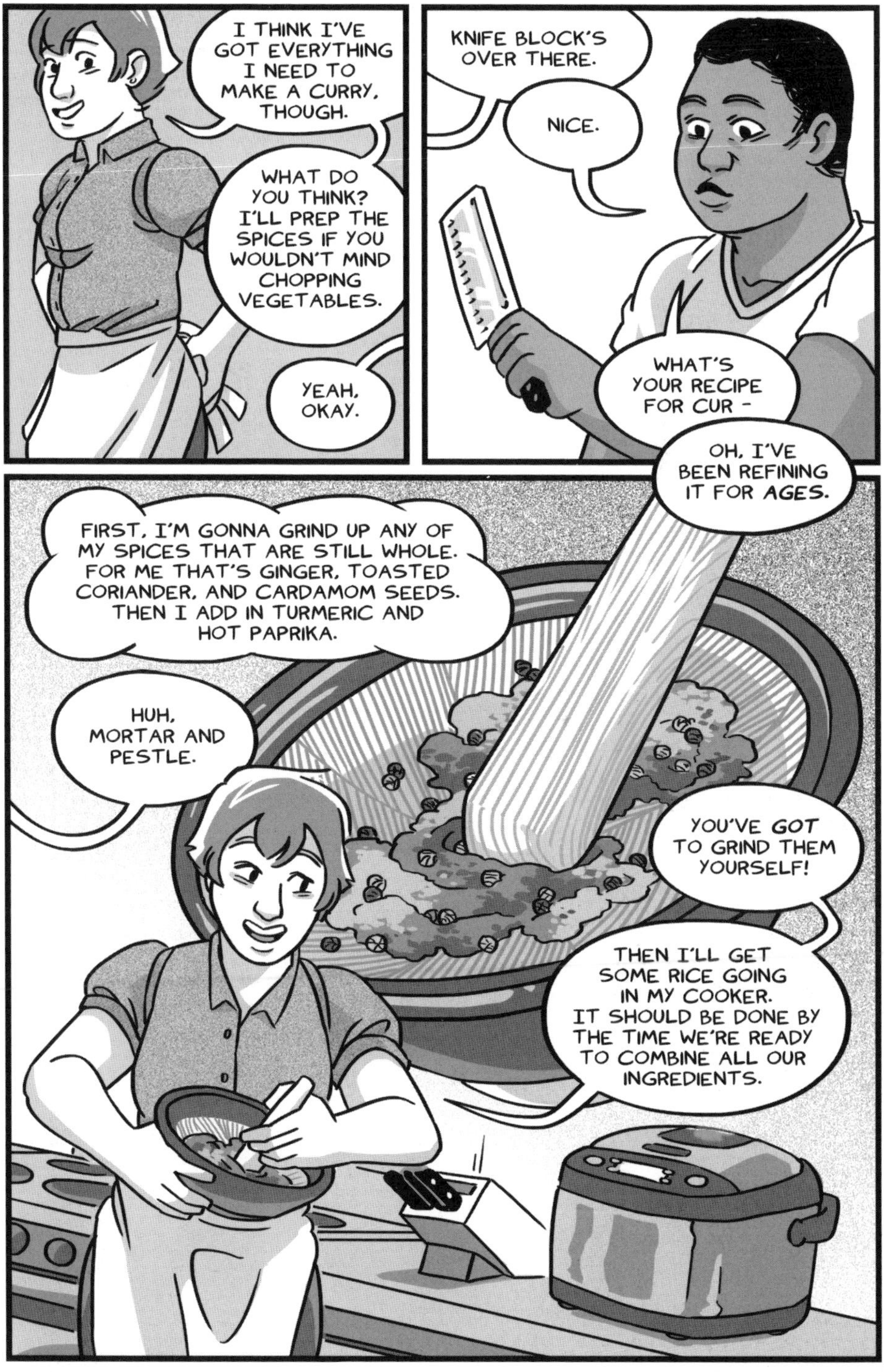
I THINK I'VE GOT EVERYTHING I NEED TO MAKE A CURRY, THOUGH.
WHAT DO YOU THINK? I'LL PREP THE SPICES IF YOU WOULDN'T MIND CHOPPING VEGETABLES.
YEAH, OKAY.
KNIFE BLOCK'S OVER THERE.
NICE.
WHAT'S YOUR RECIPE FOR CUR -
OH, I'VE BEEN REFINING IT FOR AGES.
FIRST, I'M GONNA GRIND UP ANY OF MY SPICES THAT ARE STILL WHOLE. FOR ME THAT'S GINGER, TOASTED CORIANDER, AND CARDAMOM SEEDS. THEN I ADD IN TURMERIC AND HOT PAPRIKA.
HUH, MORTAR AND PESTLE.
YOU'VE GOT TO GRIND THEM YOURSELF!
THEN I'LL GET SOME RICE GOING IN MY COOKER. IT SHOULD BE DONE BY THE TIME WE'RE READY TO COMBINE ALL OUR INGREDIENTS.

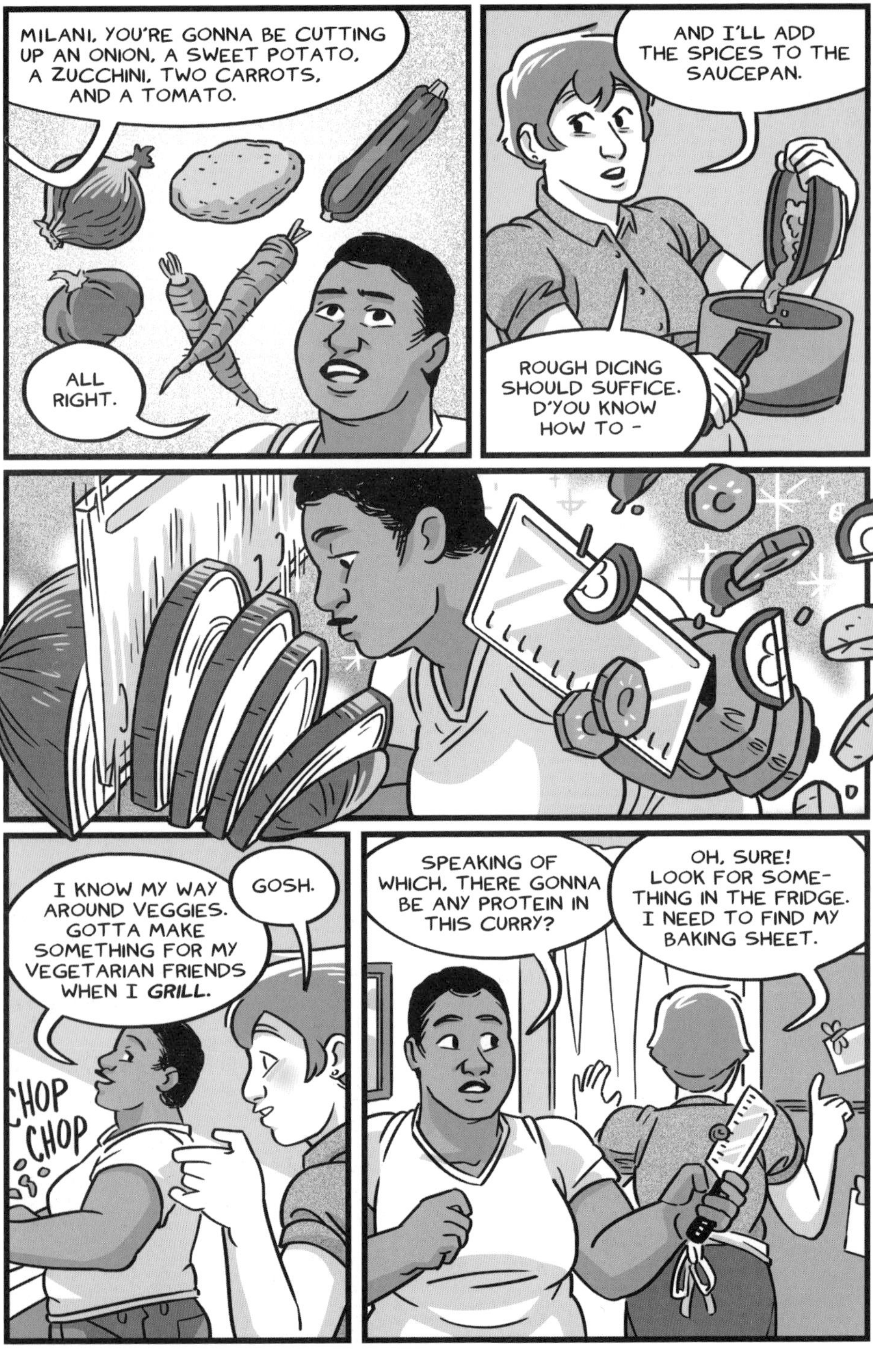
MILANI, YOU'RE GONNA BE CUTTING UP AN ONION, A SWEET POTATO, A ZUCCHINI, TWO CARROTS, AND A TOMATO.
ALL RIGHT.
AND I'LL ADD THE SPICES TO THE SAUCEPAN.
ROUGH DICING SHOULD SUFFICE. D'YOU KNOW HOW TO -
I KNOW MY WAY AROUND VEGGIES. GOTTA MAKE SOMETHING FOR MY VEGETARIAN FRIENDS WHEN I **GRILL.**
GOSH.
CHOP CHOP
SPEAKING OF WHICH, THERE GONNA BE ANY PROTEIN IN THIS CURRY?
OH, SURE! LOOK FOR SOME-THING IN THE FRIDGE. I NEED TO FIND MY BAKING SHEET.

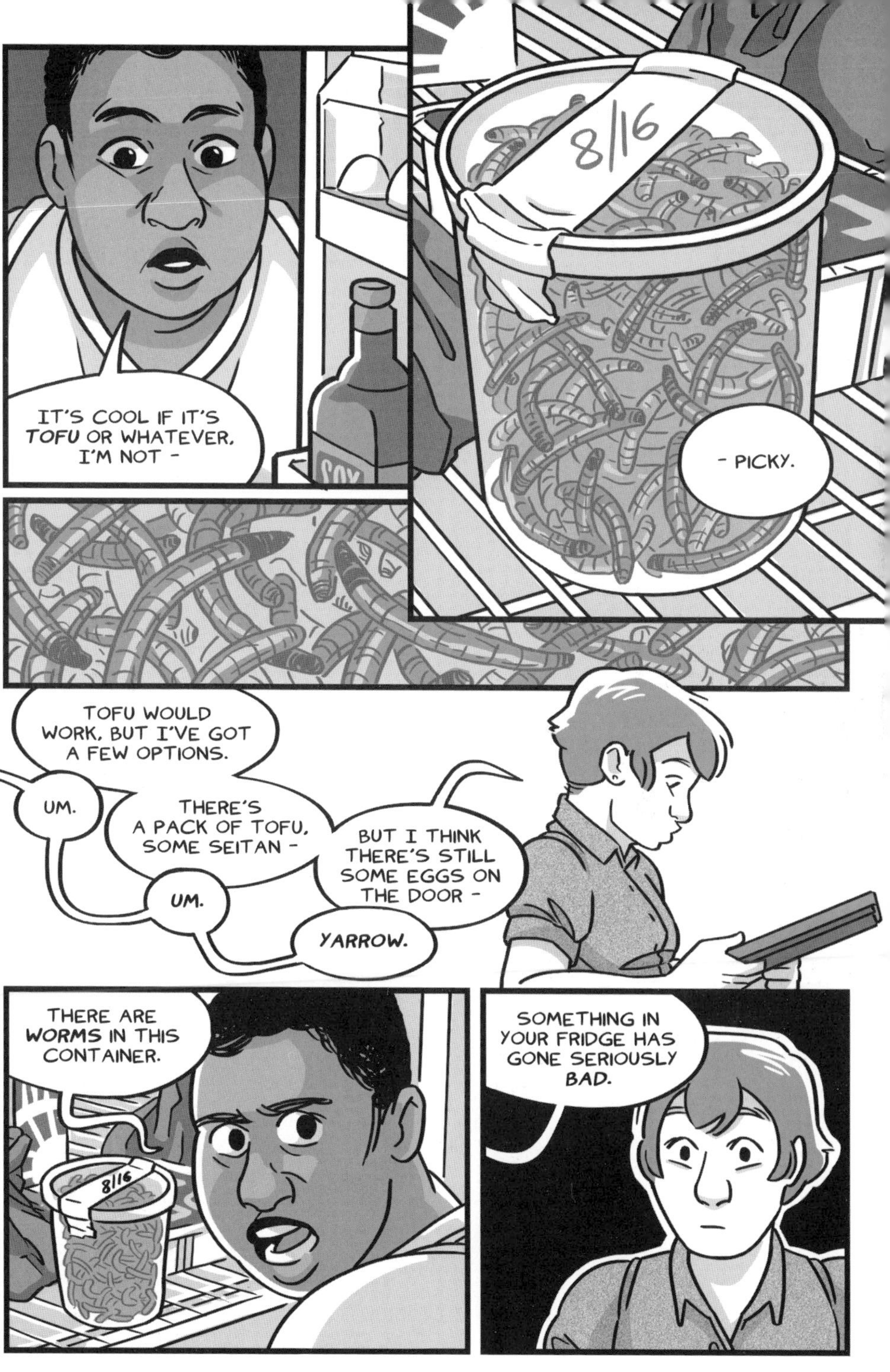
IT'S COOL IF IT'S *TOFU* OR WHATEVER, I'M NOT -
8/16
- PICKY.
SOY
TOFU WOULD WORK, BUT I'VE GOT A FEW OPTIONS.
UM.
THERE'S A PACK OF TOFU, SOME SEITAN -
UM.
BUT I THINK THERE'S STILL SOME EGGS ON THE DOOR -
YARROW.
THERE ARE **WORMS** IN THIS CONTAINER.
8/16
SOMETHING IN YOUR FRIDGE HAS GONE SERIOUSLY **BAD.**

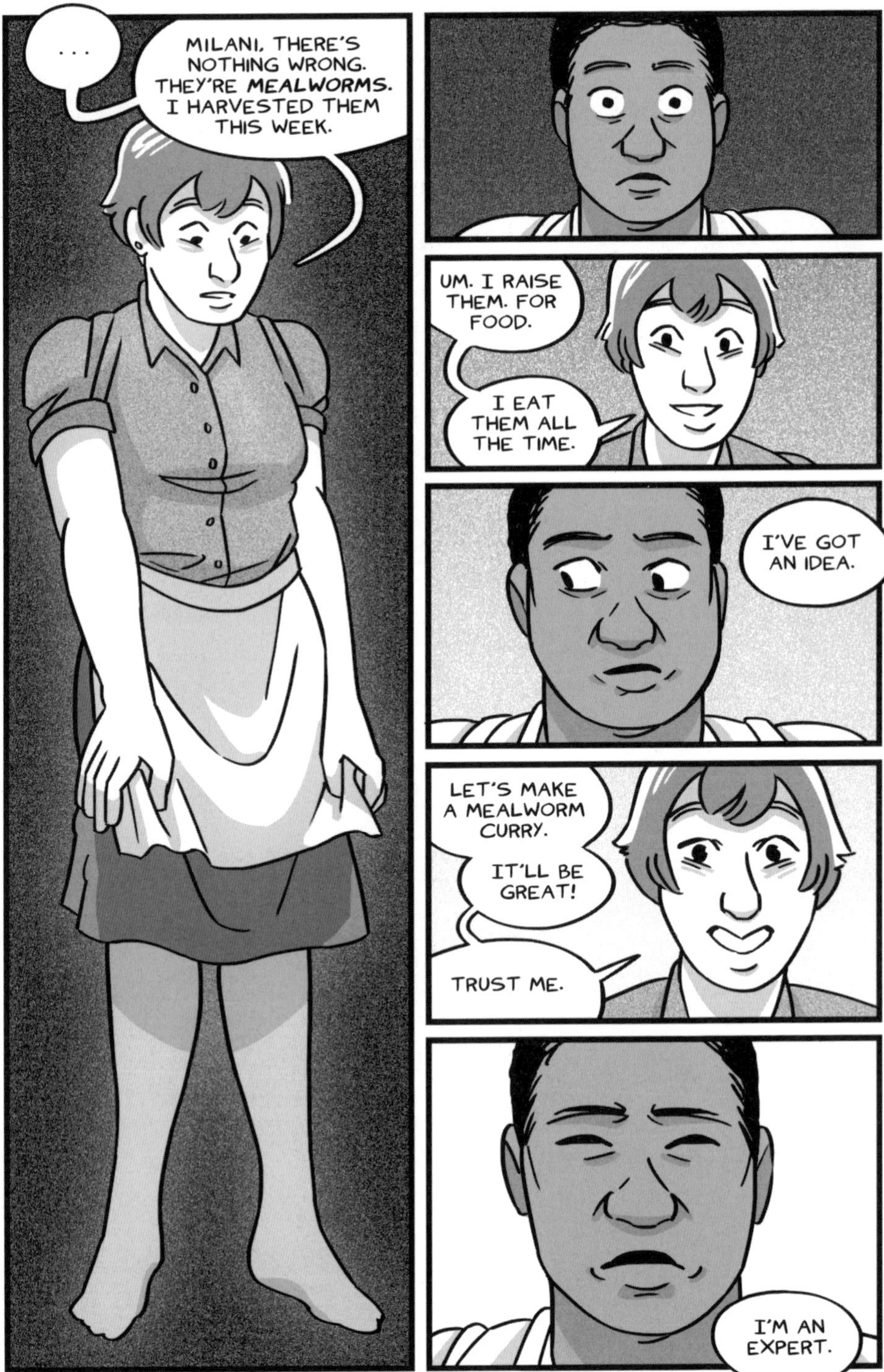
. . .
MILANI, THERE'S NOTHING WRONG. THEY'RE MEALWORMS. I HARVESTED THEM THIS WEEK.
UM. I RAISE THEM. FOR FOOD.
I EAT THEM ALL THE TIME.
I'VE GOT AN IDEA.
LET'S MAKE A MEALWORM CURRY.
IT'LL BE GREAT!
TRUST ME.
I'M AN EXPERT.

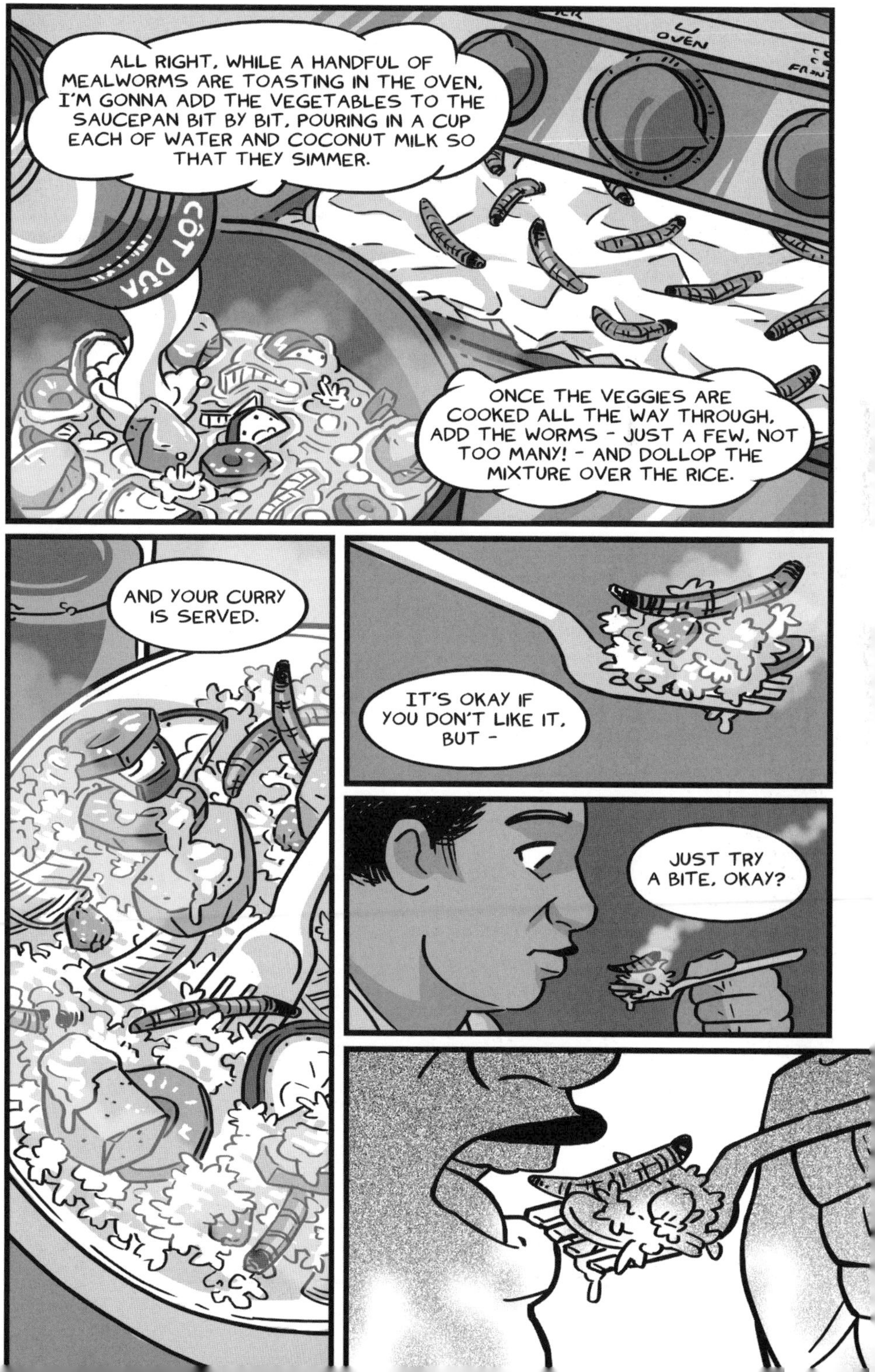
ALL RIGHT, WHILE A HANDFUL OF MEALWORMS ARE TOASTING IN THE OVEN, I'M GONNA ADD THE VEGETABLES TO THE SAUCEPAN BIT BY BIT, POURING IN A CUP EACH OF WATER AND COCONUT MILK SO THAT THEY SIMMER.
OVEN
CÔT DỪA
ONCE THE VEGGIES ARE COOKED ALL THE WAY THROUGH, ADD THE WORMS - JUST A FEW, NOT TOO MANY! - AND DOLLOP THE MIXTURE OVER THE RICE.
AND YOUR CURRY IS SERVED.
IT'S OKAY IF YOU DON'T LIKE IT, BUT -
JUST TRY A BITE, OKAY?

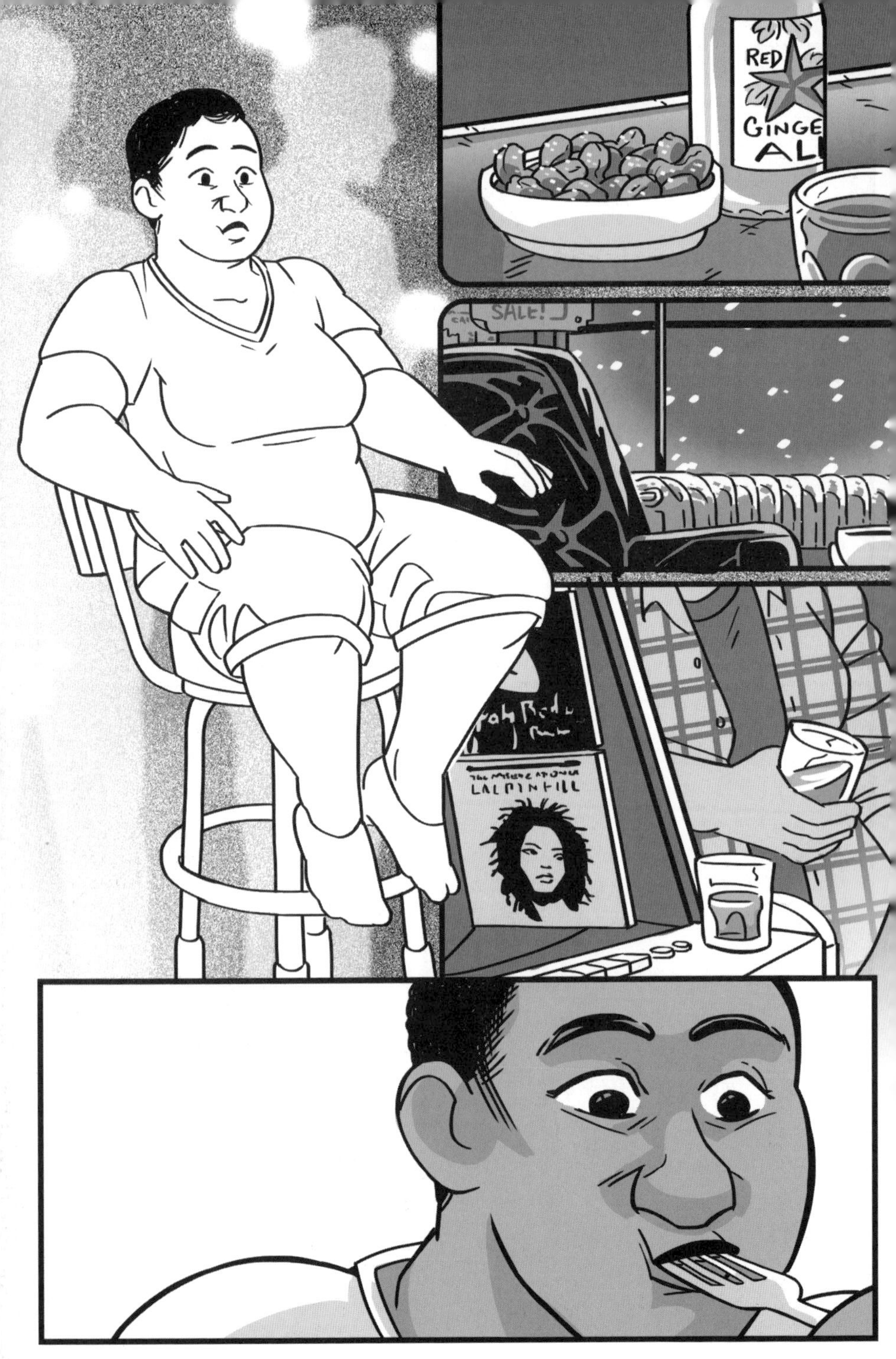
RED
GINGE
AL
SALE!

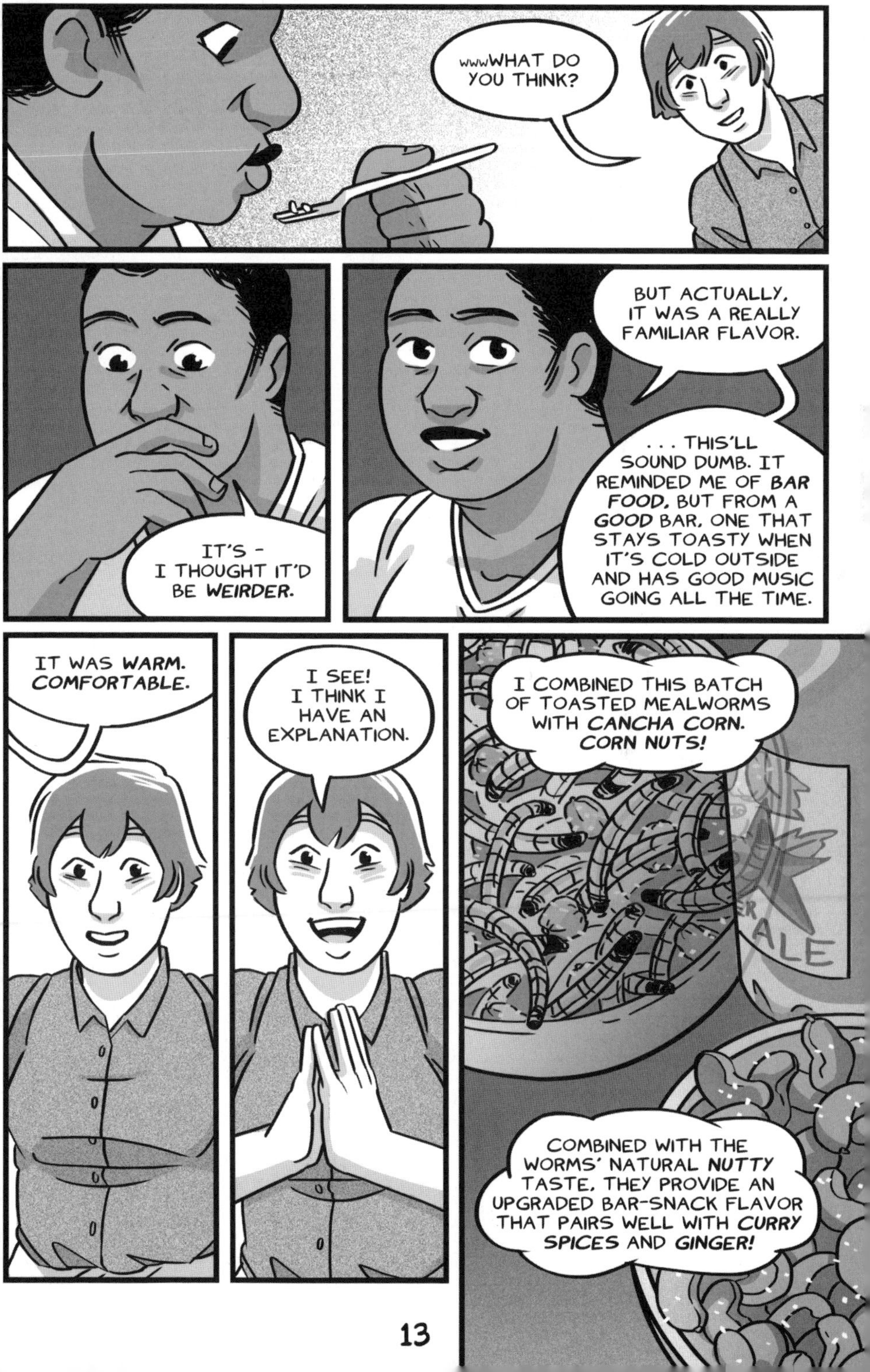
wwwWHAT DO YOU THINK?
IT'S - I THOUGHT IT'D BE **WEIRDER**.
BUT ACTUALLY, IT WAS A REALLY FAMILIAR FLAVOR.
. . . THIS'LL SOUND DUMB. IT REMINDED ME OF ***BAR FOOD***, BUT FROM A ***GOOD*** BAR, ONE THAT STAYS TOASTY WHEN IT'S COLD OUTSIDE AND HAS GOOD MUSIC GOING ALL THE TIME.
IT WAS **WARM**. ***COMFORTABLE***.
I SEE! I THINK I HAVE AN EXPLANATION.
I COMBINED THIS BATCH OF TOASTED MEALWORMS WITH ***CANCHA CORN***. ***CORN NUTS!***
ALE
COMBINED WITH THE WORMS' NATURAL ***NUTTY*** TASTE, THEY PROVIDE AN UPGRADED BAR-SNACK FLAVOR THAT PAIRS WELL WITH ***CURRY SPICES*** AND ***GINGER!***

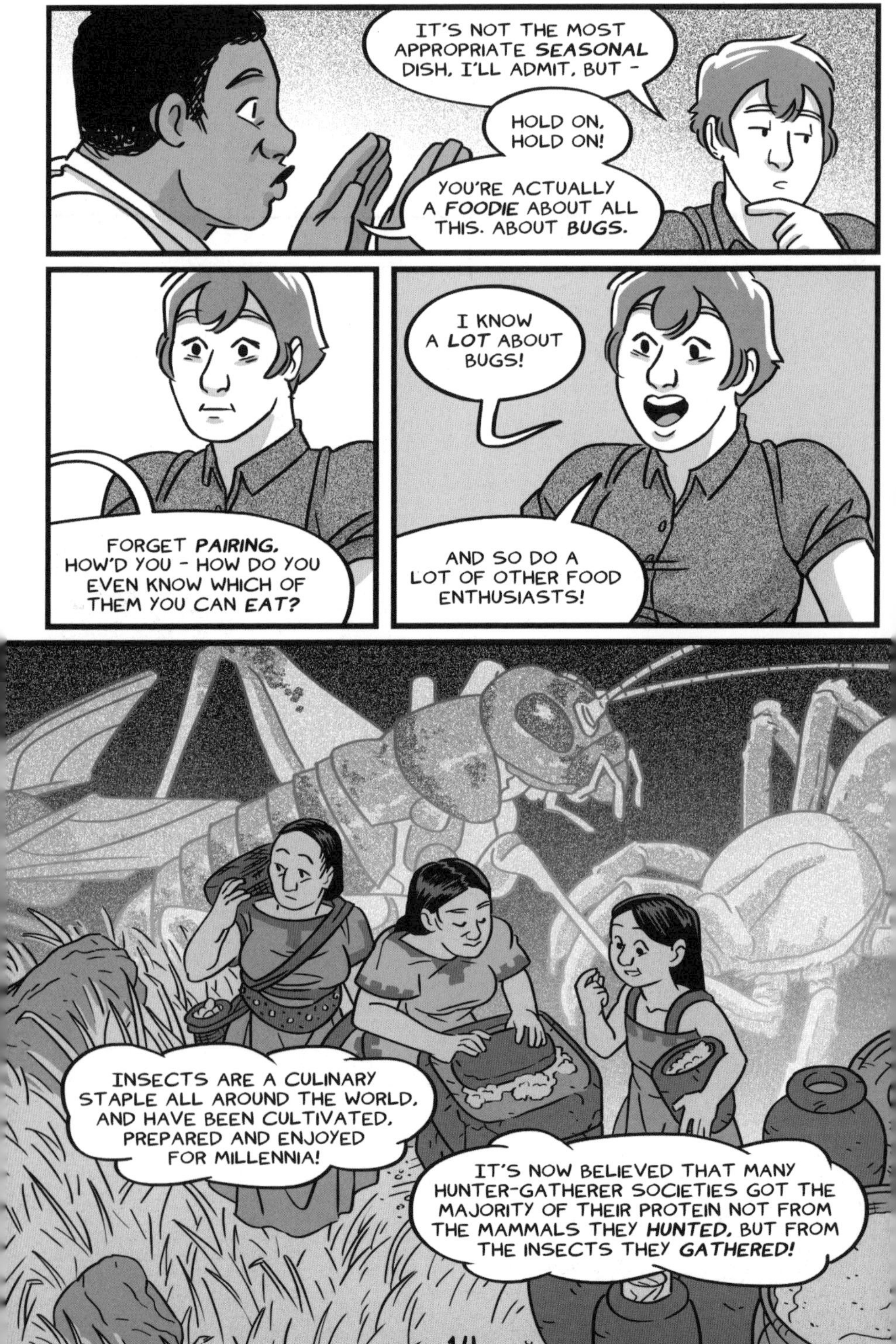
IT'S NOT THE MOST APPROPRIATE **SEASONAL** DISH, I'LL ADMIT, BUT -
HOLD ON, HOLD ON!
YOU'RE ACTUALLY A *FOODIE* ABOUT ALL THIS. ABOUT **BUGS.**
FORGET **PAIRING.** HOW'D YOU - HOW DO YOU EVEN KNOW WHICH OF THEM YOU CAN **EAT?**
I KNOW A ***LOT*** ABOUT BUGS!
AND SO DO A LOT OF OTHER FOOD ENTHUSIASTS!
INSECTS ARE A CULINARY STAPLE ALL AROUND THE WORLD, AND HAVE BEEN CULTIVATED, PREPARED AND ENJOYED FOR MILLENNIA!
IT'S NOW BELIEVED THAT MANY HUNTER-GATHERER SOCIETIES GOT THE MAJORITY OF THEIR PROTEIN NOT FROM THE MAMMALS THEY ***HUNTED,*** BUT FROM THE INSECTS THEY ***GATHERED!***

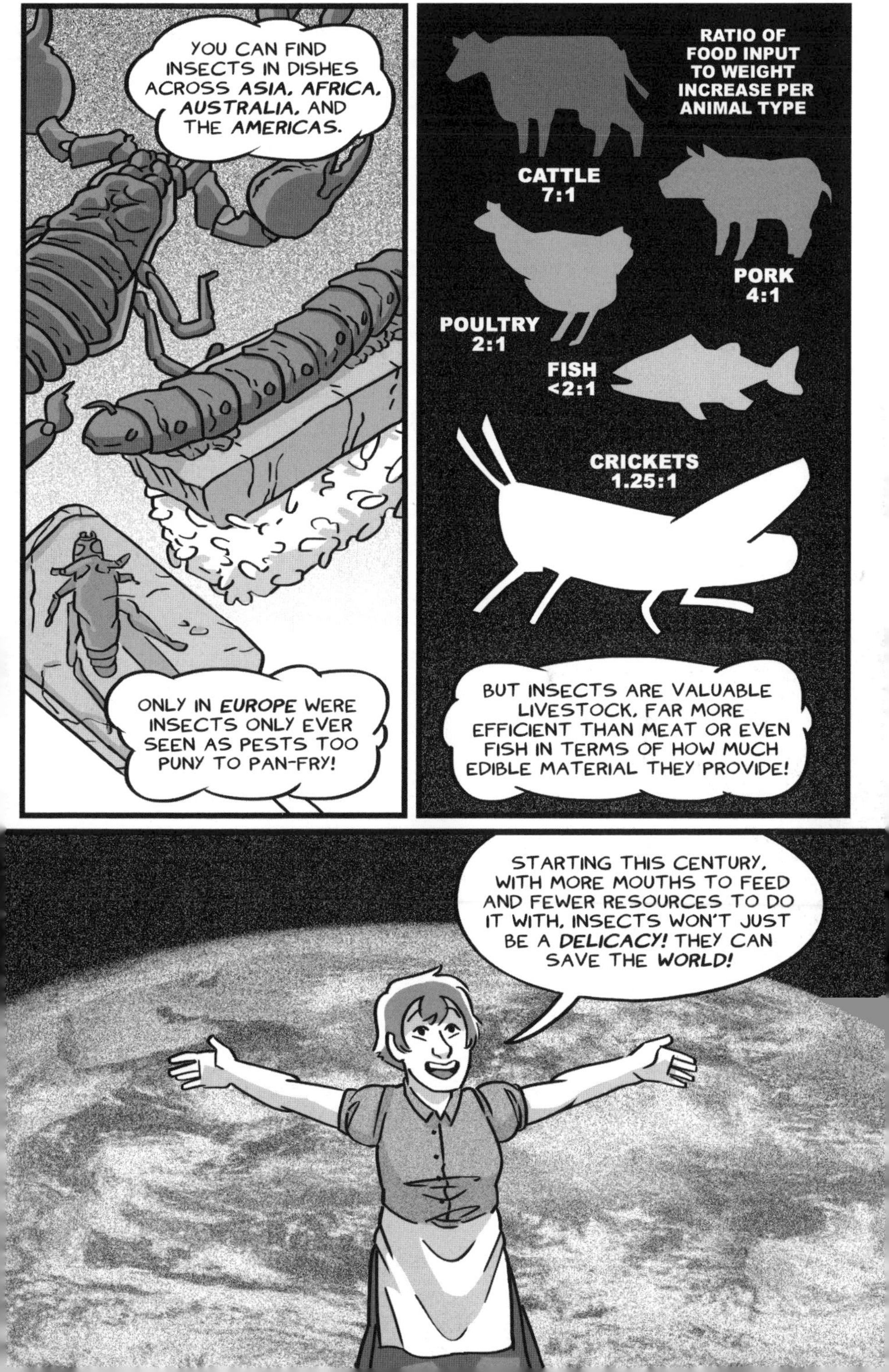
YOU CAN FIND INSECTS IN DISHES ACROSS ASIA, AFRICA, AUSTRALIA, AND THE AMERICAS.
ONLY IN EUROPE WERE INSECTS ONLY EVER SEEN AS PESTS TOO PUNY TO PAN-FRY!
RATIO OF FOOD INPUT TO WEIGHT INCREASE PER ANIMAL TYPE
CATTLE 7:1
PORK 4:1
POULTRY 2:1
FISH <2:1
CRICKETS 1.25:1
BUT INSECTS ARE VALUABLE LIVESTOCK, FAR MORE EFFICIENT THAN MEAT OR EVEN FISH IN TERMS OF HOW MUCH EDIBLE MATERIAL THEY PROVIDE!
STARTING THIS CENTURY, WITH MORE MOUTHS TO FEED AND FEWER RESOURCES TO DO IT WITH, INSECTS WON'T JUST BE A DELICACY! THEY CAN SAVE THE WORLD!

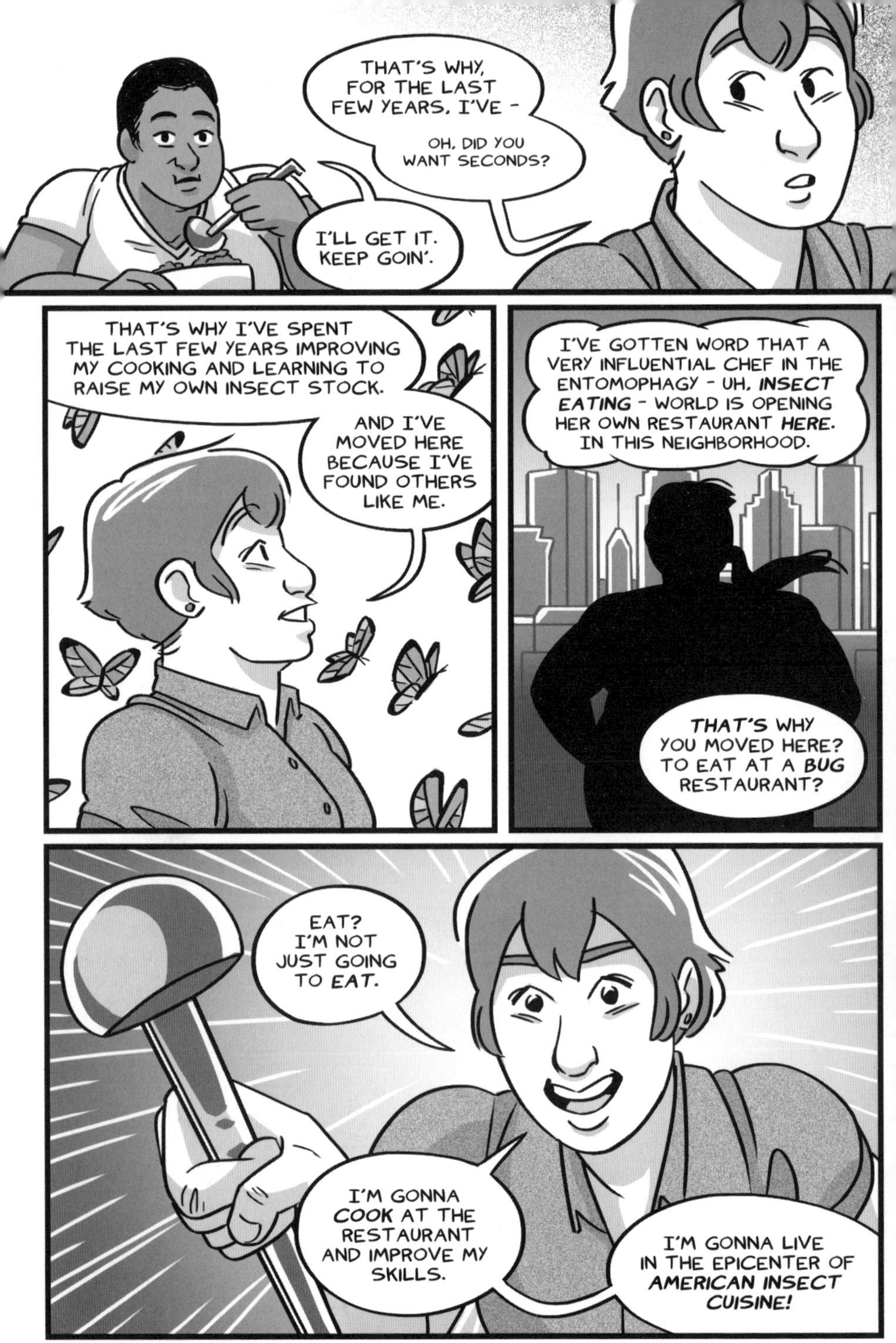

THAT'S WHY, FOR THE LAST FEW YEARS, I'VE -
OH, DID YOU WANT SECONDS?
I'LL GET IT. KEEP GOIN'.
THAT'S WHY I'VE SPENT THE LAST FEW YEARS IMPROVING MY COOKING AND LEARNING TO RAISE MY OWN INSECT STOCK.
AND I'VE MOVED HERE BECAUSE I'VE FOUND OTHERS LIKE ME.
I'VE GOTTEN WORD THAT A VERY INFLUENTIAL CHEF IN THE ENTOMOPHAGY - UH, *INSECT EATING* - WORLD IS OPENING HER OWN RESTAURANT *HERE*. IN THIS NEIGHBORHOOD.
THAT'S WHY YOU MOVED HERE? TO EAT AT A *BUG* RESTAURANT?
EAT? I'M NOT JUST GOING TO *EAT*.
I'M GONNA *COOK* AT THE RESTAURANT AND IMPROVE MY SKILLS.
I'M GONNA LIVE IN THE EPICENTER OF *AMERICAN INSECT CUISINE!*

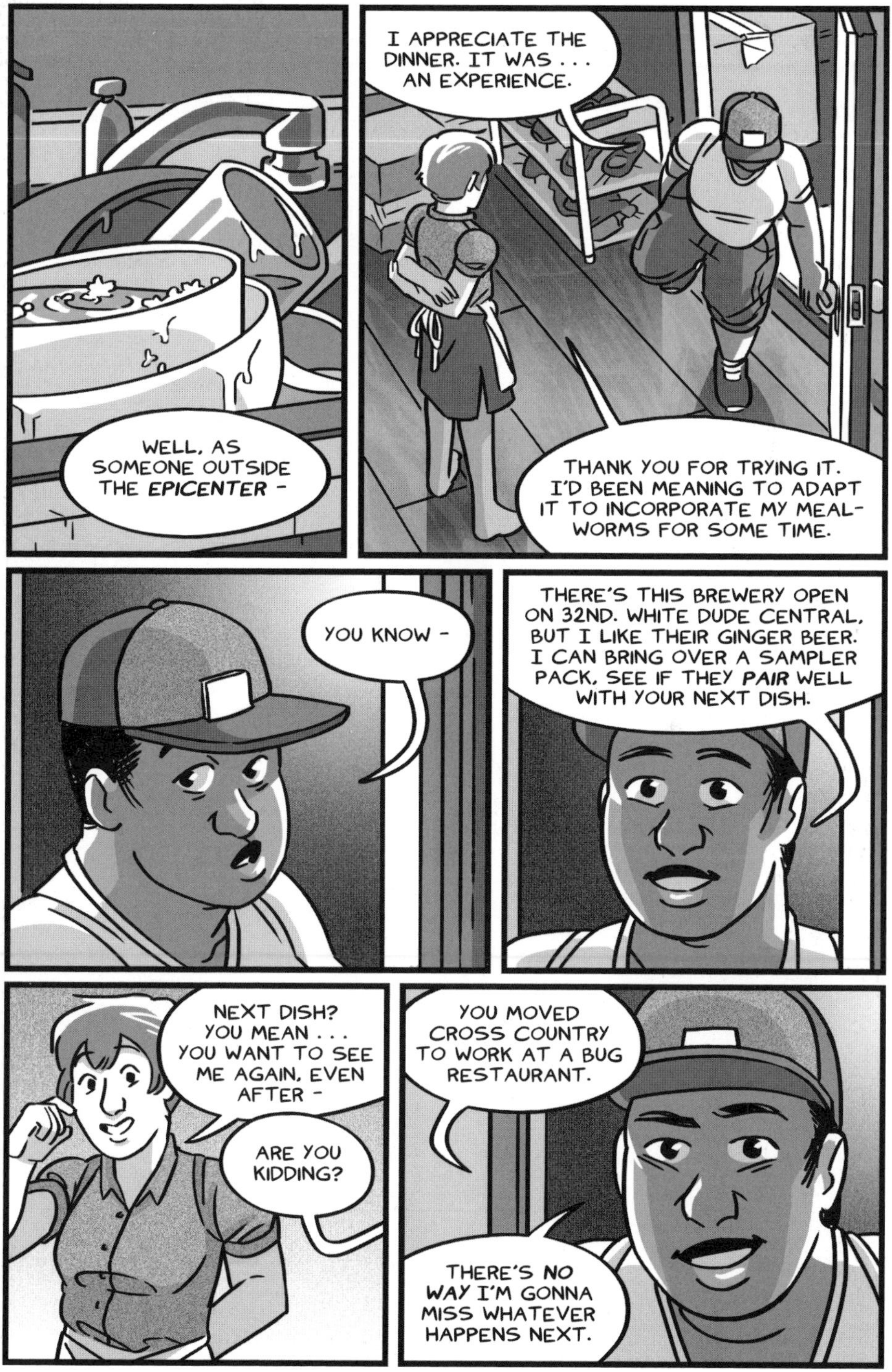
WELL, AS SOMEONE OUTSIDE THE **EPICENTER** –
I APPRECIATE THE DINNER. IT WAS . . . AN EXPERIENCE.
THANK YOU FOR TRYING IT. I'D BEEN MEANING TO ADAPT IT TO INCORPORATE MY MEAL-WORMS FOR SOME TIME.
YOU KNOW –
THERE'S THIS BREWERY OPEN ON 32ND. WHITE DUDE CENTRAL, BUT I LIKE THEIR GINGER BEER. I CAN BRING OVER A SAMPLER PACK, SEE IF THEY **PAIR** WELL WITH YOUR NEXT DISH.
NEXT DISH? YOU MEAN . . . YOU WANT TO SEE ME AGAIN, EVEN AFTER –
ARE YOU KIDDING?
YOU MOVED CROSS COUNTRY TO WORK AT A BUG RESTAURANT.
THERE'S **NO WAY** I'M GONNA MISS WHATEVER HAPPENS NEXT.

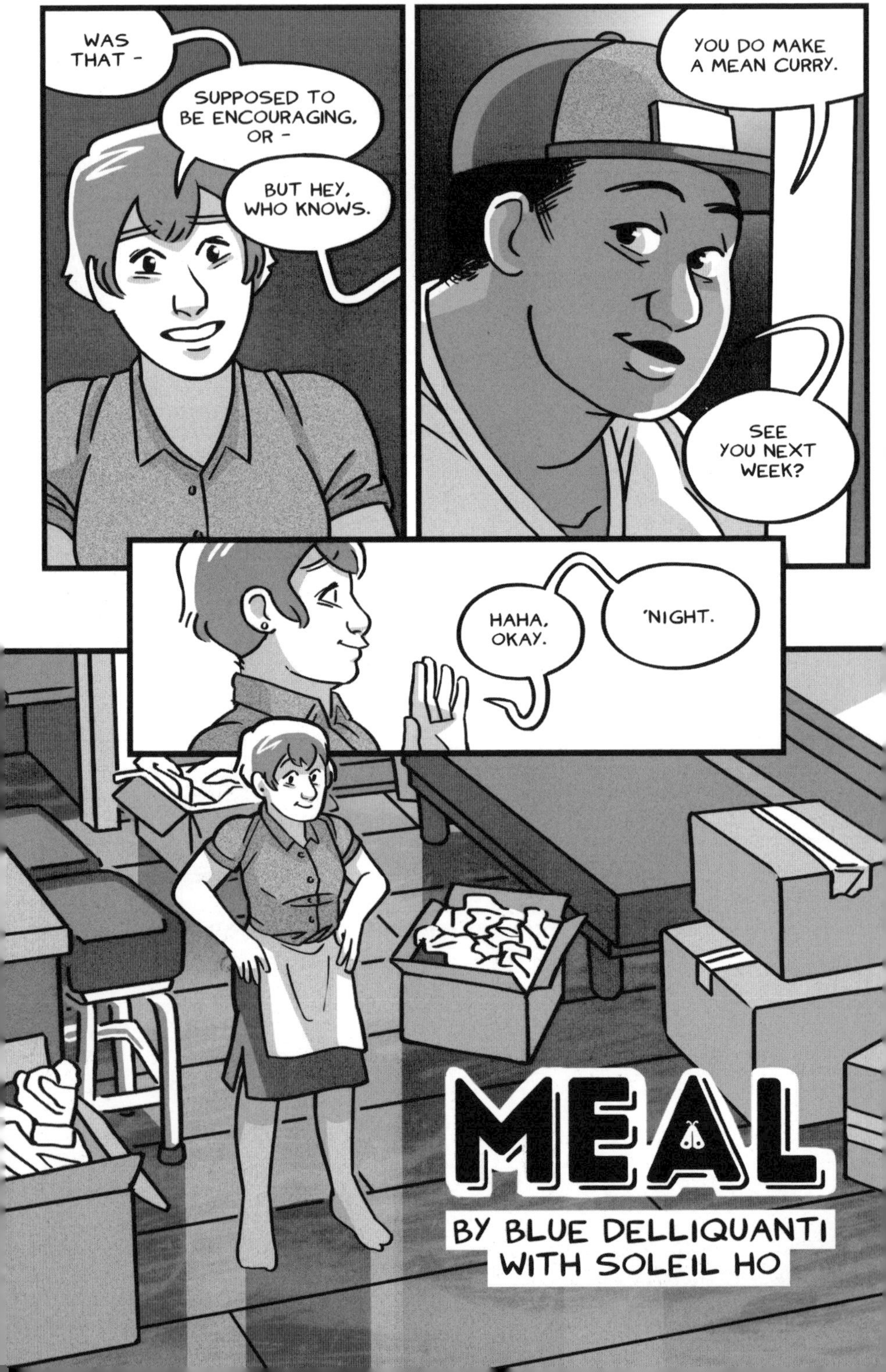
WAS THAT -
SUPPOSED TO BE ENCOURAGING, OR -
BUT HEY, WHO KNOWS.
YOU DO MAKE A MEAN CURRY.
SEE YOU NEXT WEEK?
HAHA, OKAY.
'NIGHT.
MEAL
BY BLUE DELLIQUANTI
WITH SOLEIL HO

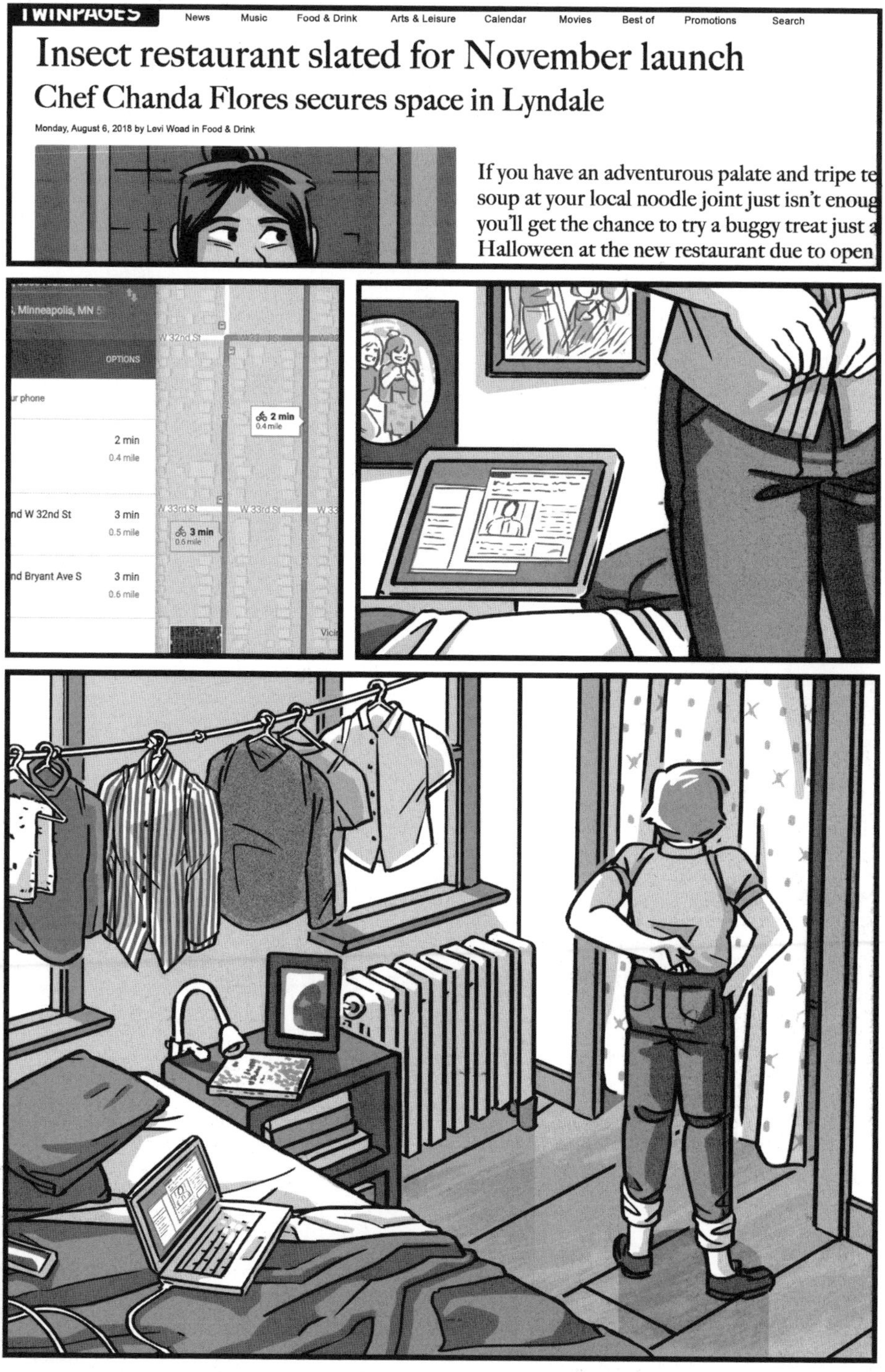
TWINPAGES
News
Music
Food & Drink
Arts & Leisure
Calendar
Movies
Best of
Promotions
Search
Insect restaurant slated for November launch
Chef Chanda Flores secures space in Lyndale
Monday, August 6, 2018 by Levi Woad in Food & Drink
If you have an adventurous palate and tripe te
soup at your local noodle joint just isn't enoug
you'll get the chance to try a buggy treat just a
Halloween at the new restaurant due to open
, Minneapolis, MN
OPTIONS
r phone
2 min
0.4 mile
nd W 32nd St
3 min
0.5 mile
nd Bryant Ave S
3 min
0.6 mile
W 32nd St
2 min
0.4 mile
W 33rd St
W 33rd St
3 min
0.6 mile

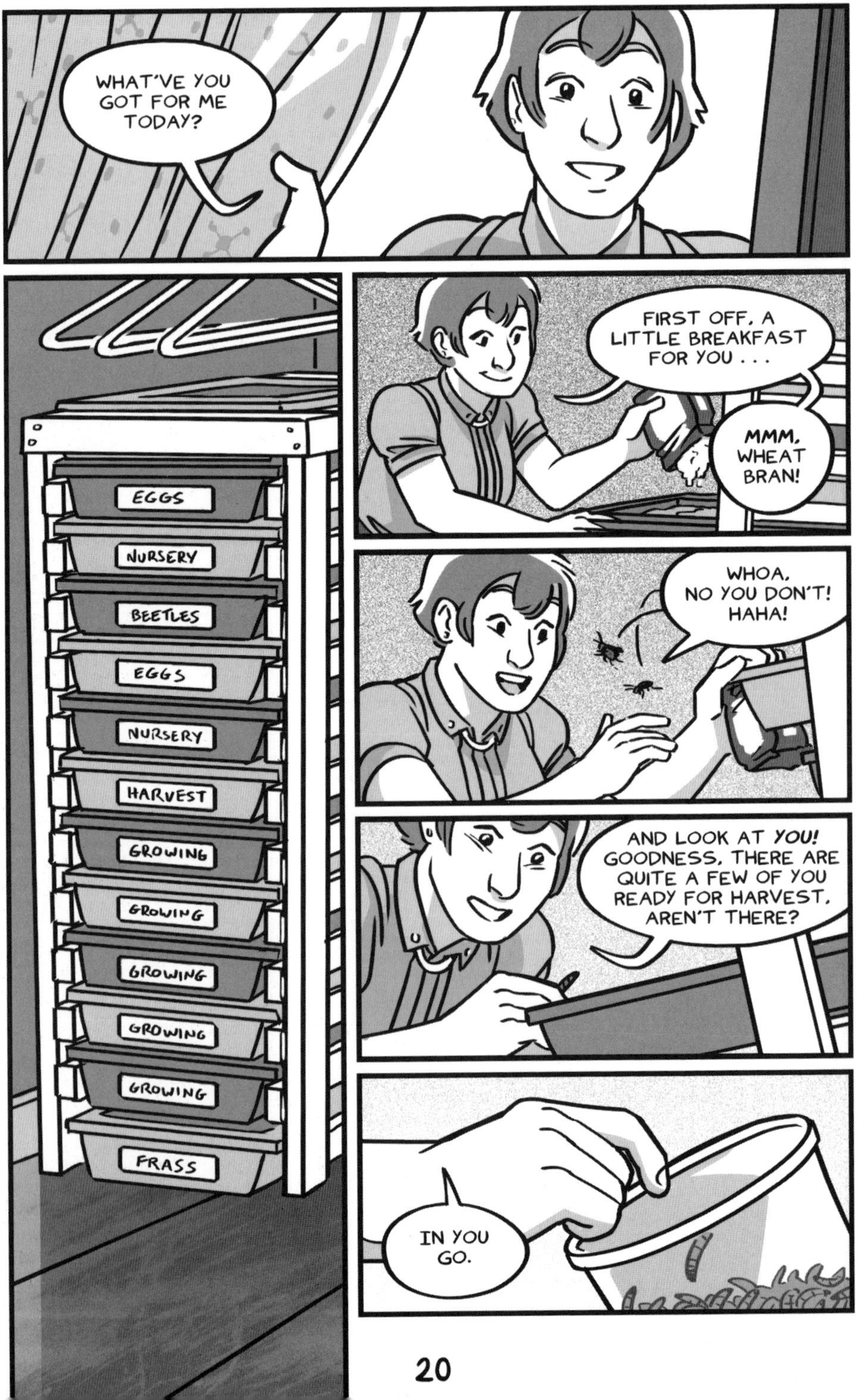
WHAT'VE YOU GOT FOR ME TODAY?
EGGS
NURSERY
BEETLES
EGGS
NURSERY
HARVEST
GROWING
GROWING
GROWING
GROWING
GROWING
FRASS
FIRST OFF, A LITTLE BREAKFAST FOR YOU . . .
MMM, WHEAT BRAN!
WHOA, NO YOU DON'T! HAHA!
AND LOOK AT YOU! GOODNESS, THERE ARE QUITE A FEW OF YOU READY FOR HARVEST, AREN'T THERE?
IN YOU GO.

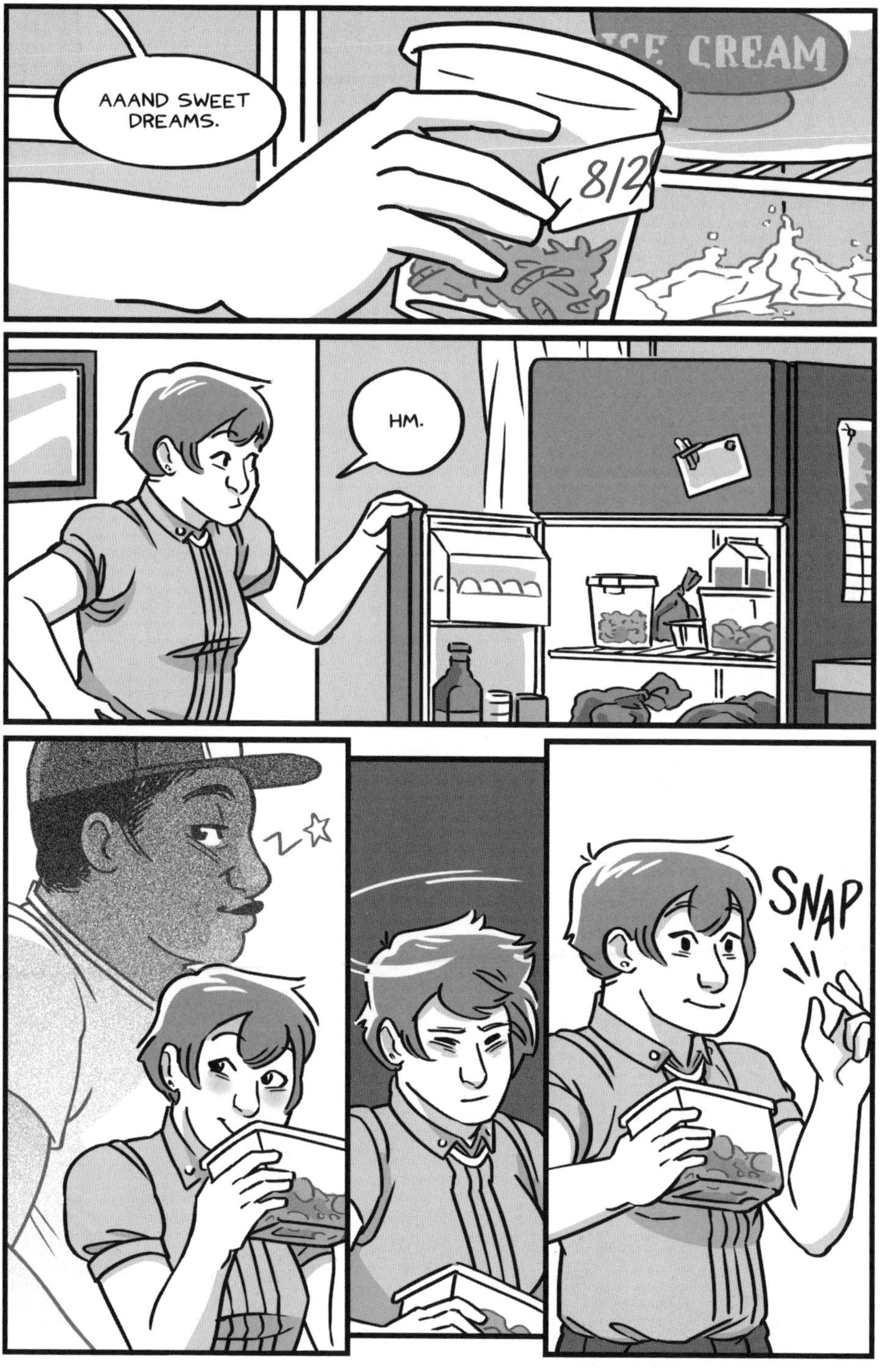
AAAND SWEET DREAMS.
ICE CREAM
8/2
HM.
SNAP

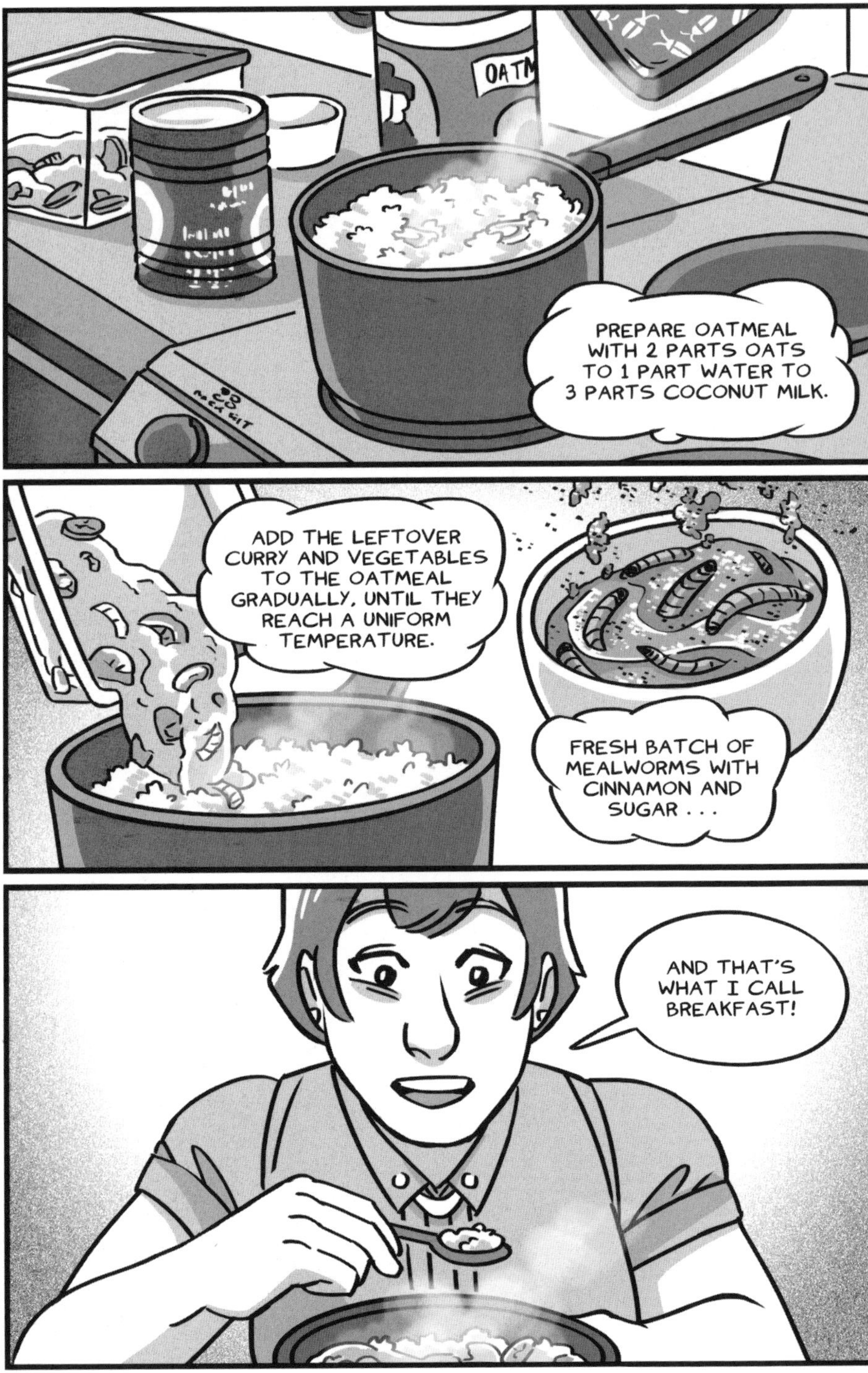
OATM
PREPARE OATMEAL WITH 2 PARTS OATS TO 1 PART WATER TO 3 PARTS COCONUT MILK.
ADD THE LEFTOVER CURRY AND VEGETABLES TO THE OATMEAL GRADUALLY, UNTIL THEY REACH A UNIFORM TEMPERATURE.
FRESH BATCH OF MEALWORMS WITH CINNAMON AND SUGAR . . .
AND THAT'S WHAT I CALL BREAKFAST!

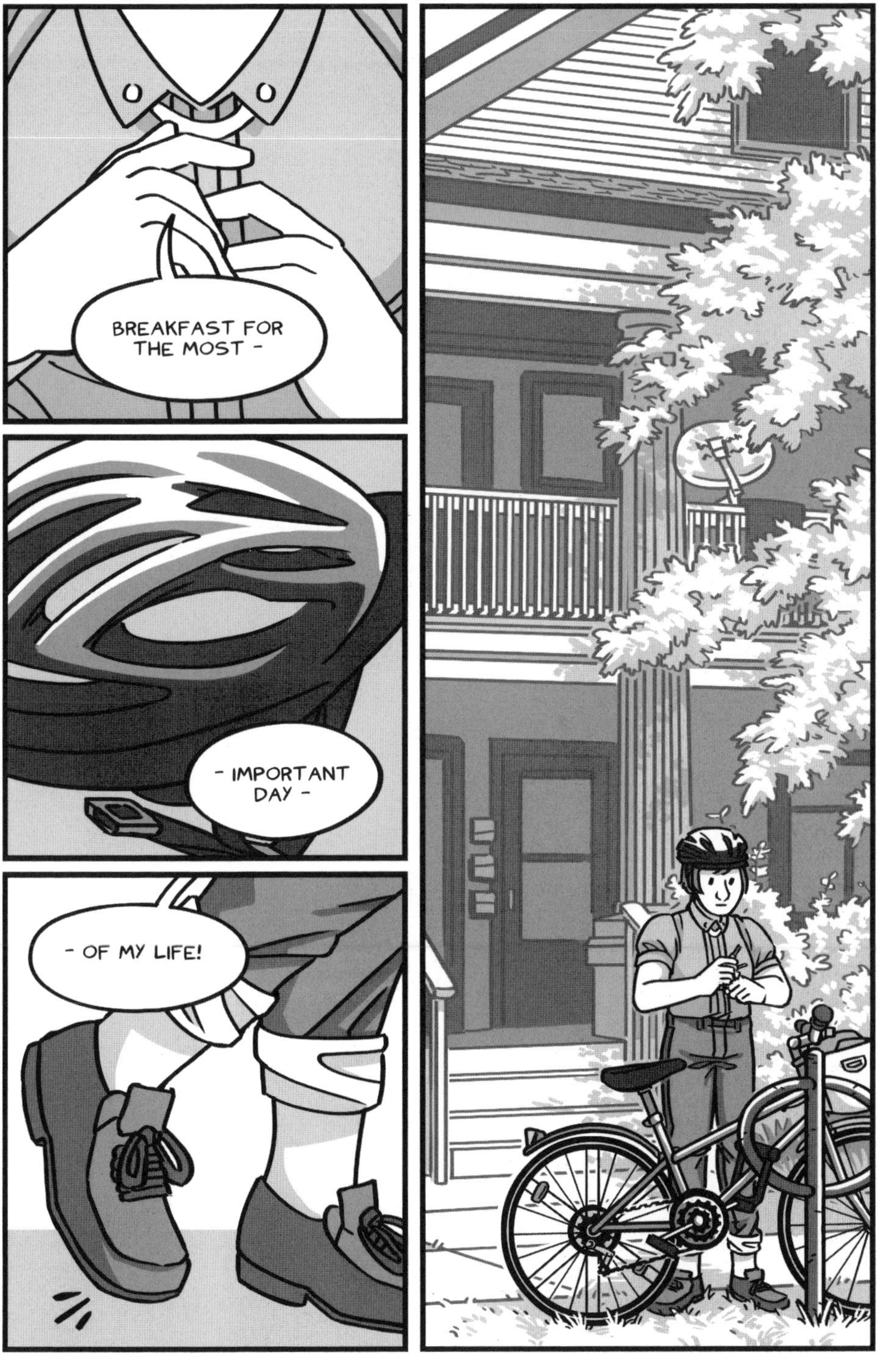
BREAKFAST FOR THE MOST -
- IMPORTANT DAY -
- OF MY LIFE!

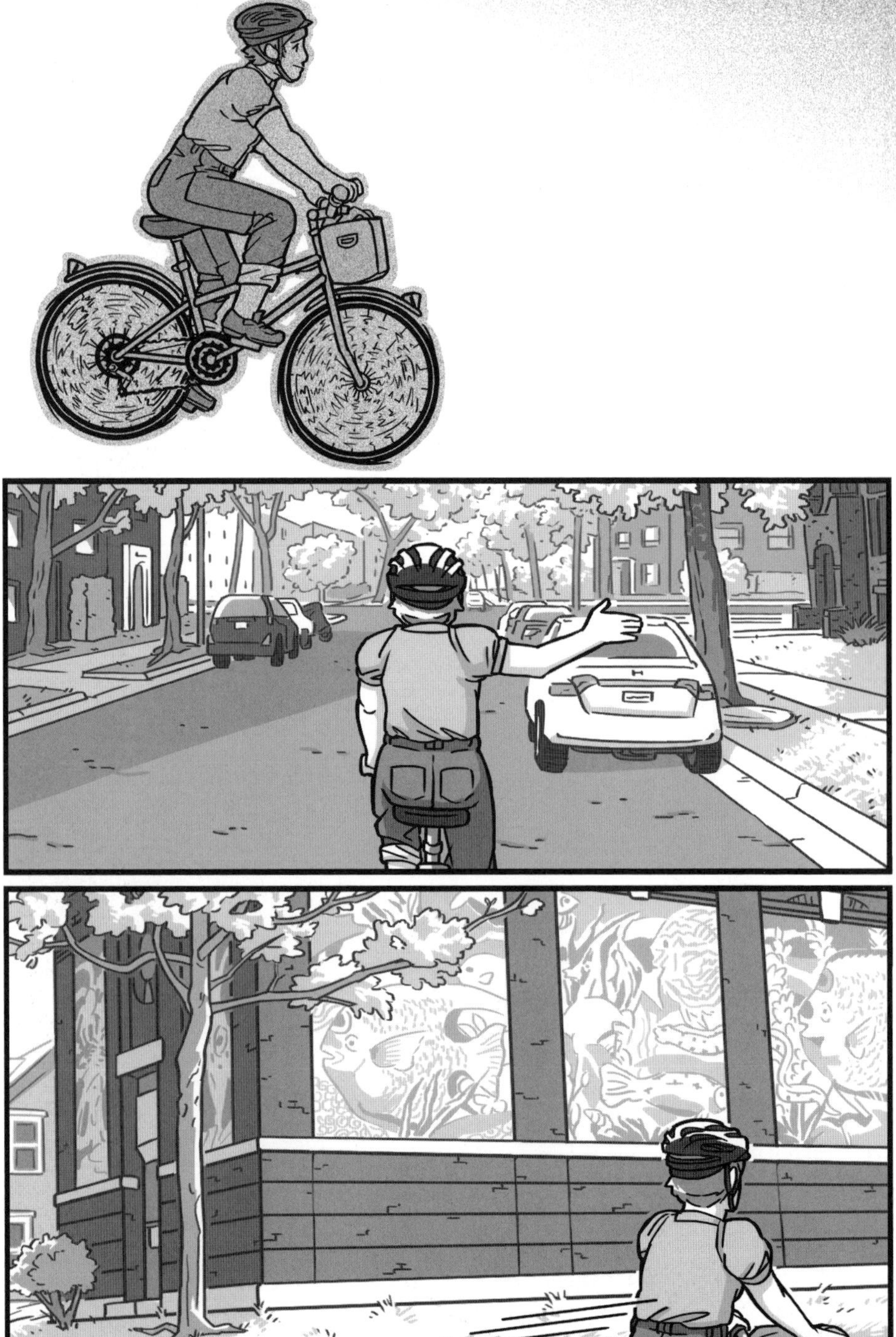

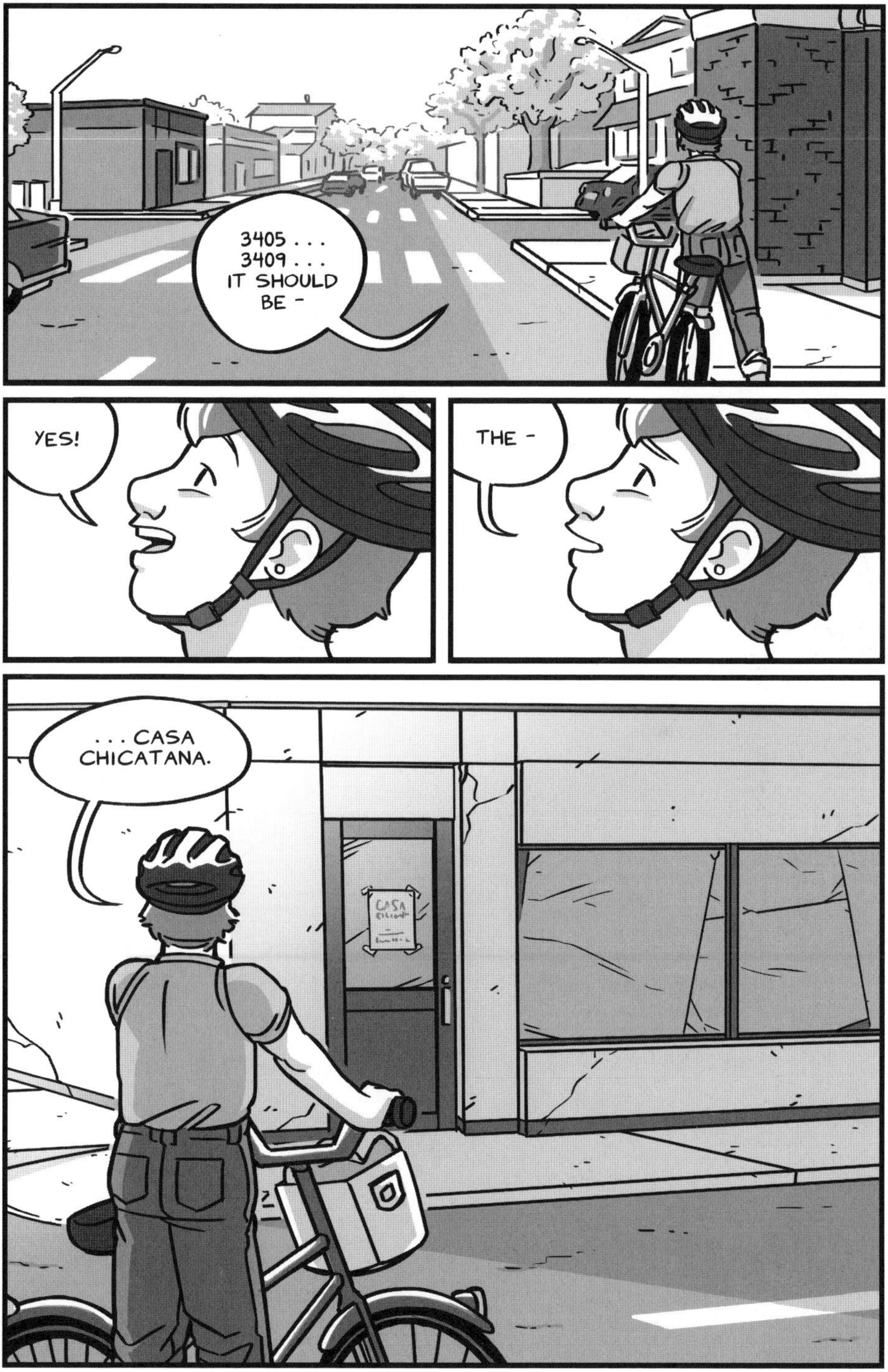
3405 . . . 3409 . . . IT SHOULD BE -
YES!
THE -
. . . CASA CHICATANA.

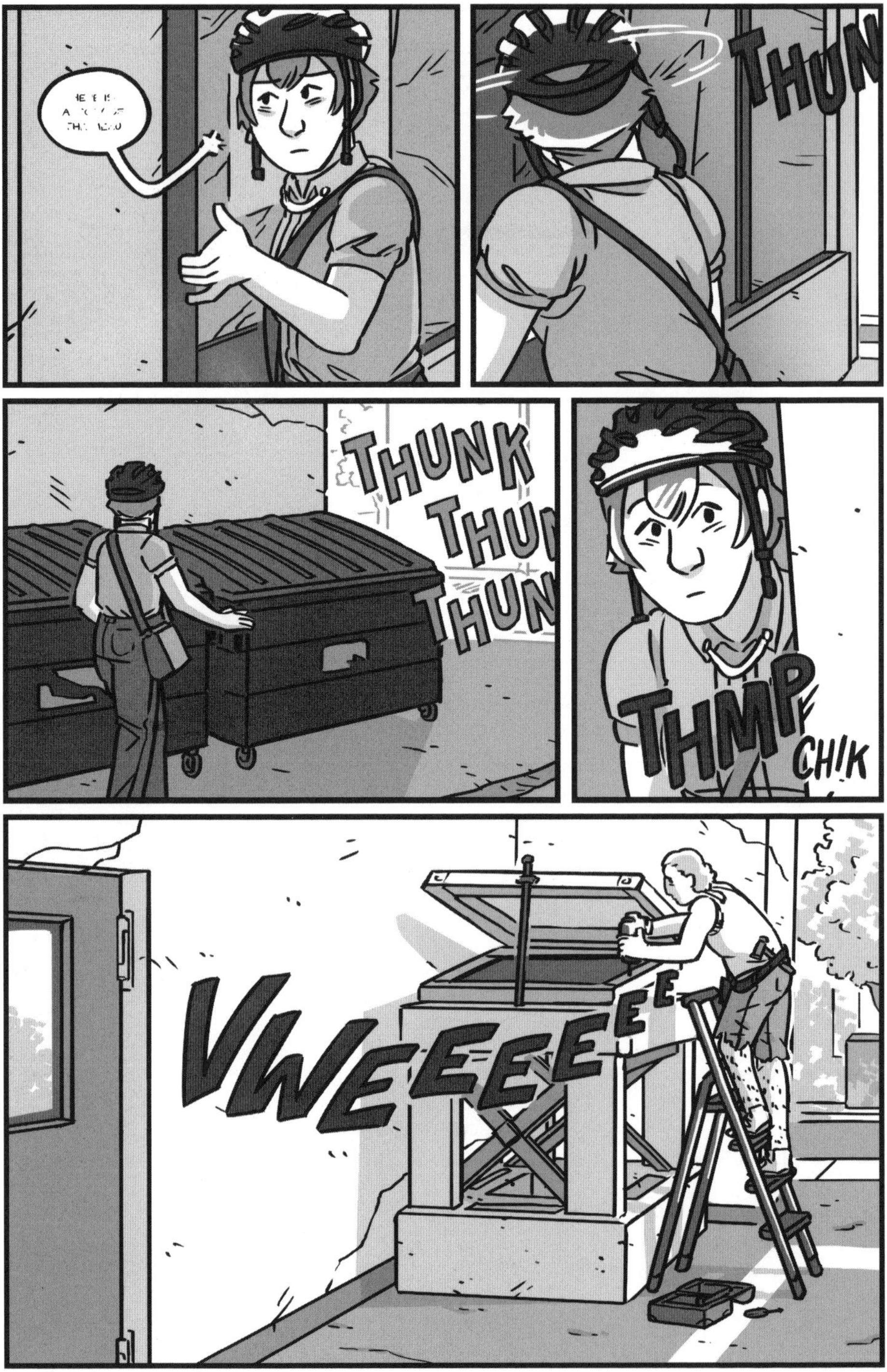
THUN
THUNK
THUN
THUN
THMP
CHIK
VWEEEEEE

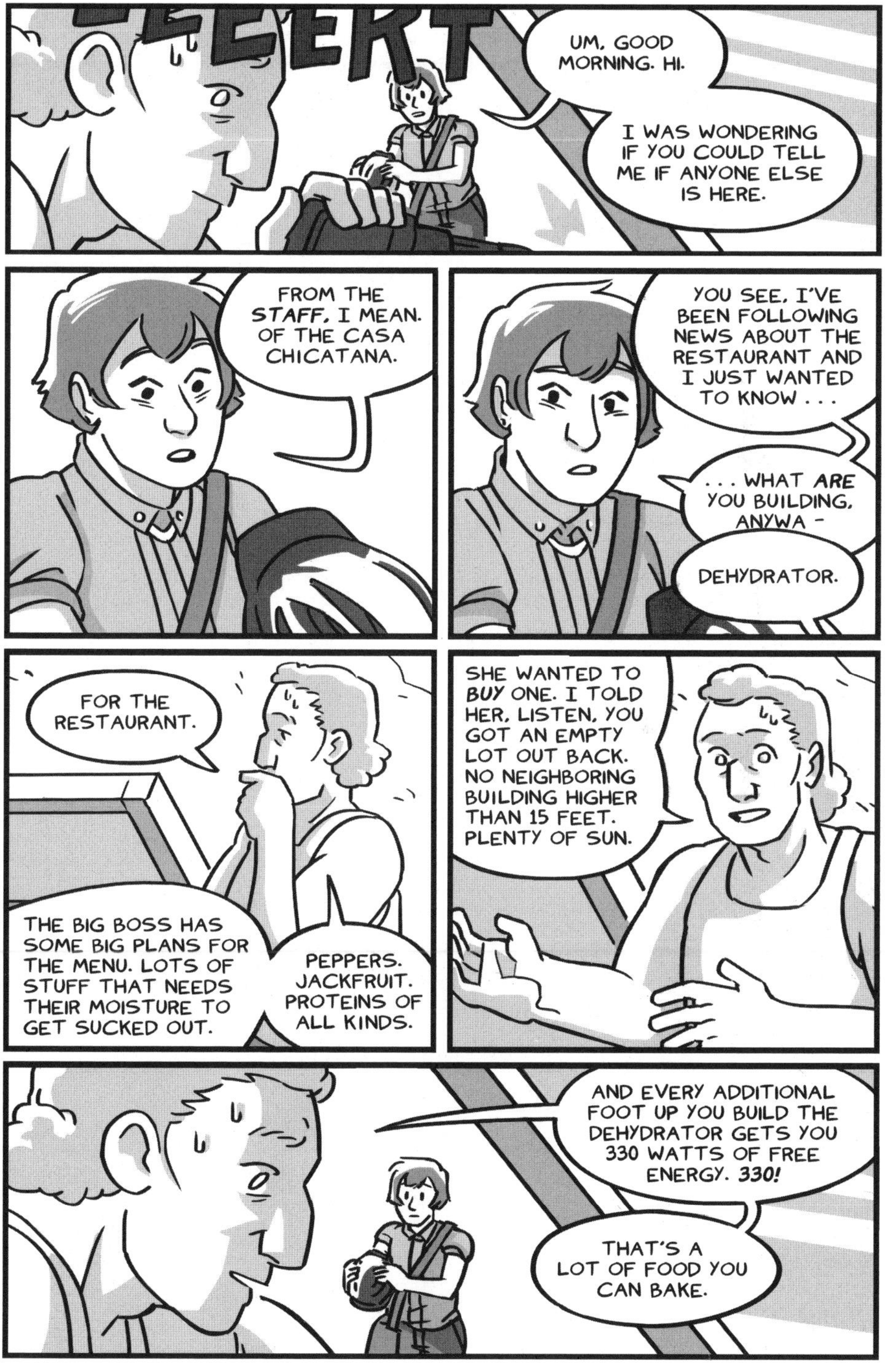
UM, GOOD MORNING. HI.
I WAS WONDERING IF YOU COULD TELL ME IF ANYONE ELSE IS HERE.
FROM THE *STAFF*, I MEAN. OF THE CASA CHICATANA.
YOU SEE, I'VE BEEN FOLLOWING NEWS ABOUT THE RESTAURANT AND I JUST WANTED TO KNOW . . .
. . . WHAT *ARE* YOU BUILDING, ANYWA –
DEHYDRATOR.
FOR THE RESTAURANT.
THE BIG BOSS HAS SOME BIG PLANS FOR THE MENU. LOTS OF STUFF THAT NEEDS THEIR MOISTURE TO GET SUCKED OUT.
PEPPERS. JACKFRUIT. PROTEINS OF ALL KINDS.
SHE WANTED TO *BUY* ONE. I TOLD HER, LISTEN, YOU GOT AN EMPTY LOT OUT BACK. NO NEIGHBORING BUILDING HIGHER THAN 15 FEET. PLENTY OF SUN.
AND EVERY ADDITIONAL FOOT UP YOU BUILD THE DEHYDRATOR GETS YOU 330 WATTS OF FREE ENERGY. *330!*
THAT'S A LOT OF FOOD YOU CAN BAKE.

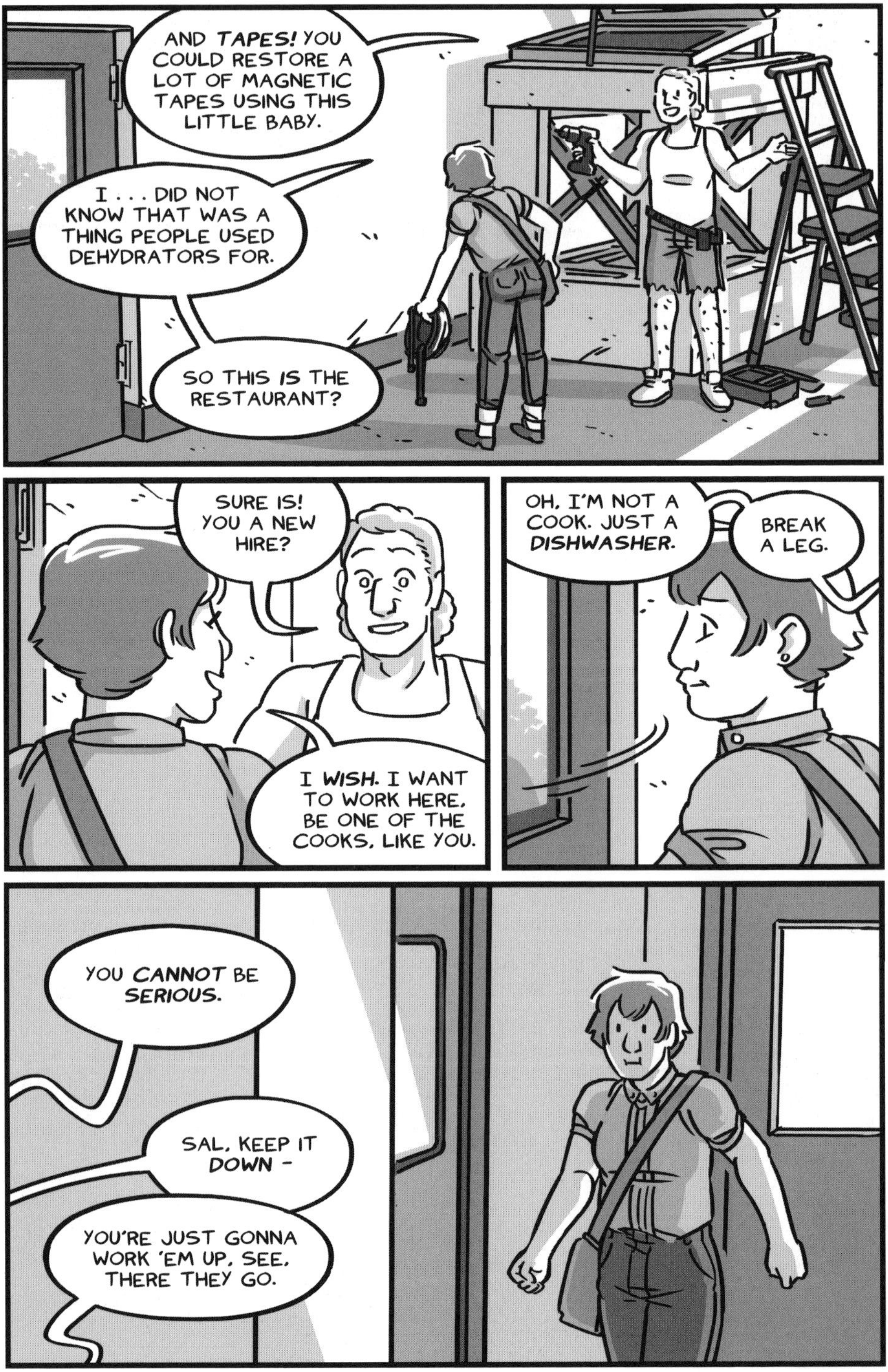
AND TAPES! YOU COULD RESTORE A LOT OF MAGNETIC TAPES USING THIS LITTLE BABY.
I . . . DID NOT KNOW THAT WAS A THING PEOPLE USED DEHYDRATORS FOR.
SO THIS IS THE RESTAURANT?
SURE IS! YOU A NEW HIRE?
I WISH. I WANT TO WORK HERE, BE ONE OF THE COOKS, LIKE YOU.
OH, I'M NOT A COOK. JUST A DISHWASHER.
BREAK A LEG.
YOU CANNOT BE SERIOUS.
SAL, KEEP IT DOWN -
YOU'RE JUST GONNA WORK 'EM UP, SEE, THERE THEY GO.

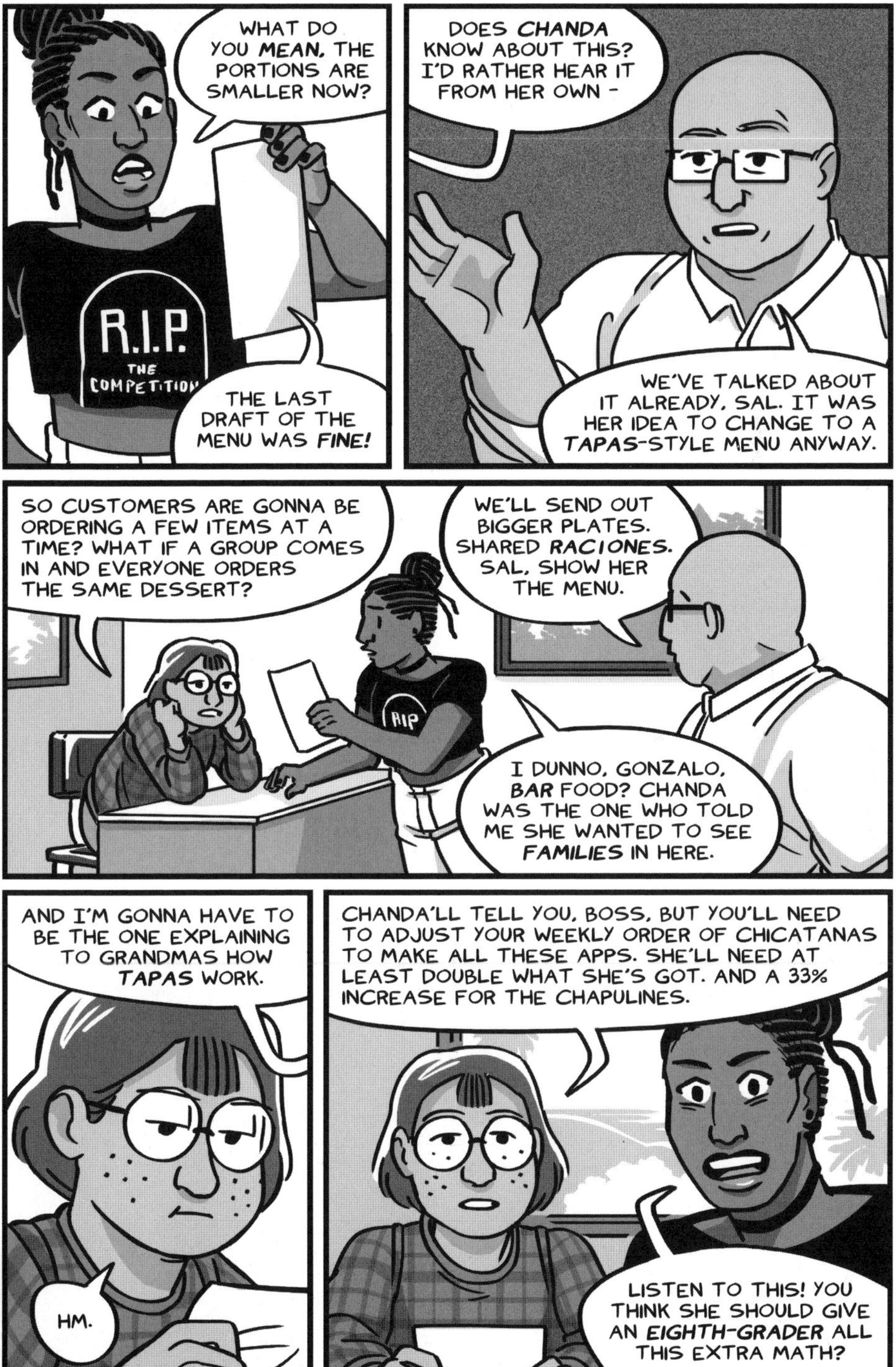
WHAT DO YOU MEAN, THE PORTIONS ARE SMALLER NOW?
R.I.P. THE COMPETITION
THE LAST DRAFT OF THE MENU WAS FINE!
DOES CHANDA KNOW ABOUT THIS? I'D RATHER HEAR IT FROM HER OWN –
WE'VE TALKED ABOUT IT ALREADY, SAL. IT WAS HER IDEA TO CHANGE TO A TAPAS-STYLE MENU ANYWAY.
SO CUSTOMERS ARE GONNA BE ORDERING A FEW ITEMS AT A TIME? WHAT IF A GROUP COMES IN AND EVERYONE ORDERS THE SAME DESSERT?
WE'LL SEND OUT BIGGER PLATES. SHARED RACIONES. SAL, SHOW HER THE MENU.
RIP
I DUNNO, GONZALO, BAR FOOD? CHANDA WAS THE ONE WHO TOLD ME SHE WANTED TO SEE FAMILIES IN HERE.
AND I'M GONNA HAVE TO BE THE ONE EXPLAINING TO GRANDMAS HOW TAPAS WORK.
HM.
CHANDA'LL TELL YOU, BOSS, BUT YOU'LL NEED TO ADJUST YOUR WEEKLY ORDER OF CHICATANAS TO MAKE ALL THESE APPS. SHE'LL NEED AT LEAST DOUBLE WHAT SHE'S GOT. AND A 33% INCREASE FOR THE CHAPULINES.
LISTEN TO THIS! YOU THINK SHE SHOULD GIVE AN EIGHTH-GRADER ALL THIS EXTRA MATH?

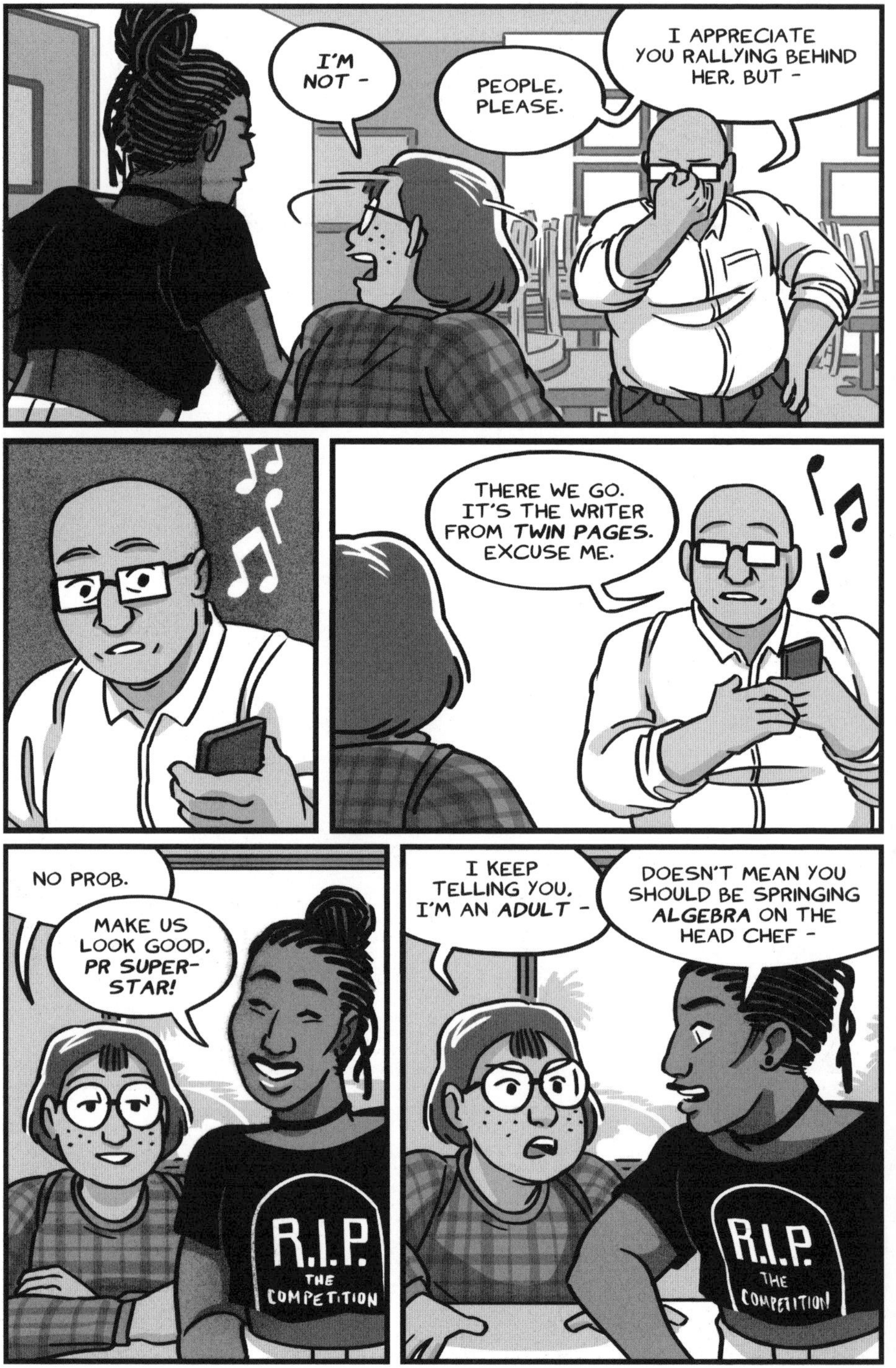
I'M NOT -
PEOPLE, PLEASE.
I APPRECIATE YOU RALLYING BEHIND HER, BUT -
THERE WE GO. IT'S THE WRITER FROM **TWIN PAGES**. EXCUSE ME.
NO PROB.
MAKE US LOOK GOOD, **PR SUPER-STAR!**
R.I.P. THE COMPETITION
I KEEP TELLING YOU, I'M AN *ADULT* -
DOESN'T MEAN YOU SHOULD BE SPRINGING **ALGEBRA** ON THE HEAD CHEF -
R.I.P. THE COMPETITION

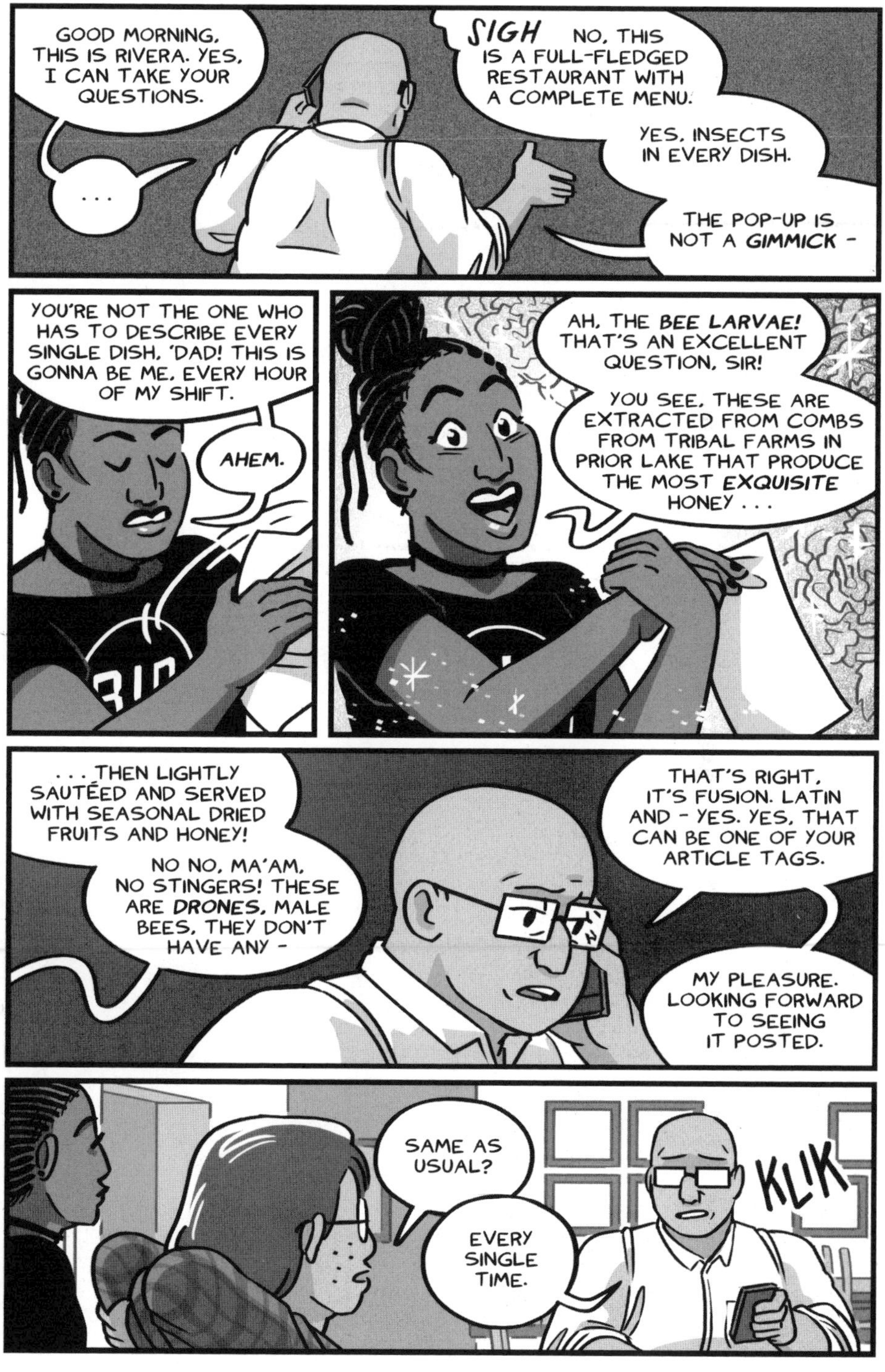
GOOD MORNING, THIS IS RIVERA. YES, I CAN TAKE YOUR QUESTIONS.
...
SIGH NO, THIS IS A FULL-FLEDGED RESTAURANT WITH A COMPLETE MENU.
YES, INSECTS IN EVERY DISH.
THE POP-UP IS NOT A GIMMICK -
YOU'RE NOT THE ONE WHO HAS TO DESCRIBE EVERY SINGLE DISH, 'DAD! THIS IS GONNA BE ME, EVERY HOUR OF MY SHIFT.
AHEM.
AH, THE BEE LARVAE! THAT'S AN EXCELLENT QUESTION, SIR!
YOU SEE, THESE ARE EXTRACTED FROM COMBS FROM TRIBAL FARMS IN PRIOR LAKE THAT PRODUCE THE MOST EXQUISITE HONEY . . .
. . . THEN LIGHTLY SAUTÉED AND SERVED WITH SEASONAL DRIED FRUITS AND HONEY!
NO NO, MA'AM, NO STINGERS! THESE ARE DRONES, MALE BEES, THEY DON'T HAVE ANY -
THAT'S RIGHT, IT'S FUSION. LATIN AND - YES. YES, THAT CAN BE ONE OF YOUR ARTICLE TAGS.
MY PLEASURE. LOOKING FORWARD TO SEEING IT POSTED.
SAME AS USUAL?
EVERY SINGLE TIME.
KLIK

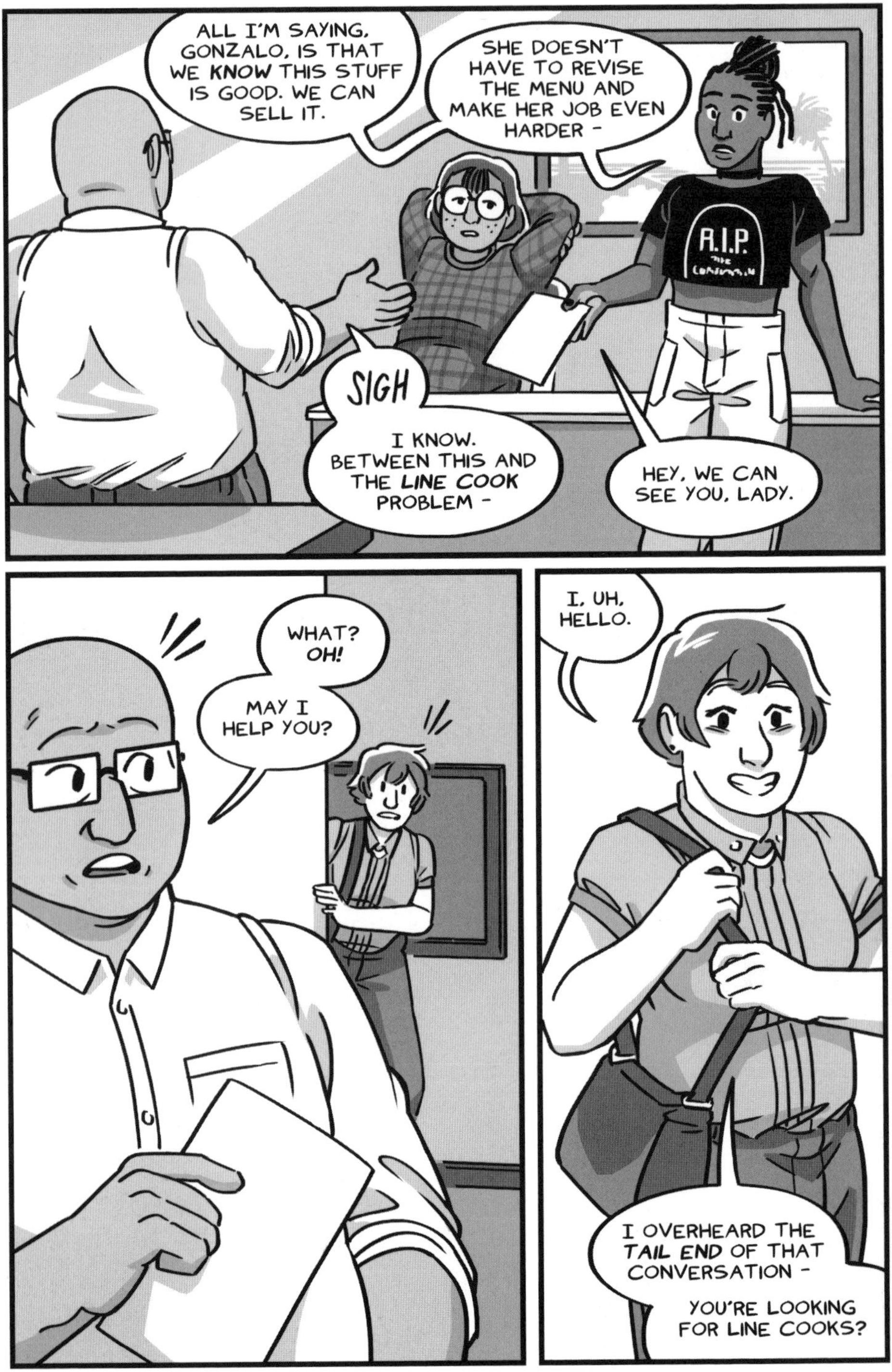
ALL I'M SAYING, GONZALO, IS THAT WE **KNOW** THIS STUFF IS GOOD. WE CAN SELL IT.
SHE DOESN'T HAVE TO REVISE THE MENU AND MAKE HER JOB EVEN HARDER -
R.I.P.
SIGH
I KNOW. BETWEEN THIS AND THE ***LINE COOK*** PROBLEM -
HEY, WE CAN SEE YOU, LADY.
WHAT? ***OH!***
MAY I HELP YOU?
I, UH, HELLO.
I OVERHEARD THE ***TAIL END*** OF THAT CONVERSATION -
YOU'RE LOOKING FOR LINE COOKS?

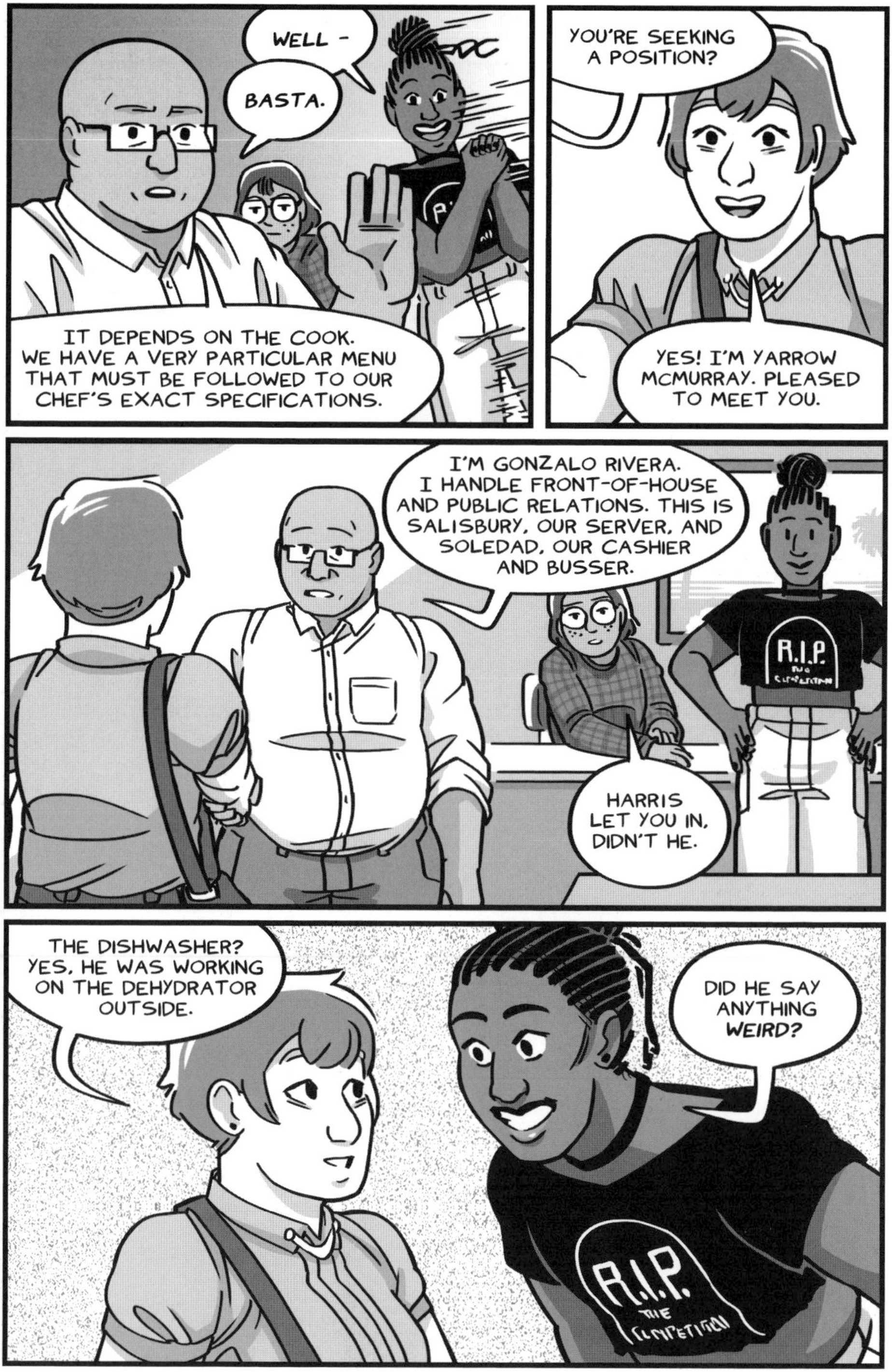
WELL -
BASTA.
IT DEPENDS ON THE COOK. WE HAVE A VERY PARTICULAR MENU THAT MUST BE FOLLOWED TO OUR CHEF'S EXACT SPECIFICATIONS.
YOU'RE SEEKING A POSITION?
YES! I'M YARROW MCMURRAY. PLEASED TO MEET YOU.
I'M GONZALO RIVERA. I HANDLE FRONT-OF-HOUSE AND PUBLIC RELATIONS. THIS IS SALISBURY, OUR SERVER, AND SOLEDAD, OUR CASHIER AND BUSSER.
R.I.P.
HARRIS LET YOU IN, DIDN'T HE.
THE DISHWASHER? YES, HE WAS WORKING ON THE DEHYDRATOR OUTSIDE.
DID HE SAY ANYTHING **WEIRD?**
R.I.P.

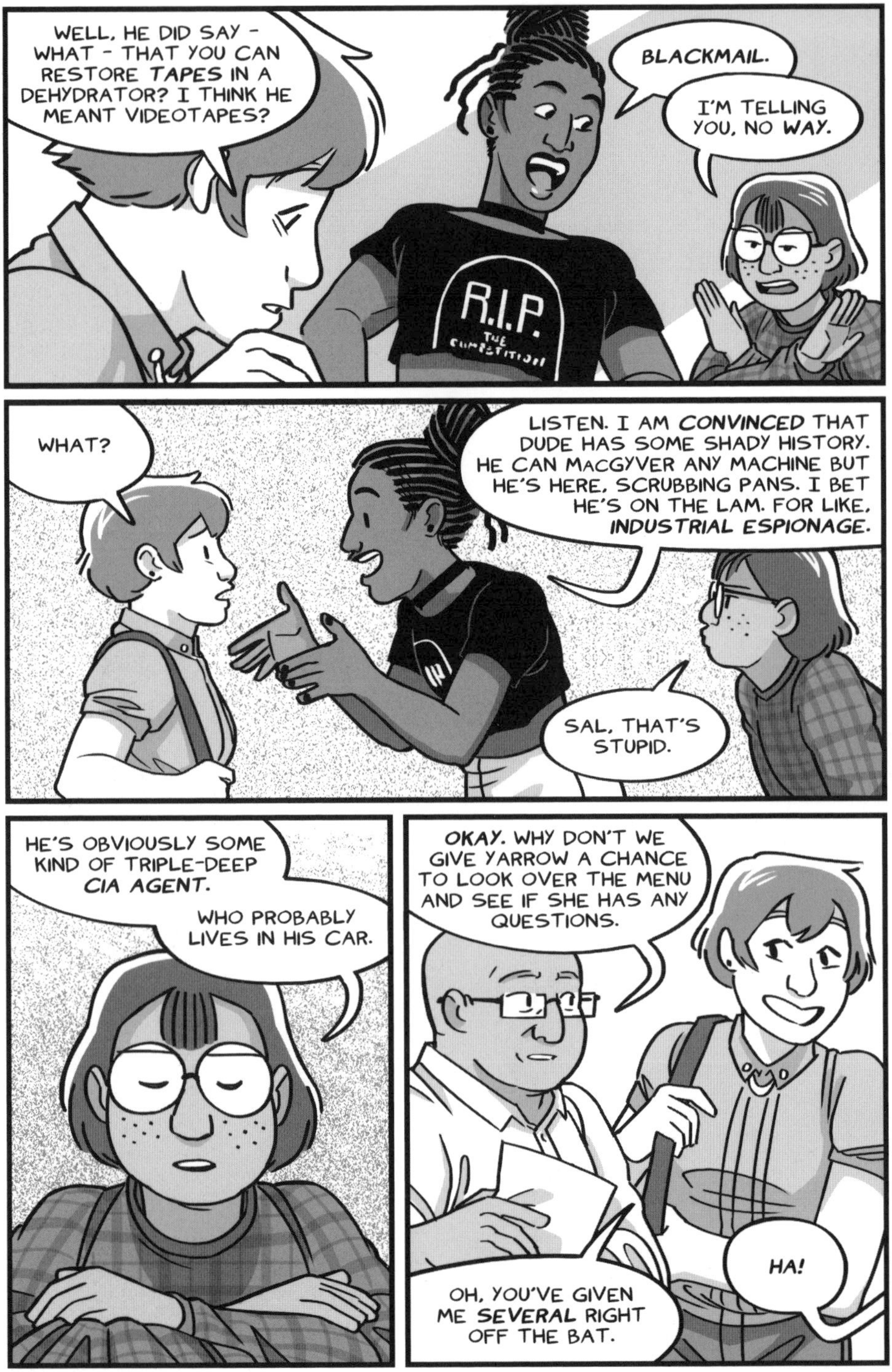
WELL, HE DID SAY - WHAT - THAT YOU CAN RESTORE TAPES IN A DEHYDRATOR? I THINK HE MEANT VIDEOTAPES?
BLACKMAIL.
I'M TELLING YOU, NO WAY.
R.I.P. THE COMPETITION
WHAT?
LISTEN. I AM CONVINCED THAT DUDE HAS SOME SHADY HISTORY. HE CAN MACGYVER ANY MACHINE BUT HE'S HERE, SCRUBBING PANS. I BET HE'S ON THE LAM. FOR LIKE, INDUSTRIAL ESPIONAGE.
SAL, THAT'S STUPID.
HE'S OBVIOUSLY SOME KIND OF TRIPLE-DEEP CIA AGENT.
WHO PROBABLY LIVES IN HIS CAR.
OKAY. WHY DON'T WE GIVE YARROW A CHANCE TO LOOK OVER THE MENU AND SEE IF SHE HAS ANY QUESTIONS.
HA!
OH, YOU'VE GIVEN ME SEVERAL RIGHT OFF THE BAT.

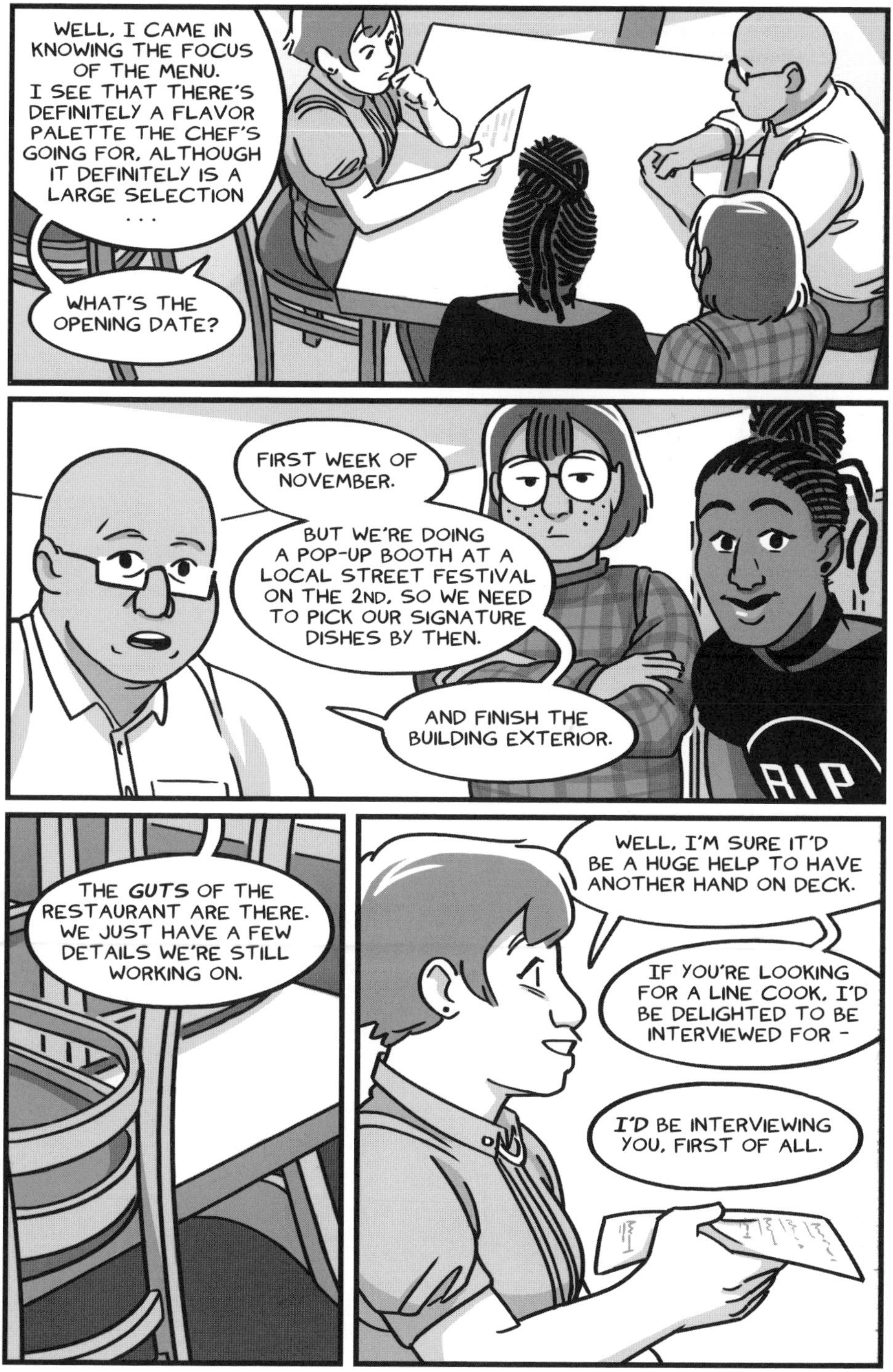
WELL, I CAME IN KNOWING THE FOCUS OF THE MENU. I SEE THAT THERE'S DEFINITELY A FLAVOR PALETTE THE CHEF'S GOING FOR, ALTHOUGH IT DEFINITELY IS A LARGE SELECTION . . .
WHAT'S THE OPENING DATE?
FIRST WEEK OF NOVEMBER.
BUT WE'RE DOING A POP-UP BOOTH AT A LOCAL STREET FESTIVAL ON THE 2ND, SO WE NEED TO PICK OUR SIGNATURE DISHES BY THEN.
AND FINISH THE BUILDING EXTERIOR.
RIP
THE *GUTS* OF THE RESTAURANT ARE THERE. WE JUST HAVE A FEW DETAILS WE'RE STILL WORKING ON.
WELL, I'M SURE IT'D BE A HUGE HELP TO HAVE ANOTHER HAND ON DECK.
IF YOU'RE LOOKING FOR A LINE COOK, I'D BE DELIGHTED TO BE INTERVIEWED FOR -
I'D BE INTERVIEWING YOU, FIRST OF ALL.

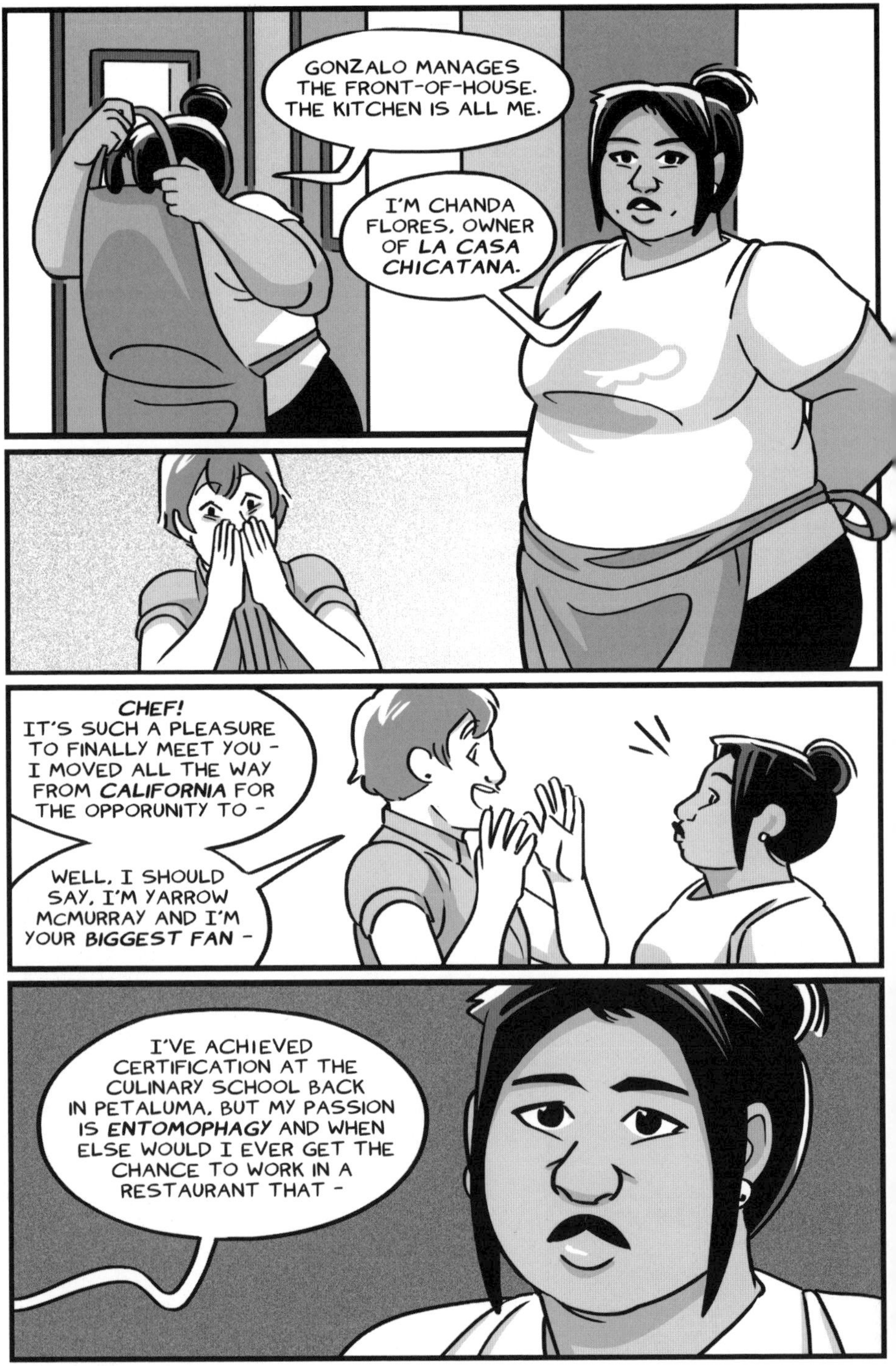
GONZALO MANAGES THE FRONT-OF-HOUSE. THE KITCHEN IS ALL ME.
I'M CHANDA FLORES, OWNER OF *LA CASA CHICATANA.*
CHEF! IT'S SUCH A PLEASURE TO FINALLY MEET YOU - I MOVED ALL THE WAY FROM *CALIFORNIA* FOR THE OPPORUNITY TO -
WELL, I SHOULD SAY, I'M YARROW MCMURRAY AND I'M YOUR *BIGGEST FAN* -
I'VE ACHIEVED CERTIFICATION AT THE CULINARY SCHOOL BACK IN PETALUMA, BUT MY PASSION IS *ENTOMOPHAGY* AND WHEN ELSE WOULD I EVER GET THE CHANCE TO WORK IN A RESTAURANT THAT -

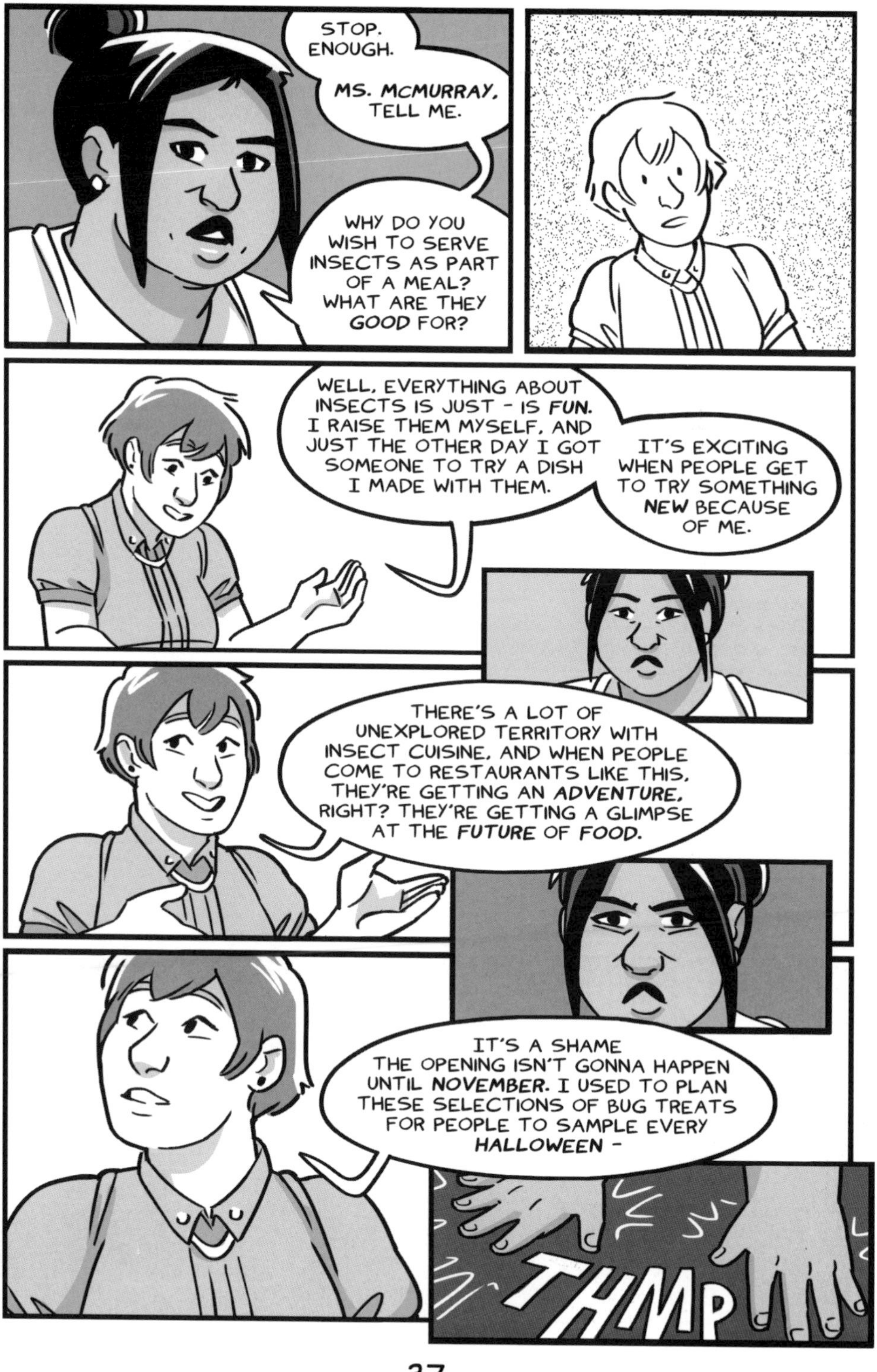
STOP. ENOUGH.
MS. MCMURRAY, TELL ME.
WHY DO YOU WISH TO SERVE INSECTS AS PART OF A MEAL? WHAT ARE THEY GOOD FOR?
WELL, EVERYTHING ABOUT INSECTS IS JUST - IS FUN. I RAISE THEM MYSELF, AND JUST THE OTHER DAY I GOT SOMEONE TO TRY A DISH I MADE WITH THEM.
IT'S EXCITING WHEN PEOPLE GET TO TRY SOMETHING NEW BECAUSE OF ME.
THERE'S A LOT OF UNEXPLORED TERRITORY WITH INSECT CUISINE, AND WHEN PEOPLE COME TO RESTAURANTS LIKE THIS, THEY'RE GETTING AN ADVENTURE, RIGHT? THEY'RE GETTING A GLIMPSE AT THE FUTURE OF FOOD.
IT'S A SHAME THE OPENING ISN'T GONNA HAPPEN UNTIL NOVEMBER. I USED TO PLAN THESE SELECTIONS OF BUG TREATS FOR PEOPLE TO SAMPLE EVERY HALLOWEEN -
THMP

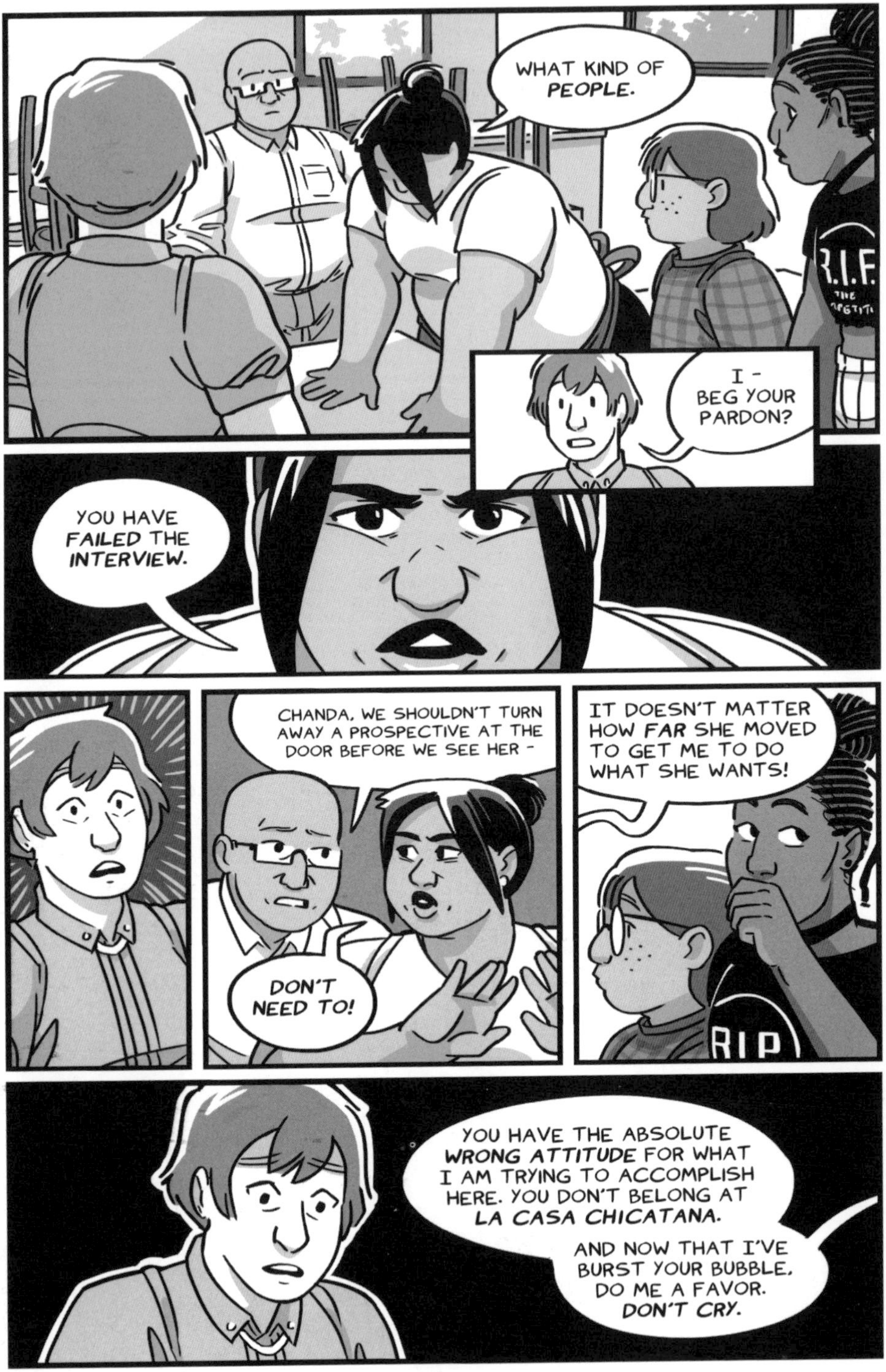
WHAT KIND OF PEOPLE.
I - BEG YOUR PARDON?
YOU HAVE FAILED THE INTERVIEW.
CHANDA, WE SHOULDN'T TURN AWAY A PROSPECTIVE AT THE DOOR BEFORE WE SEE HER -
DON'T NEED TO!
IT DOESN'T MATTER HOW FAR SHE MOVED TO GET ME TO DO WHAT SHE WANTS!
RIP
YOU HAVE THE ABSOLUTE WRONG ATTITUDE FOR WHAT I AM TRYING TO ACCOMPLISH HERE. YOU DON'T BELONG AT LA CASA CHICATANA.
AND NOW THAT I'VE BURST YOUR BUBBLE, DO ME A FAVOR. DON'T CRY.

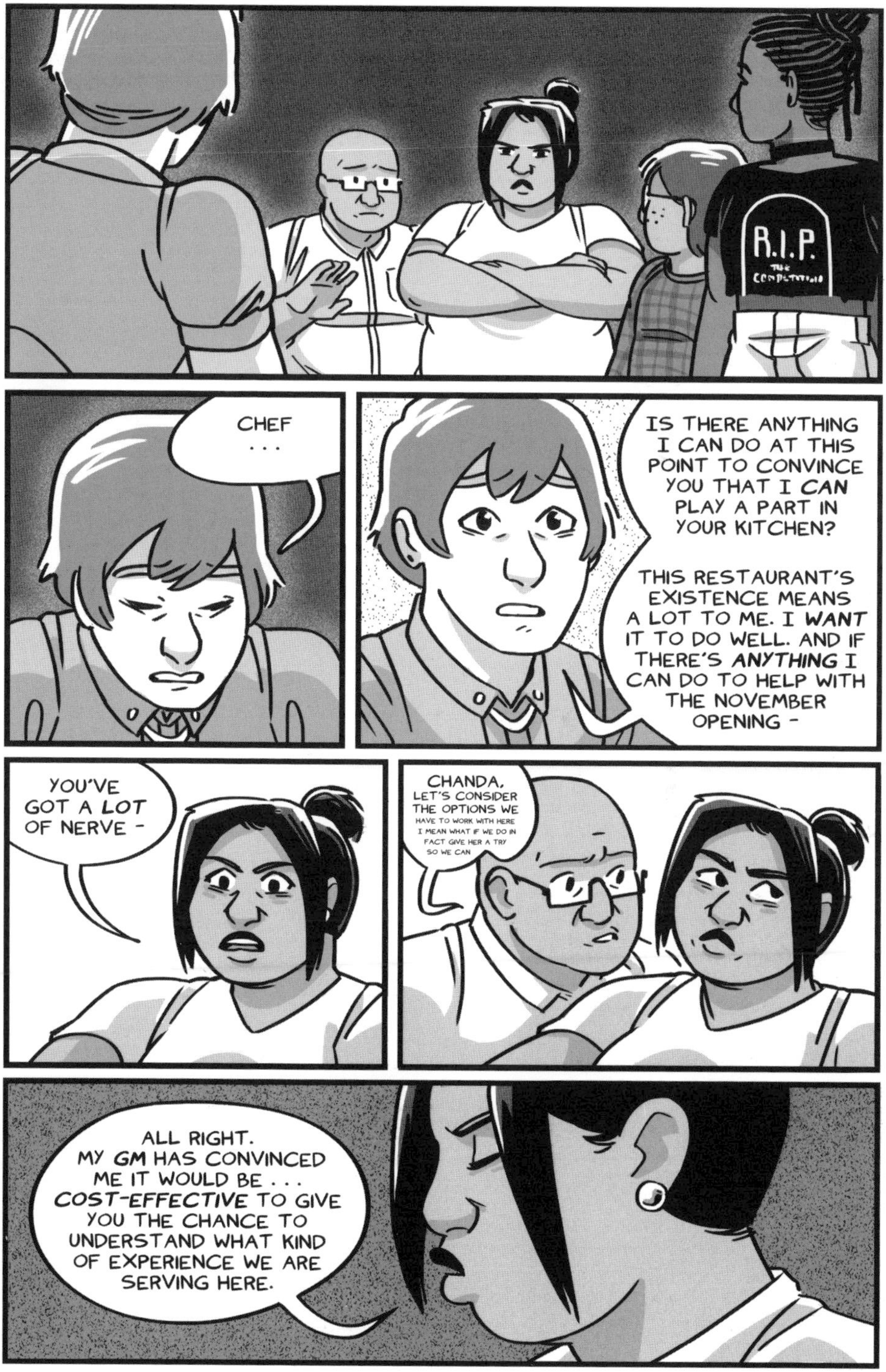
R.I.P.
CHEF . . .
IS THERE ANYTHING I CAN DO AT THIS POINT TO CONVINCE YOU THAT I *CAN* PLAY A PART IN YOUR KITCHEN?
THIS RESTAURANT'S EXISTENCE MEANS A LOT TO ME. I **WANT** IT TO DO **WELL**. AND IF THERE'S ***ANYTHING*** I CAN DO TO HELP WITH THE NOVEMBER OPENING -
YOU'VE GOT A **LOT** OF NERVE -
CHANDA, LET'S CONSIDER THE OPTIONS WE HAVE TO WORK WITH HERE I MEAN WHAT IF WE DO IN FACT GIVE HER A TRY SO WE CAN
ALL RIGHT. MY **GM** HAS CONVINCED ME IT WOULD BE . . . ***COST-EFFECTIVE*** TO GIVE YOU THE CHANCE TO UNDERSTAND WHAT KIND OF EXPERIENCE WE ARE SERVING HERE.

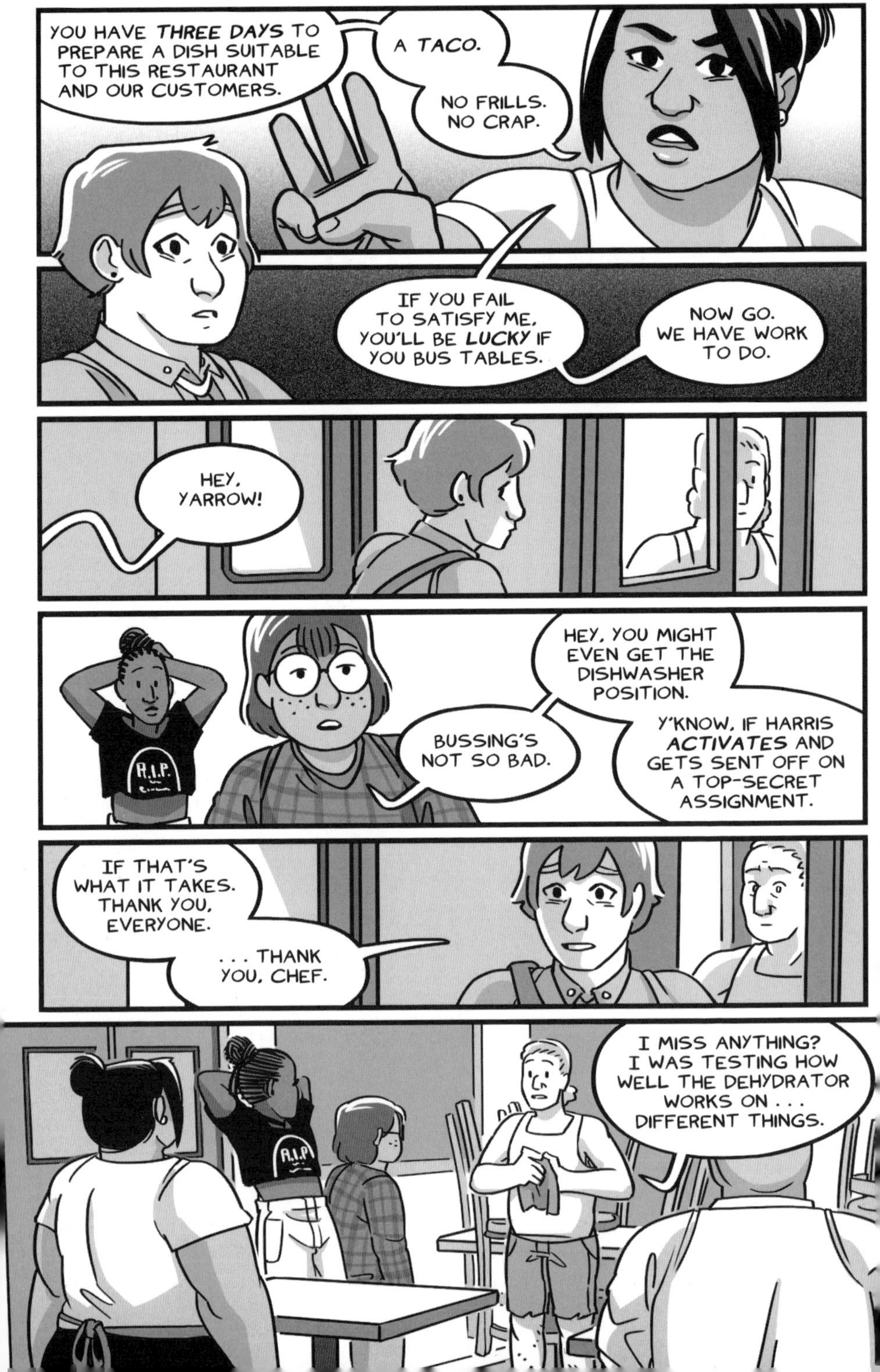
YOU HAVE THREE DAYS TO PREPARE A DISH SUITABLE TO THIS RESTAURANT AND OUR CUSTOMERS.
A TACO.
NO FRILLS. NO CRAP.
IF YOU FAIL TO SATISFY ME, YOU'LL BE LUCKY IF YOU BUS TABLES.
NOW GO. WE HAVE WORK TO DO.
HEY, YARROW!
BUSSING'S NOT SO BAD.
HEY, YOU MIGHT EVEN GET THE DISHWASHER POSITION.
Y'KNOW, IF HARRIS ACTIVATES AND GETS SENT OFF ON A TOP-SECRET ASSIGNMENT.
R.I.P.
IF THAT'S WHAT IT TAKES. THANK YOU, EVERYONE.
. . . THANK YOU, CHEF.
R.I.P.
I MISS ANYTHING? I WAS TESTING HOW WELL THE DEHYDRATOR WORKS ON . . . DIFFERENT THINGS.

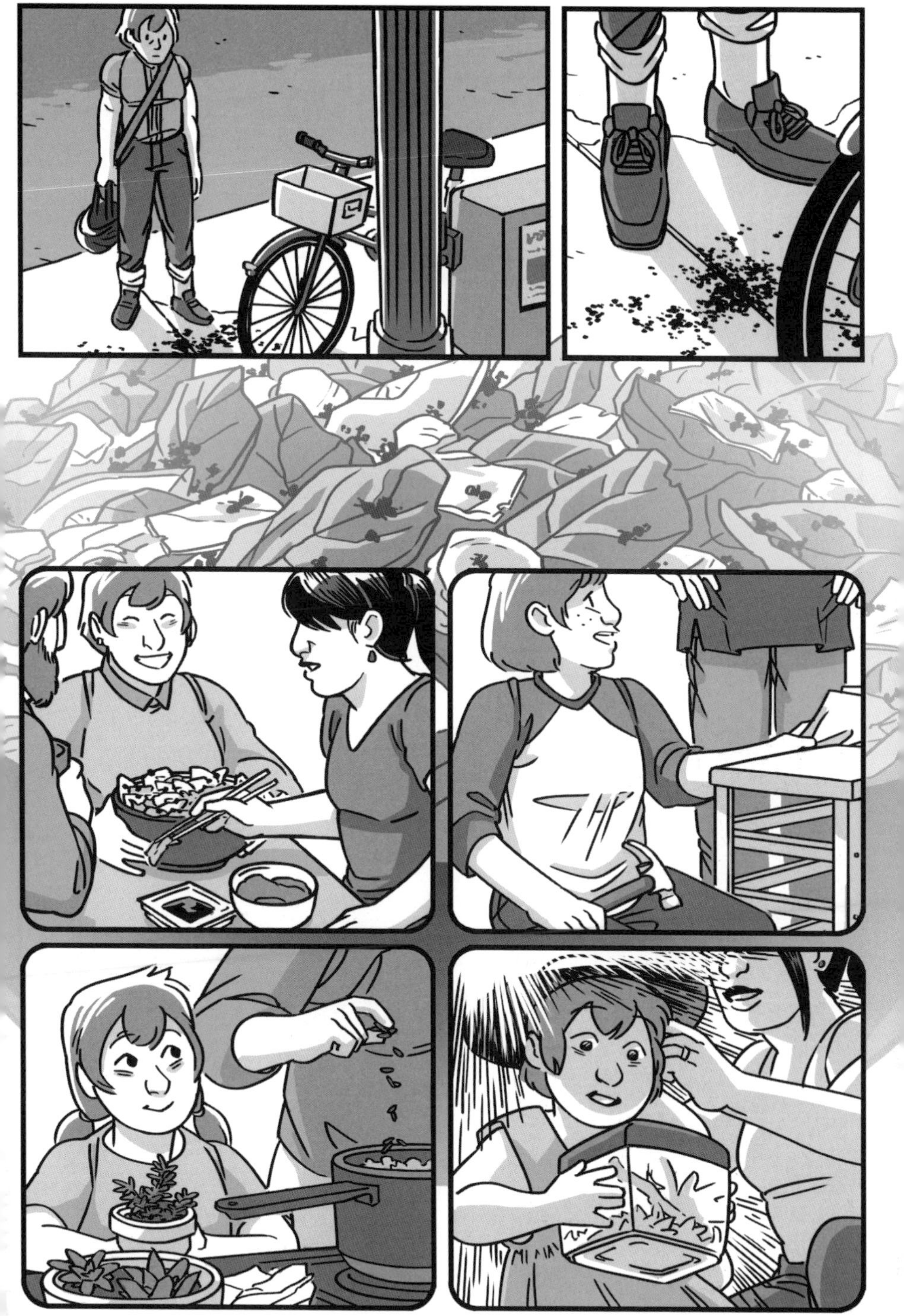

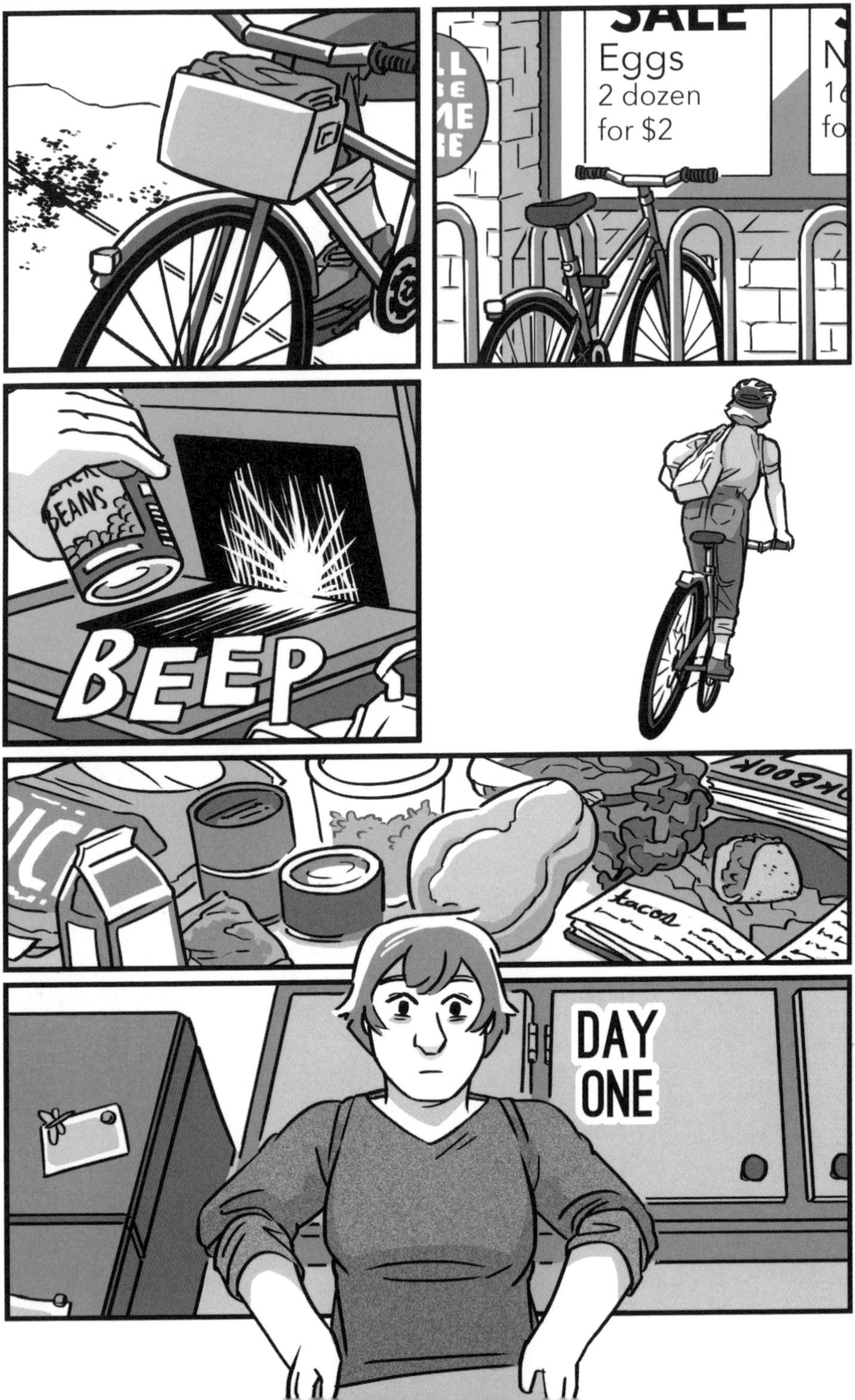
SALE
Eggs
2 dozen
for $2
BEANS
BEEP
tacos
DAY ONE

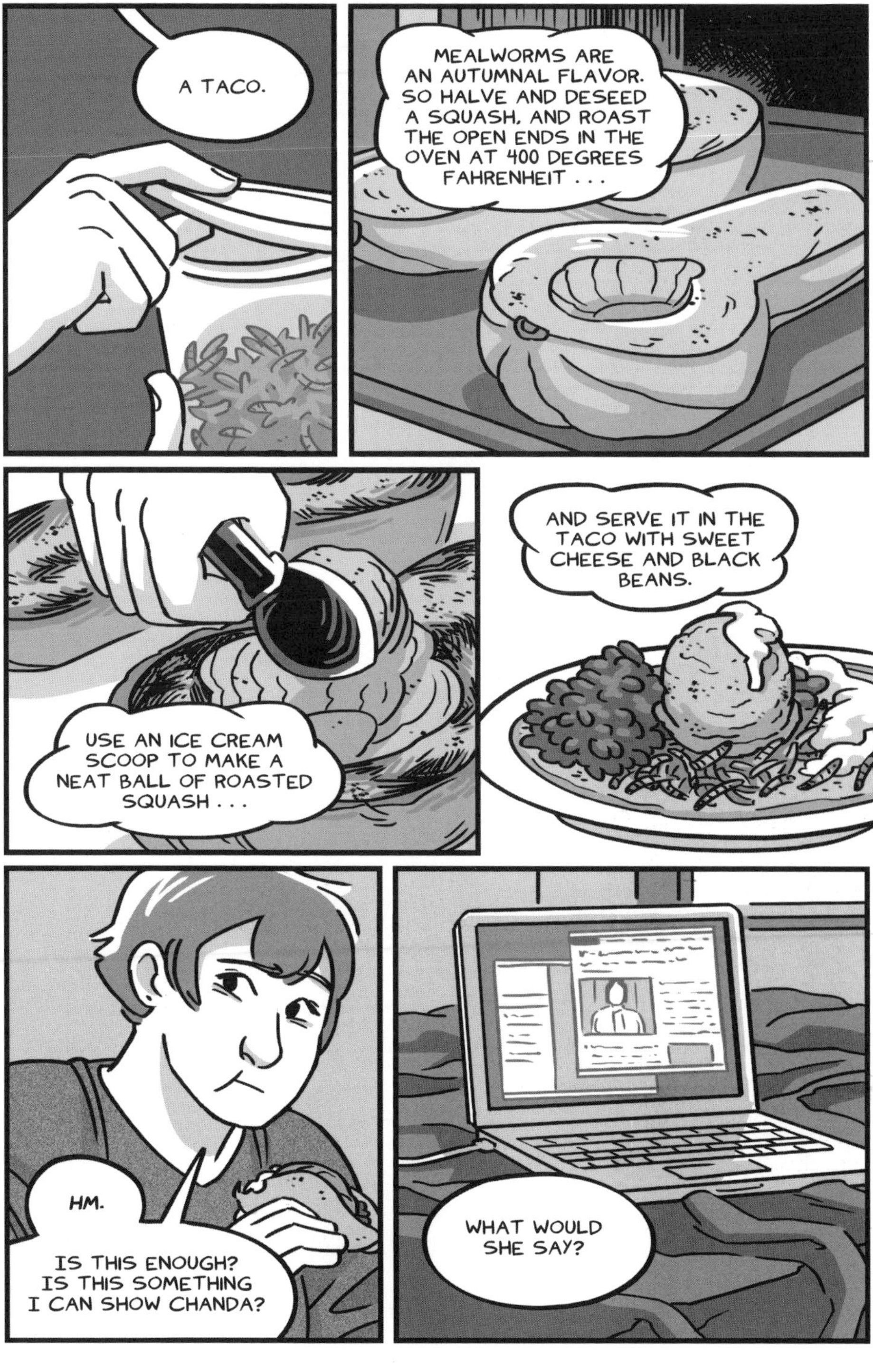
A TACO.
MEALWORMS ARE AN AUTUMNAL FLAVOR. SO HALVE AND DESEED A SQUASH, AND ROAST THE OPEN ENDS IN THE OVEN AT 400 DEGREES FAHRENHEIT . . .
USE AN ICE CREAM SCOOP TO MAKE A NEAT BALL OF ROASTED SQUASH . . .
AND SERVE IT IN THE TACO WITH SWEET CHEESE AND BLACK BEANS.
HM.
IS THIS ENOUGH? IS THIS SOMETHING I CAN SHOW CHANDA?
WHAT WOULD SHE SAY?

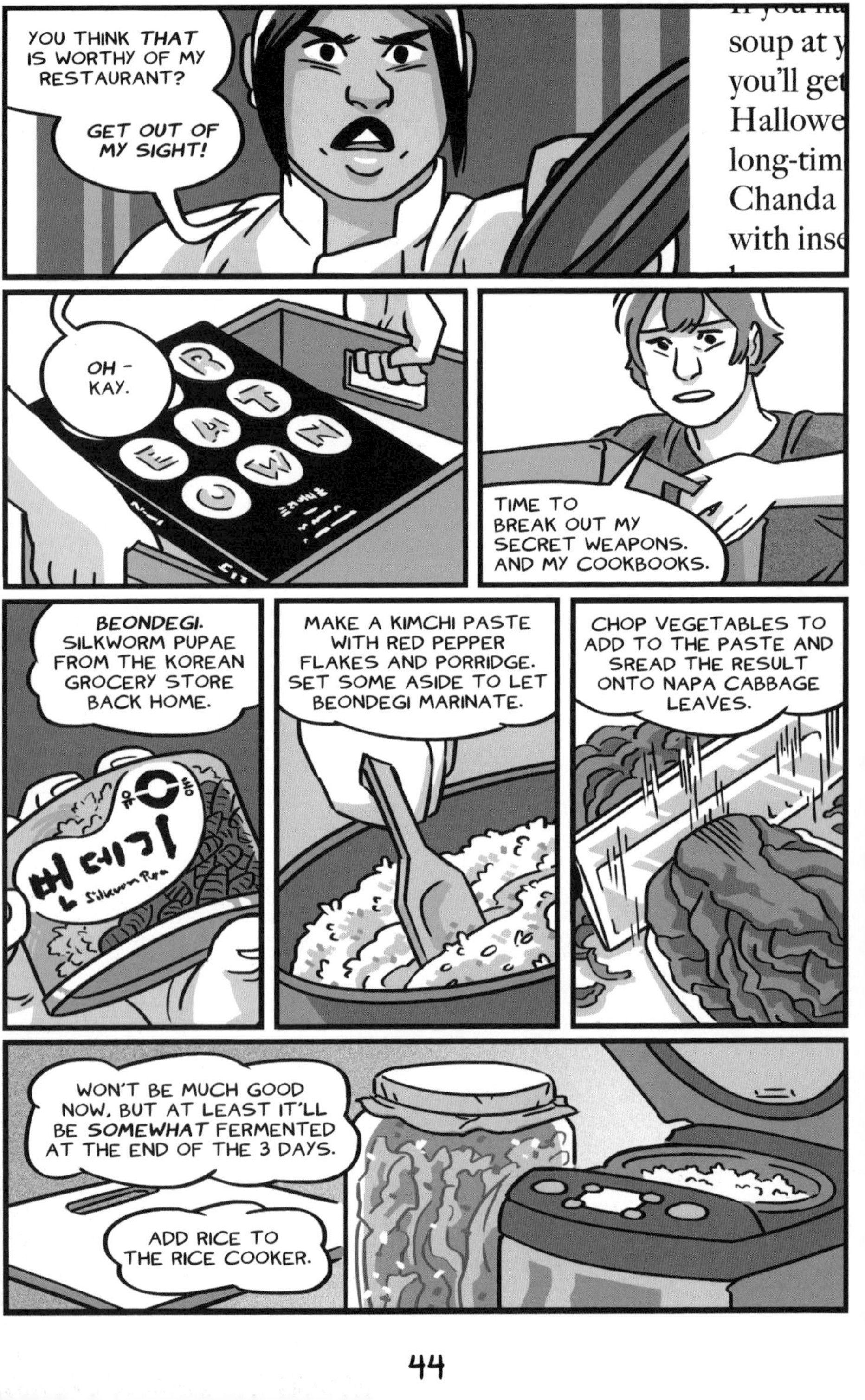
YOU THINK *THAT* IS WORTHY OF MY RESTAURANT?
GET OUT OF MY SIGHT!
soup at y
you'll get
Hallowe
long-tim
Chanda
with ins
OH - KAY.
TIME TO BREAK OUT MY SECRET WEAPONS. AND MY COOKBOOKS.
BEONDEGI. SILKWORM PUPAE FROM THE KOREAN GROCERY STORE BACK HOME.
번데기
Silkworm Pupa
MAKE A KIMCHI PASTE WITH RED PEPPER FLAKES AND PORRIDGE. SET SOME ASIDE TO LET BEONDEGI MARINATE.
CHOP VEGETABLES TO ADD TO THE PASTE AND SREAD THE RESULT ONTO NAPA CABBAGE LEAVES.
WON'T BE MUCH GOOD NOW, BUT AT LEAST IT'LL BE *SOMEWHAT* FERMENTED AT THE END OF THE 3 DAYS.
ADD RICE TO THE RICE COOKER.

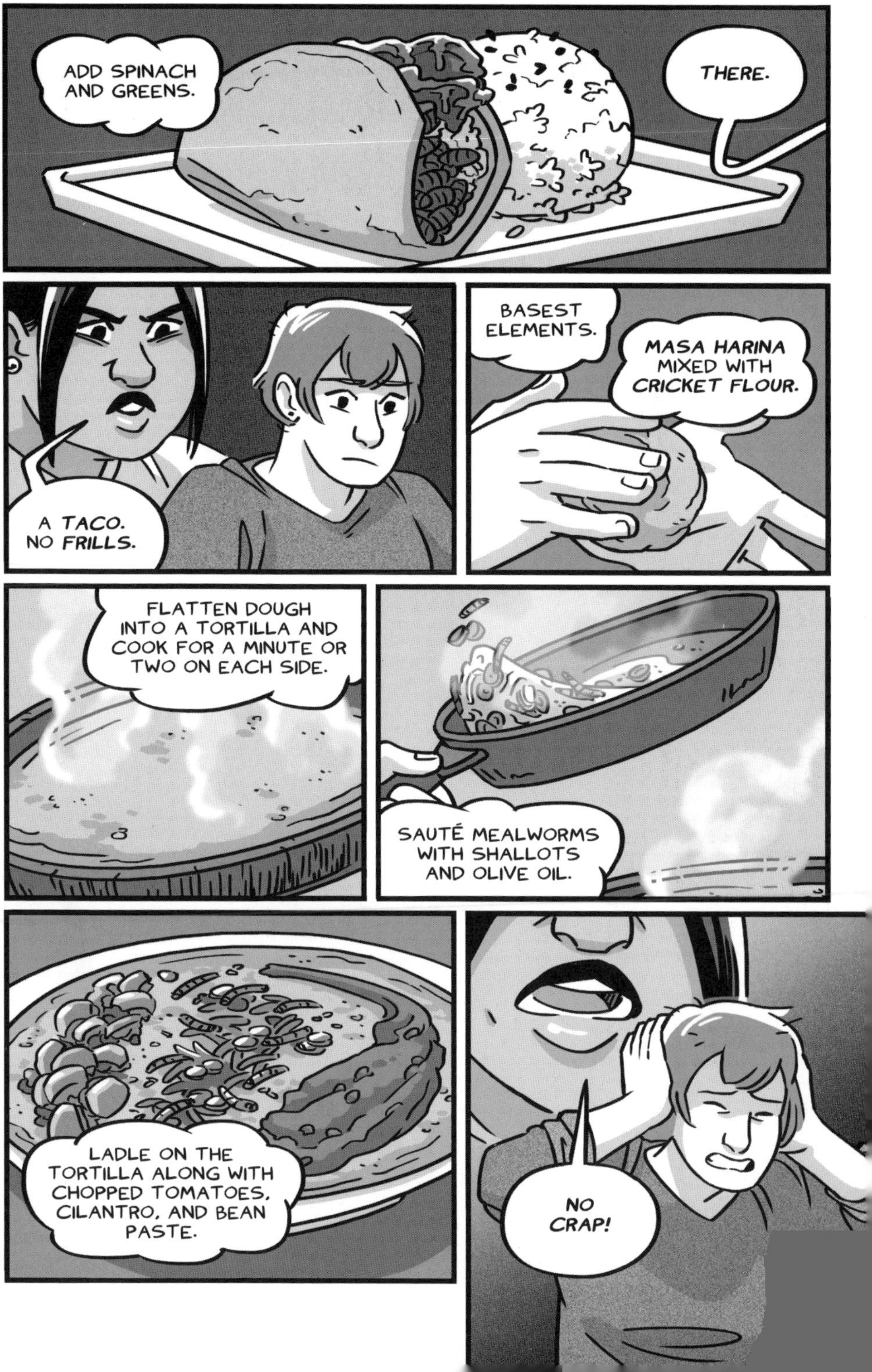
ADD SPINACH AND GREENS.
THERE.
A TACO. NO FRILLS.
BASEST ELEMENTS.
MASA HARINA MIXED WITH CRICKET FLOUR.
FLATTEN DOUGH INTO A TORTILLA AND COOK FOR A MINUTE OR TWO ON EACH SIDE.
SAUTÉ MEALWORMS WITH SHALLOTS AND OLIVE OIL.
LADLE ON THE TORTILLA ALONG WITH CHOPPED TOMATOES, CILANTRO, AND BEAN PASTE.
NO CRAP!

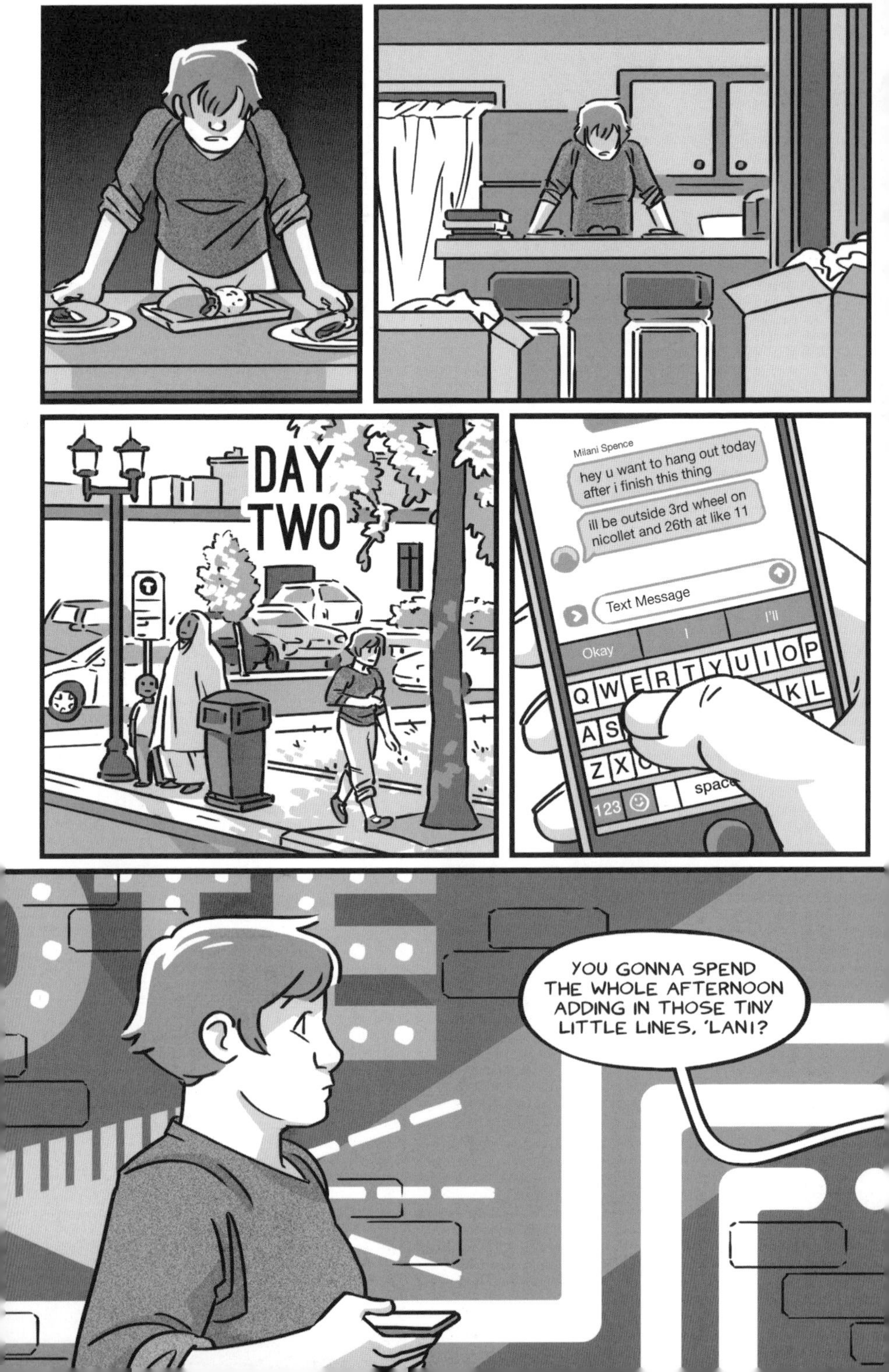
DAY TWO
Milani Spence
hey u want to hang out today after i finish this thing
ill be outside 3rd wheel on nicollet and 26th at like 11
Text Message
Okay
I
I'll
YOU GONNA SPEND THE WHOLE AFTERNOON ADDING IN THOSE TINY LITTLE LINES, 'LANI?

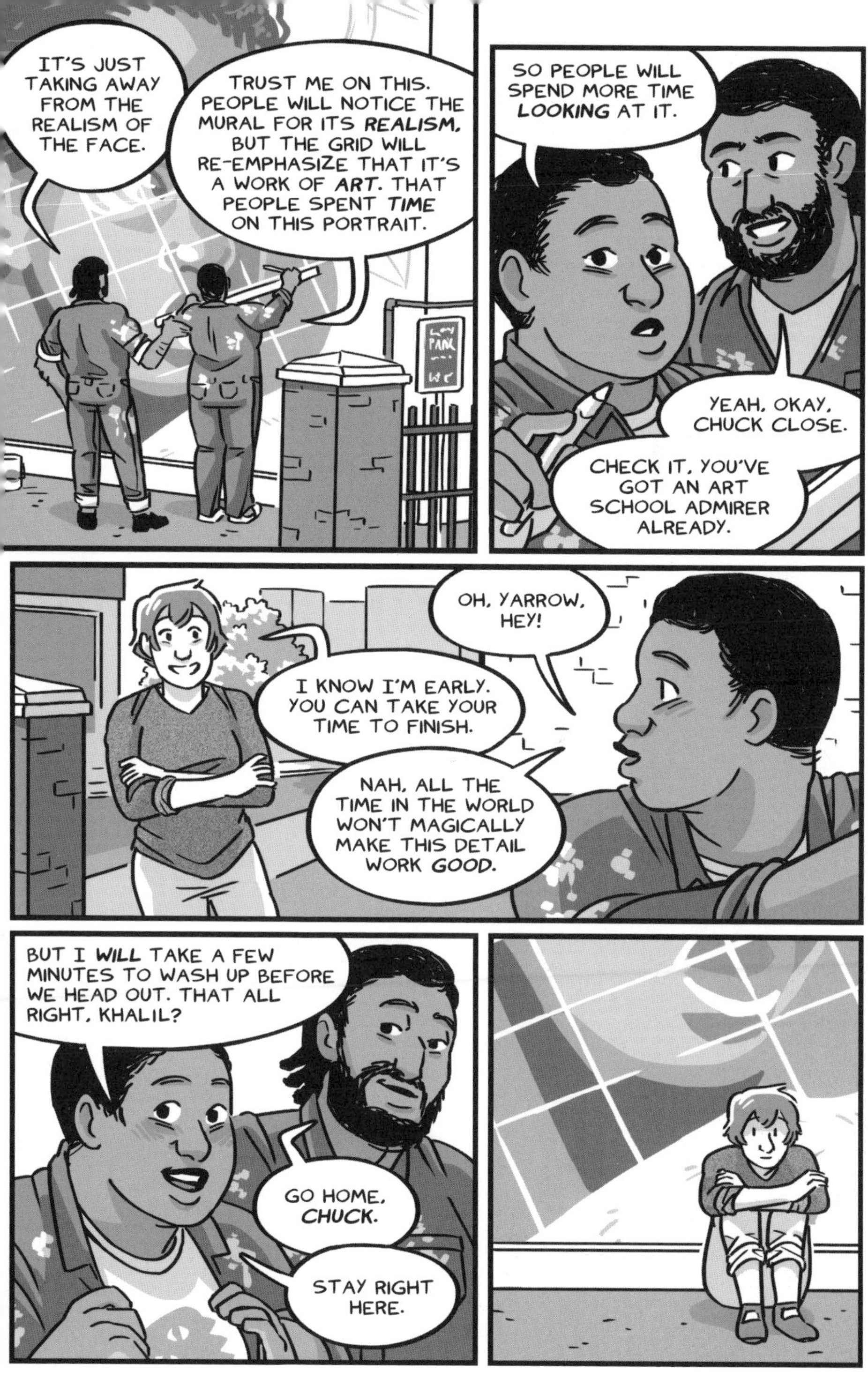
IT'S JUST TAKING AWAY FROM THE REALISM OF THE FACE.
TRUST ME ON THIS. PEOPLE WILL NOTICE THE MURAL FOR ITS ***REALISM,*** BUT THE GRID WILL RE-EMPHASIZE THAT IT'S A WORK OF ***ART***. THAT PEOPLE SPENT ***TIME*** ON THIS PORTRAIT.
SO PEOPLE WILL SPEND MORE TIME ***LOOKING*** AT IT.
YEAH, OKAY, CHUCK CLOSE.
CHECK IT, YOU'VE GOT AN ART SCHOOL ADMIRER ALREADY.
OH, YARROW, HEY!
I KNOW I'M EARLY. YOU CAN TAKE YOUR TIME TO FINISH.
NAH, ALL THE TIME IN THE WORLD WON'T MAGICALLY MAKE THIS DETAIL WORK ***GOOD***.
BUT I ***WILL*** TAKE A FEW MINUTES TO WASH UP BEFORE WE HEAD OUT. THAT ALL RIGHT, KHALIL?
GO HOME, ***CHUCK***.
STAY RIGHT HERE.

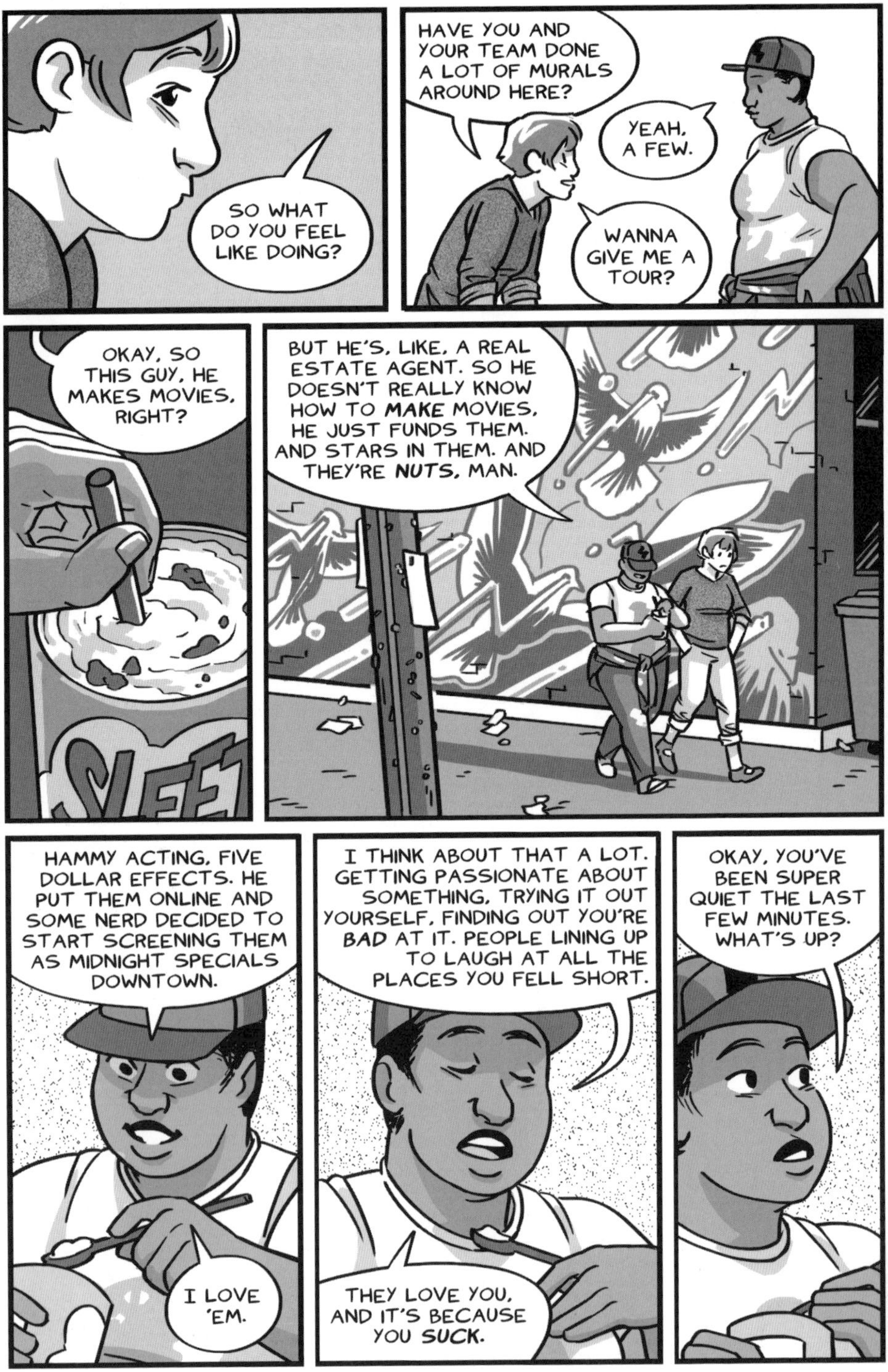
SO WHAT DO YOU FEEL LIKE DOING?
HAVE YOU AND YOUR TEAM DONE A LOT OF MURALS AROUND HERE?
YEAH, A FEW.
WANNA GIVE ME A TOUR?
OKAY, SO THIS GUY, HE MAKES MOVIES, RIGHT?
BUT HE'S, LIKE, A REAL ESTATE AGENT. SO HE DOESN'T REALLY KNOW HOW TO MAKE MOVIES, HE JUST FUNDS THEM. AND STARS IN THEM. AND THEY'RE NUTS, MAN.
HAMMY ACTING, FIVE DOLLAR EFFECTS. HE PUT THEM ONLINE AND SOME NERD DECIDED TO START SCREENING THEM AS MIDNIGHT SPECIALS DOWNTOWN.
I LOVE 'EM.
I THINK ABOUT THAT A LOT. GETTING PASSIONATE ABOUT SOMETHING, TRYING IT OUT YOURSELF, FINDING OUT YOU'RE BAD AT IT. PEOPLE LINING UP TO LAUGH AT ALL THE PLACES YOU FELL SHORT.
THEY LOVE YOU, AND IT'S BECAUSE YOU SUCK.
OKAY, YOU'VE BEEN SUPER QUIET THE LAST FEW MINUTES. WHAT'S UP?

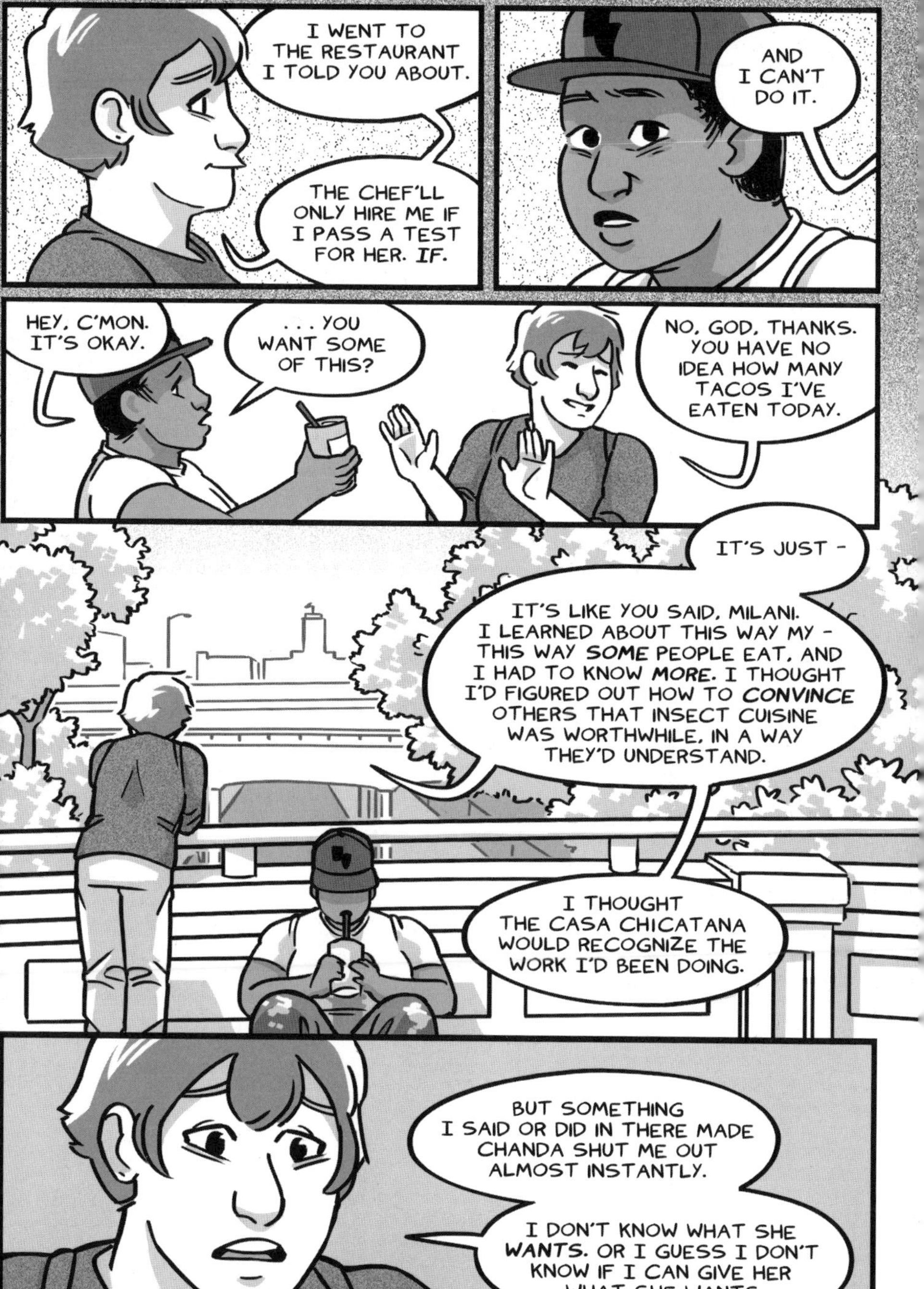
I WENT TO THE RESTAURANT I TOLD YOU ABOUT.
THE CHEF'LL ONLY HIRE ME IF I PASS A TEST FOR HER. *IF*.
AND I CAN'T DO IT.
HEY, C'MON. IT'S OKAY.
. . . YOU WANT SOME OF THIS?
NO, GOD, THANKS. YOU HAVE NO IDEA HOW MANY TACOS I'VE EATEN TODAY.
IT'S JUST -
IT'S LIKE YOU SAID, MILANI. I LEARNED ABOUT THIS WAY MY - THIS WAY **SOME** PEOPLE EAT, AND I HAD TO KNOW **MORE**. I THOUGHT I'D FIGURED OUT HOW TO **CONVINCE** OTHERS THAT INSECT CUISINE WAS WORTHWHILE, IN A WAY THEY'D UNDERSTAND.
I THOUGHT THE CASA CHICATANA WOULD RECOGNIZE THE WORK I'D BEEN DOING.
BUT SOMETHING I SAID OR DID IN THERE MADE CHANDA SHUT ME OUT ALMOST INSTANTLY.
I DON'T KNOW WHAT SHE **WANTS**. OR I GUESS I DON'T KNOW IF I CAN GIVE HER WHAT SHE WANTS.

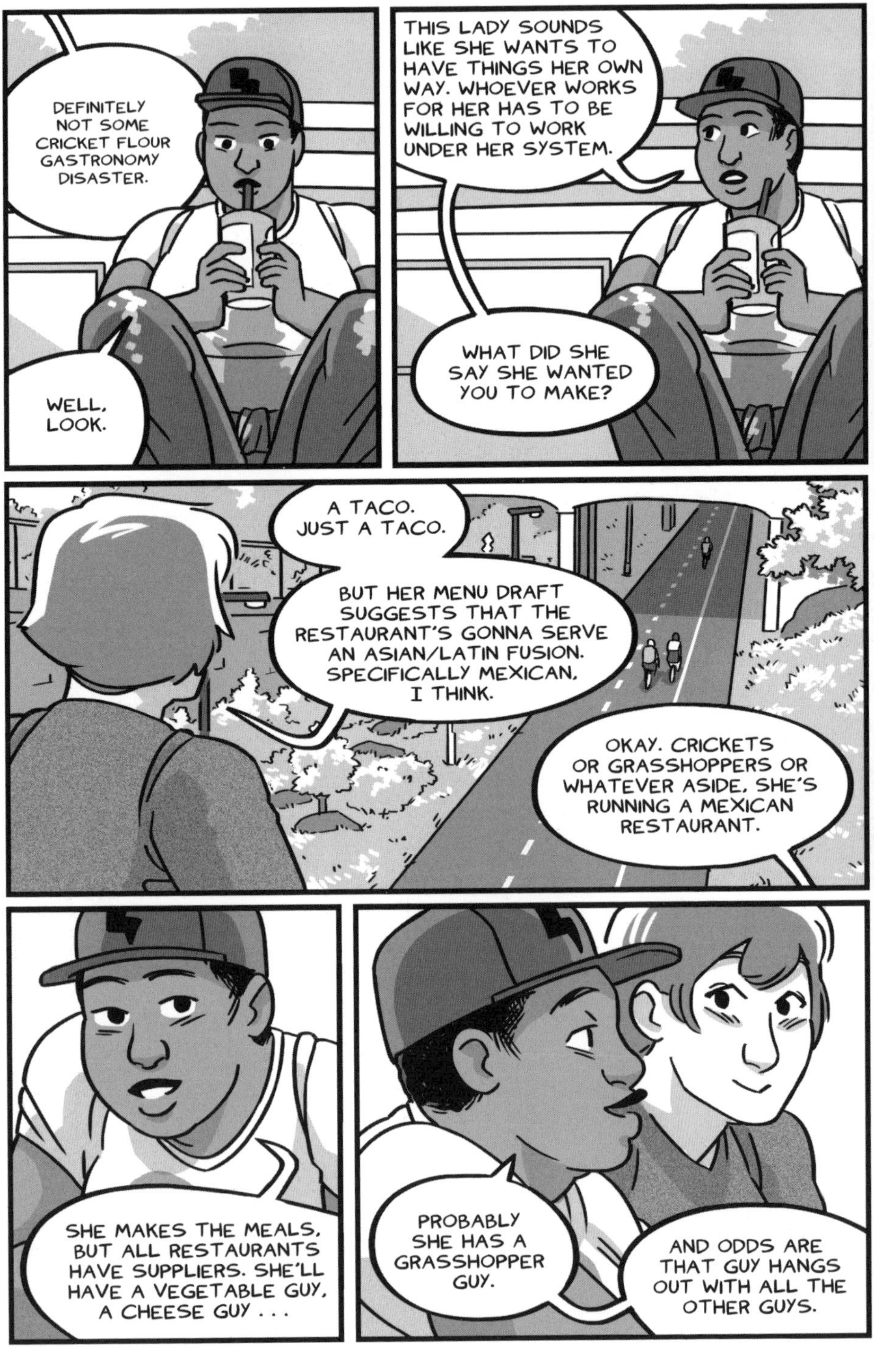
DEFINITELY NOT SOME CRICKET FLOUR GASTRONOMY DISASTER.
WELL, LOOK.
THIS LADY SOUNDS LIKE SHE WANTS TO HAVE THINGS HER OWN WAY. WHOEVER WORKS FOR HER HAS TO BE WILLING TO WORK UNDER HER SYSTEM.
WHAT DID SHE SAY SHE WANTED YOU TO MAKE?
A TACO. JUST A TACO.
BUT HER MENU DRAFT SUGGESTS THAT THE RESTAURANT'S GONNA SERVE AN ASIAN/LATIN FUSION. SPECIFICALLY MEXICAN, I THINK.
OKAY. CRICKETS OR GRASSHOPPERS OR WHATEVER ASIDE, SHE'S RUNNING A MEXICAN RESTAURANT.
SHE MAKES THE MEALS, BUT ALL RESTAURANTS HAVE SUPPLIERS. SHE'LL HAVE A VEGETABLE GUY, A CHEESE GUY . . .
PROBABLY SHE HAS A GRASSHOPPER GUY.
AND ODDS ARE THAT GUY HANGS OUT WITH ALL THE OTHER GUYS.

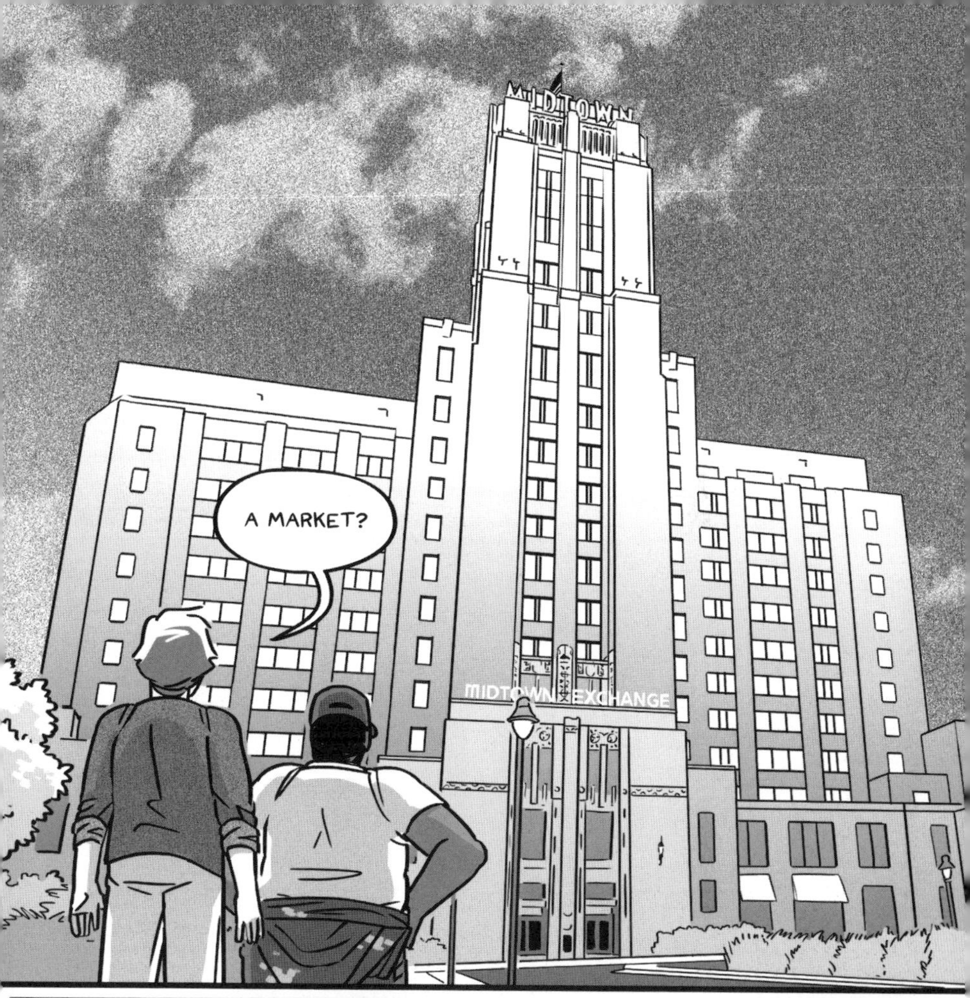
MIDTOWN
MIDTOWN EXCHANGE
A MARKET?

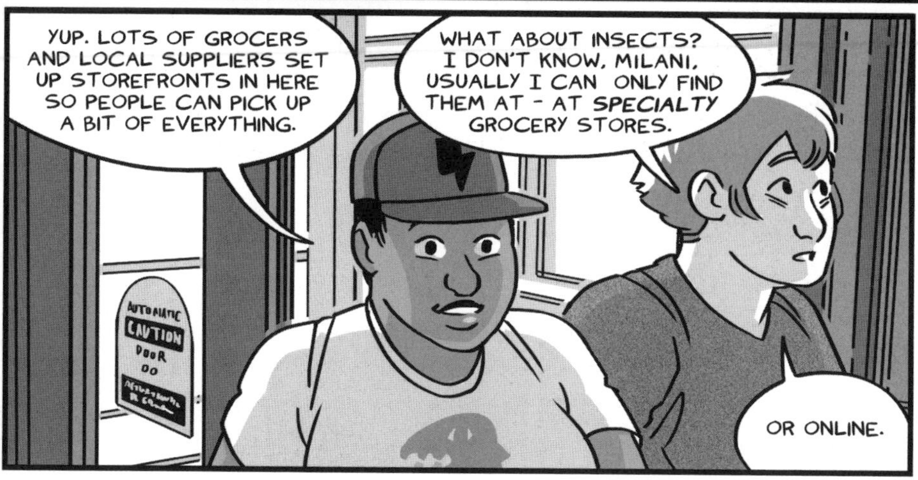
YUP. LOTS OF GROCERS AND LOCAL SUPPLIERS SET UP STOREFRONTS IN HERE SO PEOPLE CAN PICK UP A BIT OF EVERYTHING.
WHAT ABOUT INSECTS? I DON'T KNOW, MILANI, USUALLY I CAN ONLY FIND THEM AT - AT *SPECIALTY* GROCERY STORES.
OR ONLINE.
AUTOMATIC CAUTION DOOR

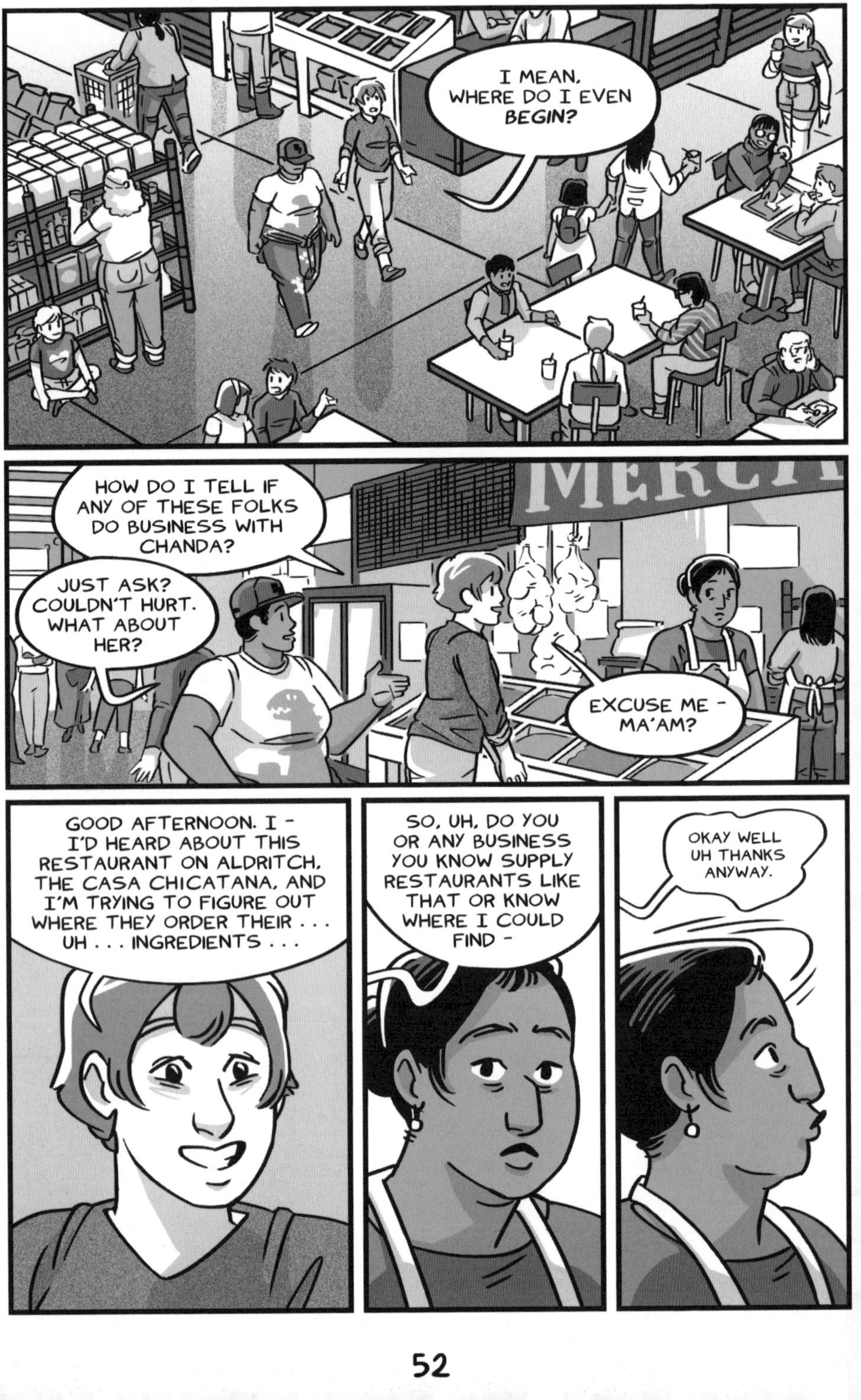
I MEAN, WHERE DO I EVEN BEGIN?
MERC
HOW DO I TELL IF ANY OF THESE FOLKS DO BUSINESS WITH CHANDA?
JUST ASK? COULDN'T HURT. WHAT ABOUT HER?
EXCUSE ME - MA'AM?
GOOD AFTERNOON. I - I'D HEARD ABOUT THIS RESTAURANT ON ALDRITCH, THE CASA CHICATANA, AND I'M TRYING TO FIGURE OUT WHERE THEY ORDER THEIR . . . UH . . . INGREDIENTS . . .
SO, UH, DO YOU OR ANY BUSINESS YOU KNOW SUPPLY RESTAURANTS LIKE THAT OR KNOW WHERE I COULD FIND -
OKAY WELL UH THANKS ANYWAY.

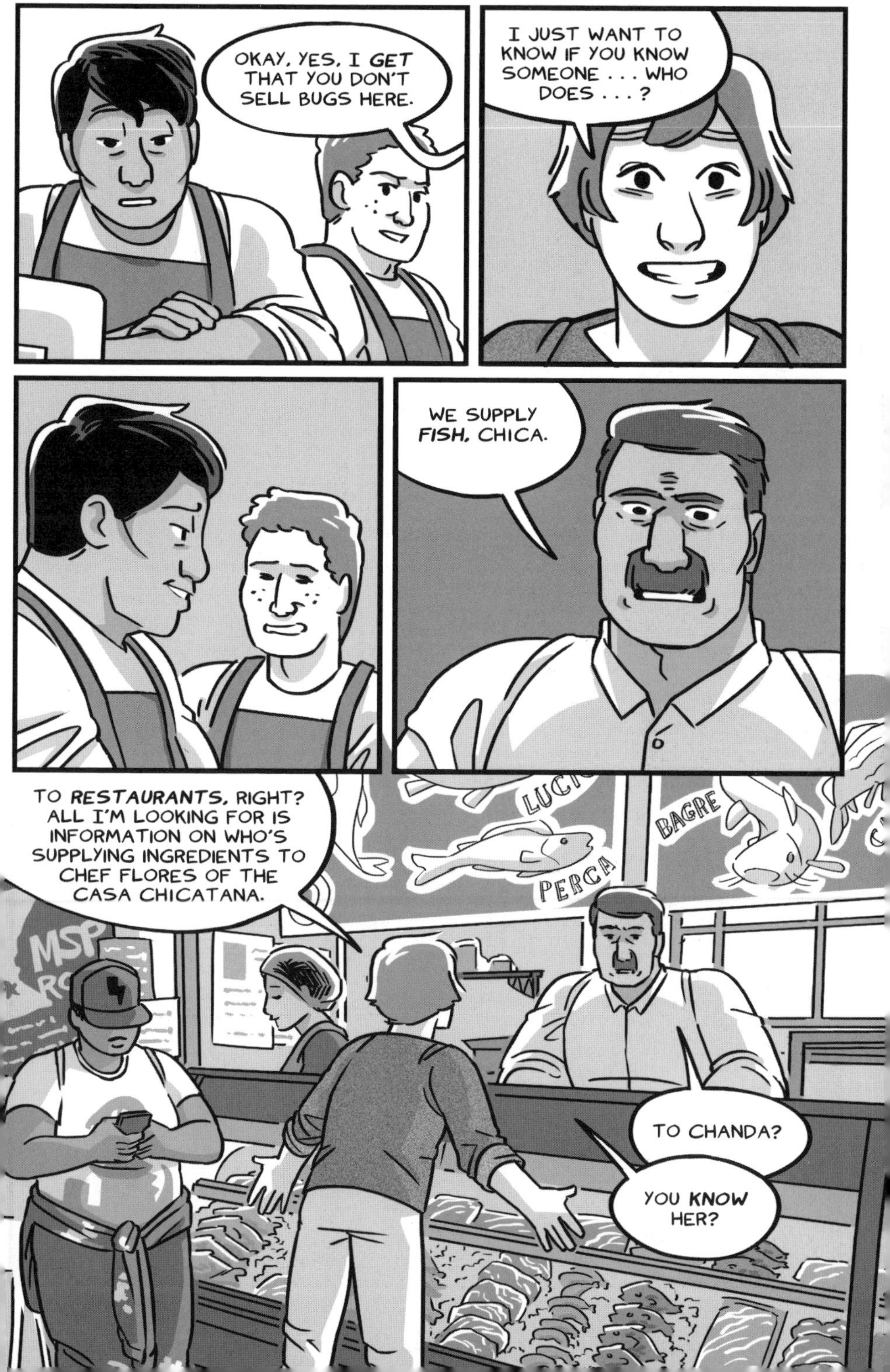
OKAY, YES, I GET THAT YOU DON'T SELL BUGS HERE.
I JUST WANT TO KNOW IF YOU KNOW SOMEONE . . . WHO DOES . . . ?
WE SUPPLY FISH, CHICA.
TO RESTAURANTS, RIGHT? ALL I'M LOOKING FOR IS INFORMATION ON WHO'S SUPPLYING INGREDIENTS TO CHEF FLORES OF THE CASA CHICATANA.
BAGRE
PERCA
TO CHANDA?
YOU KNOW HER?

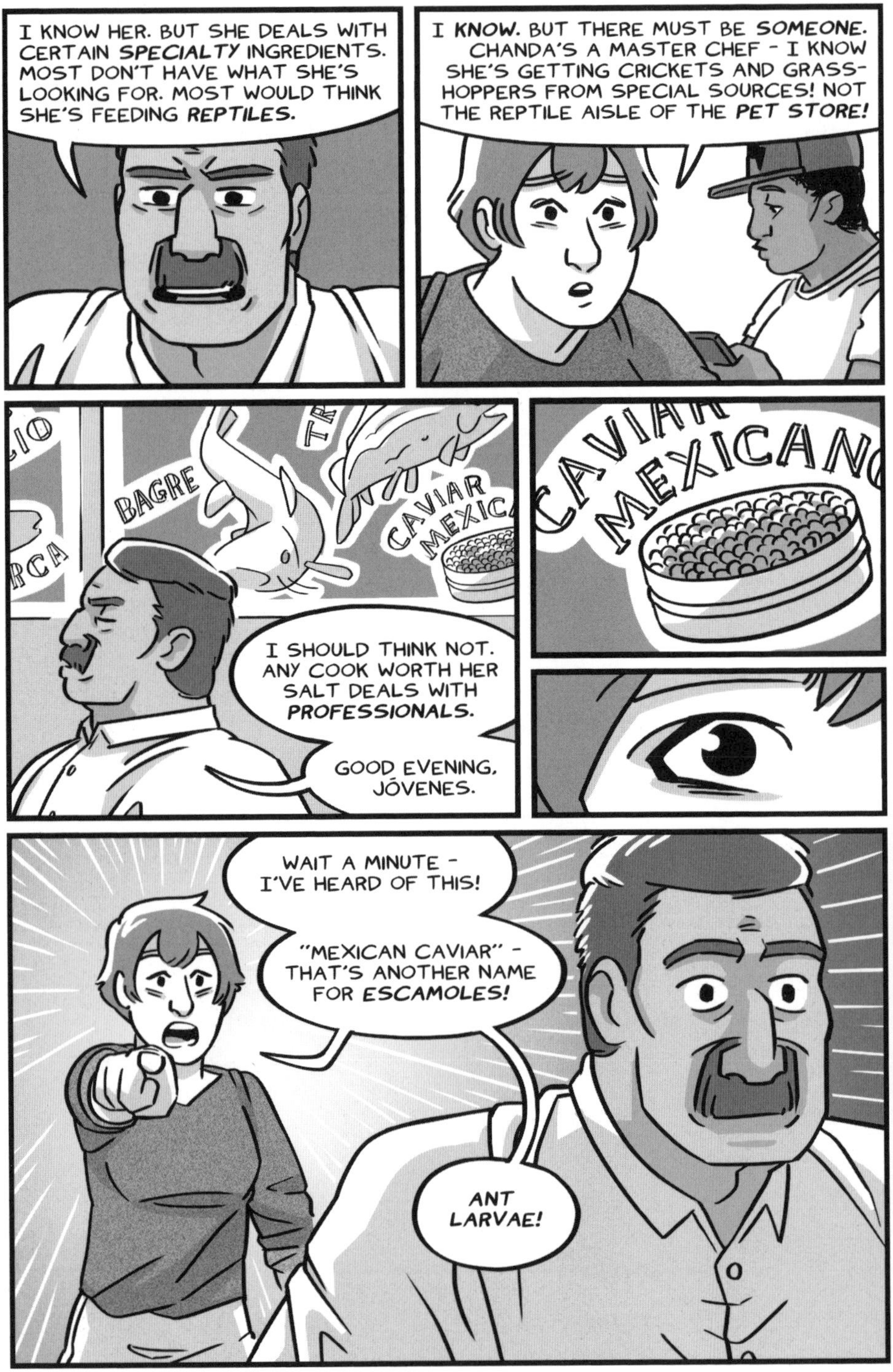
I KNOW HER. BUT SHE DEALS WITH CERTAIN *SPECIALTY* INGREDIENTS. MOST DON'T HAVE WHAT SHE'S LOOKING FOR. MOST WOULD THINK SHE'S FEEDING *REPTILES.*
I *KNOW.* BUT THERE MUST BE *SOMEONE.* CHANDA'S A MASTER CHEF - I KNOW SHE'S GETTING CRICKETS AND GRASS-HOPPERS FROM SPECIAL SOURCES! NOT THE REPTILE AISLE OF THE *PET STORE!*
BAGRE
CAVIAR MEXIC
I SHOULD THINK NOT. ANY COOK WORTH HER SALT DEALS WITH *PROFESSIONALS.*
GOOD EVENING, JÓVENES.
CAVIAR MEXICANO
WAIT A MINUTE - I'VE HEARD OF THIS!
"MEXICAN CAVIAR" - THAT'S ANOTHER NAME FOR *ESCAMOLES!*
ANT LARVAE!

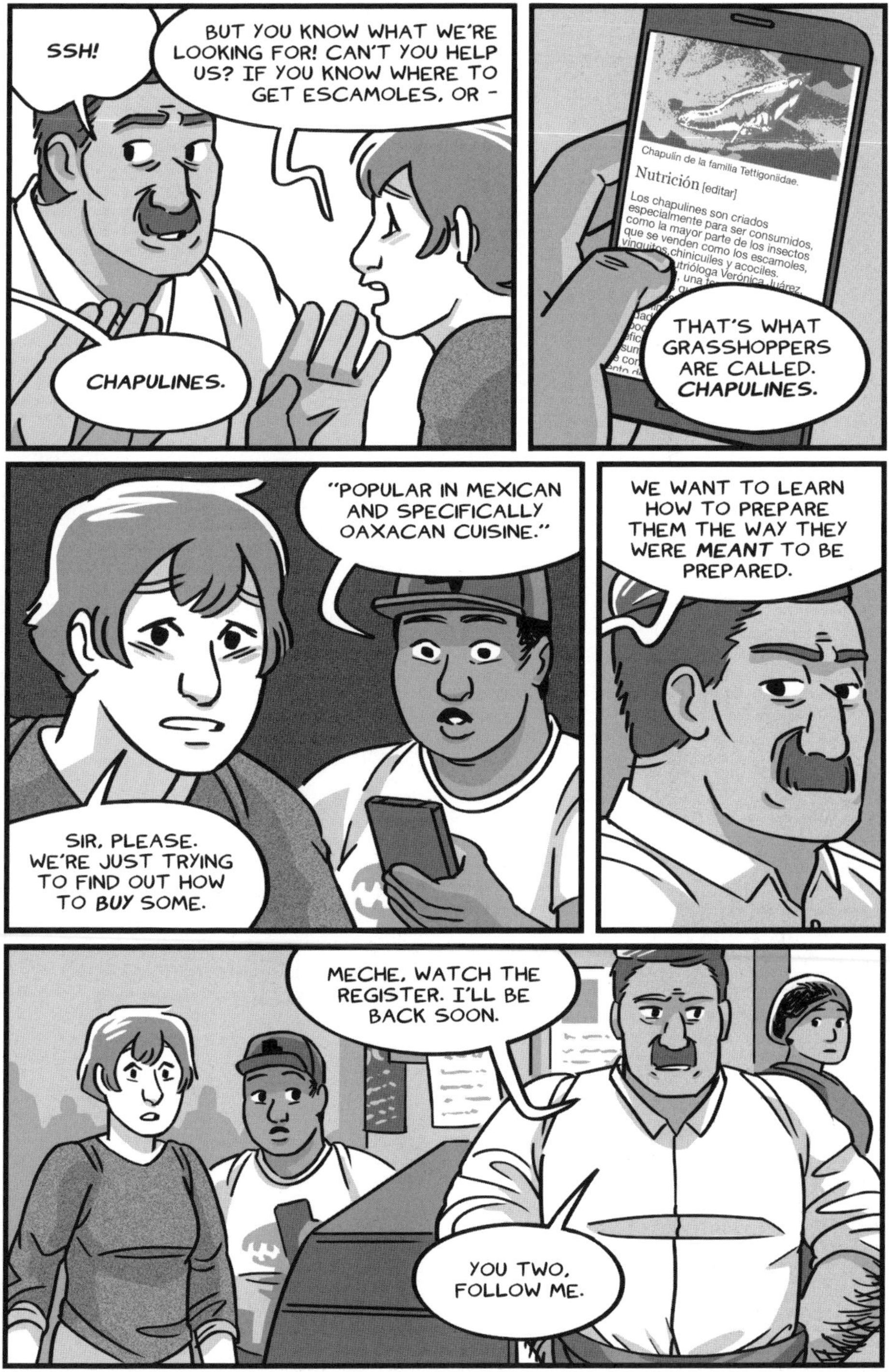
SSH!
BUT YOU KNOW WHAT WE'RE LOOKING FOR! CAN'T YOU HELP US? IF YOU KNOW WHERE TO GET ESCAMOLES, OR -
CHAPULINES.
Chapulín de la familia Tettigoniidae.
Nutrición [editar]
Los chapulines son criados especialmente para ser consumidos, como la mayor parte de los insectos que se venden como los escamoles, vinguitos, chinicuiles y acociles.
THAT'S WHAT GRASSHOPPERS ARE CALLED. CHAPULINES.
"POPULAR IN MEXICAN AND SPECIFICALLY OAXACAN CUISINE."
SIR, PLEASE. WE'RE JUST TRYING TO FIND OUT HOW TO BUY SOME.
WE WANT TO LEARN HOW TO PREPARE THEM THE WAY THEY WERE MEANT TO BE PREPARED.
MECHE, WATCH THE REGISTER. I'LL BE BACK SOON.
YOU TWO, FOLLOW ME.

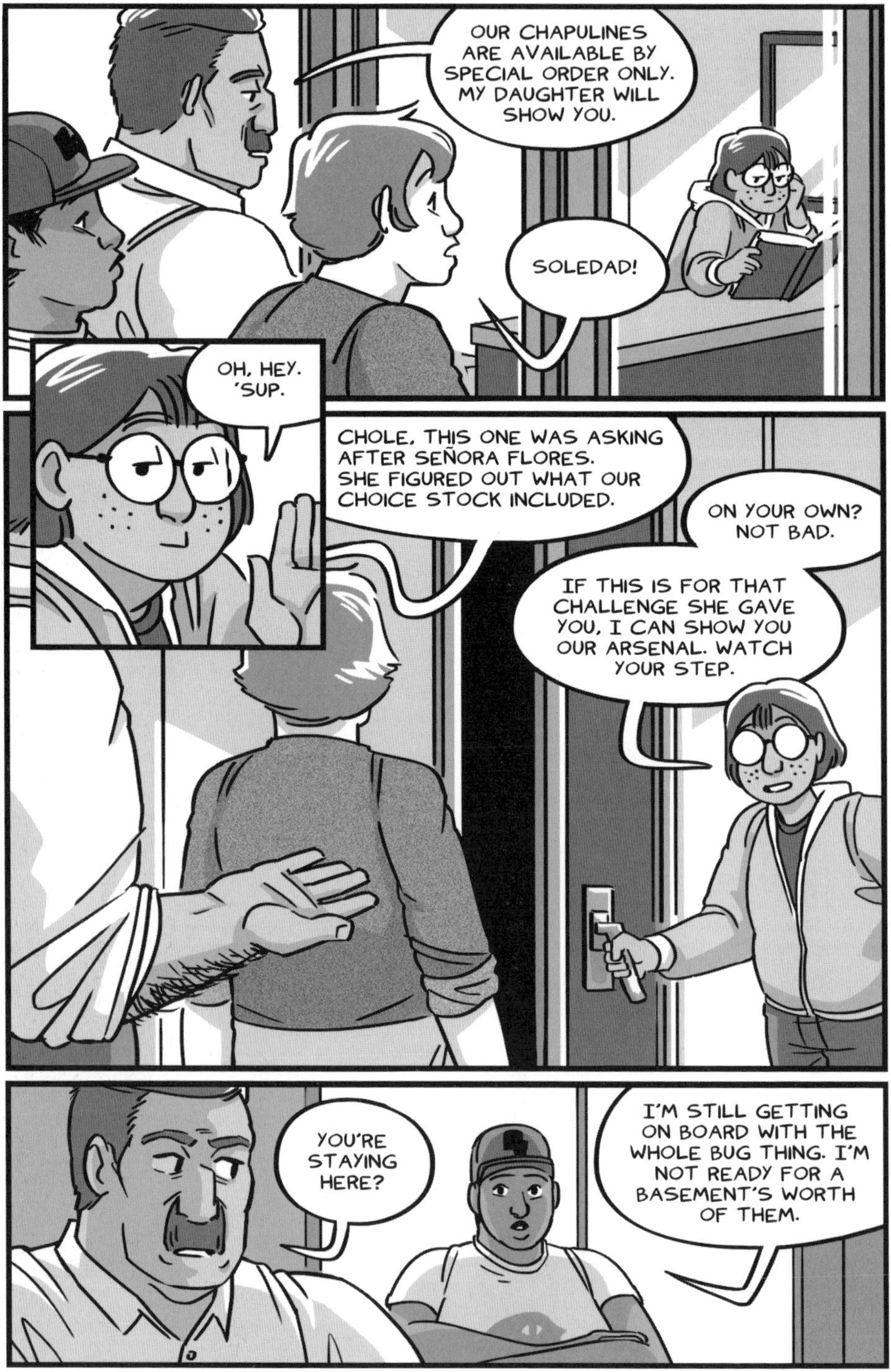
OUR CHAPULINES ARE AVAILABLE BY SPECIAL ORDER ONLY. MY DAUGHTER WILL SHOW YOU.
SOLEDAD!
OH, HEY. 'SUP.
CHOLE, THIS ONE WAS ASKING AFTER SEÑORA FLORES. SHE FIGURED OUT WHAT OUR CHOICE STOCK INCLUDED.
ON YOUR OWN? NOT BAD.
IF THIS IS FOR THAT CHALLENGE SHE GAVE YOU, I CAN SHOW YOU OUR ARSENAL. WATCH YOUR STEP.
YOU'RE STAYING HERE?
I'M STILL GETTING ON BOARD WITH THE WHOLE BUG THING. I'M NOT READY FOR A BASEMENT'S WORTH OF THEM.

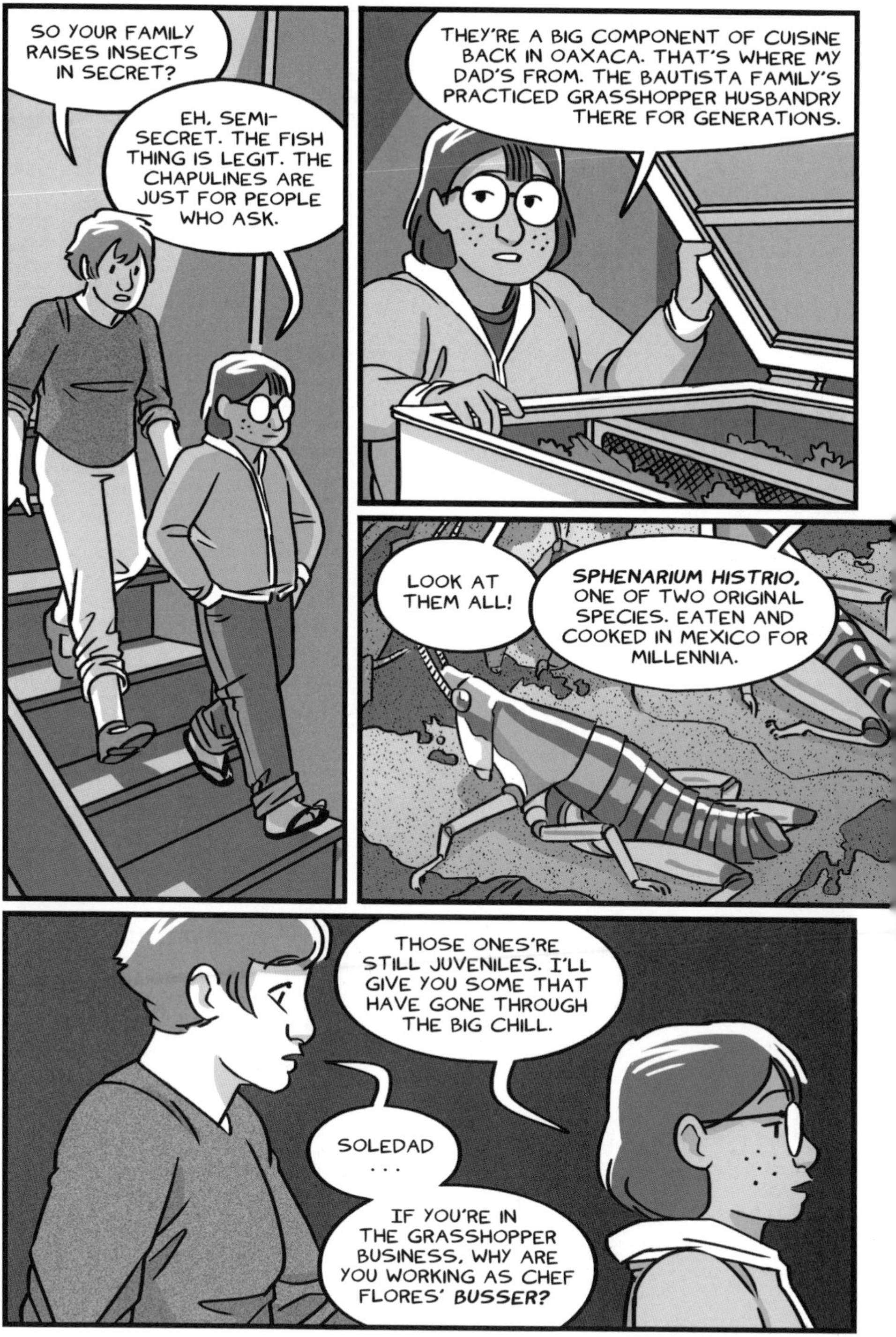

SO YOUR FAMILY RAISES INSECTS IN SECRET?
EH, SEMI-SECRET. THE FISH THING IS LEGIT. THE CHAPULINES ARE JUST FOR PEOPLE WHO ASK.
THEY'RE A BIG COMPONENT OF CUISINE BACK IN OAXACA. THAT'S WHERE MY DAD'S FROM. THE BAUTISTA FAMILY'S PRACTICED GRASSHOPPER HUSBANDRY THERE FOR GENERATIONS.
LOOK AT THEM ALL!
SPHENARIUM HISTRIO, ONE OF TWO ORIGINAL SPECIES. EATEN AND COOKED IN MEXICO FOR MILLENNIA.
THOSE ONES'RE STILL JUVENILES. I'LL GIVE YOU SOME THAT HAVE GONE THROUGH THE BIG CHILL.
SOLEDAD . . .
IF YOU'RE IN THE GRASSHOPPER BUSINESS, WHY ARE YOU WORKING AS CHEF FLORES' *BUSSER?*

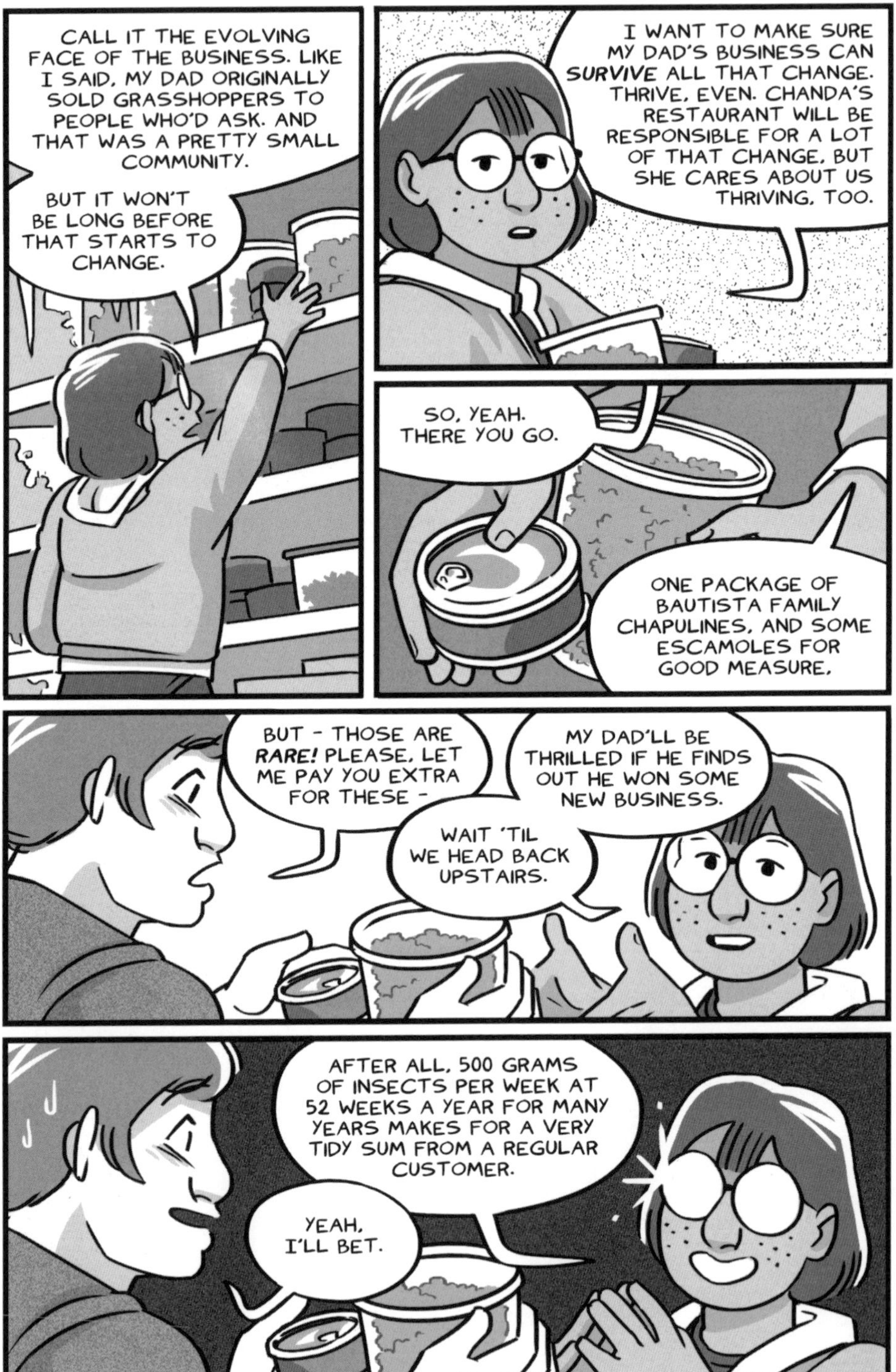
CALL IT THE EVOLVING FACE OF THE BUSINESS. LIKE I SAID, MY DAD ORIGINALLY SOLD GRASSHOPPERS TO PEOPLE WHO'D ASK. AND THAT WAS A PRETTY SMALL COMMUNITY.
BUT IT WON'T BE LONG BEFORE THAT STARTS TO CHANGE.
I WANT TO MAKE SURE MY DAD'S BUSINESS CAN *SURVIVE* ALL THAT CHANGE. THRIVE, EVEN. CHANDA'S RESTAURANT WILL BE RESPONSIBLE FOR A LOT OF THAT CHANGE, BUT SHE CARES ABOUT US THRIVING, TOO.
SO, YEAH. THERE YOU GO.
ONE PACKAGE OF BAUTISTA FAMILY CHAPULINES, AND SOME ESCAMOLES FOR GOOD MEASURE.
BUT - THOSE ARE *RARE!* PLEASE, LET ME PAY YOU EXTRA FOR THESE -
MY DAD'LL BE THRILLED IF HE FINDS OUT HE WON SOME NEW BUSINESS.
WAIT 'TIL WE HEAD BACK UPSTAIRS.
AFTER ALL, 500 GRAMS OF INSECTS PER WEEK AT 52 WEEKS A YEAR FOR MANY YEARS MAKES FOR A VERY TIDY SUM FROM A REGULAR CUSTOMER.
YEAH, I'LL BET.

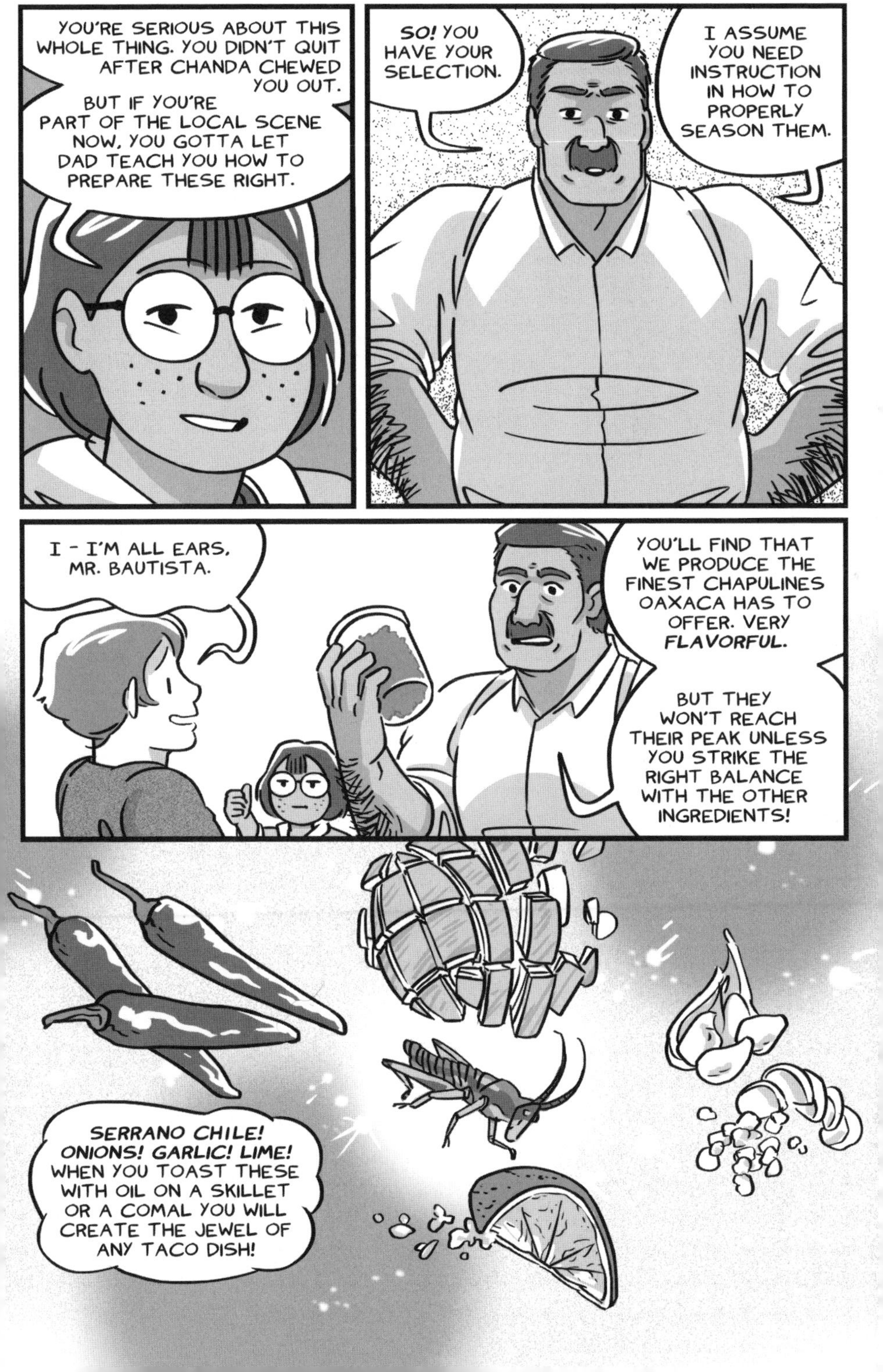
YOU'RE SERIOUS ABOUT THIS WHOLE THING. YOU DIDN'T QUIT AFTER CHANDA CHEWED YOU OUT.
BUT IF YOU'RE PART OF THE LOCAL SCENE NOW, YOU GOTTA LET DAD TEACH YOU HOW TO PREPARE THESE RIGHT.
SO! YOU HAVE YOUR SELECTION.
I ASSUME YOU NEED INSTRUCTION IN HOW TO PROPERLY SEASON THEM.
I - I'M ALL EARS, MR. BAUTISTA.
YOU'LL FIND THAT WE PRODUCE THE FINEST CHAPULINES OAXACA HAS TO OFFER. VERY FLAVORFUL.
BUT THEY WON'T REACH THEIR PEAK UNLESS YOU STRIKE THE RIGHT BALANCE WITH THE OTHER INGREDIENTS!
SERRANO CHILE! ONIONS! GARLIC! LIME! WHEN YOU TOAST THESE WITH OIL ON A SKILLET OR A COMAL YOU WILL CREATE THE JEWEL OF ANY TACO DISH!

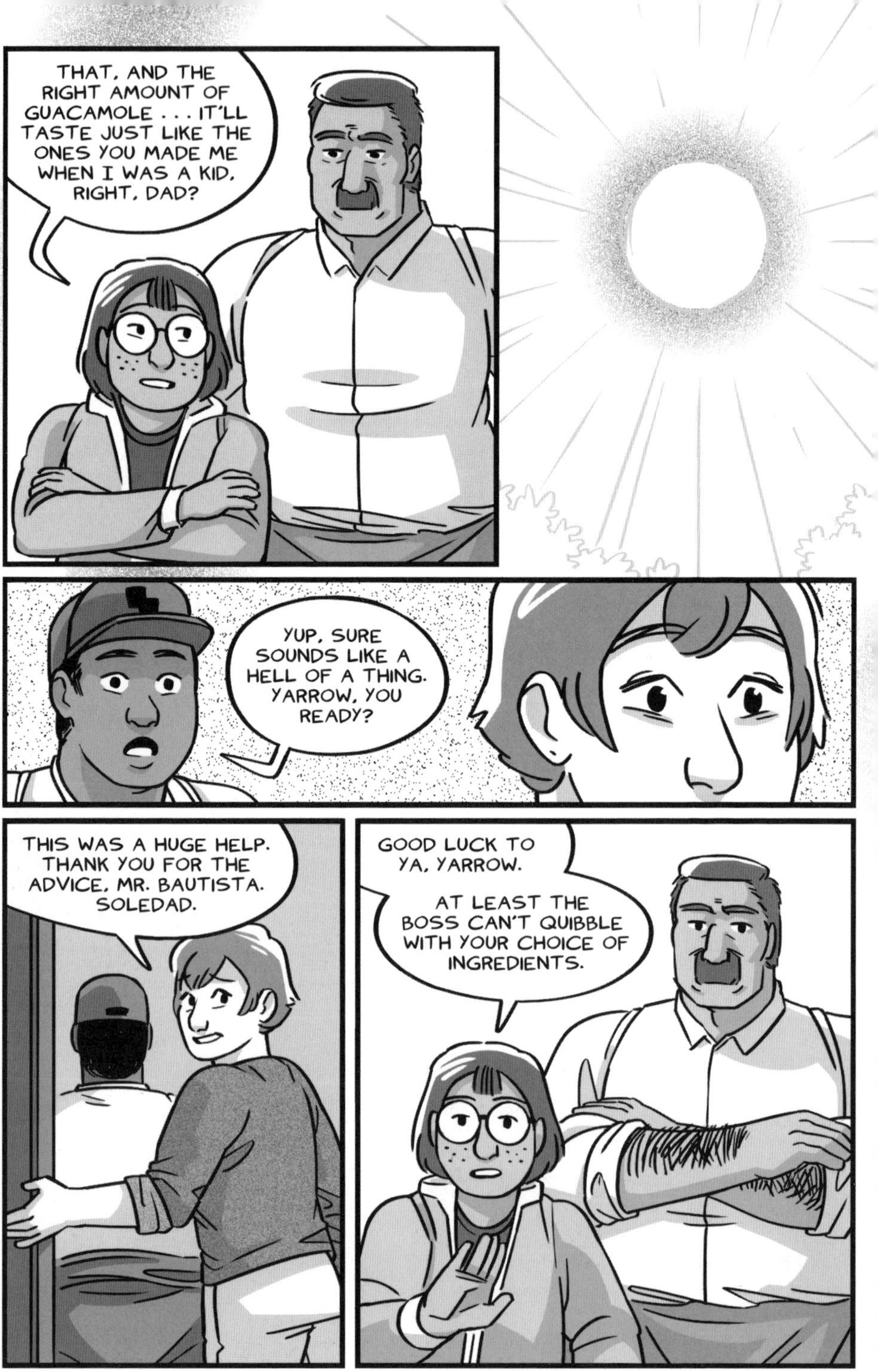
THAT, AND THE RIGHT AMOUNT OF GUACAMOLE . . . IT'LL TASTE JUST LIKE THE ONES YOU MADE ME WHEN I WAS A KID, RIGHT, DAD?
YUP, SURE SOUNDS LIKE A HELL OF A THING. YARROW, YOU READY?
THIS WAS A HUGE HELP. THANK YOU FOR THE ADVICE, MR. BAUTISTA. SOLEDAD.
GOOD LUCK TO YA, YARROW.
AT LEAST THE BOSS CAN'T QUIBBLE WITH YOUR CHOICE OF INGREDIENTS.

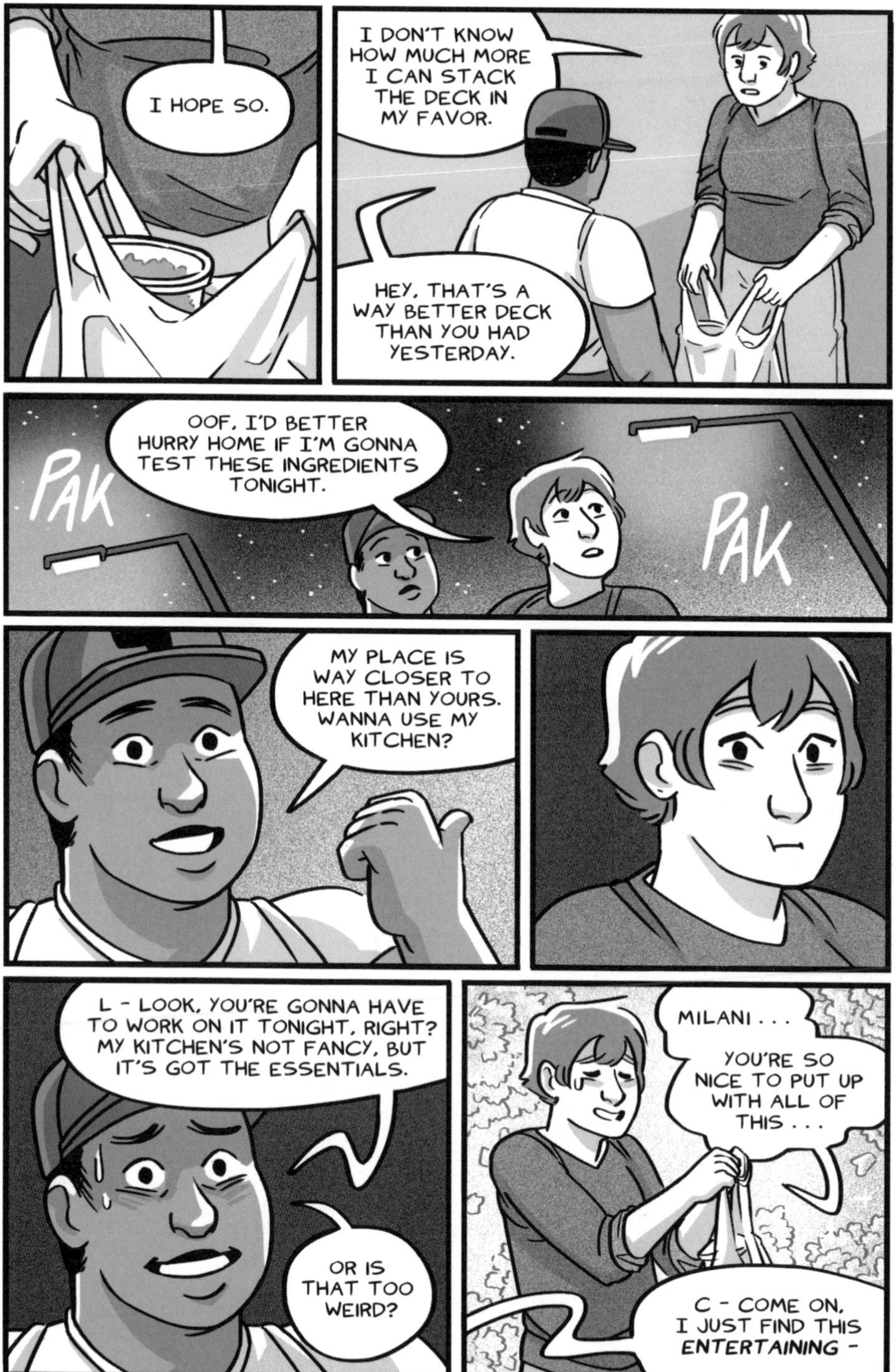
I HOPE SO.
I DON'T KNOW HOW MUCH MORE I CAN STACK THE DECK IN MY FAVOR.
HEY, THAT'S A WAY BETTER DECK THAN YOU HAD YESTERDAY.
OOF, I'D BETTER HURRY HOME IF I'M GONNA TEST THESE INGREDIENTS TONIGHT.
PAK
PAK
MY PLACE IS WAY CLOSER TO HERE THAN YOURS. WANNA USE MY KITCHEN?
L - LOOK, YOU'RE GONNA HAVE TO WORK ON IT TONIGHT, RIGHT? MY KITCHEN'S NOT FANCY, BUT IT'S GOT THE ESSENTIALS.
OR IS THAT TOO WEIRD?
MILANI . . .
YOU'RE SO NICE TO PUT UP WITH ALL OF THIS . . .
C - COME ON, I JUST FIND THIS *ENTERTAINING* -

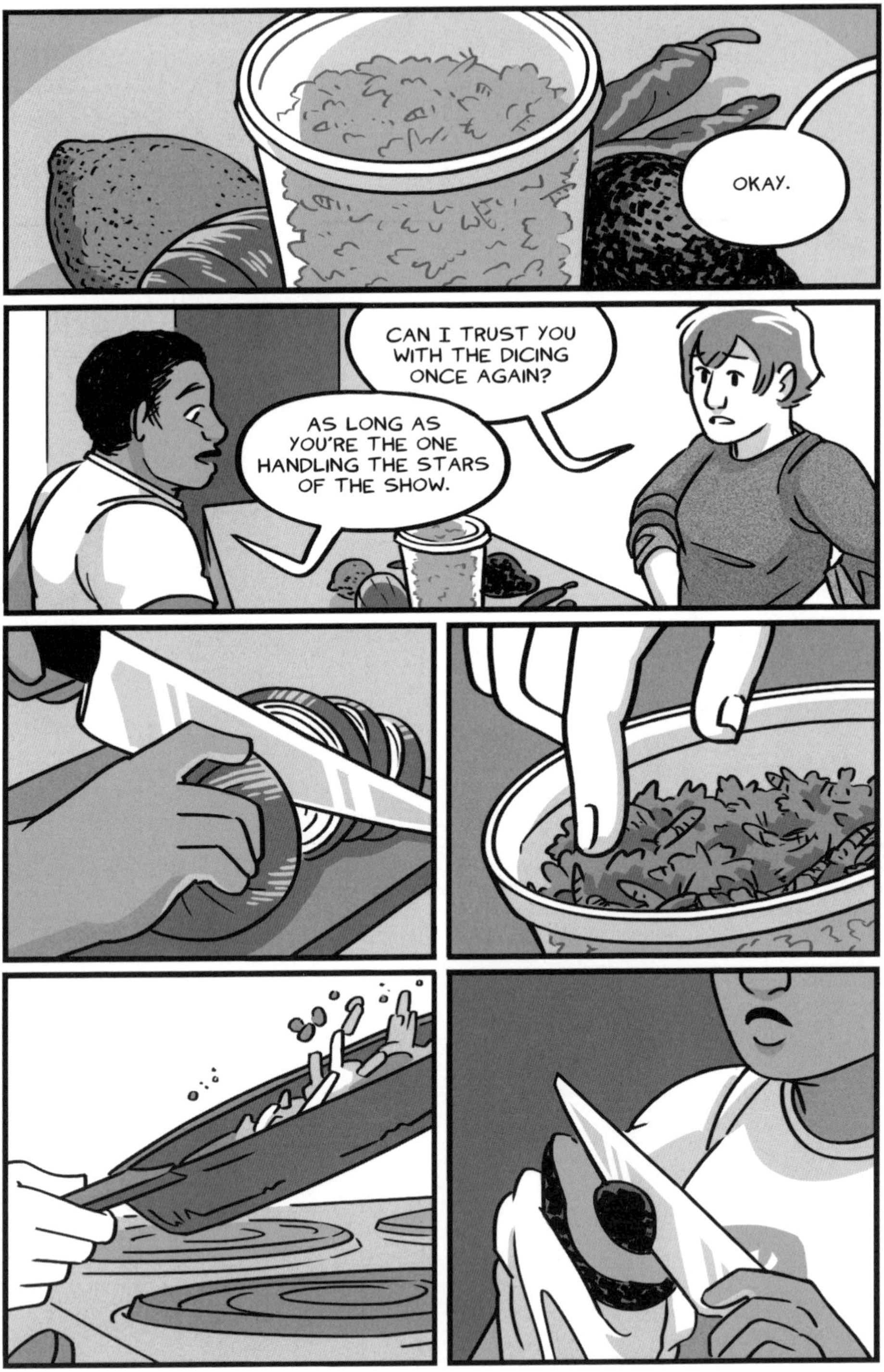
OKAY.
CAN I TRUST YOU WITH THE DICING ONCE AGAIN?
AS LONG AS YOU'RE THE ONE HANDLING THE STARS OF THE SHOW.

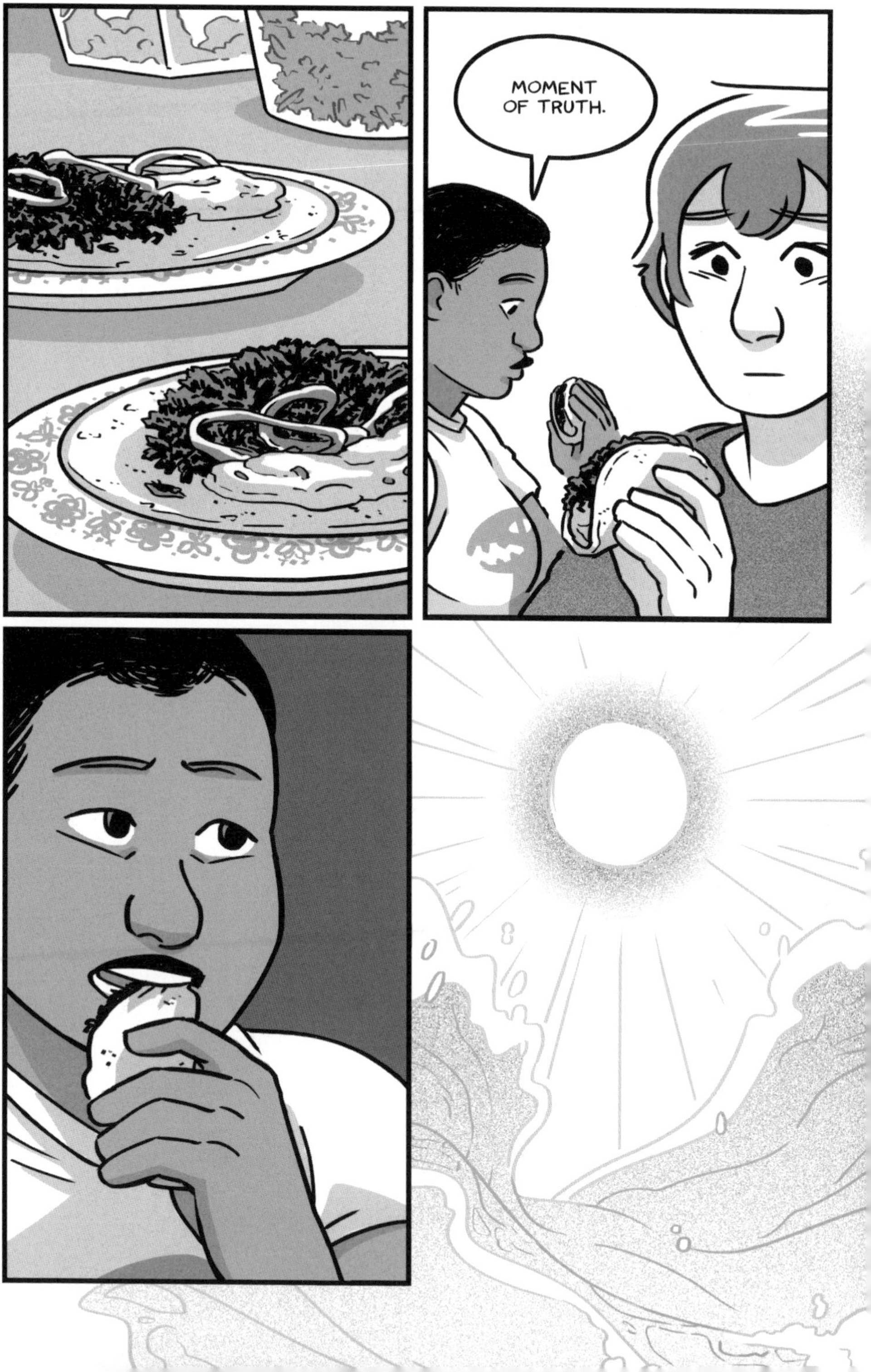
MOMENT OF TRUTH.

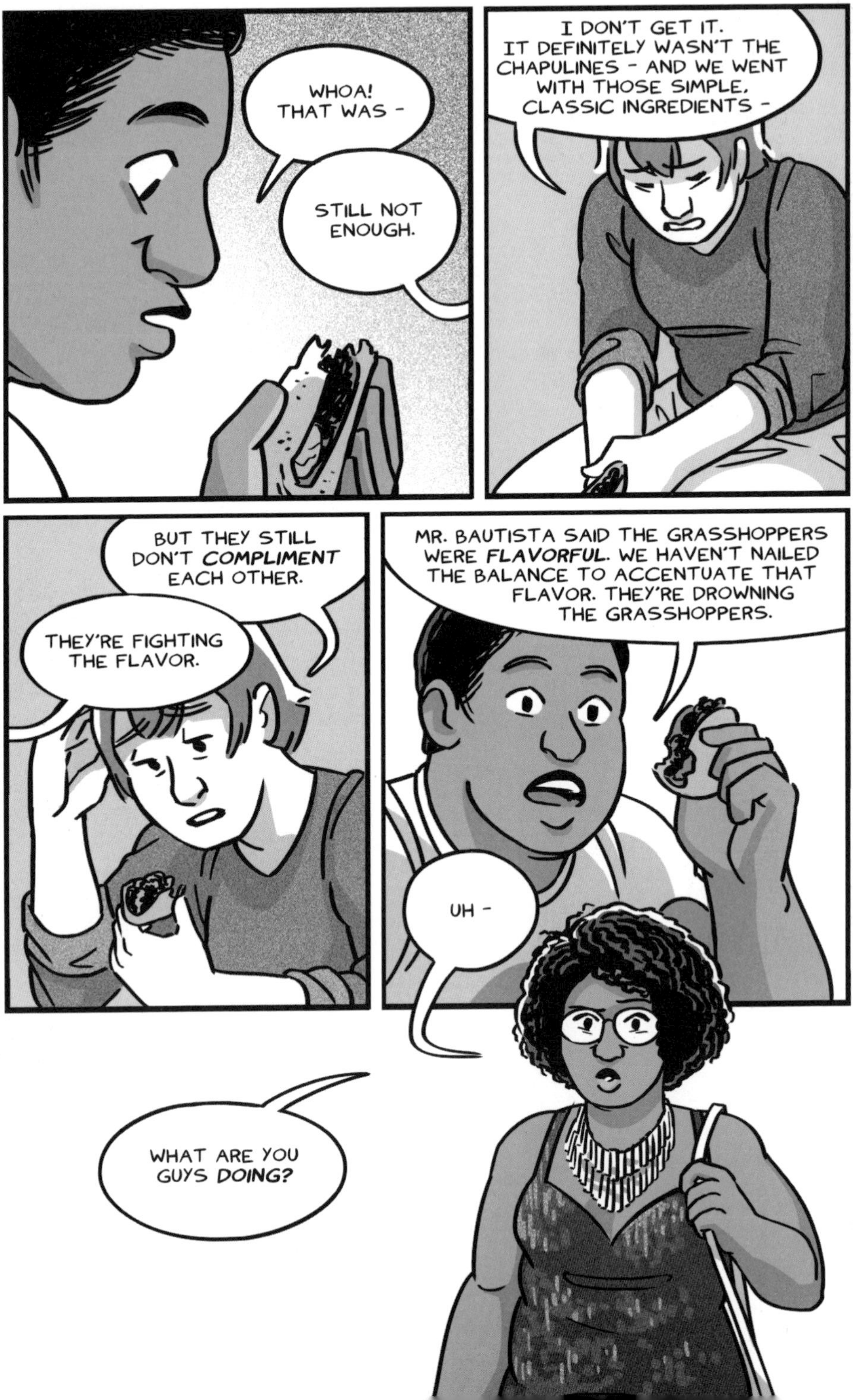
WHOA! THAT WAS -
STILL NOT ENOUGH.
I DON'T GET IT. IT DEFINITELY WASN'T THE CHAPULINES - AND WE WENT WITH THOSE SIMPLE, CLASSIC INGREDIENTS -
BUT THEY STILL DON'T **COMPLIMENT** EACH OTHER.
THEY'RE FIGHTING THE FLAVOR.
MR. BAUTISTA SAID THE GRASSHOPPERS WERE **FLAVORFUL**. WE HAVEN'T NAILED THE BALANCE TO ACCENTUATE THAT FLAVOR. THEY'RE DROWNING THE GRASSHOPPERS.
UH -
WHAT ARE YOU GUYS **DOING?**

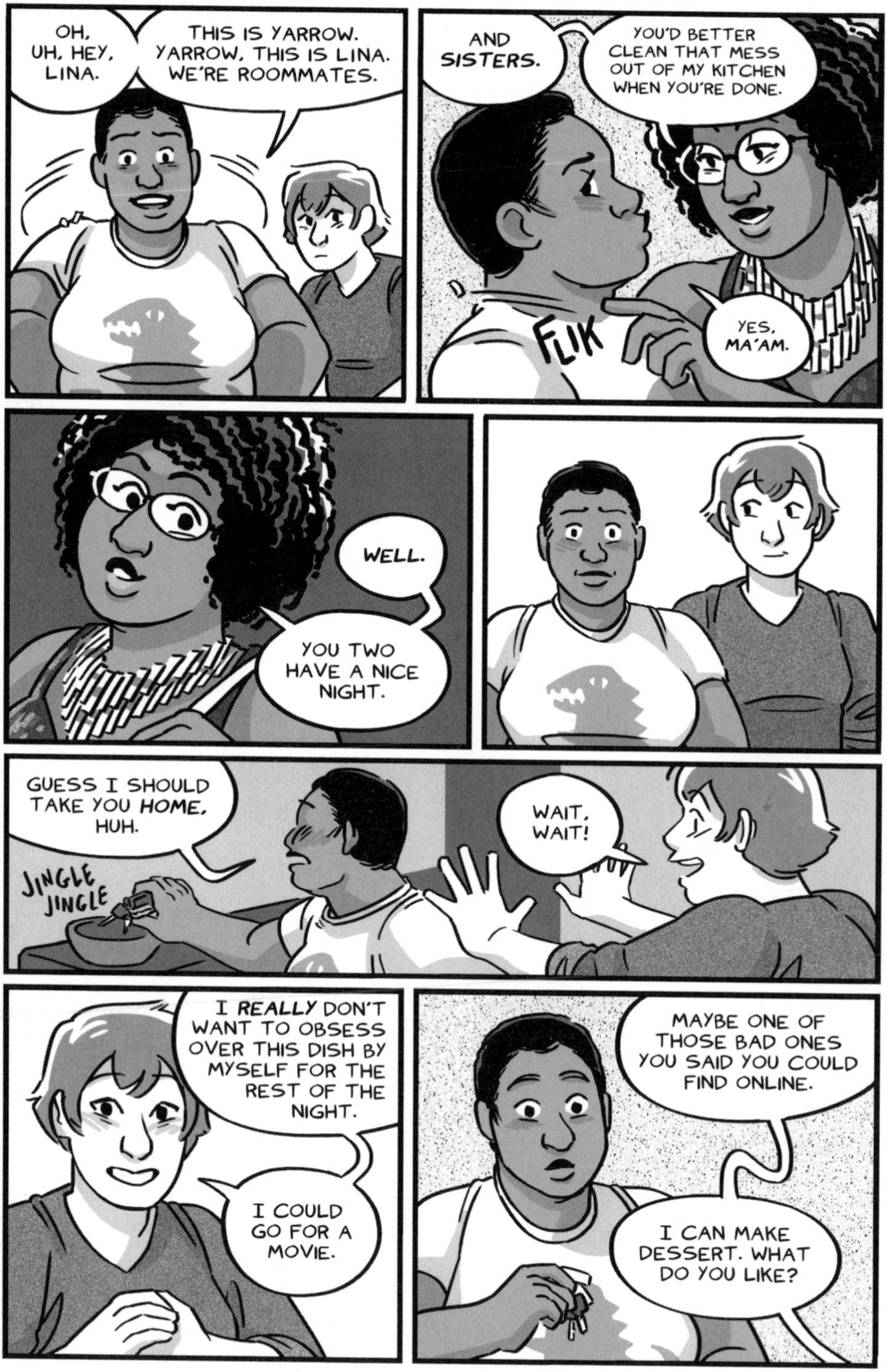
OH, UH, HEY, LINA.
THIS IS YARROW. YARROW, THIS IS LINA. WE'RE ROOMMATES.
AND SISTERS.
YOU'D BETTER CLEAN THAT MESS OUT OF MY KITCHEN WHEN YOU'RE DONE.
FLIK
YES, MA'AM.
WELL.
YOU TWO HAVE A NICE NIGHT.
GUESS I SHOULD TAKE YOU HOME, HUH.
JINGLE JINGLE
WAIT, WAIT!
I REALLY DON'T WANT TO OBSESS OVER THIS DISH BY MYSELF FOR THE REST OF THE NIGHT.
I COULD GO FOR A MOVIE.
MAYBE ONE OF THOSE BAD ONES YOU SAID YOU COULD FIND ONLINE.
I CAN MAKE DESSERT. WHAT DO YOU LIKE?

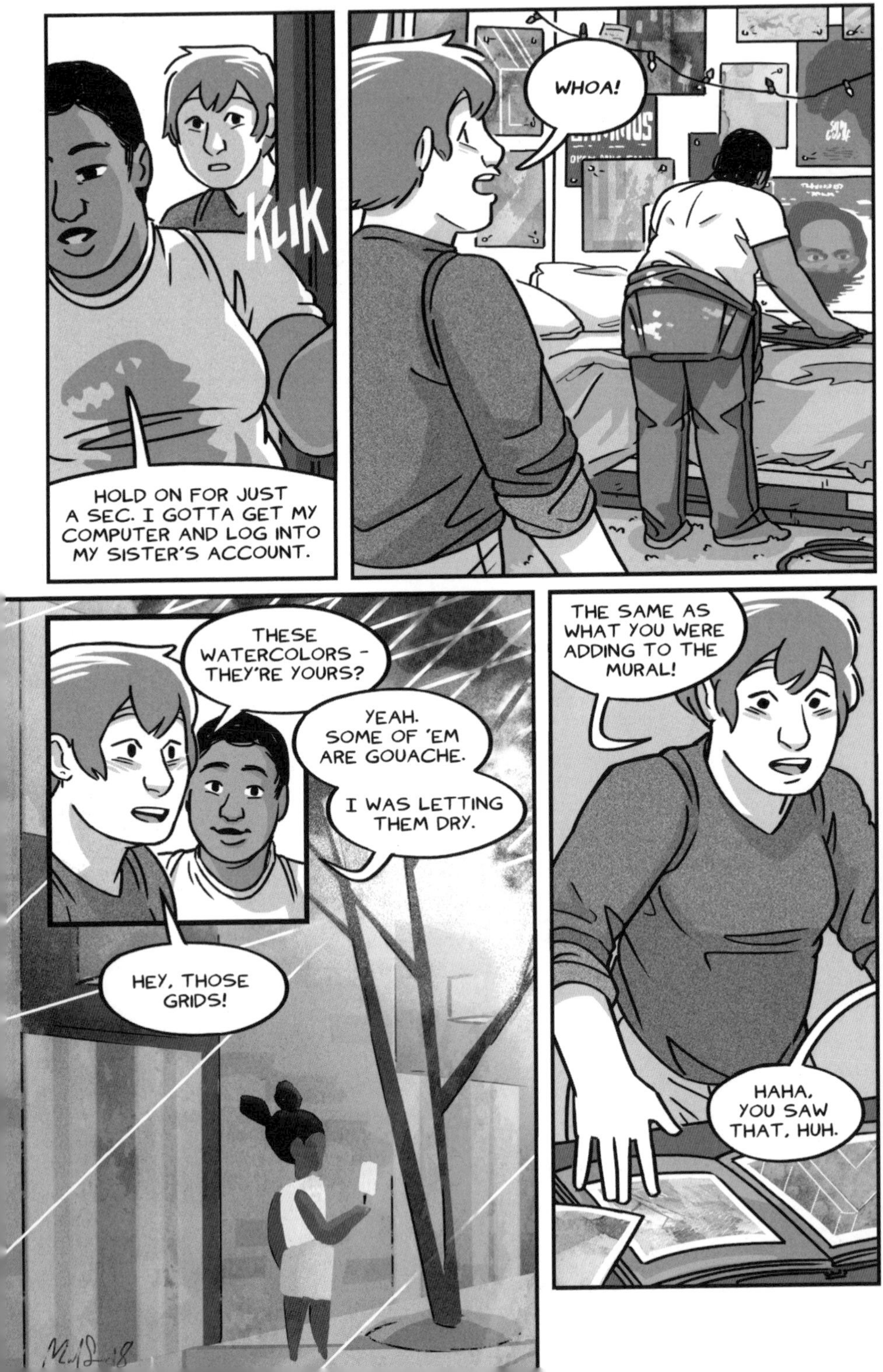
KLIK
HOLD ON FOR JUST A SEC. I GOTTA GET MY COMPUTER AND LOG INTO MY SISTER'S ACCOUNT.
WHOA!
THESE WATERCOLORS - THEY'RE YOURS?
YEAH. SOME OF 'EM ARE GOUACHE.
I WAS LETTING THEM DRY.
HEY, THOSE GRIDS!
THE SAME AS WHAT YOU WERE ADDING TO THE MURAL!
HAHA, YOU SAW THAT, HUH.

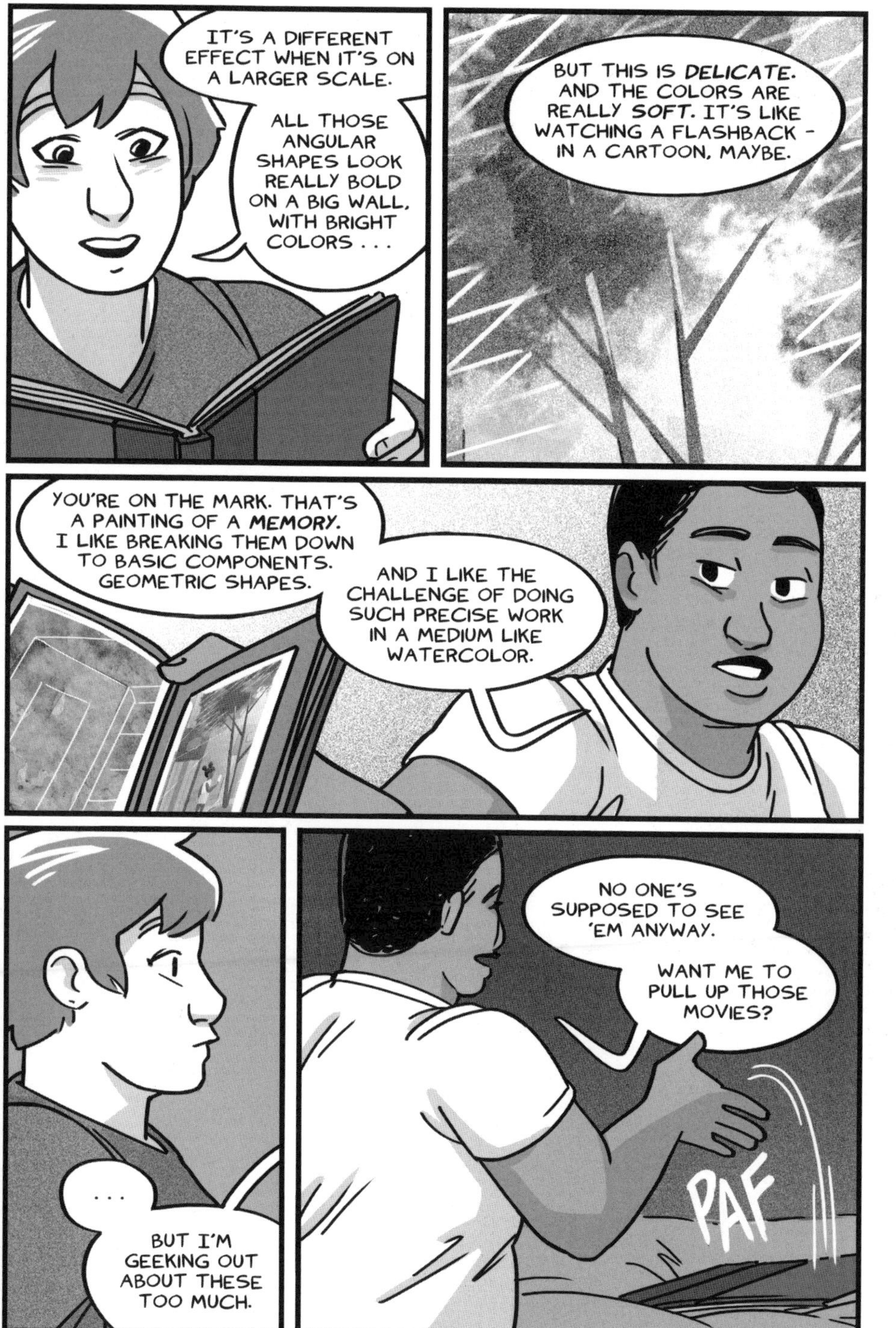
IT'S A DIFFERENT EFFECT WHEN IT'S ON A LARGER SCALE.
ALL THOSE ANGULAR SHAPES LOOK REALLY BOLD ON A BIG WALL, WITH BRIGHT COLORS . . .
BUT THIS IS *DELICATE*. AND THE COLORS ARE REALLY *SOFT*. IT'S LIKE WATCHING A FLASHBACK - IN A CARTOON, MAYBE.
YOU'RE ON THE MARK. THAT'S A PAINTING OF A *MEMORY*. I LIKE BREAKING THEM DOWN TO BASIC COMPONENTS. GEOMETRIC SHAPES.
AND I LIKE THE CHALLENGE OF DOING SUCH PRECISE WORK IN A MEDIUM LIKE WATERCOLOR.
. . .
BUT I'M GEEKING OUT ABOUT THESE TOO MUCH.
NO ONE'S SUPPOSED TO SEE 'EM ANYWAY.
WANT ME TO PULL UP THOSE MOVIES?
PAF

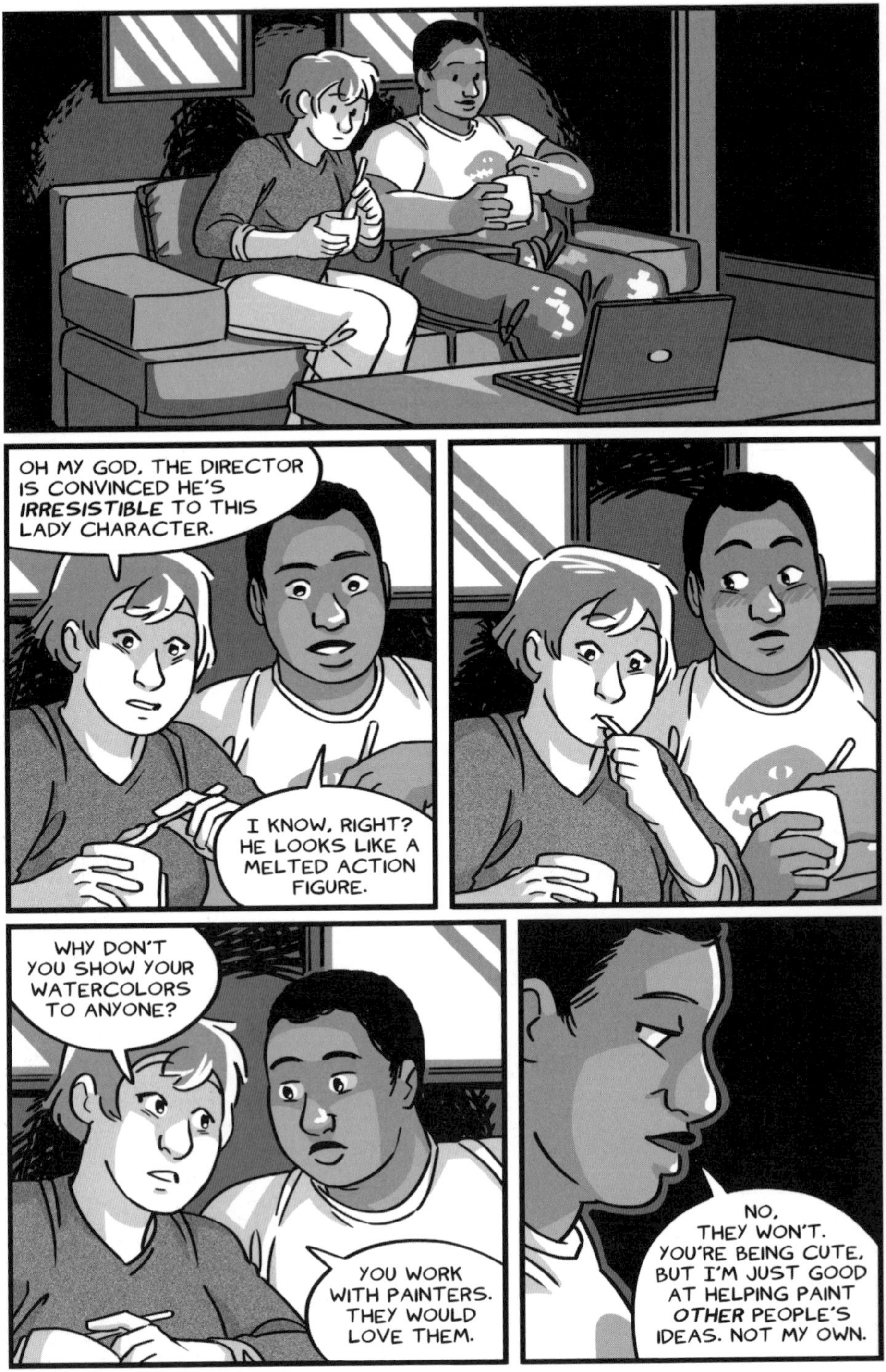
OH MY GOD, THE DIRECTOR IS CONVINCED HE'S *IRRESISTIBLE* TO THIS LADY CHARACTER.
I KNOW, RIGHT? HE LOOKS LIKE A MELTED ACTION FIGURE.
WHY DON'T YOU SHOW YOUR WATERCOLORS TO ANYONE?
YOU WORK WITH PAINTERS. THEY WOULD LOVE THEM.
NO, THEY WON'T. YOU'RE BEING CUTE, BUT I'M JUST GOOD AT HELPING PAINT *OTHER* PEOPLE'S IDEAS. NOT MY OWN.

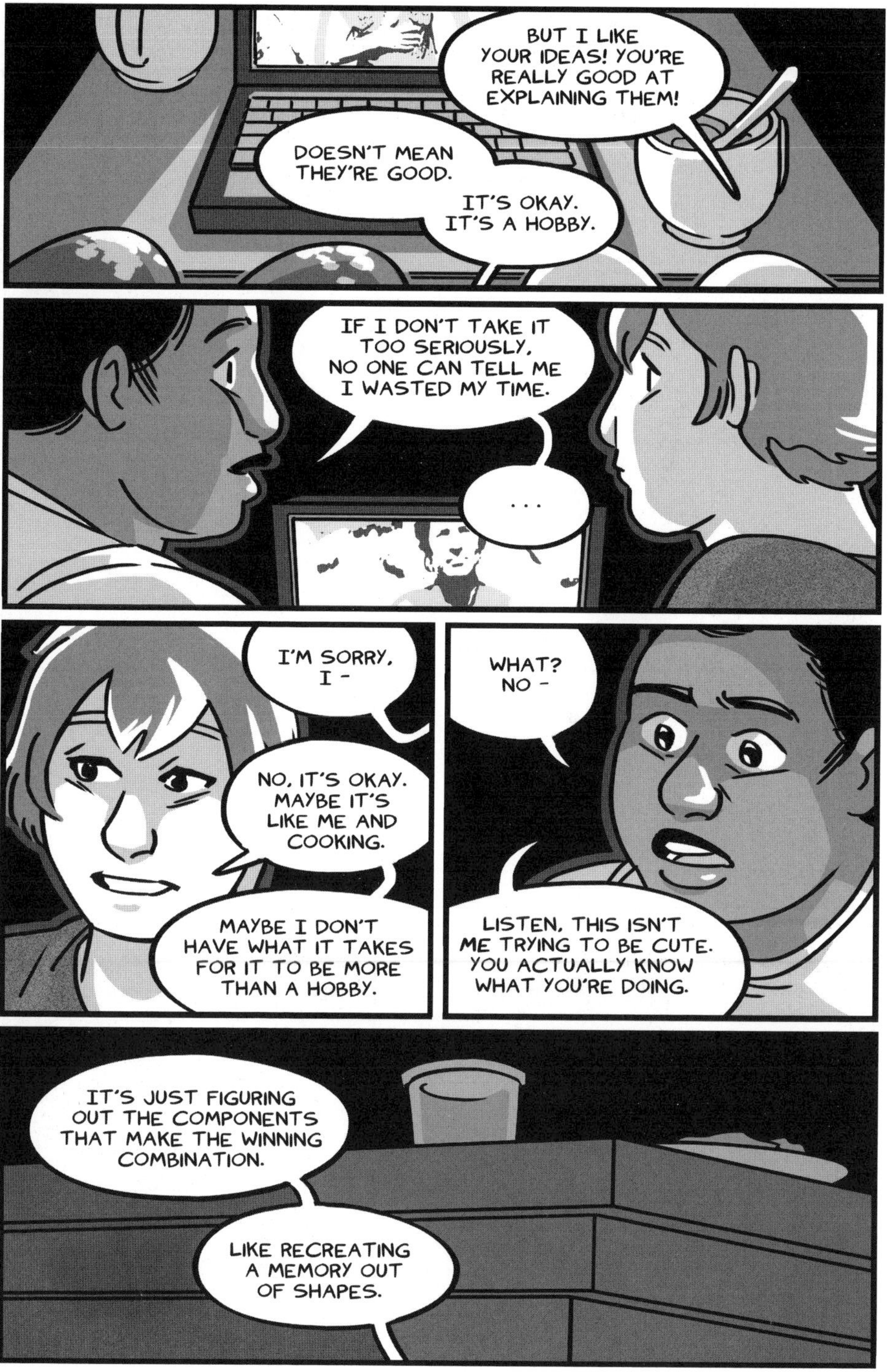
BUT I LIKE YOUR IDEAS! YOU'RE REALLY GOOD AT EXPLAINING THEM!
DOESN'T MEAN THEY'RE GOOD.
IT'S OKAY. IT'S A HOBBY.
IF I DON'T TAKE IT TOO SERIOUSLY, NO ONE CAN TELL ME I WASTED MY TIME.
. . .
I'M SORRY, I -
NO, IT'S OKAY. MAYBE IT'S LIKE ME AND COOKING.
MAYBE I DON'T HAVE WHAT IT TAKES FOR IT TO BE MORE THAN A HOBBY.
WHAT? NO -
LISTEN, THIS ISN'T ME TRYING TO BE CUTE. YOU ACTUALLY KNOW WHAT YOU'RE DOING.
IT'S JUST FIGURING OUT THE COMPONENTS THAT MAKE THE WINNING COMBINATION.
LIKE RECREATING A MEMORY OUT OF SHAPES.

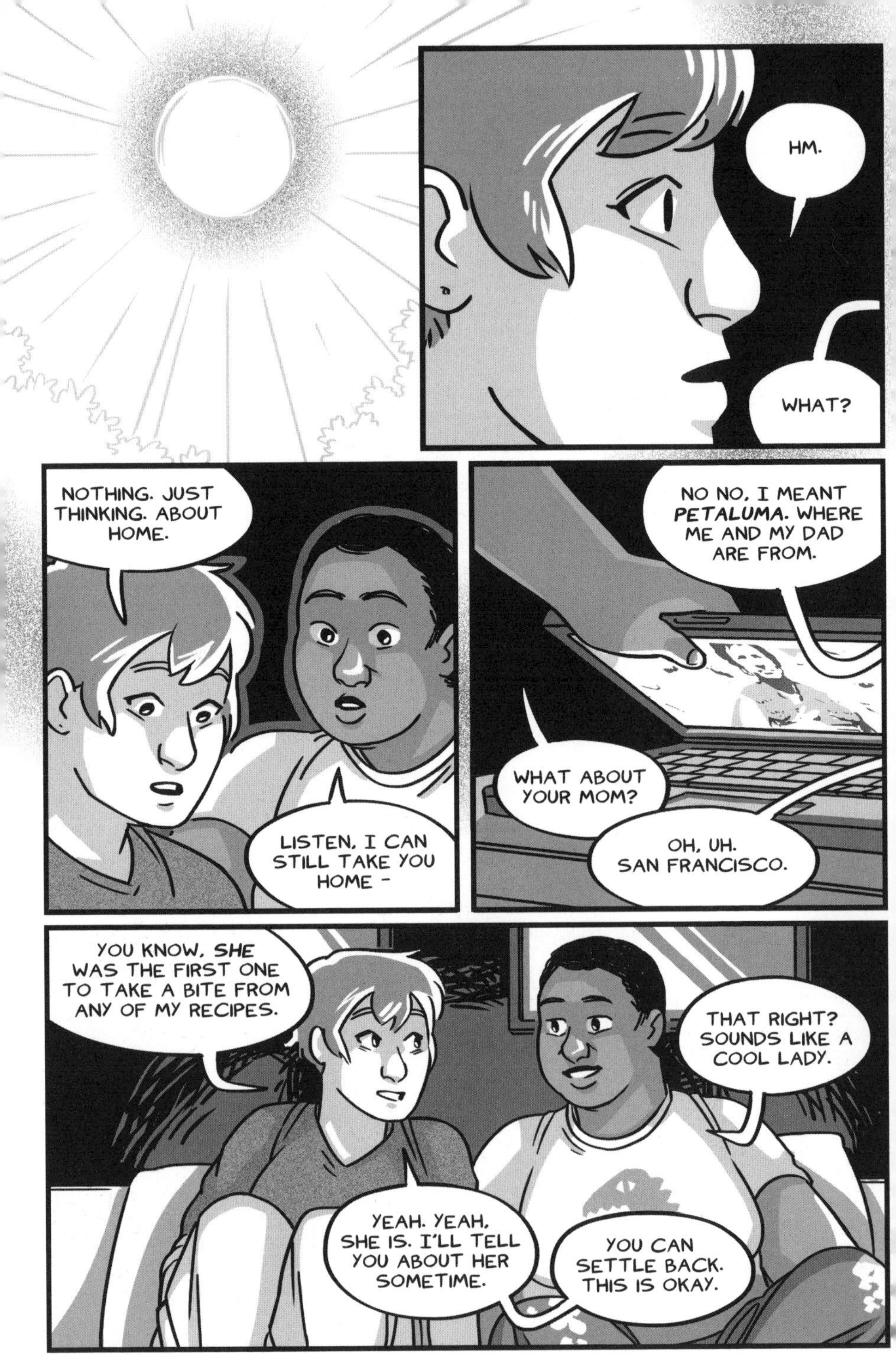
HM.
WHAT?
NOTHING. JUST THINKING. ABOUT HOME.
LISTEN, I CAN STILL TAKE YOU HOME -
NO NO, I MEANT *PETALUMA*. WHERE ME AND MY DAD ARE FROM.
WHAT ABOUT YOUR MOM?
OH, UH. SAN FRANCISCO.
YOU KNOW, *SHE* WAS THE FIRST ONE TO TAKE A BITE FROM ANY OF MY RECIPES.
THAT RIGHT? SOUNDS LIKE A COOL LADY.
YEAH. YEAH, SHE IS. I'LL TELL YOU ABOUT HER SOMETIME.
YOU CAN SETTLE BACK. THIS IS OKAY.

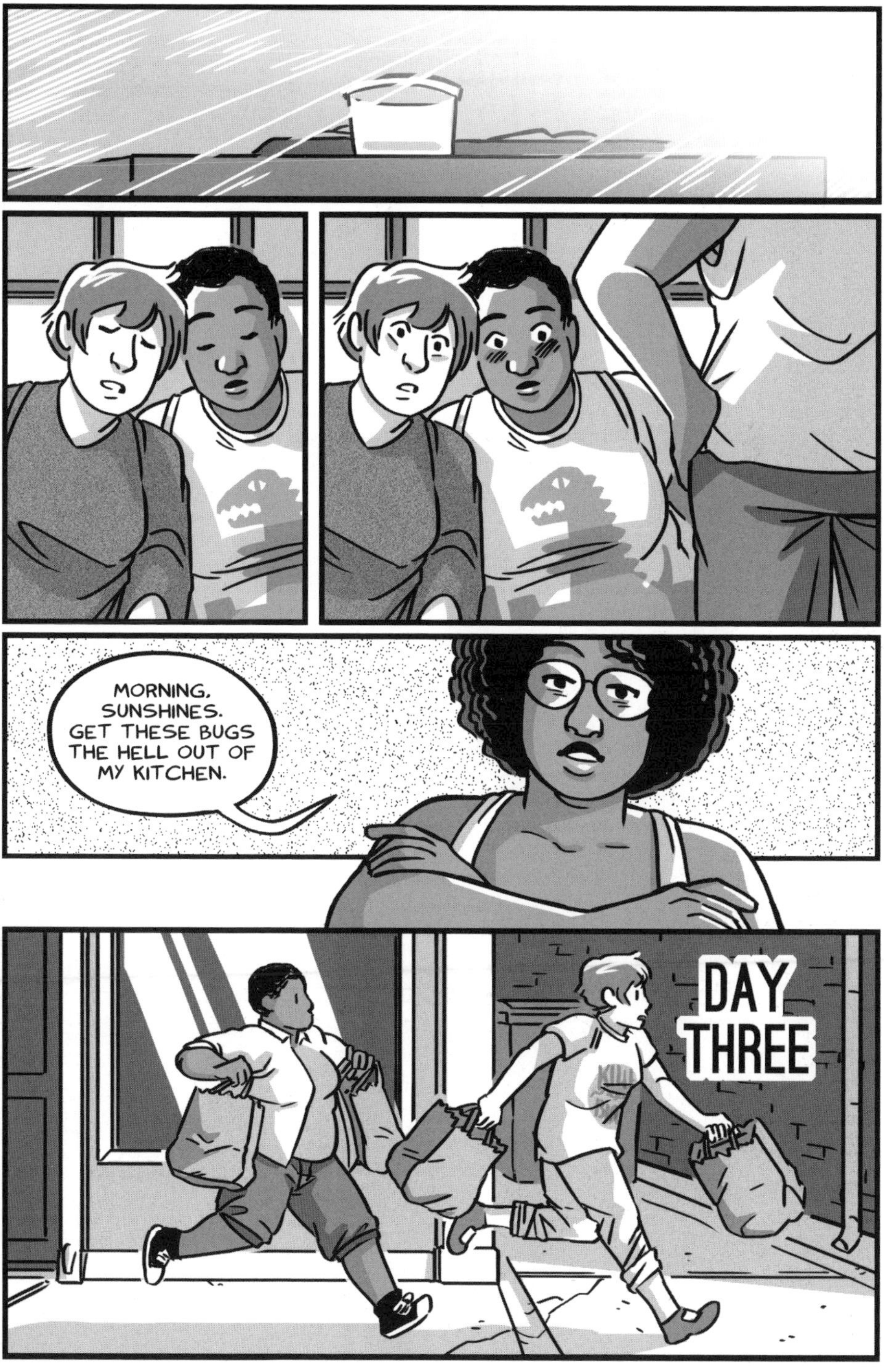
MORNING, SUNSHINES. GET THESE BUGS THE HELL OUT OF MY KITCHEN.
DAY THREE

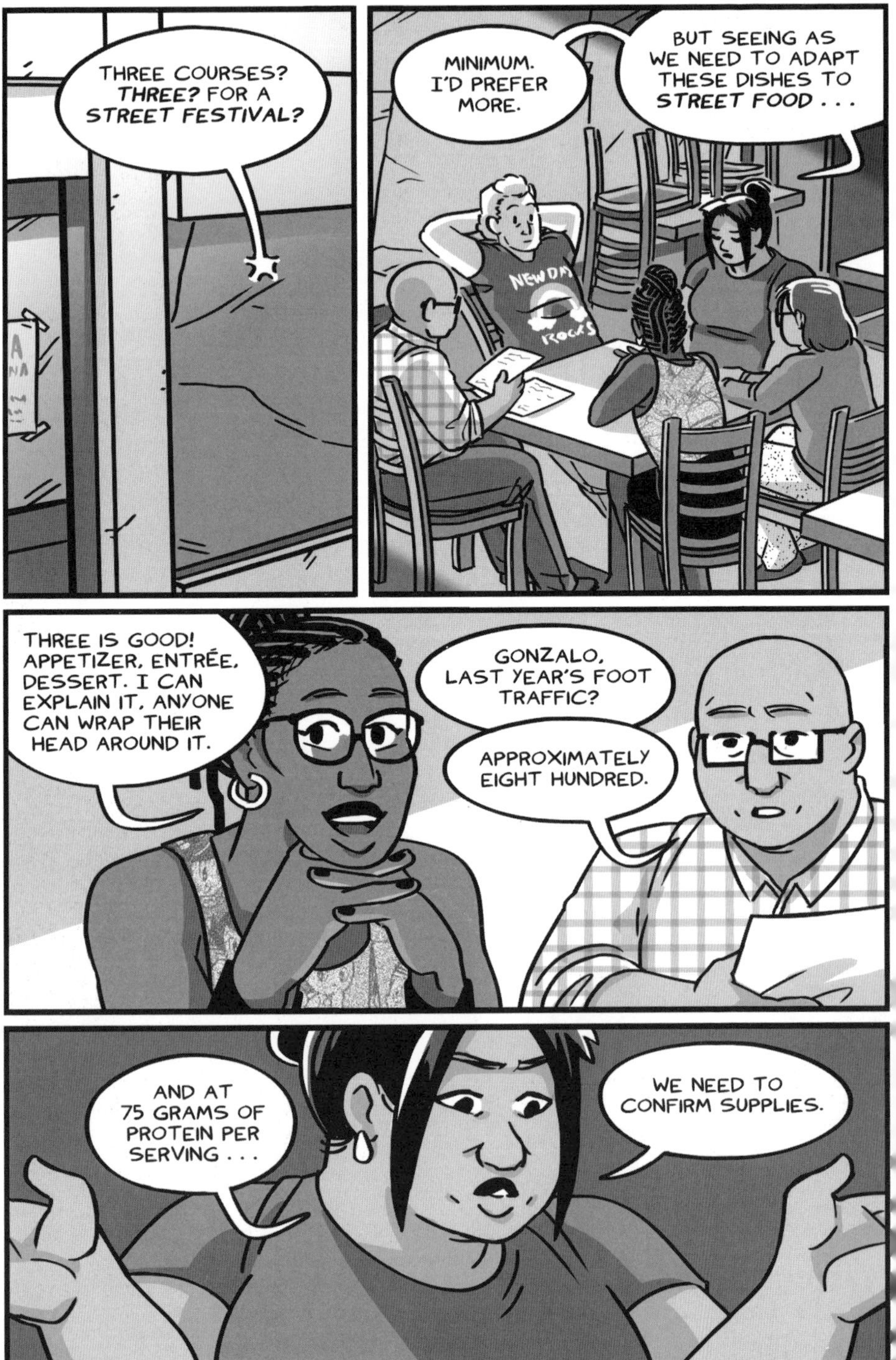
THREE COURSES? *THREE?* FOR A STREET FESTIVAL?
MINIMUM. I'D PREFER MORE.
BUT SEEING AS WE NEED TO ADAPT THESE DISHES TO *STREET FOOD* . . .
NEW DAY ROCKS
THREE IS GOOD! APPETIZER, ENTRÉE, DESSERT. I CAN EXPLAIN IT, ANYONE CAN WRAP THEIR HEAD AROUND IT.
GONZALO, LAST YEAR'S FOOT TRAFFIC?
APPROXIMATELY EIGHT HUNDRED.
AND AT 75 GRAMS OF PROTEIN PER SERVING . . .
WE NEED TO CONFIRM SUPPLIES.

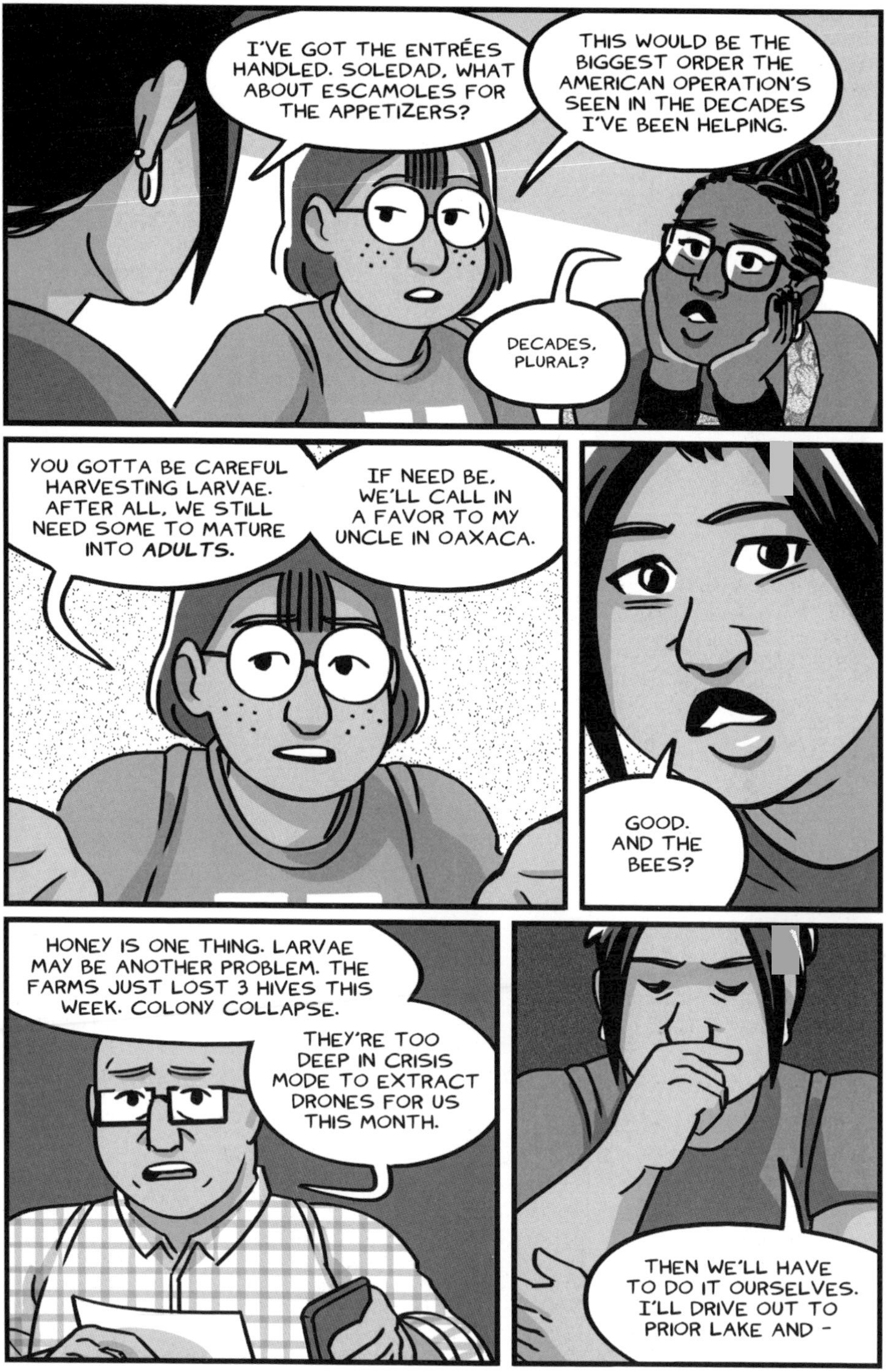
I'VE GOT THE ENTRÉES HANDLED. SOLEDAD, WHAT ABOUT ESCAMOLES FOR THE APPETIZERS?
THIS WOULD BE THE BIGGEST ORDER THE AMERICAN OPERATION'S SEEN IN THE DECADES I'VE BEEN HELPING.
DECADES, PLURAL?
YOU GOTTA BE CAREFUL HARVESTING LARVAE. AFTER ALL, WE STILL NEED SOME TO MATURE INTO *ADULTS*.
IF NEED BE, WE'LL CALL IN A FAVOR TO MY UNCLE IN OAXACA.
GOOD. AND THE BEES?
HONEY IS ONE THING. LARVAE MAY BE ANOTHER PROBLEM. THE FARMS JUST LOST 3 HIVES THIS WEEK. COLONY COLLAPSE.
THEY'RE TOO DEEP IN CRISIS MODE TO EXTRACT DRONES FOR US THIS MONTH.
THEN WE'LL HAVE TO DO IT OURSELVES. I'LL DRIVE OUT TO PRIOR LAKE AND –

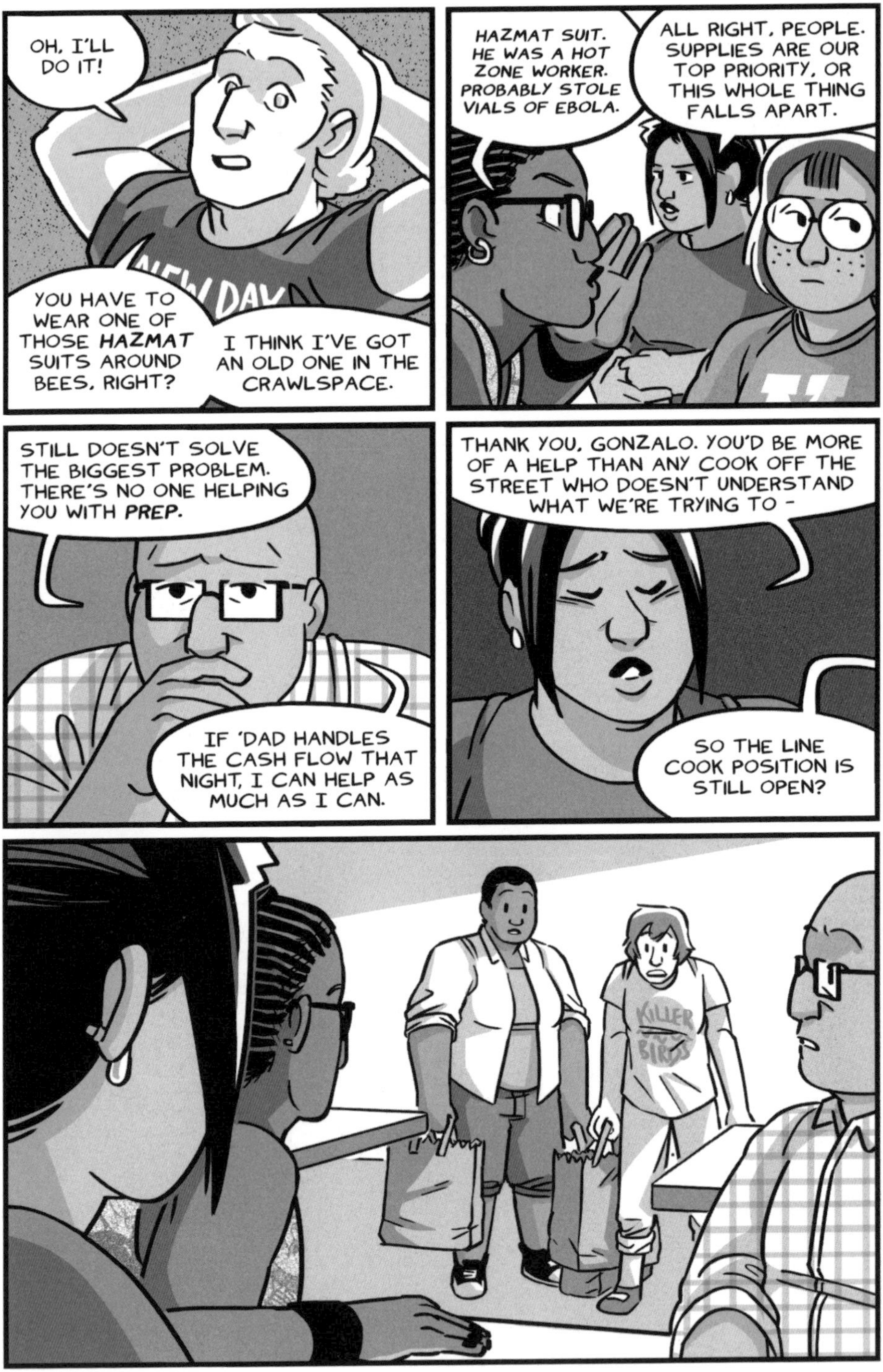
OH, I'LL DO IT!
YOU HAVE TO WEAR ONE OF THOSE HAZMAT SUITS AROUND BEES, RIGHT?
I THINK I'VE GOT AN OLD ONE IN THE CRAWLSPACE.
NEW DAY
HAZMAT SUIT. HE WAS A HOT ZONE WORKER. PROBABLY STOLE VIALS OF EBOLA.
ALL RIGHT, PEOPLE. SUPPLIES ARE OUR TOP PRIORITY, OR THIS WHOLE THING FALLS APART.
STILL DOESN'T SOLVE THE BIGGEST PROBLEM. THERE'S NO ONE HELPING YOU WITH PREP.
IF 'DAD HANDLES THE CASH FLOW THAT NIGHT, I CAN HELP AS MUCH AS I CAN.
THANK YOU, GONZALO. YOU'D BE MORE OF A HELP THAN ANY COOK OFF THE STREET WHO DOESN'T UNDERSTAND WHAT WE'RE TRYING TO -
SO THE LINE COOK POSITION IS STILL OPEN?
KILLER BIRDS

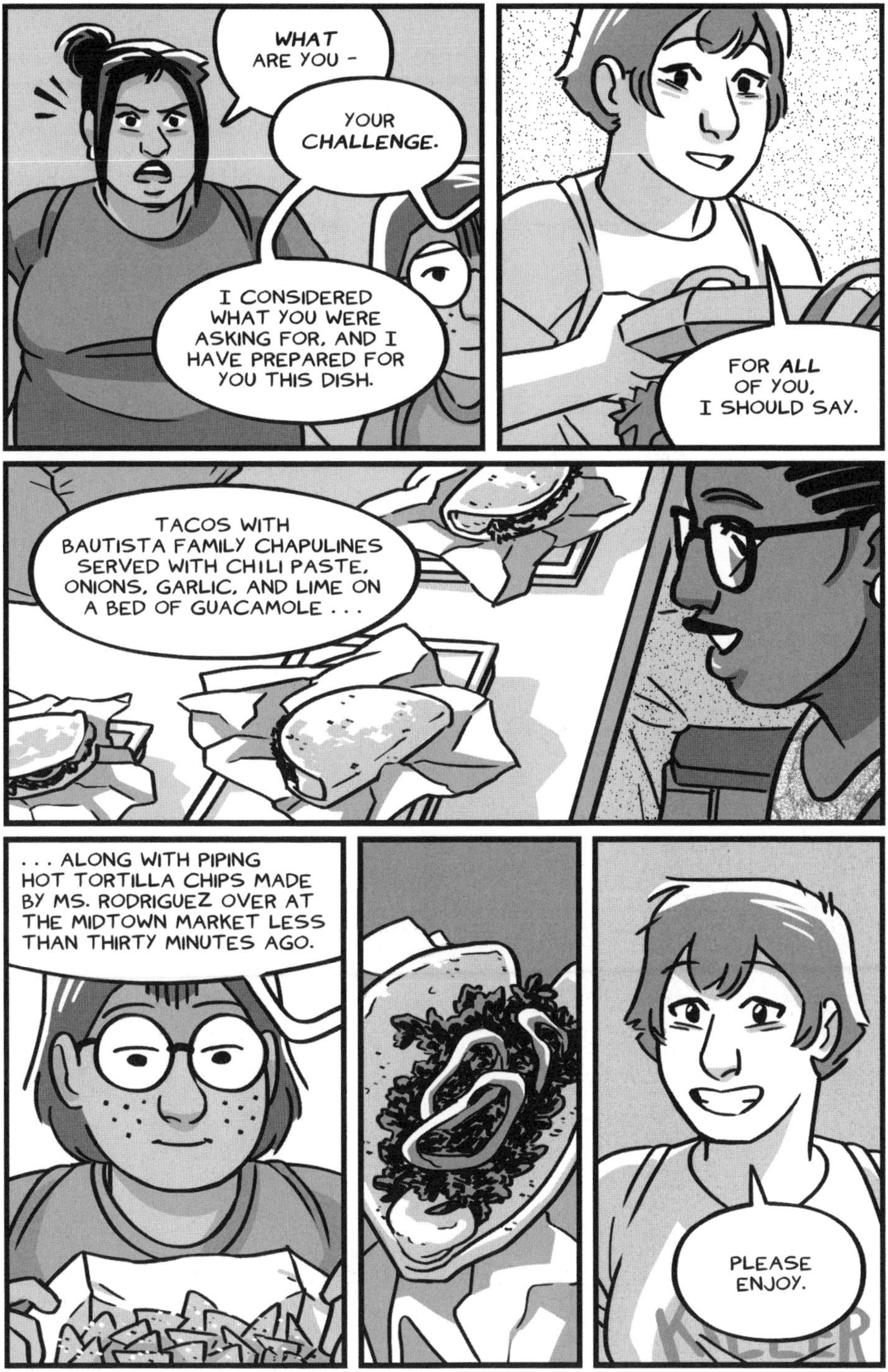
WHAT ARE YOU -
YOUR CHALLENGE.
I CONSIDERED WHAT YOU WERE ASKING FOR, AND I HAVE PREPARED FOR YOU THIS DISH.
FOR ALL OF YOU, I SHOULD SAY.
TACOS WITH BAUTISTA FAMILY CHAPULINES SERVED WITH CHILI PASTE, ONIONS, GARLIC, AND LIME ON A BED OF GUACAMOLE . . .
. . . ALONG WITH PIPING HOT TORTILLA CHIPS MADE BY MS. RODRIGUEZ OVER AT THE MIDTOWN MARKET LESS THAN THIRTY MINUTES AGO.
PLEASE ENJOY.

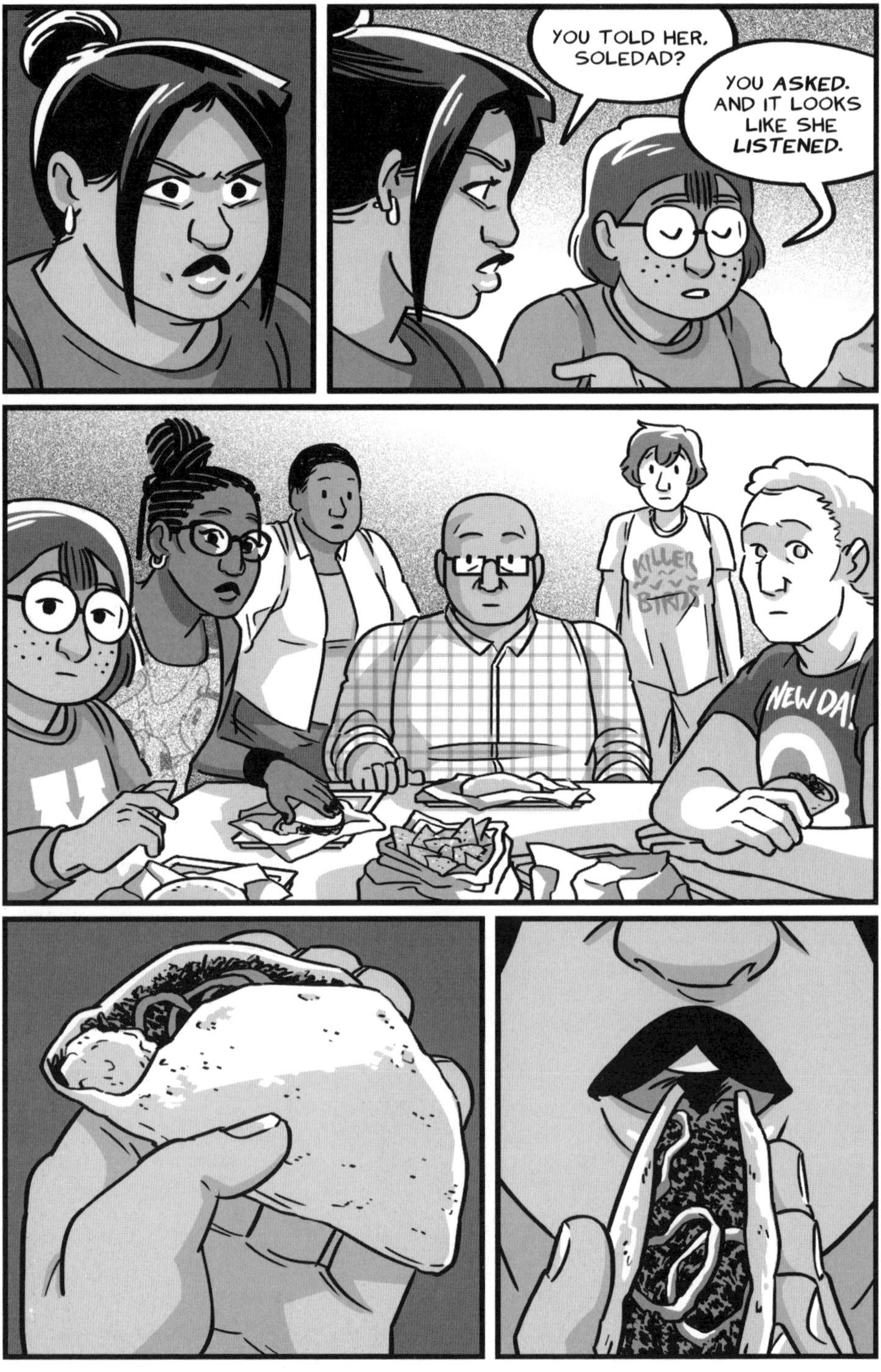
YOU TOLD HER, SOLEDAD?
YOU ASKED. AND IT LOOKS LIKE SHE LISTENED.
KILLER BIRDS
NEW DA

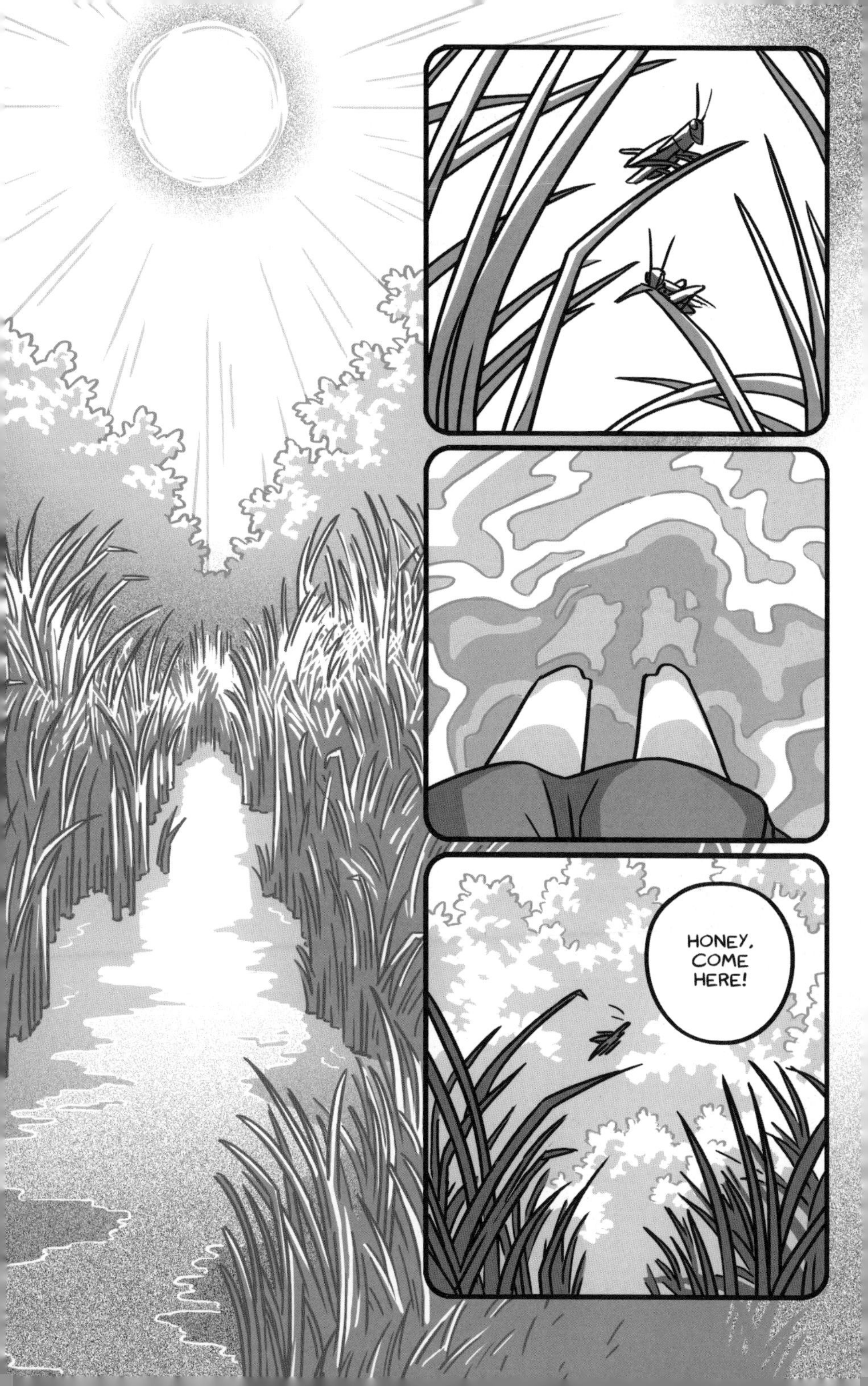
HONEY, COME HERE!

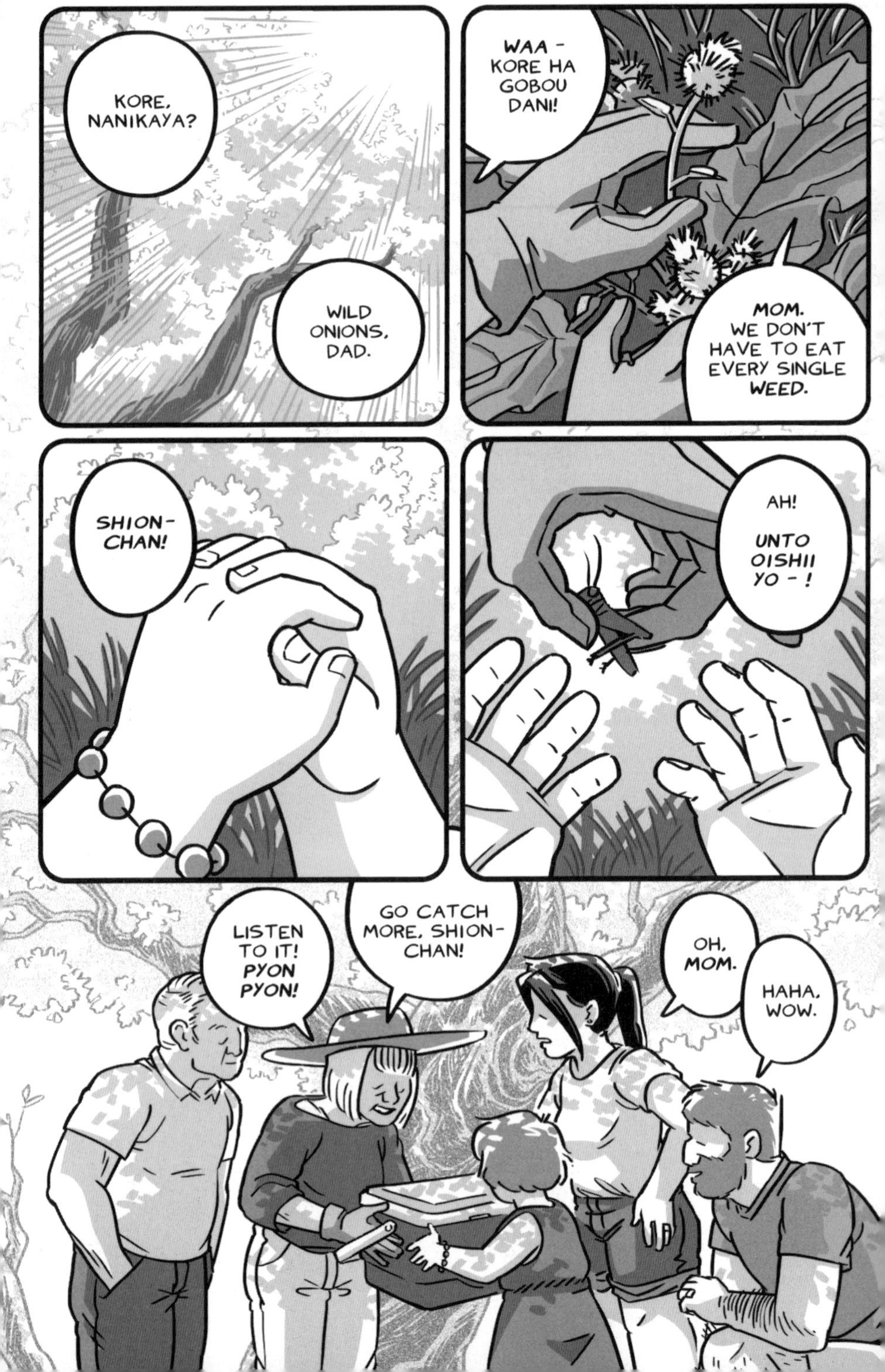
KORE, NANIKAYA?
WILD ONIONS, DAD.
WAA-KORE HA GOBOU DANI!
MOM. WE DON'T HAVE TO EAT EVERY SINGLE WEED.
SHION-CHAN!
AH!
UNTO OISHII YO-!
LISTEN TO IT! PYON PYON!
GO CATCH MORE, SHION-CHAN!
OH, MOM.
HAHA, WOW.

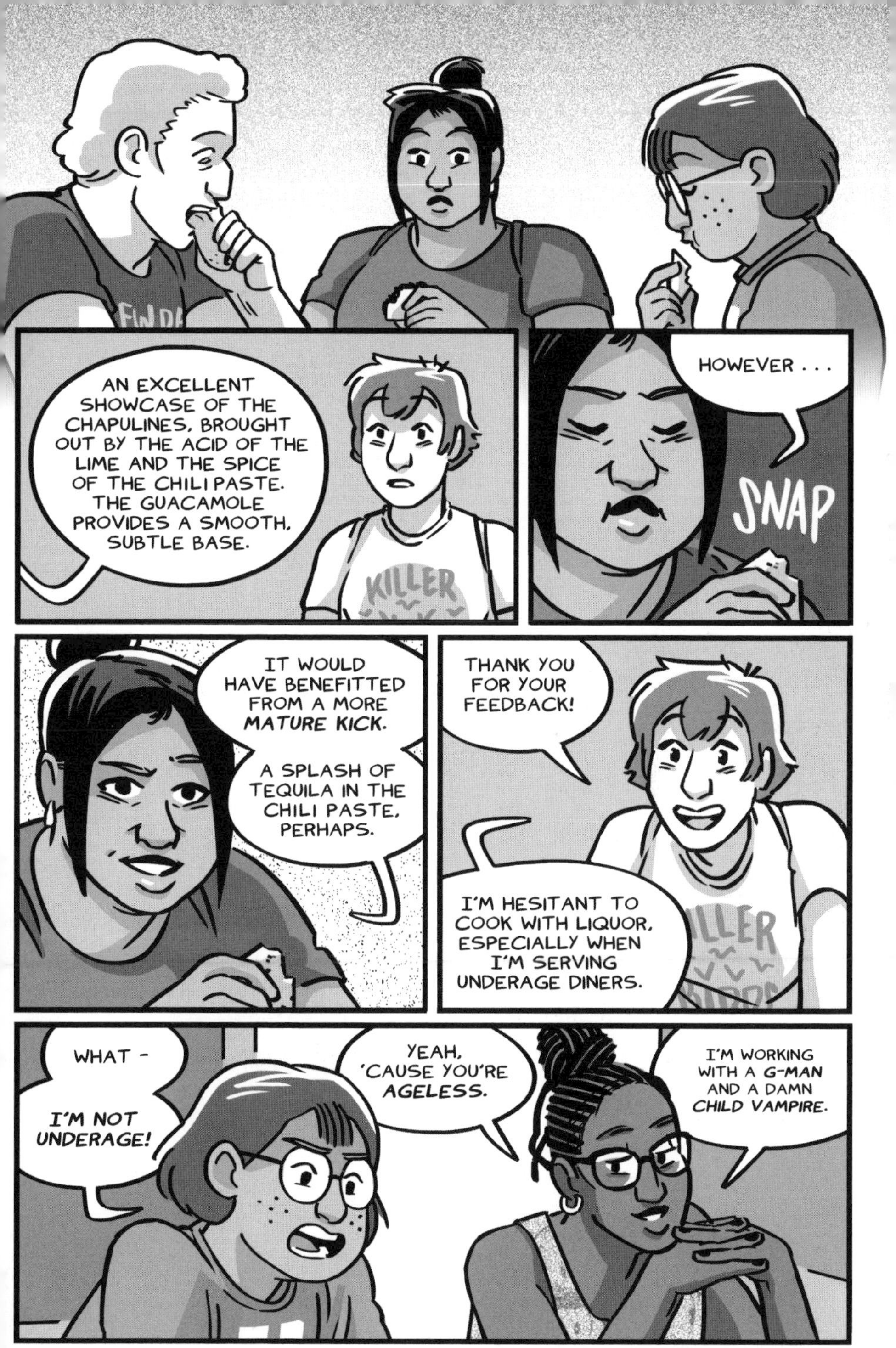
AN EXCELLENT SHOWCASE OF THE CHAPULINES, BROUGHT OUT BY THE ACID OF THE LIME AND THE SPICE OF THE CHILI PASTE. THE GUACAMOLE PROVIDES A SMOOTH, SUBTLE BASE.
KILLER
HOWEVER . . .
SNAP
IT WOULD HAVE BENEFITTED FROM A MORE *MATURE KICK.*
A SPLASH OF TEQUILA IN THE CHILI PASTE, PERHAPS.
THANK YOU FOR YOUR FEEDBACK!
I'M HESITANT TO COOK WITH LIQUOR, ESPECIALLY WHEN I'M SERVING UNDERAGE DINERS.
WHAT -
I'M NOT UNDERAGE!
YEAH, 'CAUSE YOU'RE *AGELESS.*
I'M WORKING WITH A *G-MAN* AND A DAMN *CHILD VAMPIRE.*

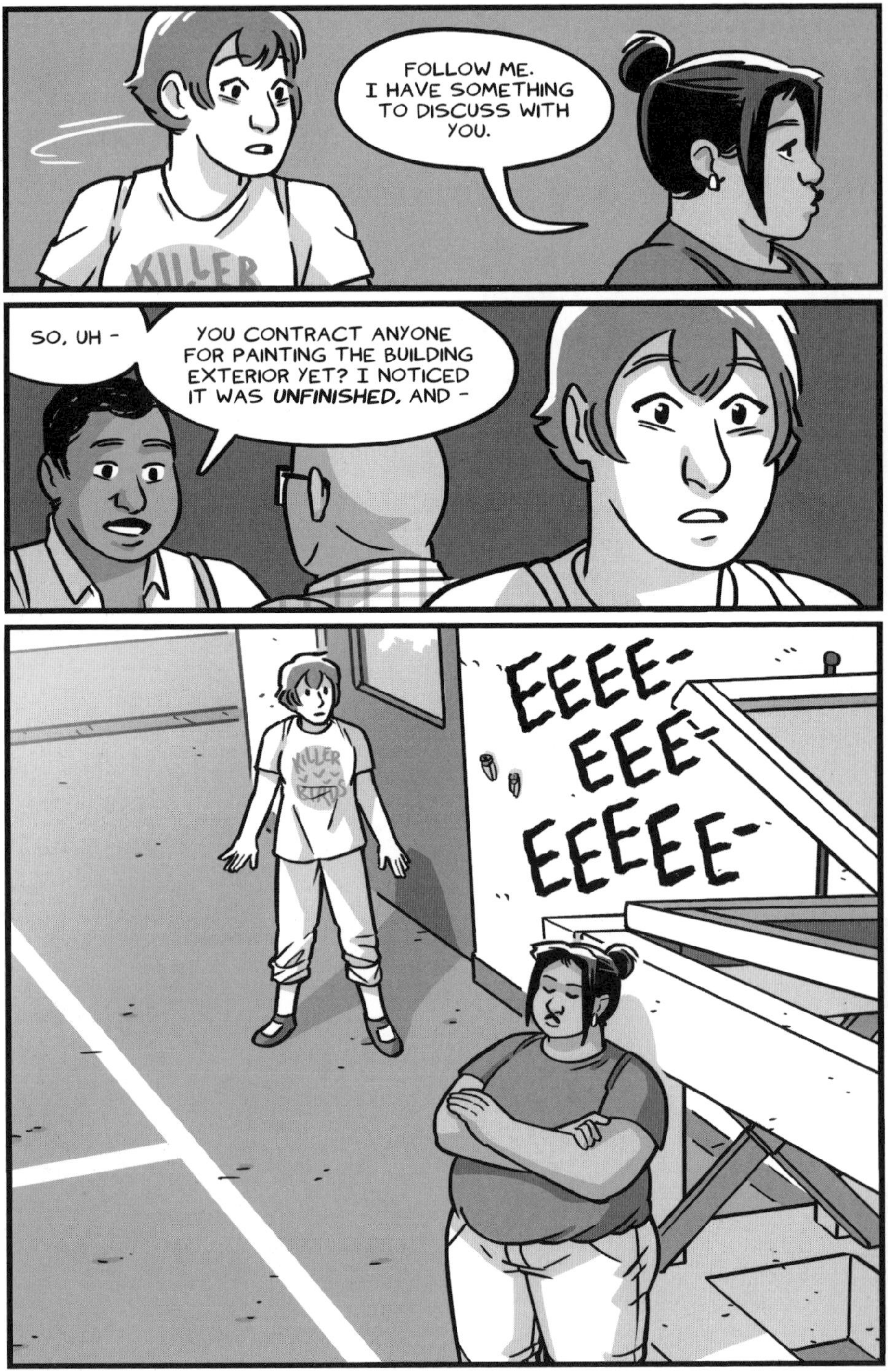
FOLLOW ME. I HAVE SOMETHING TO DISCUSS WITH YOU.
KILLER
SO, UH -
YOU CONTRACT ANYONE FOR PAINTING THE BUILDING EXTERIOR YET? I NOTICED IT WAS **UNFINISHED**, AND -
KILLER BIRDS
EEEE-
EEE-
EEEEE-

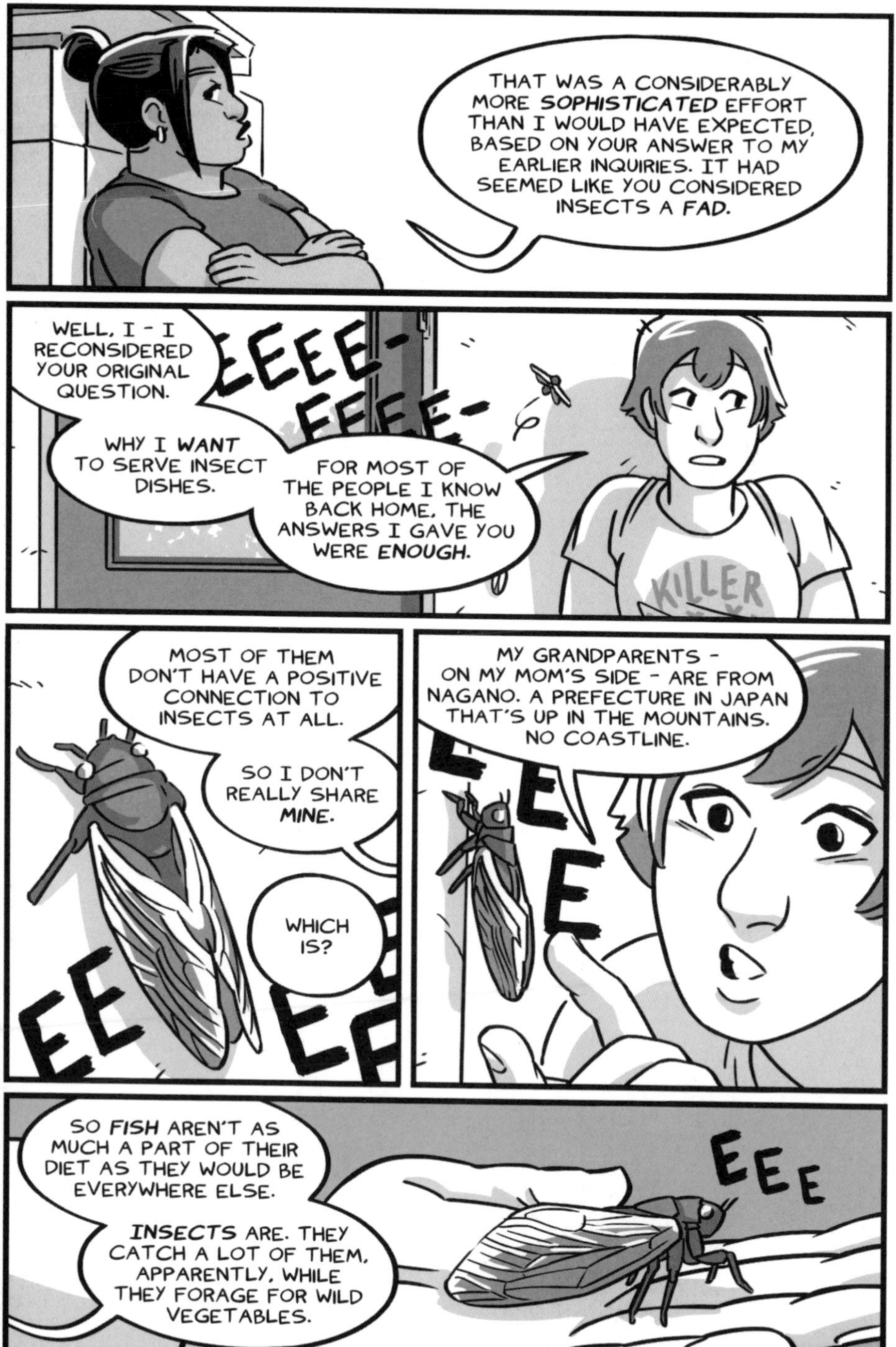
THAT WAS A CONSIDERABLY MORE SOPHISTICATED EFFORT THAN I WOULD HAVE EXPECTED, BASED ON YOUR ANSWER TO MY EARLIER INQUIRIES. IT HAD SEEMED LIKE YOU CONSIDERED INSECTS A FAD.
WELL, I - I RECONSIDERED YOUR ORIGINAL QUESTION.
EEEE-
EEEE-
WHY I WANT TO SERVE INSECT DISHES.
FOR MOST OF THE PEOPLE I KNOW BACK HOME, THE ANSWERS I GAVE YOU WERE ENOUGH.
KILLER
MOST OF THEM DON'T HAVE A POSITIVE CONNECTION TO INSECTS AT ALL.
SO I DON'T REALLY SHARE MINE.
WHICH IS?
EE
EE
MY GRANDPARENTS - ON MY MOM'S SIDE - ARE FROM NAGANO. A PREFECTURE IN JAPAN THAT'S UP IN THE MOUNTAINS. NO COASTLINE.
E
E
SO FISH AREN'T AS MUCH A PART OF THEIR DIET AS THEY WOULD BE EVERYWHERE ELSE.
INSECTS ARE. THEY CATCH A LOT OF THEM, APPARENTLY, WHILE THEY FORAGE FOR WILD VEGETABLES.
EEE

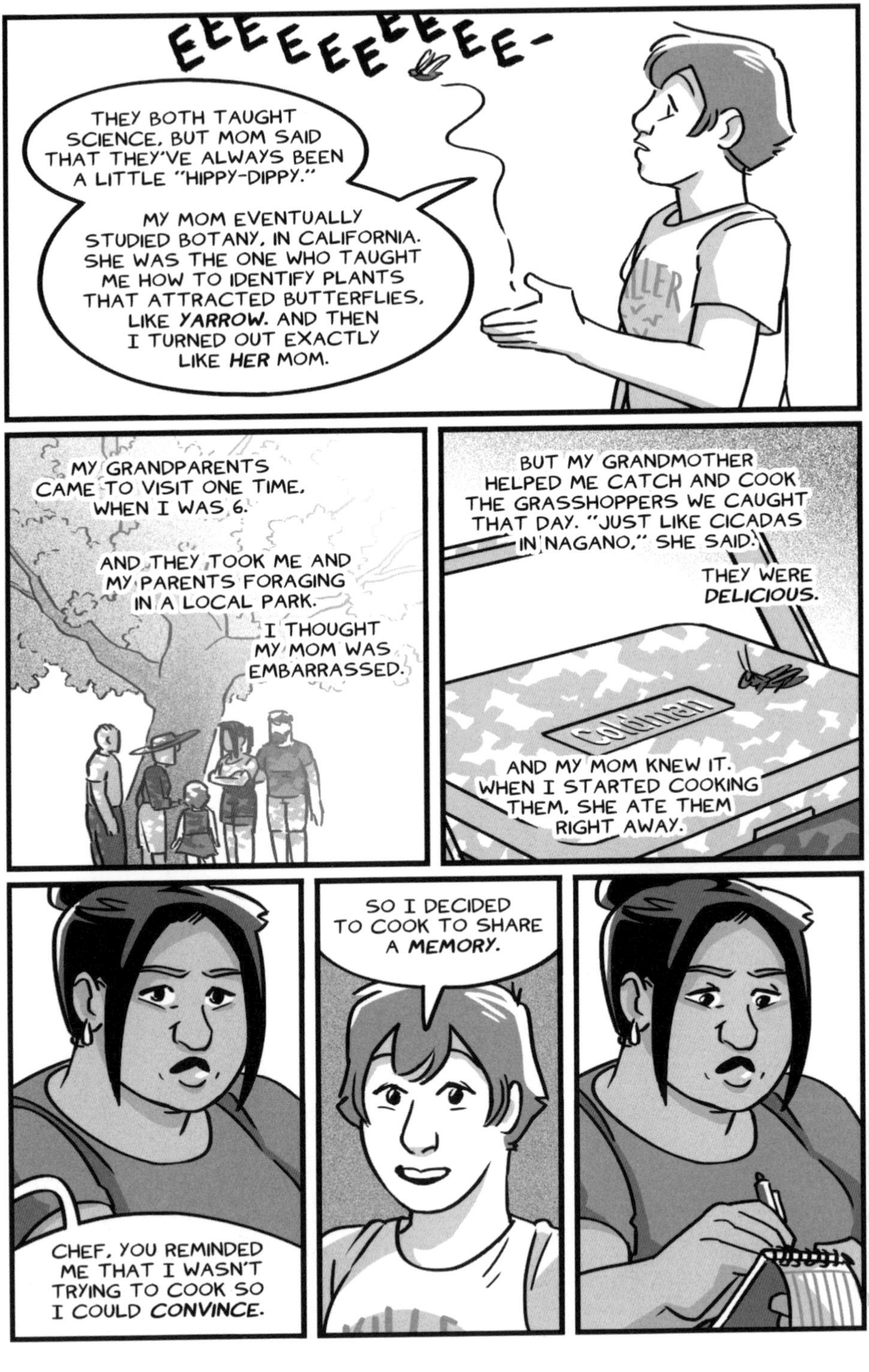
EEEEEEEEEE-
THEY BOTH TAUGHT SCIENCE, BUT MOM SAID THAT THEY'VE ALWAYS BEEN A LITTLE "HIPPY-DIPPY."
MY MOM EVENTUALLY STUDIED BOTANY, IN CALIFORNIA. SHE WAS THE ONE WHO TAUGHT ME HOW TO IDENTIFY PLANTS THAT ATTRACTED BUTTERFLIES, LIKE *YARROW*. AND THEN I TURNED OUT EXACTLY LIKE *HER* MOM.
MY GRANDPARENTS CAME TO VISIT ONE TIME, WHEN I WAS 6.
AND THEY TOOK ME AND MY PARENTS FORAGING IN A LOCAL PARK.
I THOUGHT MY MOM WAS EMBARRASSED.
BUT MY GRANDMOTHER HELPED ME CATCH AND COOK THE GRASSHOPPERS WE CAUGHT THAT DAY. "JUST LIKE CICADAS IN NAGANO," SHE SAID.
THEY WERE *DELICIOUS*.
Coleman
AND MY MOM KNEW IT. WHEN I STARTED COOKING THEM, SHE ATE THEM RIGHT AWAY.
CHEF, YOU REMINDED ME THAT I WASN'T TRYING TO COOK SO I COULD *CONVINCE*.
SO I DECIDED TO COOK TO SHARE A *MEMORY*.

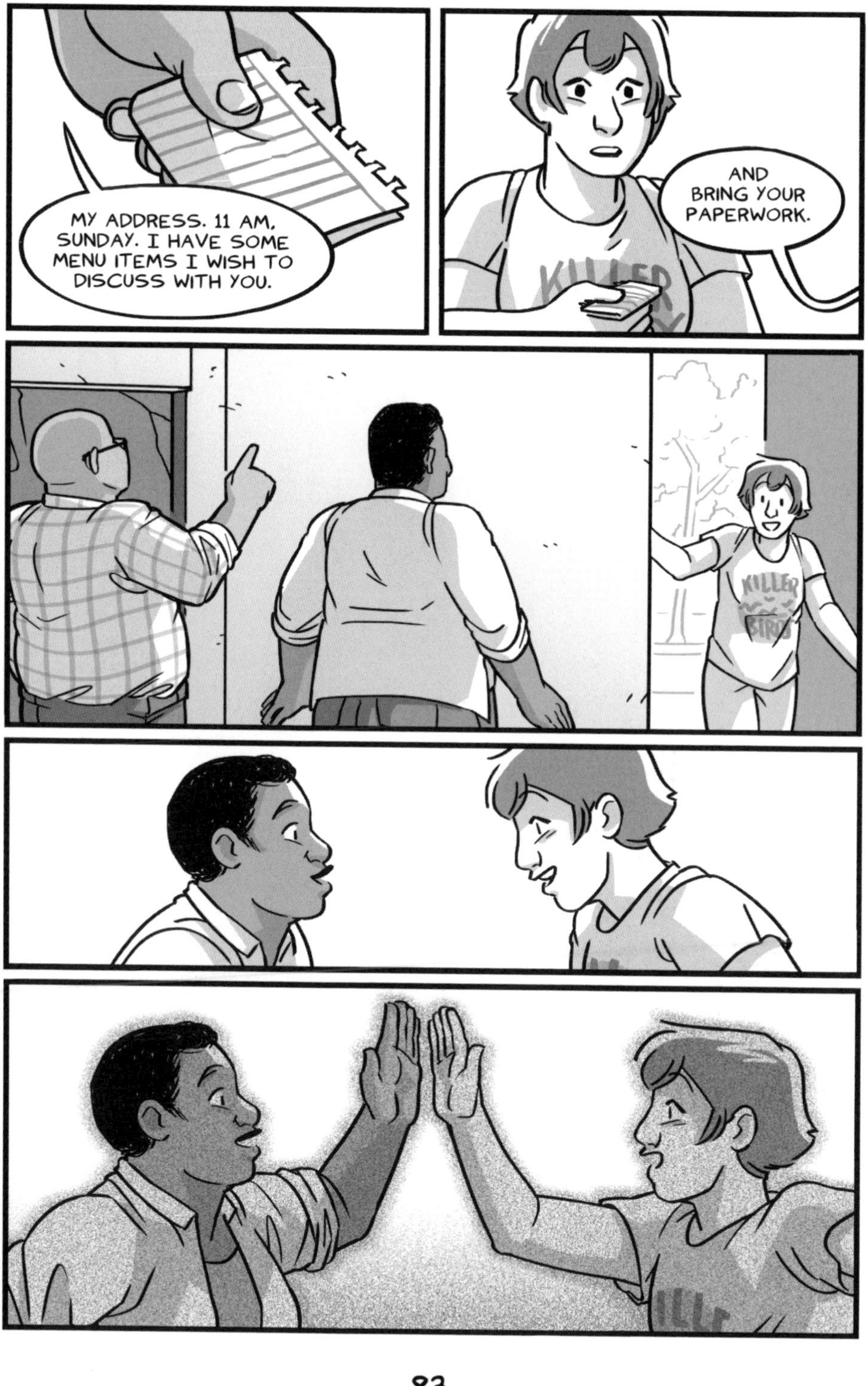
MY ADDRESS. 11 AM, SUNDAY. I HAVE SOME MENU ITEMS I WISH TO DISCUSS WITH YOU.
AND BRING YOUR PAPERWORK.
KILLER BIRD

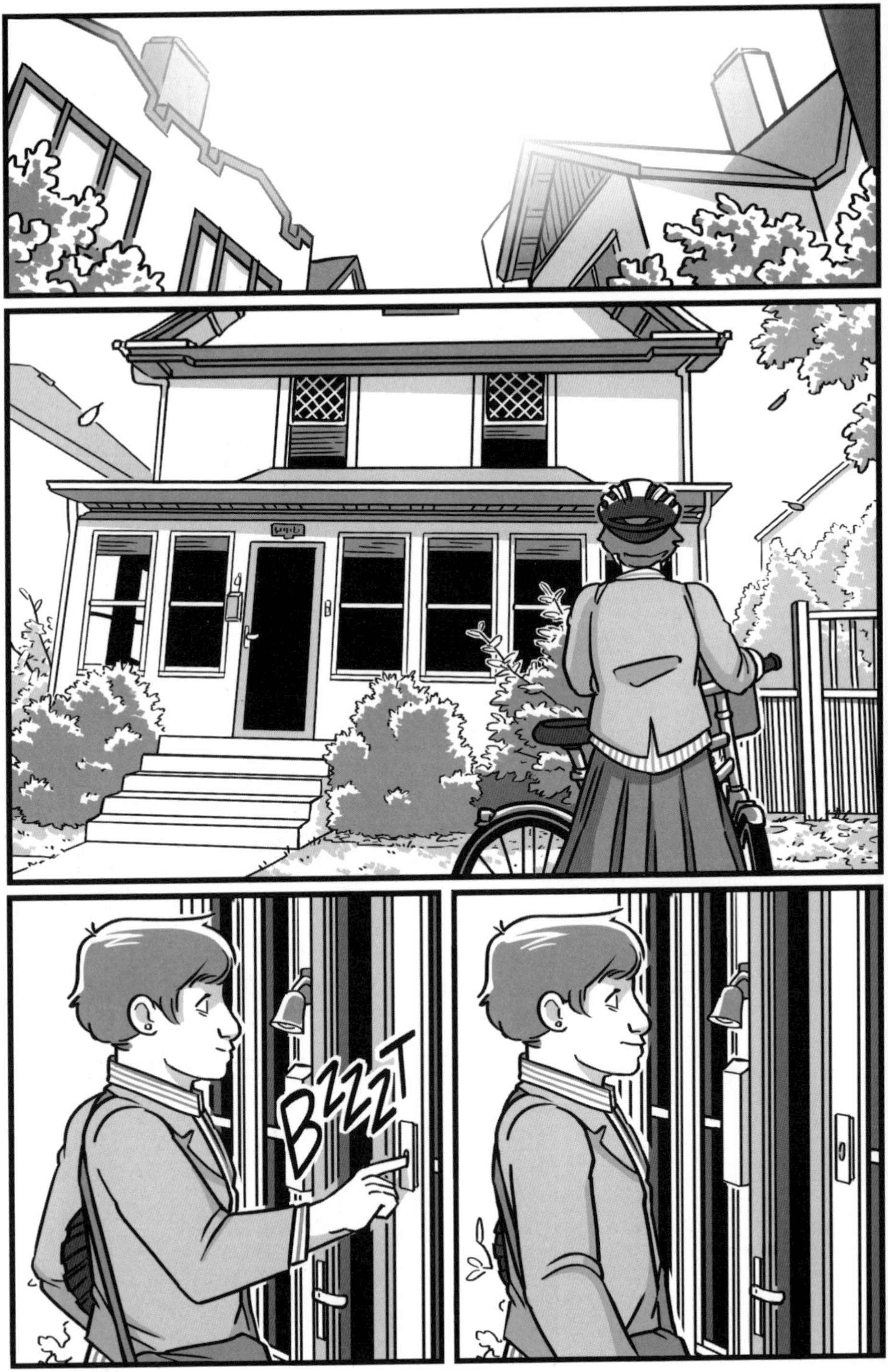
BZZZT

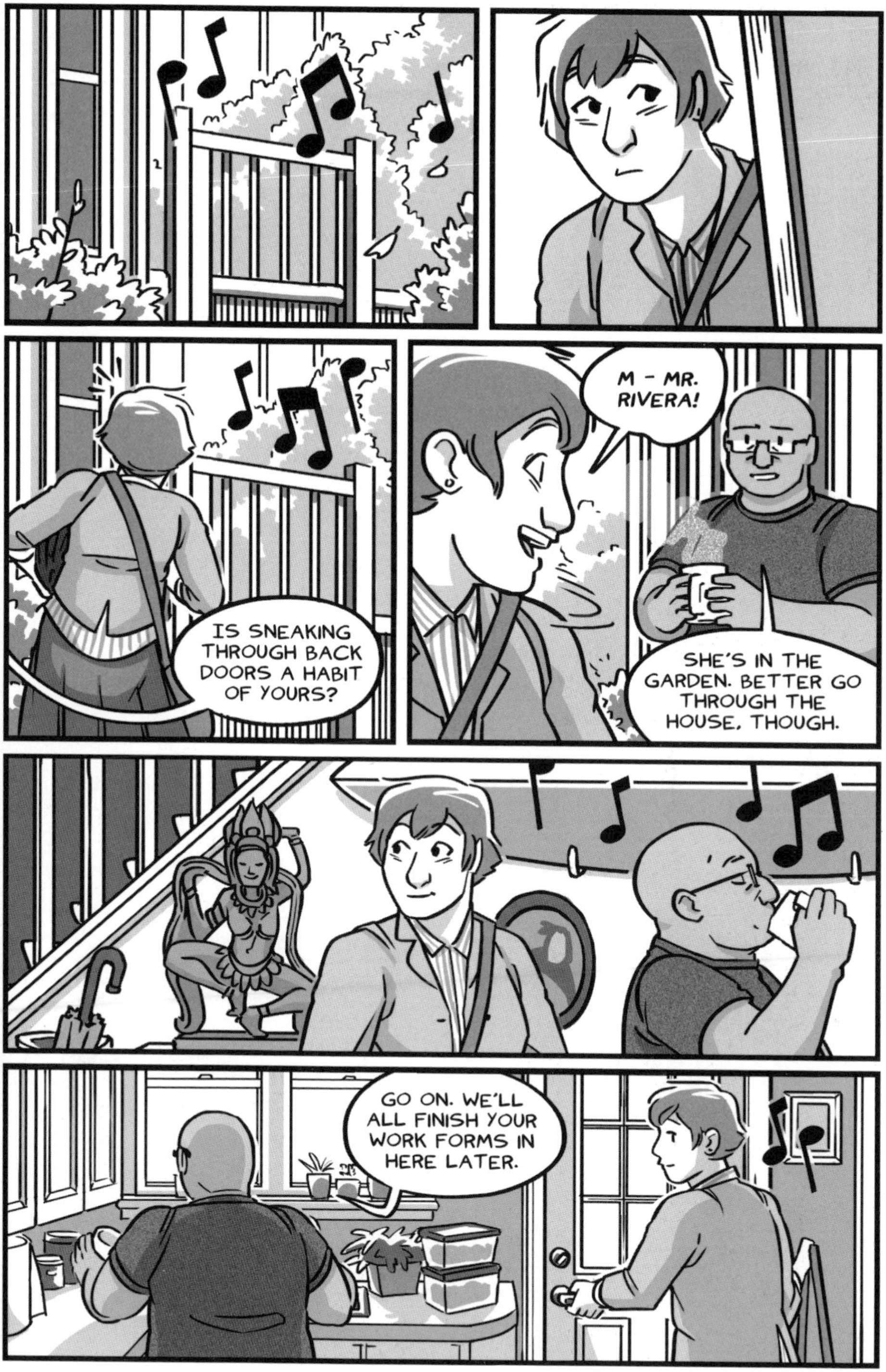
IS SNEAKING THROUGH BACK DOORS A HABIT OF YOURS?
M - MR. RIVERA!
SHE'S IN THE GARDEN. BETTER GO THROUGH THE HOUSE, THOUGH.
GO ON. WE'LL ALL FINISH YOUR WORK FORMS IN HERE LATER.

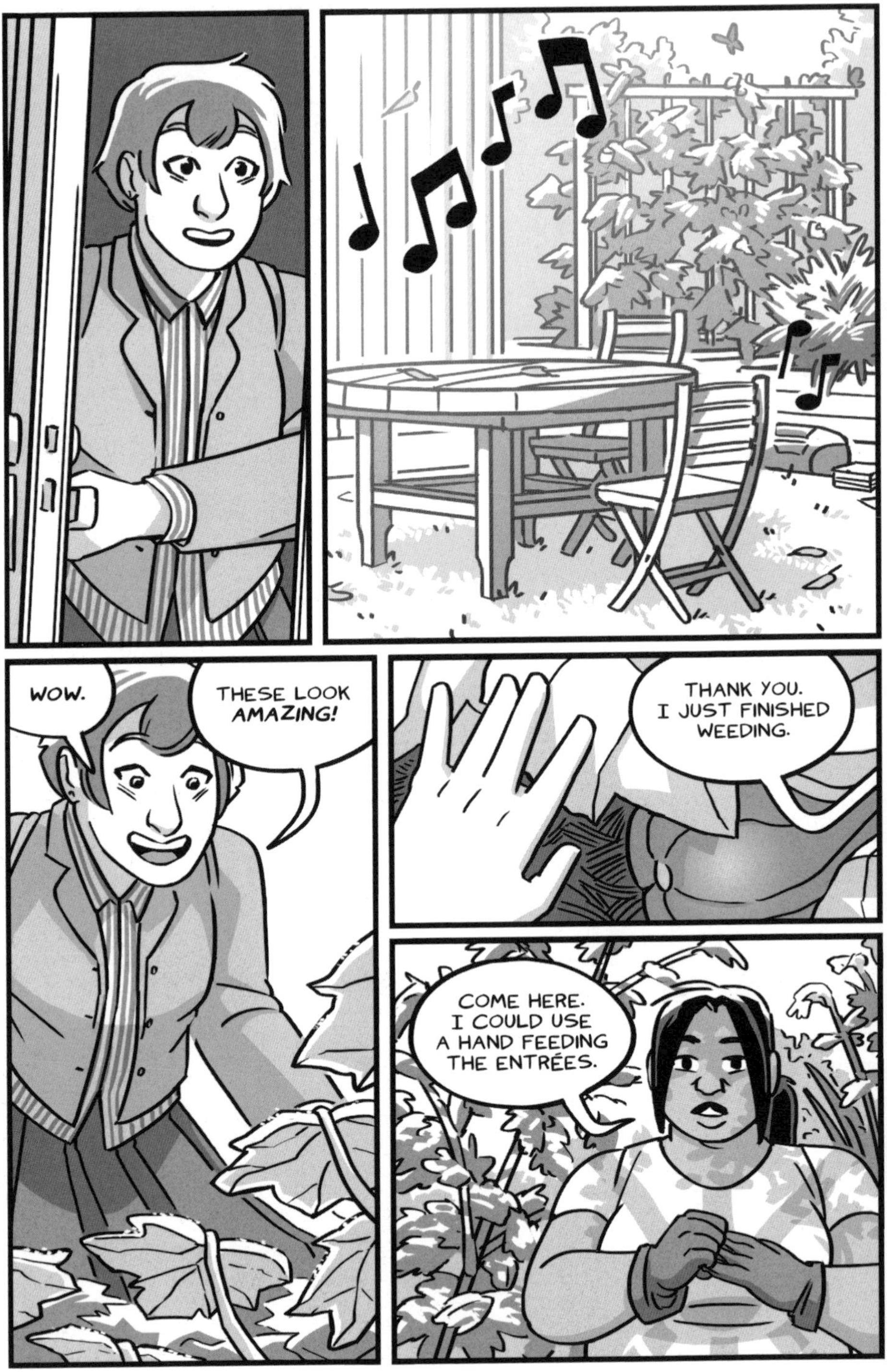
WOW.
THESE LOOK AMAZING!
THANK YOU. I JUST FINISHED WEEDING.
COME HERE. I COULD USE A HAND FEEDING THE ENTRÉES.

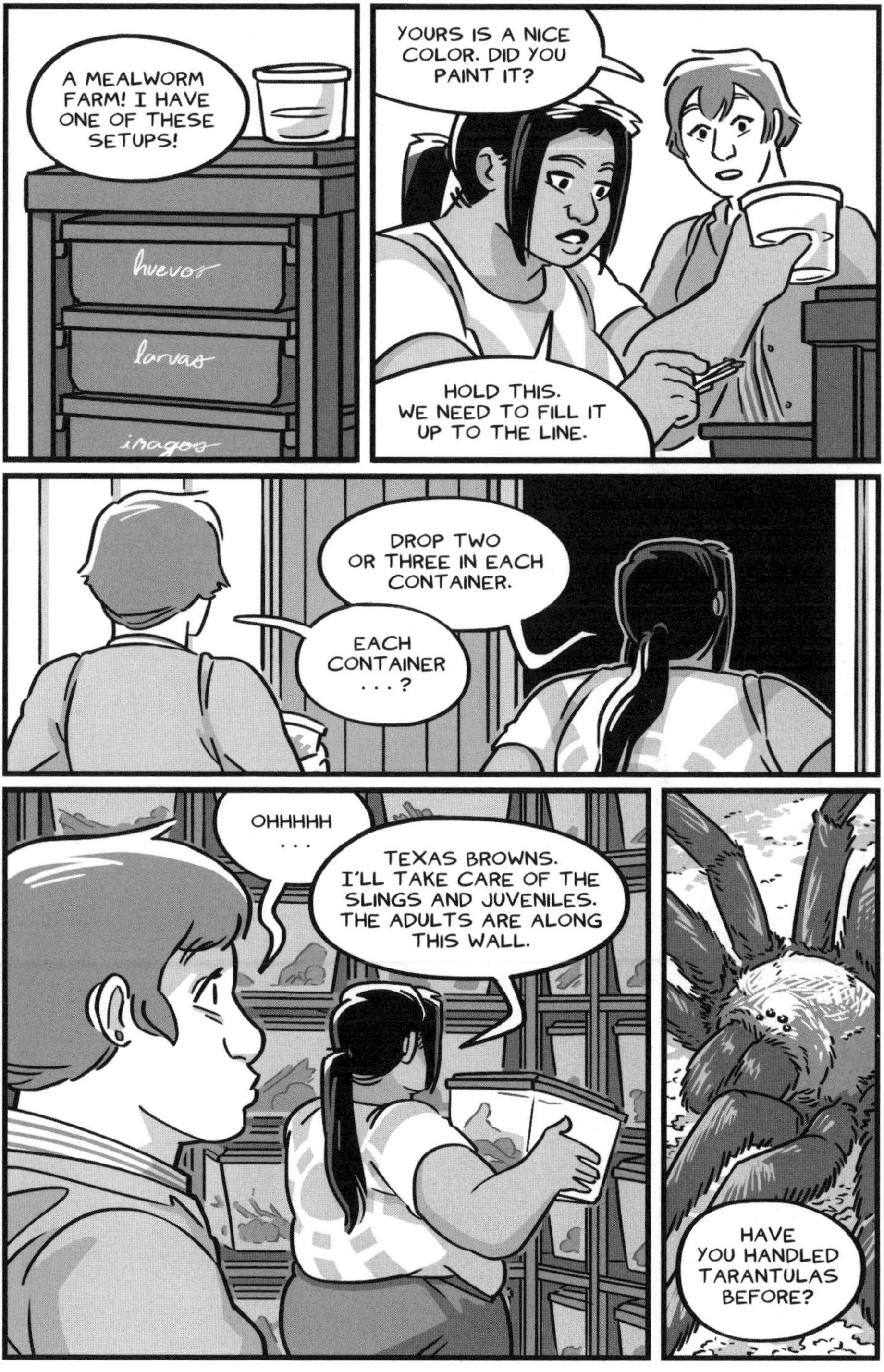
A MEALWORM FARM! I HAVE ONE OF THESE SETUPS!
huevos
larvas
imagos
YOURS IS A NICE COLOR. DID YOU PAINT IT?
HOLD THIS. WE NEED TO FILL IT UP TO THE LINE.
DROP TWO OR THREE IN EACH CONTAINER.
EACH CONTAINER . . . ?
OHHHHH . . .
TEXAS BROWNS. I'LL TAKE CARE OF THE SLINGS AND JUVENILES. THE ADULTS ARE ALONG THIS WALL.
HAVE YOU HANDLED TARANTULAS BEFORE?

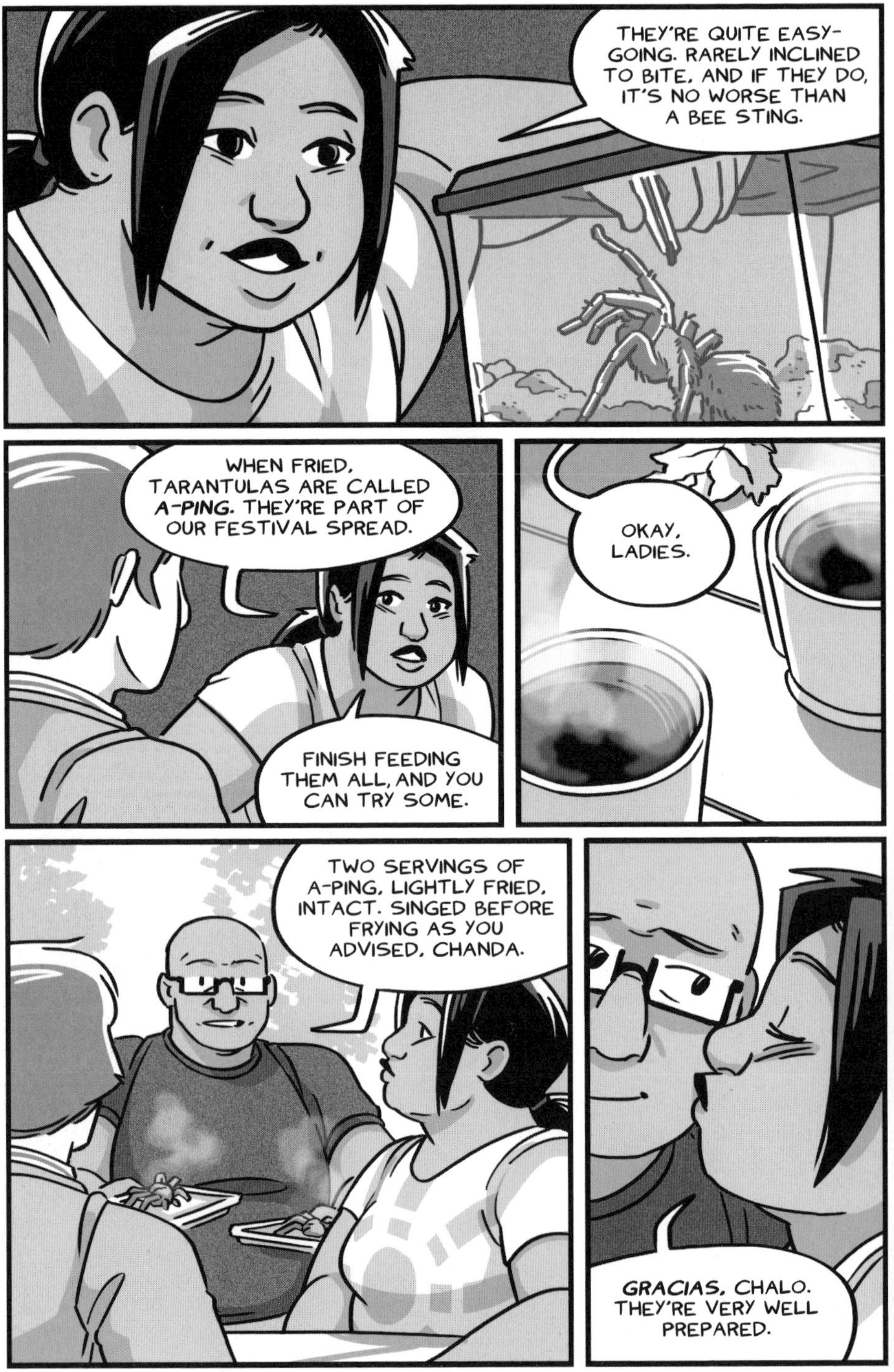
THEY'RE QUITE EASY-GOING. RARELY INCLINED TO BITE, AND IF THEY DO, IT'S NO WORSE THAN A BEE STING.
WHEN FRIED, TARANTULAS ARE CALLED *A-PING*. THEY'RE PART OF OUR FESTIVAL SPREAD.
FINISH FEEDING THEM ALL, AND YOU CAN TRY SOME.
OKAY, LADIES.
TWO SERVINGS OF A-PING, LIGHTLY FRIED, INTACT. SINGED BEFORE FRYING AS YOU ADVISED, CHANDA.
GRACIAS, CHALO. THEY'RE VERY WELL PREPARED.

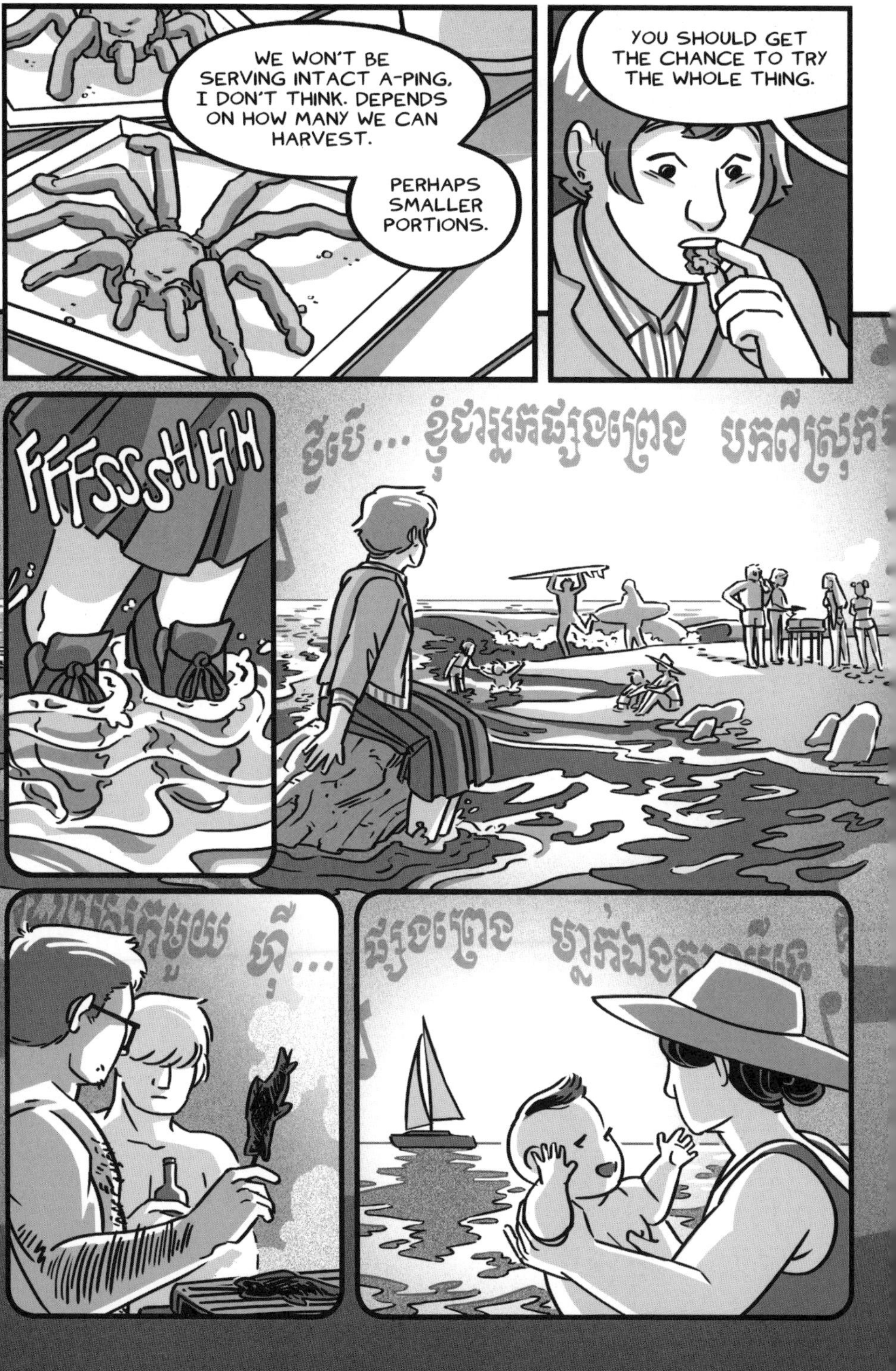
WE WON'T BE SERVING INTACT A-PING, I DON'T THINK. DEPENDS ON HOW MANY WE CAN HARVEST.
PERHAPS SMALLER PORTIONS.
YOU SHOULD GET THE CHANCE TO TRY THE WHOLE THING.
FFFSSSHHH

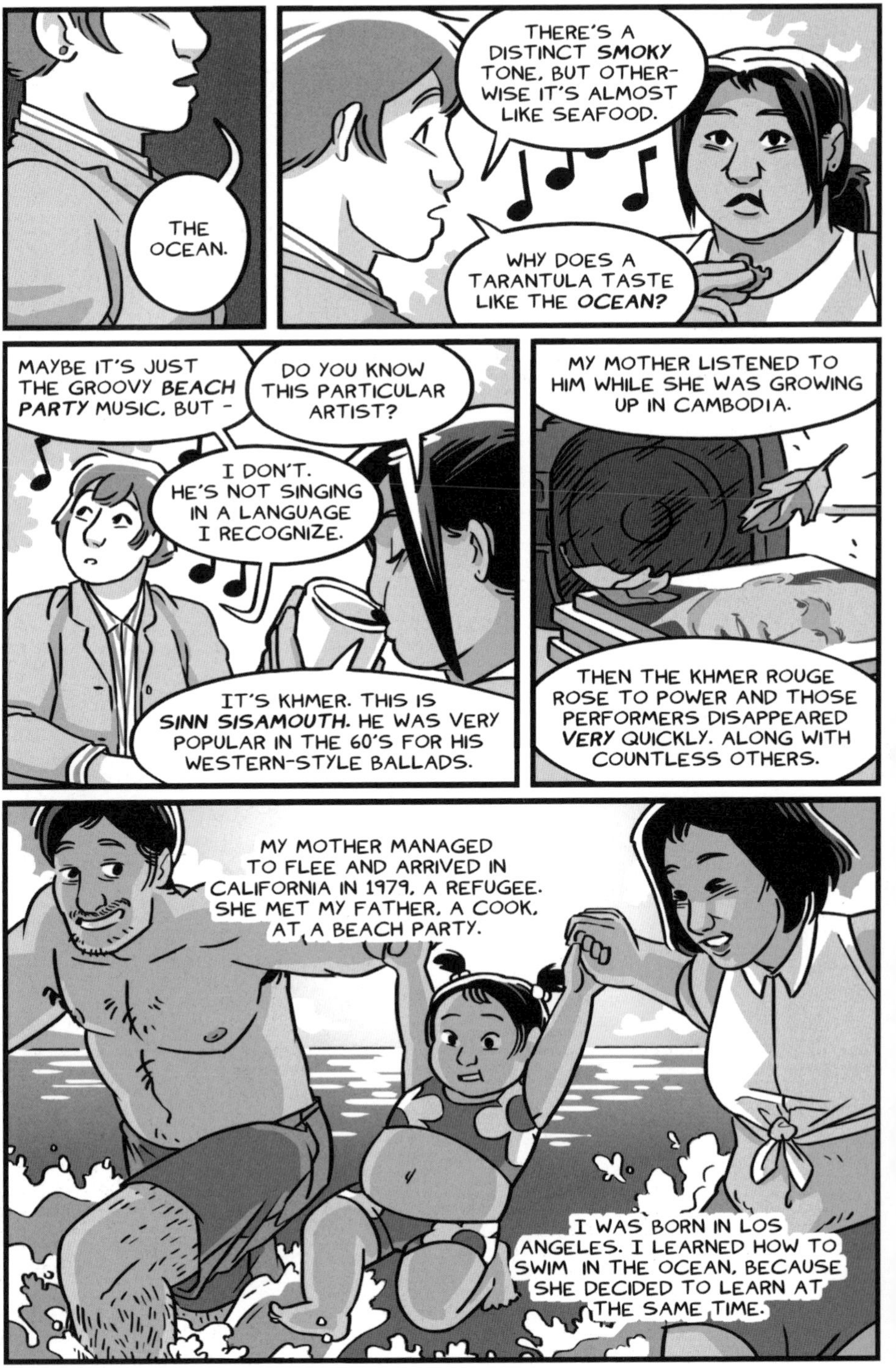
THE OCEAN.
THERE'S A DISTINCT SMOKY TONE, BUT OTHERWISE IT'S ALMOST LIKE SEAFOOD.
WHY DOES A TARANTULA TASTE LIKE THE OCEAN?
MAYBE IT'S JUST THE GROOVY BEACH PARTY MUSIC, BUT -
DO YOU KNOW THIS PARTICULAR ARTIST?
I DON'T. HE'S NOT SINGING IN A LANGUAGE I RECOGNIZE.
IT'S KHMER. THIS IS SINN SISAMOUTH. HE WAS VERY POPULAR IN THE 60'S FOR HIS WESTERN-STYLE BALLADS.
MY MOTHER LISTENED TO HIM WHILE SHE WAS GROWING UP IN CAMBODIA.
THEN THE KHMER ROUGE ROSE TO POWER AND THOSE PERFORMERS DISAPPEARED VERY QUICKLY. ALONG WITH COUNTLESS OTHERS.
MY MOTHER MANAGED TO FLEE AND ARRIVED IN CALIFORNIA IN 1979, A REFUGEE. SHE MET MY FATHER, A COOK, AT A BEACH PARTY.
I WAS BORN IN LOS ANGELES. I LEARNED HOW TO SWIM IN THE OCEAN, BECAUSE SHE DECIDED TO LEARN AT THE SAME TIME.

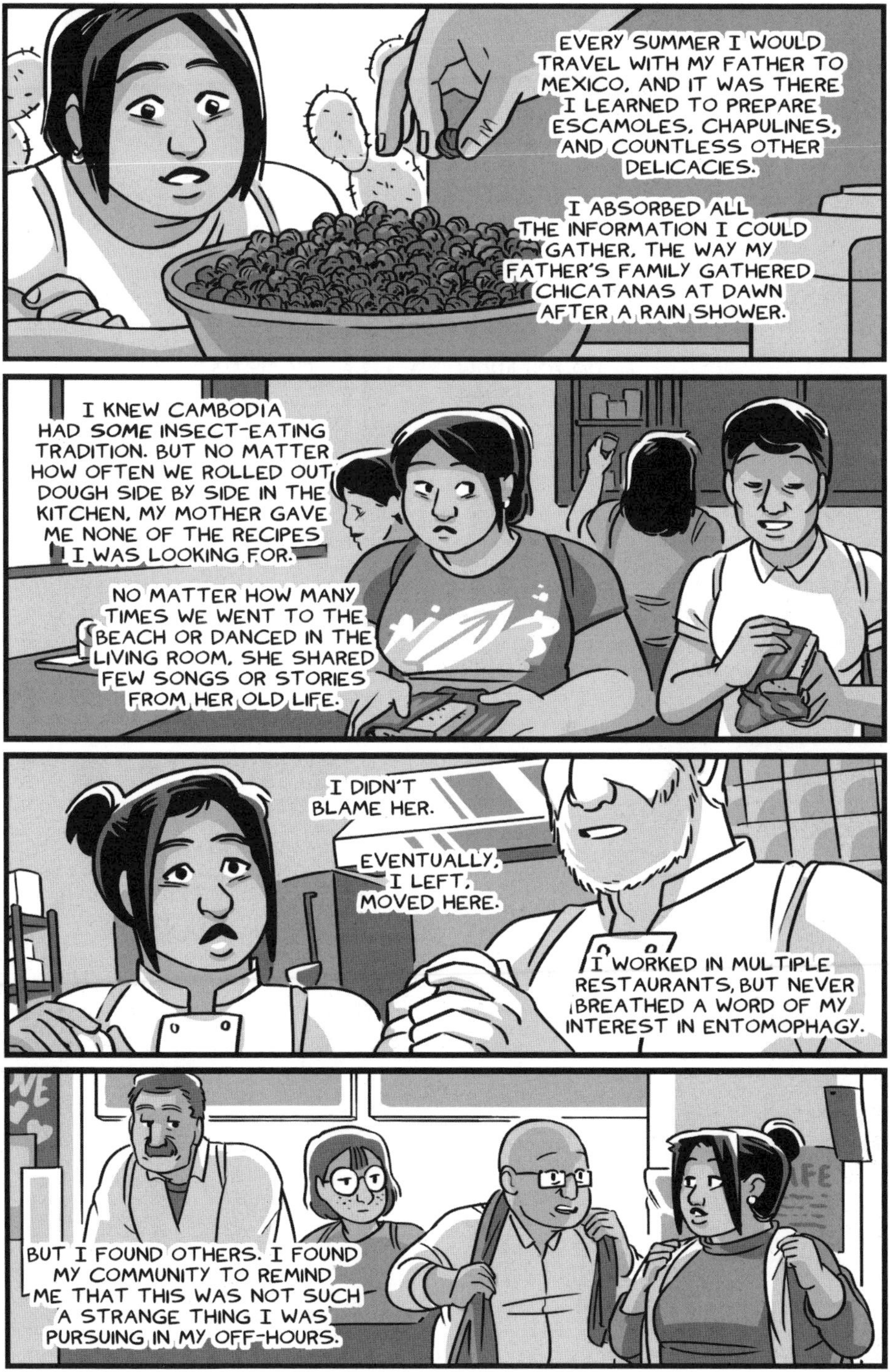
EVERY SUMMER I WOULD TRAVEL WITH MY FATHER TO MEXICO, AND IT WAS THERE I LEARNED TO PREPARE ESCAMOLES, CHAPULINES, AND COUNTLESS OTHER DELICACIES.
I ABSORBED ALL THE INFORMATION I COULD GATHER, THE WAY MY FATHER'S FAMILY GATHERED CHICATANAS AT DAWN AFTER A RAIN SHOWER.
I KNEW CAMBODIA HAD *SOME* INSECT-EATING TRADITION. BUT NO MATTER HOW OFTEN WE ROLLED OUT DOUGH SIDE BY SIDE IN THE KITCHEN, MY MOTHER GAVE ME NONE OF THE RECIPES I WAS LOOKING FOR.
NO MATTER HOW MANY TIMES WE WENT TO THE BEACH OR DANCED IN THE LIVING ROOM, SHE SHARED FEW SONGS OR STORIES FROM HER OLD LIFE.
I DIDN'T BLAME HER.
EVENTUALLY, I LEFT, MOVED HERE.
I WORKED IN MULTIPLE RESTAURANTS, BUT NEVER BREATHED A WORD OF MY INTEREST IN ENTOMOPHAGY.
BUT I FOUND OTHERS. I FOUND MY COMMUNITY TO REMIND ME THAT THIS WAS NOT SUCH A STRANGE THING I WAS PURSUING IN MY OFF-HOURS.

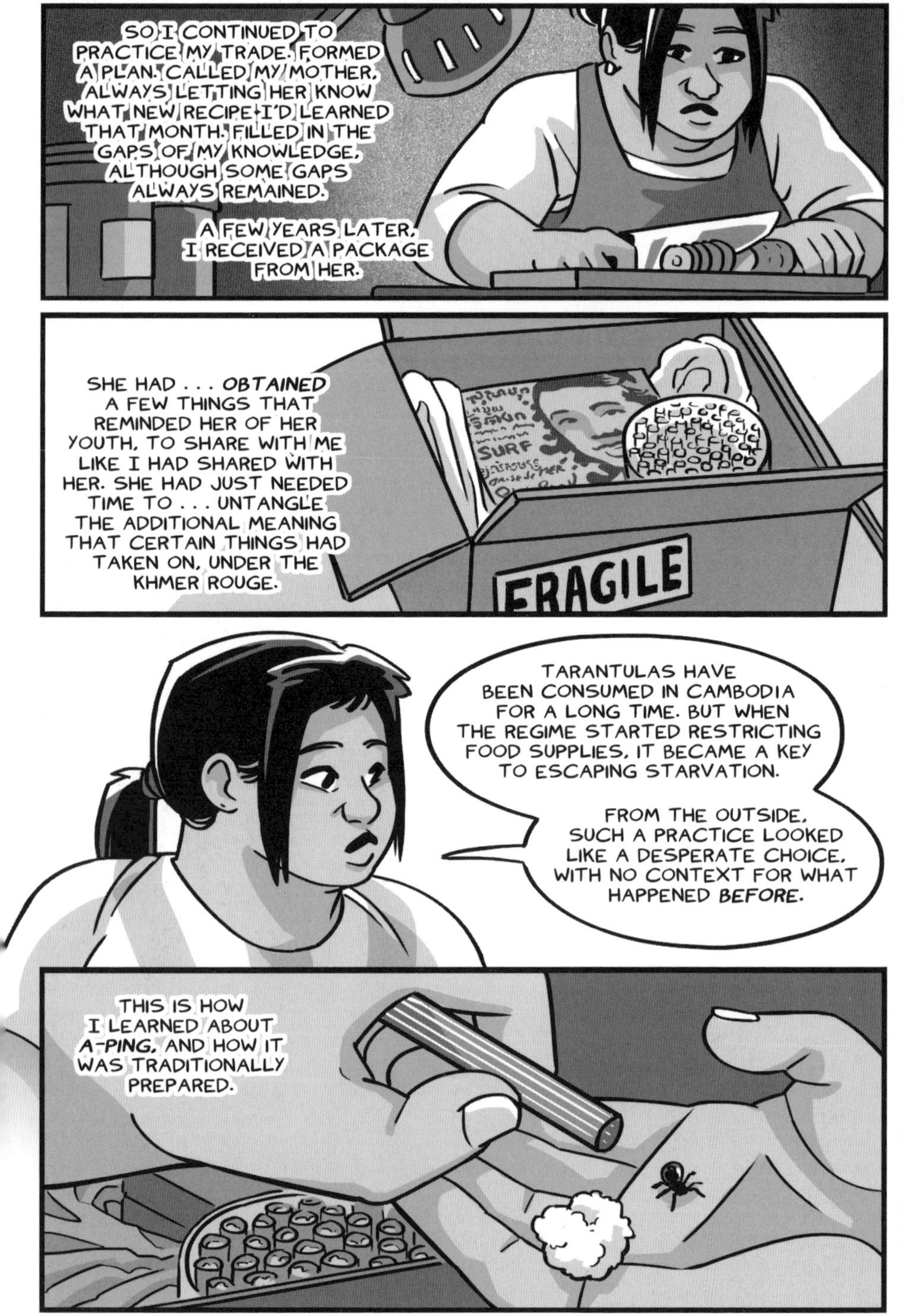
SO I CONTINUED TO PRACTICE MY TRADE. FORMED A PLAN. CALLED MY MOTHER, ALWAYS LETTING HER KNOW WHAT NEW RECIPE I'D LEARNED THAT MONTH. FILLED IN THE GAPS OF MY KNOWLEDGE, ALTHOUGH SOME GAPS ALWAYS REMAINED.
A FEW YEARS LATER, I RECEIVED A PACKAGE FROM HER.
SHE HAD . . . *OBTAINED* A FEW THINGS THAT REMINDED HER OF HER YOUTH, TO SHARE WITH ME LIKE I HAD SHARED WITH HER. SHE HAD JUST NEEDED TIME TO . . . UNTANGLE THE ADDITIONAL MEANING THAT CERTAIN THINGS HAD TAKEN ON, UNDER THE KHMER ROUGE.
SURF
FRAGILE
TARANTULAS HAVE BEEN CONSUMED IN CAMBODIA FOR A LONG TIME. BUT WHEN THE REGIME STARTED RESTRICTING FOOD SUPPLIES, IT BECAME A KEY TO ESCAPING STARVATION.
FROM THE OUTSIDE, SUCH A PRACTICE LOOKED LIKE A DESPERATE CHOICE, WITH NO CONTEXT FOR WHAT HAPPENED *BEFORE*.
THIS IS HOW I LEARNED ABOUT *A-PING*, AND HOW IT WAS TRADITIONALLY PREPARED.

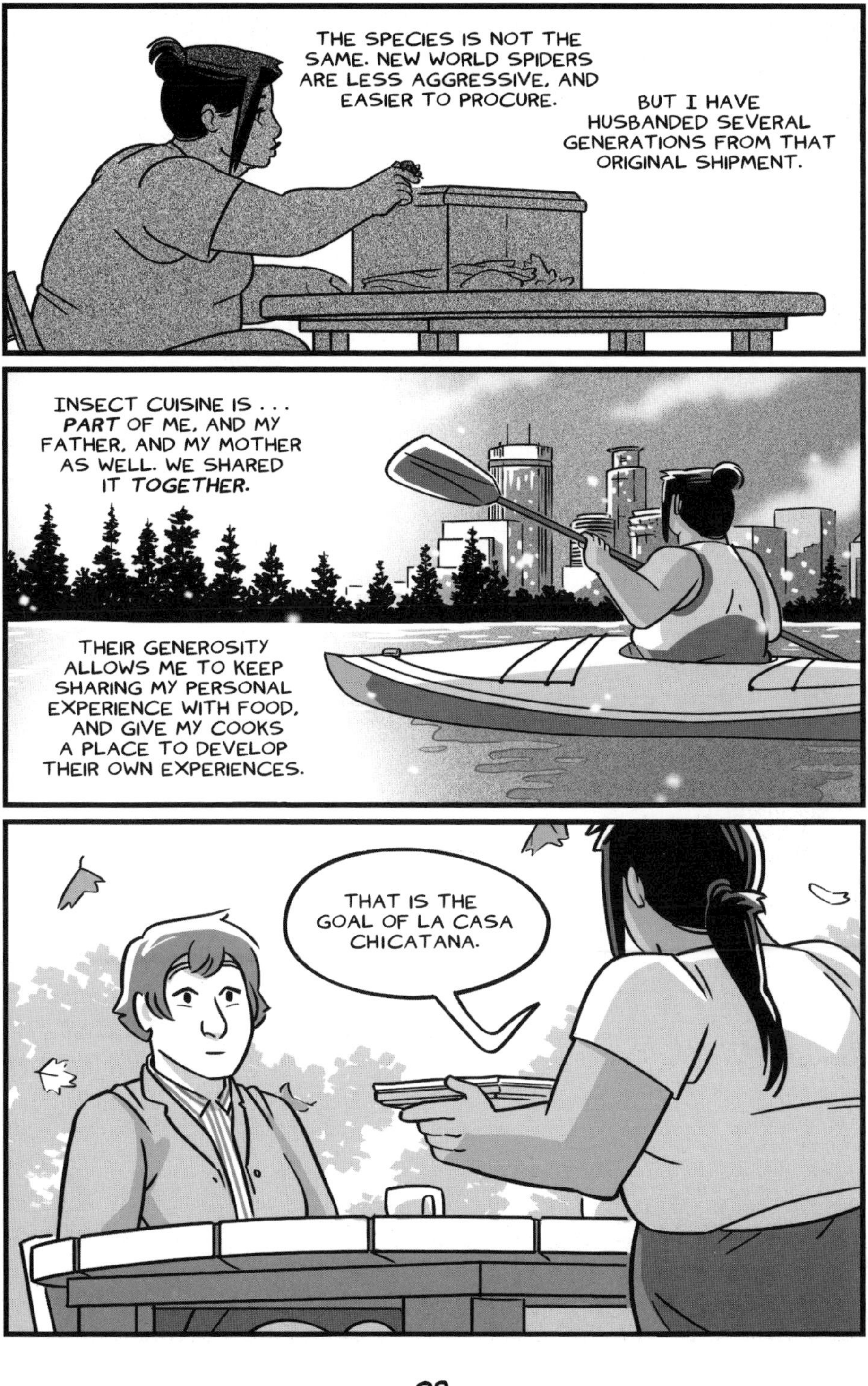
THE SPECIES IS NOT THE SAME. NEW WORLD SPIDERS ARE LESS AGGRESSIVE, AND EASIER TO PROCURE.
BUT I HAVE HUSBANDED SEVERAL GENERATIONS FROM THAT ORIGINAL SHIPMENT.
INSECT CUISINE IS . . . PART OF ME, AND MY FATHER, AND MY MOTHER AS WELL. WE SHARED IT TOGETHER.
THEIR GENEROSITY ALLOWS ME TO KEEP SHARING MY PERSONAL EXPERIENCE WITH FOOD, AND GIVE MY COOKS A PLACE TO DEVELOP THEIR OWN EXPERIENCES.
THAT IS THE GOAL OF LA CASA CHICATANA.

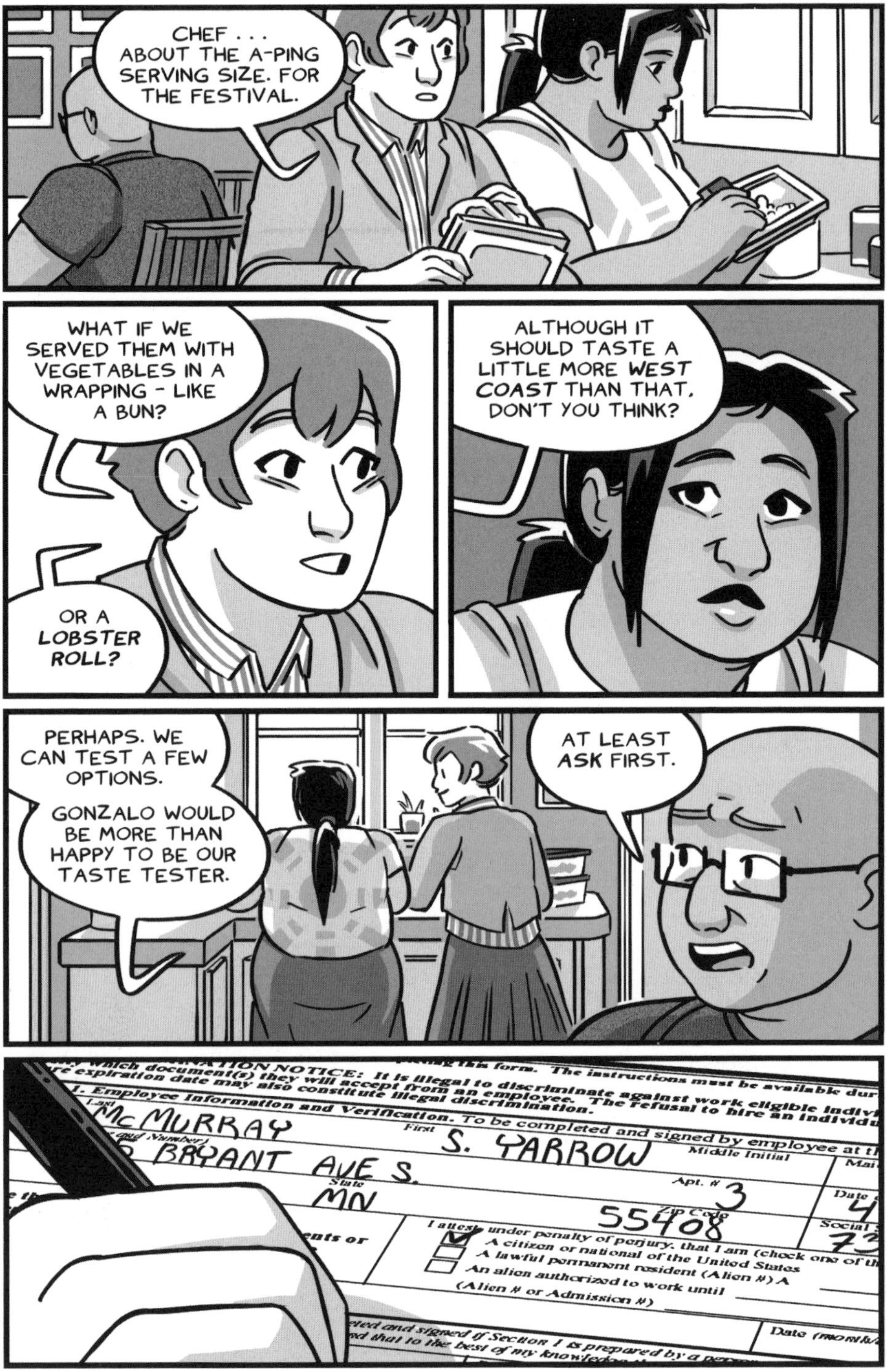
CHEF . . . ABOUT THE A-PING SERVING SIZE. FOR THE FESTIVAL.
WHAT IF WE SERVED THEM WITH VEGETABLES IN A WRAPPING – LIKE A BUN?
OR A LOBSTER ROLL?
ALTHOUGH IT SHOULD TASTE A LITTLE MORE WEST COAST THAN THAT, DON'T YOU THINK?
PERHAPS. WE CAN TEST A FEW OPTIONS.
GONZALO WOULD BE MORE THAN HAPPY TO BE OUR TASTE TESTER.
AT LEAST ASK FIRST.
McMURRAY
S. YARROW
BRYANT AVE S.
MN
3
55408
A citizen or national of the United States
A lawful permanent resident (Alien #) A
An alien authorized to work until
(Alien # or Admission #)

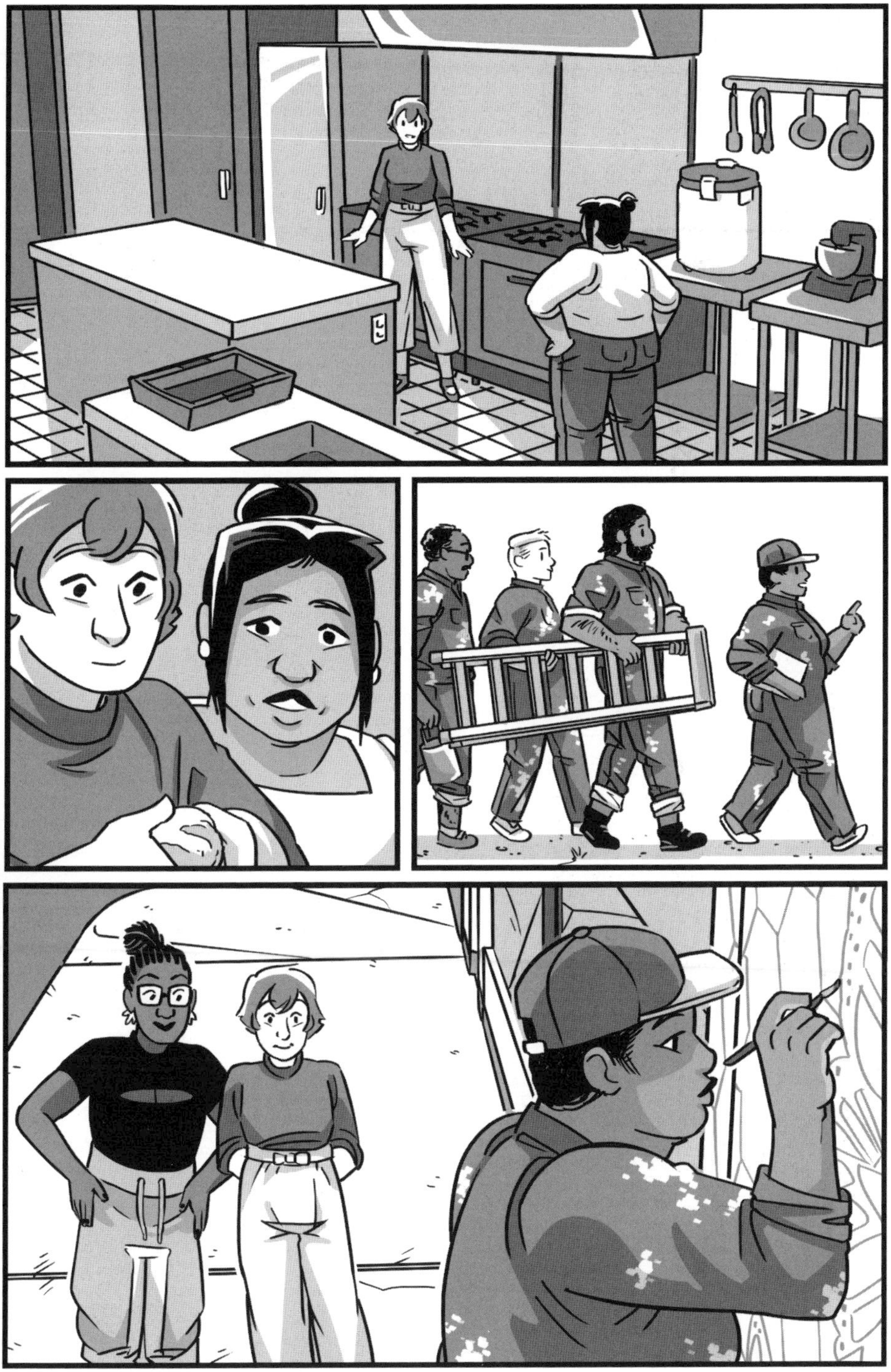

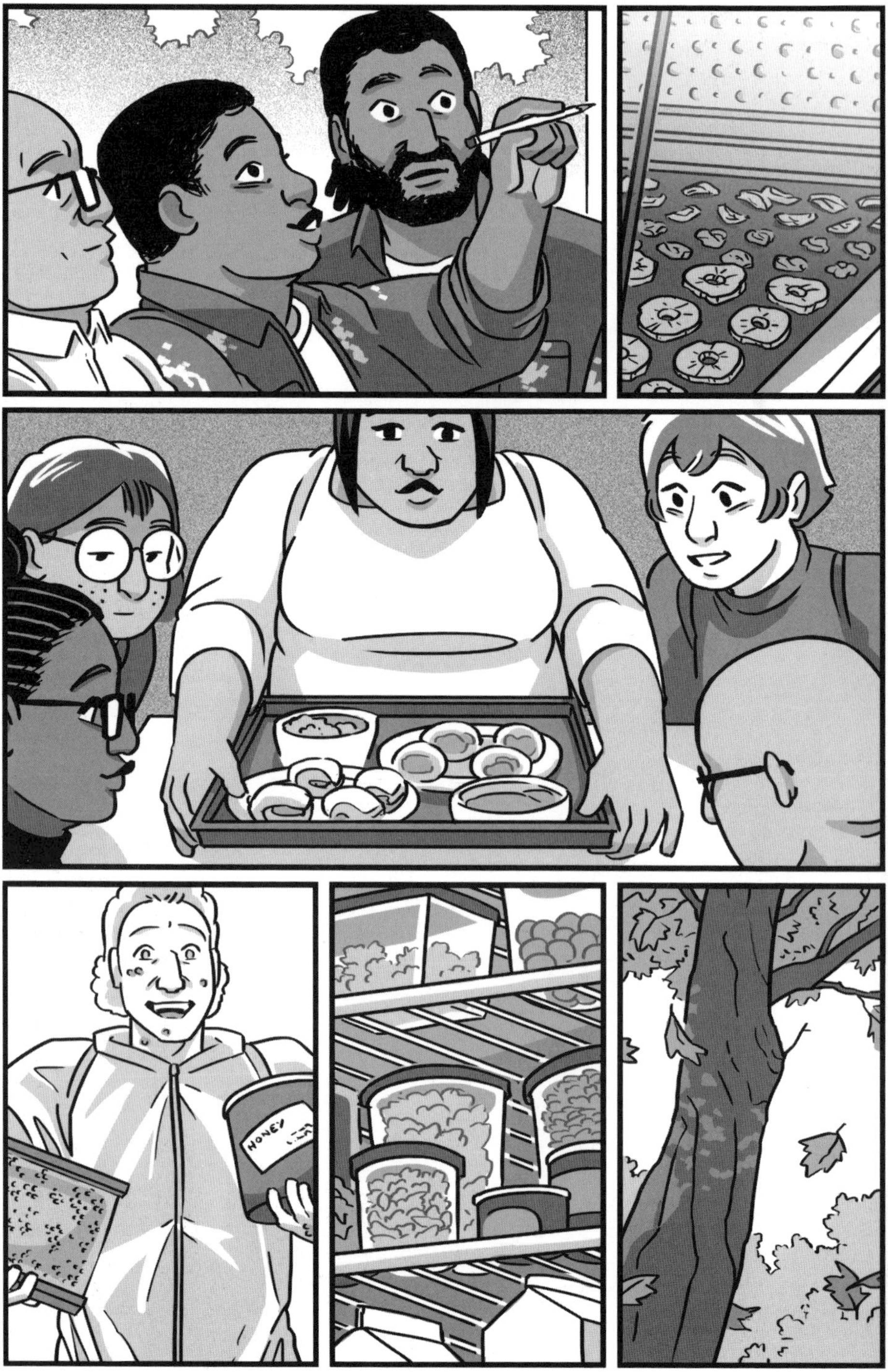
HONEY

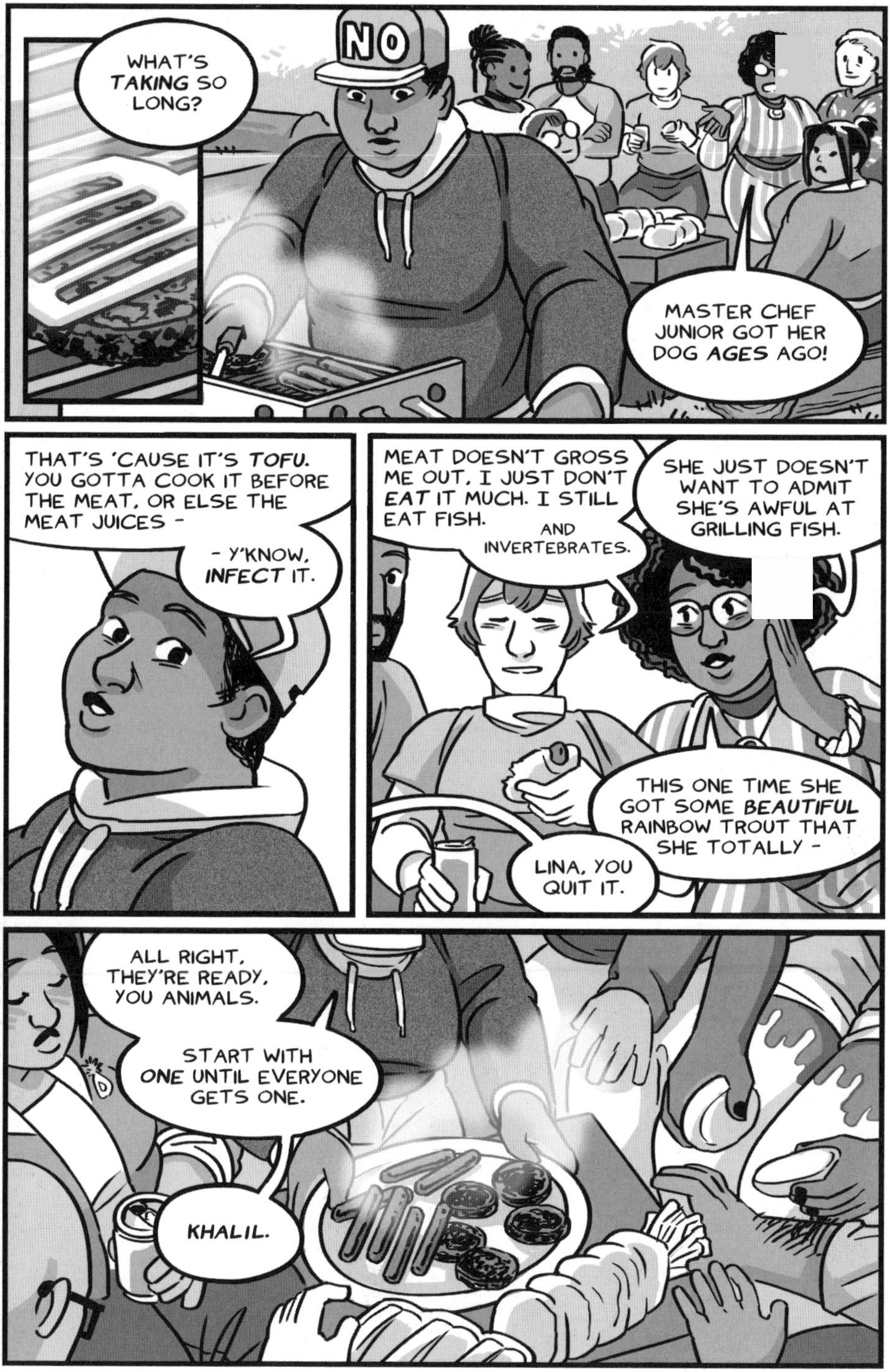
WHAT'S TAKING SO LONG?
MASTER CHEF JUNIOR GOT HER DOG AGES AGO!
THAT'S 'CAUSE IT'S TOFU. YOU GOTTA COOK IT BEFORE THE MEAT, OR ELSE THE MEAT JUICES –
– Y'KNOW, INFECT IT.
MEAT DOESN'T GROSS ME OUT, I JUST DON'T EAT IT MUCH. I STILL EAT FISH.
AND INVERTEBRATES.
SHE JUST DOESN'T WANT TO ADMIT SHE'S AWFUL AT GRILLING FISH.
THIS ONE TIME SHE GOT SOME BEAUTIFUL RAINBOW TROUT THAT SHE TOTALLY –
LINA, YOU QUIT IT.
ALL RIGHT, THEY'RE READY, YOU ANIMALS.
START WITH ONE UNTIL EVERYONE GETS ONE.
KHALIL.

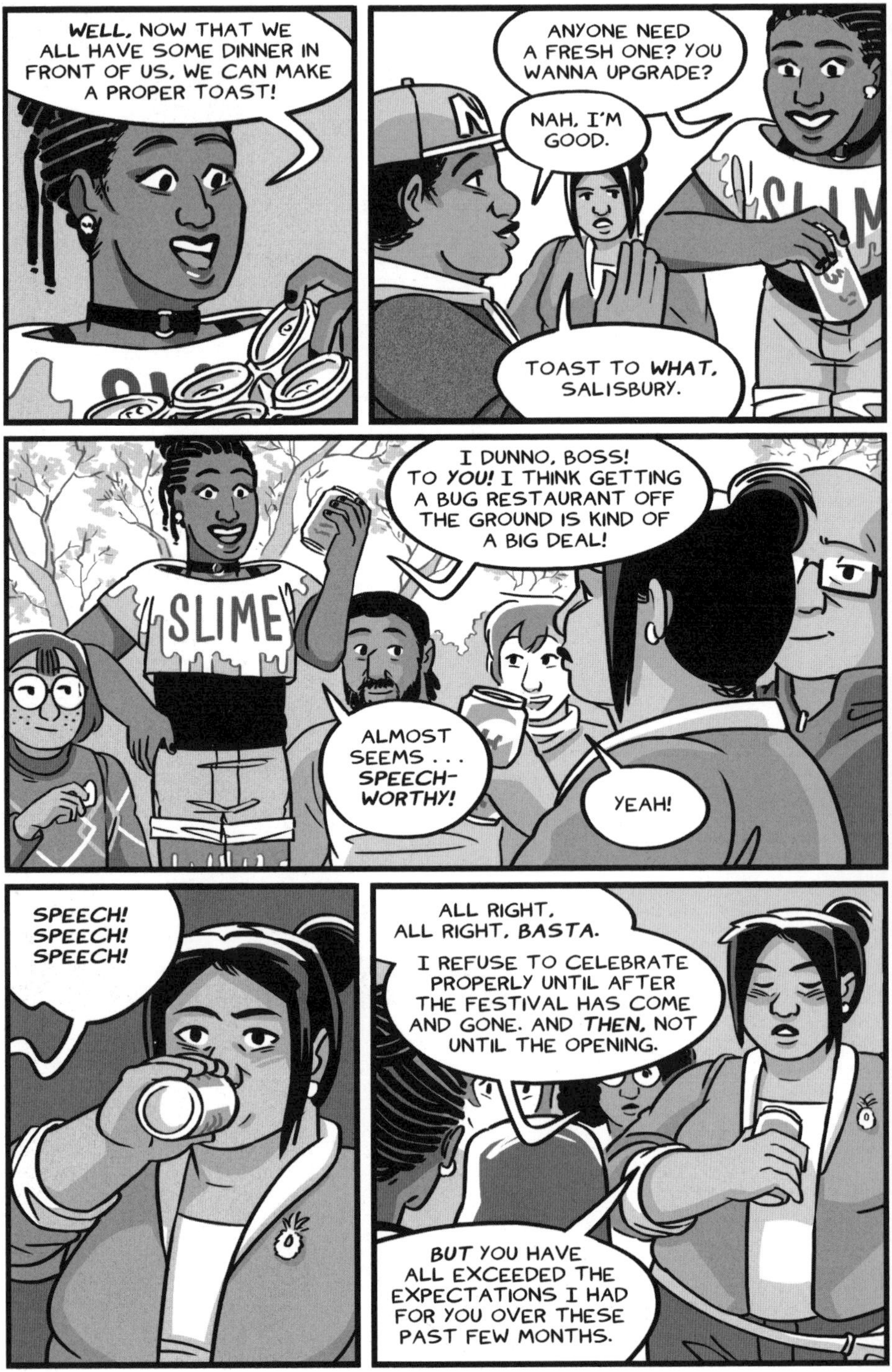
WELL, NOW THAT WE ALL HAVE SOME DINNER IN FRONT OF US, WE CAN MAKE A PROPER TOAST!
ANYONE NEED A FRESH ONE? YOU WANNA UPGRADE?
NAH, I'M GOOD.
TOAST TO WHAT, SALISBURY.
SLIME
I DUNNO, BOSS! TO YOU! I THINK GETTING A BUG RESTAURANT OFF THE GROUND IS KIND OF A BIG DEAL!
ALMOST SEEMS . . . SPEECH-WORTHY!
YEAH!
SPEECH! SPEECH! SPEECH!
ALL RIGHT, ALL RIGHT, BASTA.
I REFUSE TO CELEBRATE PROPERLY UNTIL AFTER THE FESTIVAL HAS COME AND GONE. AND THEN, NOT UNTIL THE OPENING.
BUT YOU HAVE ALL EXCEEDED THE EXPECTATIONS I HAD FOR YOU OVER THESE PAST FEW MONTHS.

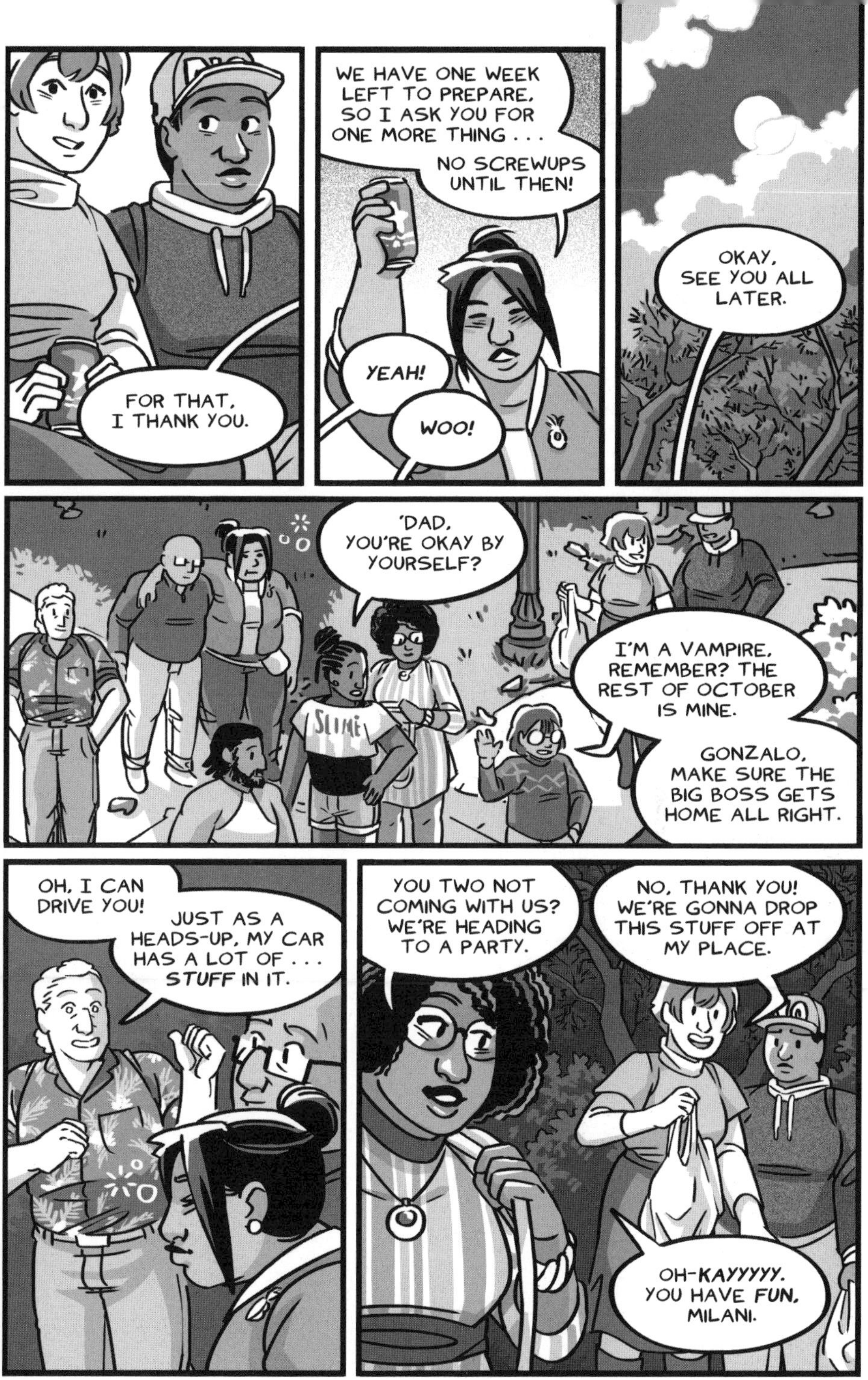
FOR THAT, I THANK YOU.
WE HAVE ONE WEEK LEFT TO PREPARE, SO I ASK YOU FOR ONE MORE THING . . .
NO SCREWUPS UNTIL THEN!
YEAH!
WOO!
OKAY, SEE YOU ALL LATER.
'DAD, YOU'RE OKAY BY YOURSELF?
I'M A VAMPIRE, REMEMBER? THE REST OF OCTOBER IS MINE.
GONZALO, MAKE SURE THE BIG BOSS GETS HOME ALL RIGHT.
SLIME
OH, I CAN DRIVE YOU!
JUST AS A HEADS-UP, MY CAR HAS A LOT OF . . . STUFF IN IT.
YOU TWO NOT COMING WITH US? WE'RE HEADING TO A PARTY.
NO, THANK YOU! WE'RE GONNA DROP THIS STUFF OFF AT MY PLACE.
OH-KAYYYYY. YOU HAVE FUN, MILANI.

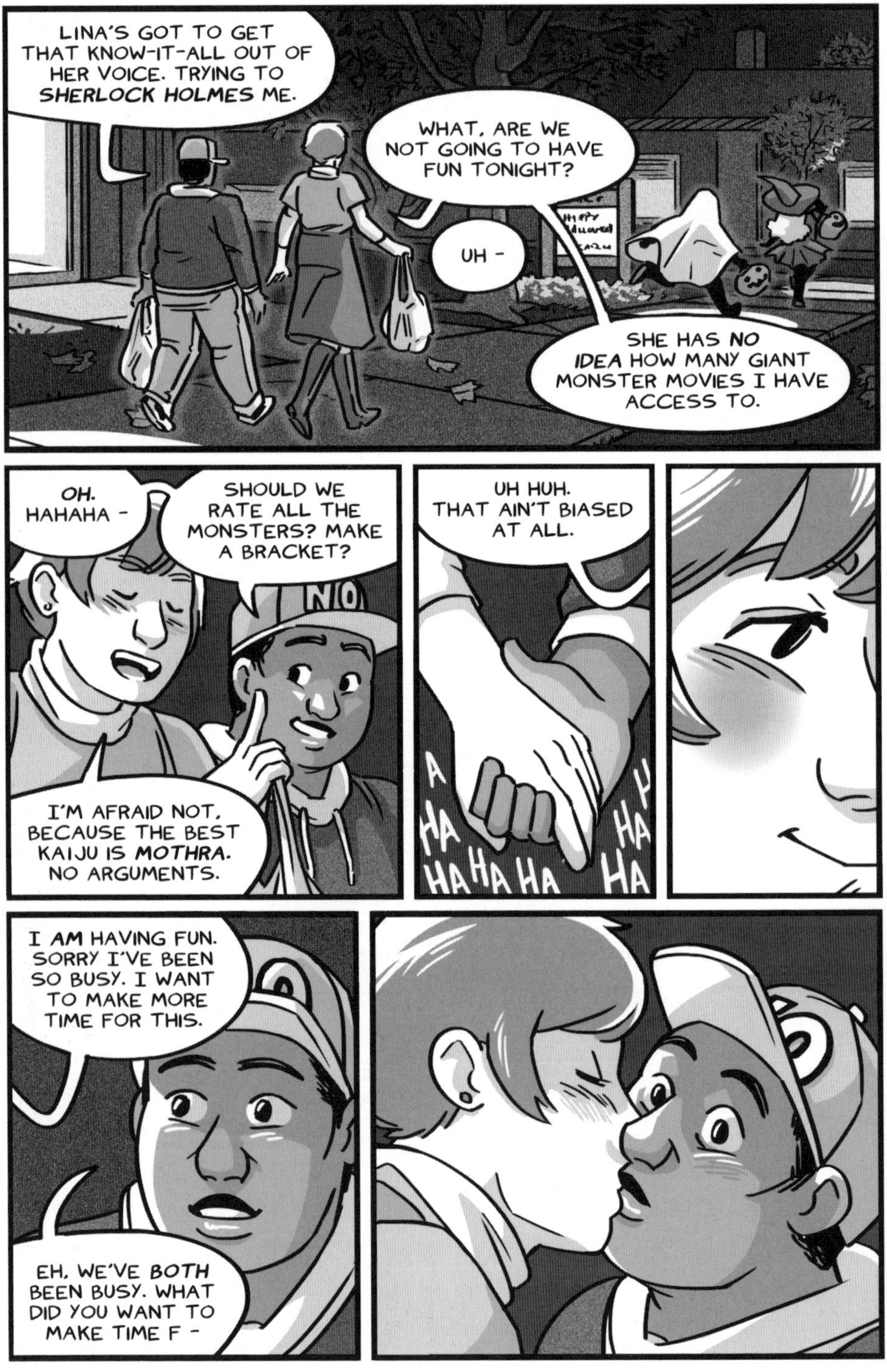
LINA'S GOT TO GET THAT KNOW-IT-ALL OUT OF HER VOICE. TRYING TO ***SHERLOCK HOLMES*** ME.
WHAT, ARE WE NOT GOING TO HAVE FUN TONIGHT?
UH -
SHE HAS ***NO IDEA*** HOW MANY GIANT MONSTER MOVIES I HAVE ACCESS TO.
OH. HAHAHA -
SHOULD WE RATE ALL THE MONSTERS? MAKE A BRACKET?
I'M AFRAID NOT, BECAUSE THE BEST KAIJU IS ***MOTHRA.*** NO ARGUMENTS.
UH HUH. THAT AIN'T BIASED AT ALL.
HA HA HA HA HA HA HA HA
I ***AM*** HAVING FUN. SORRY I'VE BEEN SO BUSY. I WANT TO MAKE MORE TIME FOR THIS.
EH, WE'VE ***BOTH*** BEEN BUSY. WHAT DID YOU WANT TO MAKE TIME F -

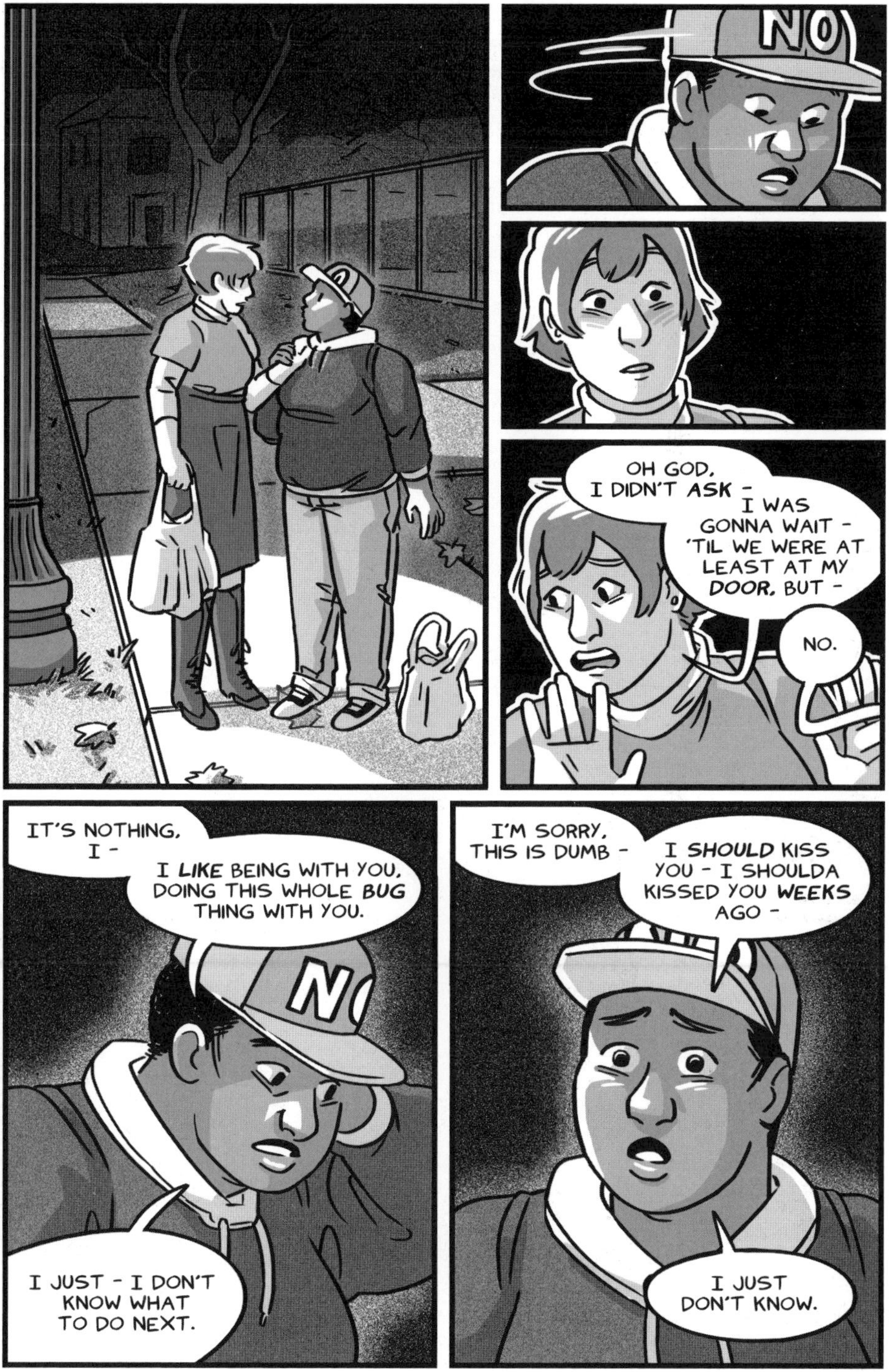
NO
OH GOD, I DIDN'T ASK -
I WAS GONNA WAIT - 'TIL WE WERE AT LEAST AT MY DOOR, BUT -
NO.
IT'S NOTHING, I -
I LIKE BEING WITH YOU, DOING THIS WHOLE BUG THING WITH YOU.
I JUST - I DON'T KNOW WHAT TO DO NEXT.
I'M SORRY, THIS IS DUMB -
I SHOULD KISS YOU - I SHOULDA KISSED YOU WEEKS AGO -
I JUST DON'T KNOW.

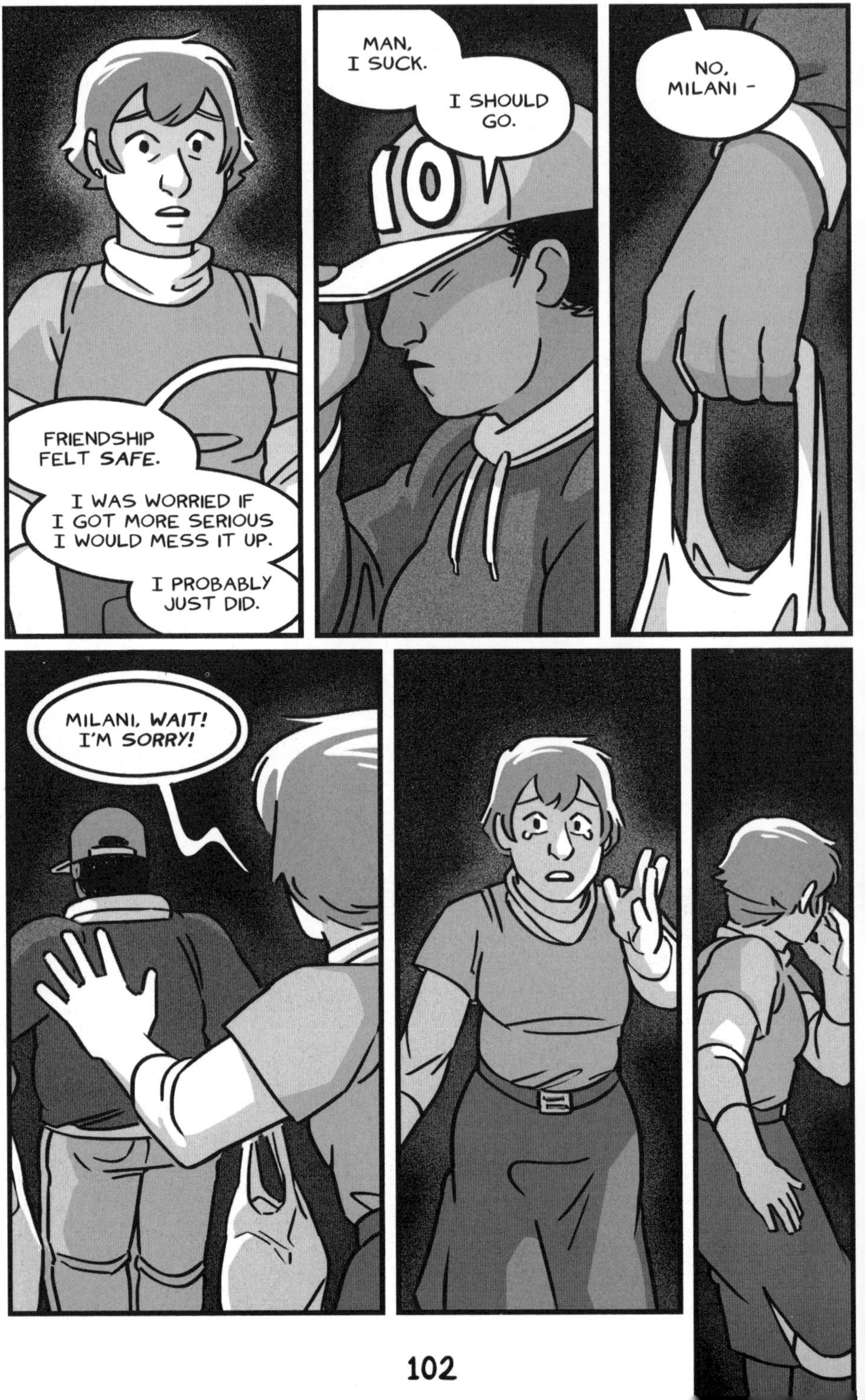
FRIENDSHIP FELT SAFE.
I WAS WORRIED IF I GOT MORE SERIOUS I WOULD MESS IT UP.
I PROBABLY JUST DID.
MAN, I SUCK.
I SHOULD GO.
NO, MILANI -
MILANI, WAIT! I'M SORRY!

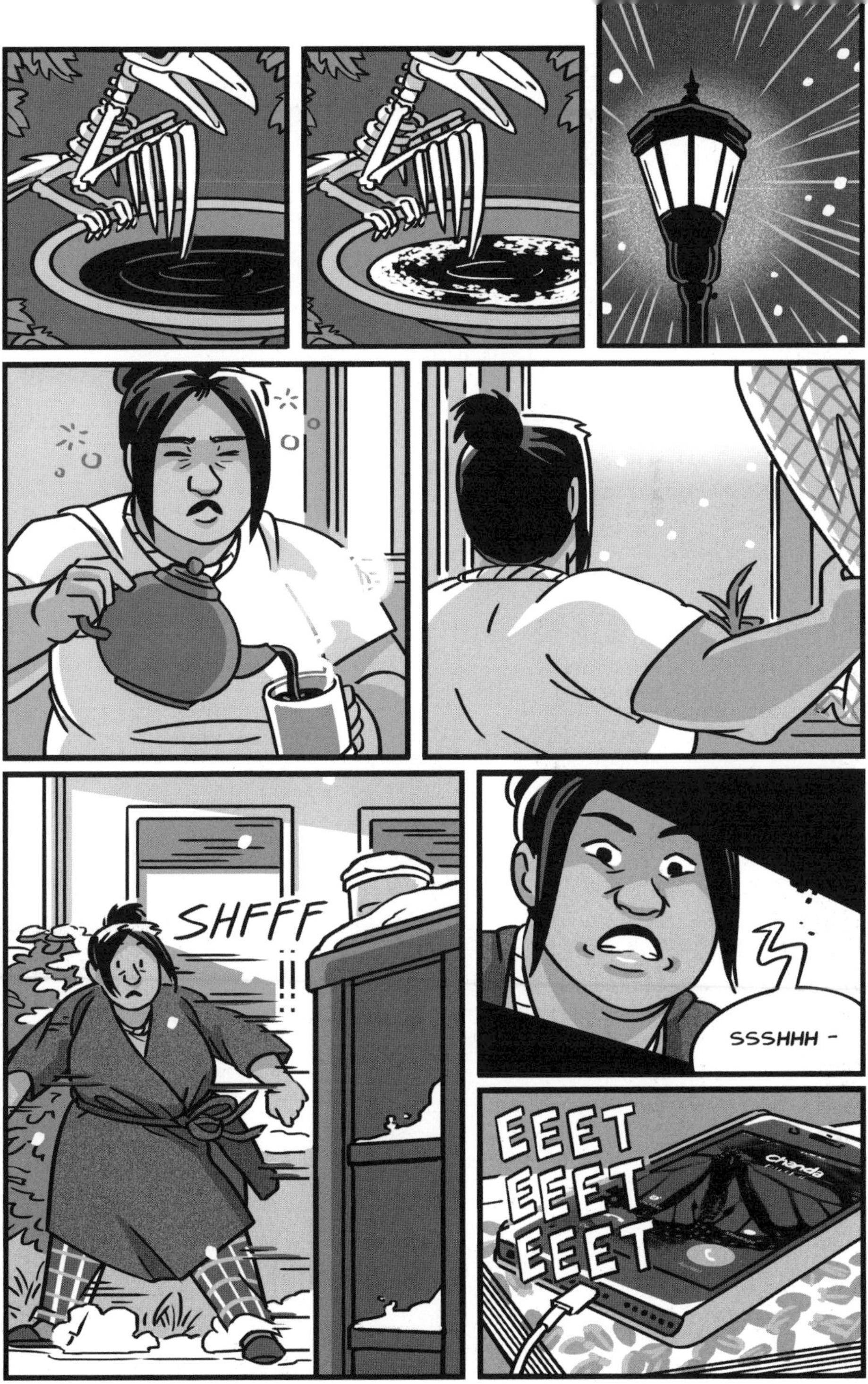
SHFFF
SSSHHH -
EEET
EEET
EEET
Chanda

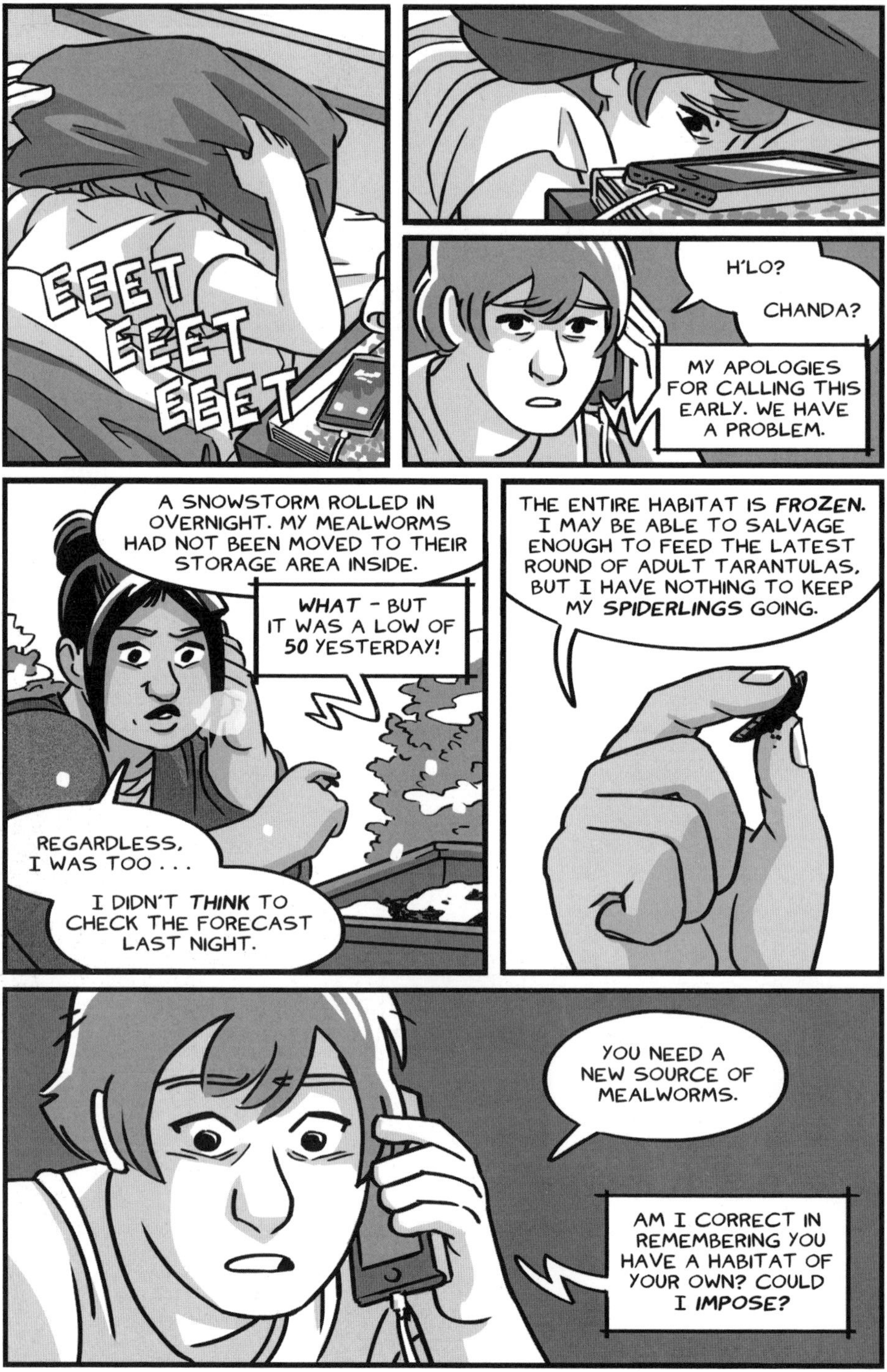
EEET EEET EEET
H'LO?
CHANDA?
MY APOLOGIES FOR CALLING THIS EARLY. WE HAVE A PROBLEM.
A SNOWSTORM ROLLED IN OVERNIGHT. MY MEALWORMS HAD NOT BEEN MOVED TO THEIR STORAGE AREA INSIDE.
WHAT - BUT IT WAS A LOW OF 50 YESTERDAY!
REGARDLESS, I WAS TOO . . .
I DIDN'T THINK TO CHECK THE FORECAST LAST NIGHT.
THE ENTIRE HABITAT IS FROZEN. I MAY BE ABLE TO SALVAGE ENOUGH TO FEED THE LATEST ROUND OF ADULT TARANTULAS, BUT I HAVE NOTHING TO KEEP MY SPIDERLINGS GOING.
YOU NEED A NEW SOURCE OF MEALWORMS.
AM I CORRECT IN REMEMBERING YOU HAVE A HABITAT OF YOUR OWN? COULD I IMPOSE?

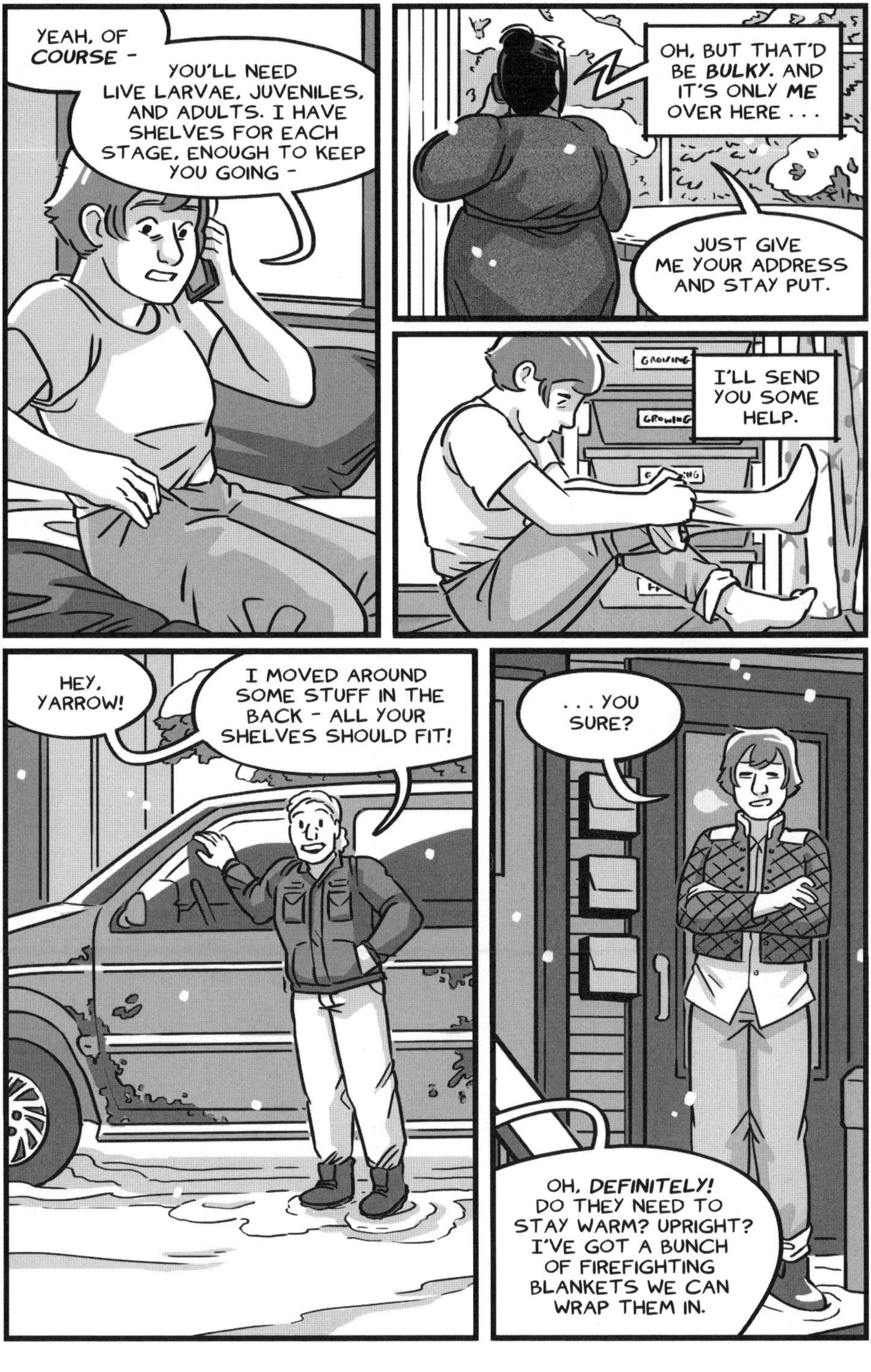
YEAH, OF *COURSE* –
YOU'LL NEED LIVE LARVAE, JUVENILES, AND ADULTS. I HAVE SHELVES FOR EACH STAGE, ENOUGH TO KEEP YOU GOING –
OH, BUT THAT'D BE ***BULKY.*** AND IT'S ONLY ***ME*** OVER HERE . . .
JUST GIVE ME YOUR ADDRESS AND STAY PUT.
GROWING
GROWING
I'LL SEND YOU SOME HELP.
HEY, YARROW!
I MOVED AROUND SOME STUFF IN THE BACK – ALL YOUR SHELVES SHOULD FIT!
. . . YOU SURE?
OH, ***DEFINITELY!*** DO THEY NEED TO STAY WARM? UPRIGHT? I'VE GOT A BUNCH OF FIREFIGHTING BLANKETS WE CAN WRAP THEM IN.

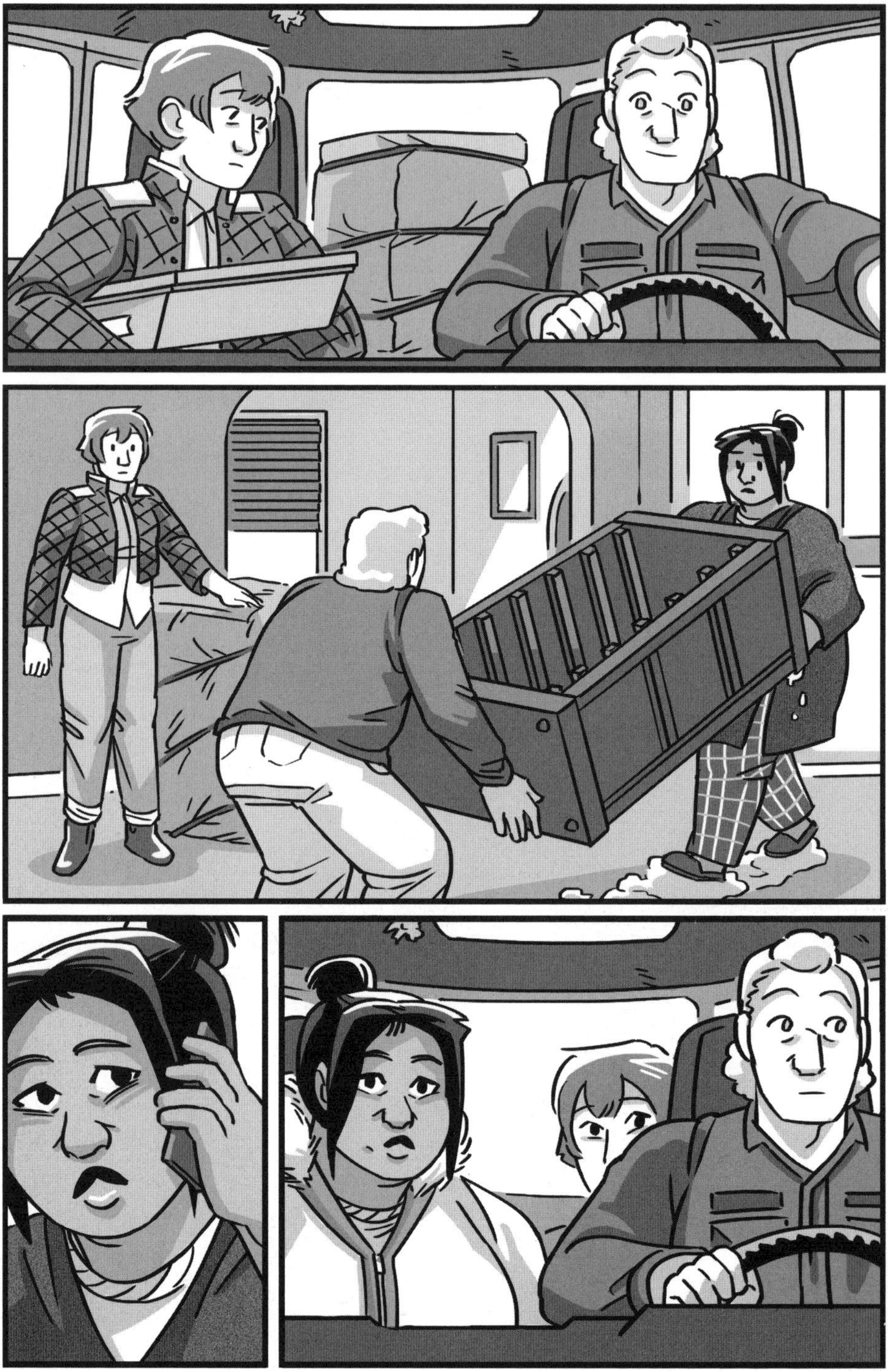

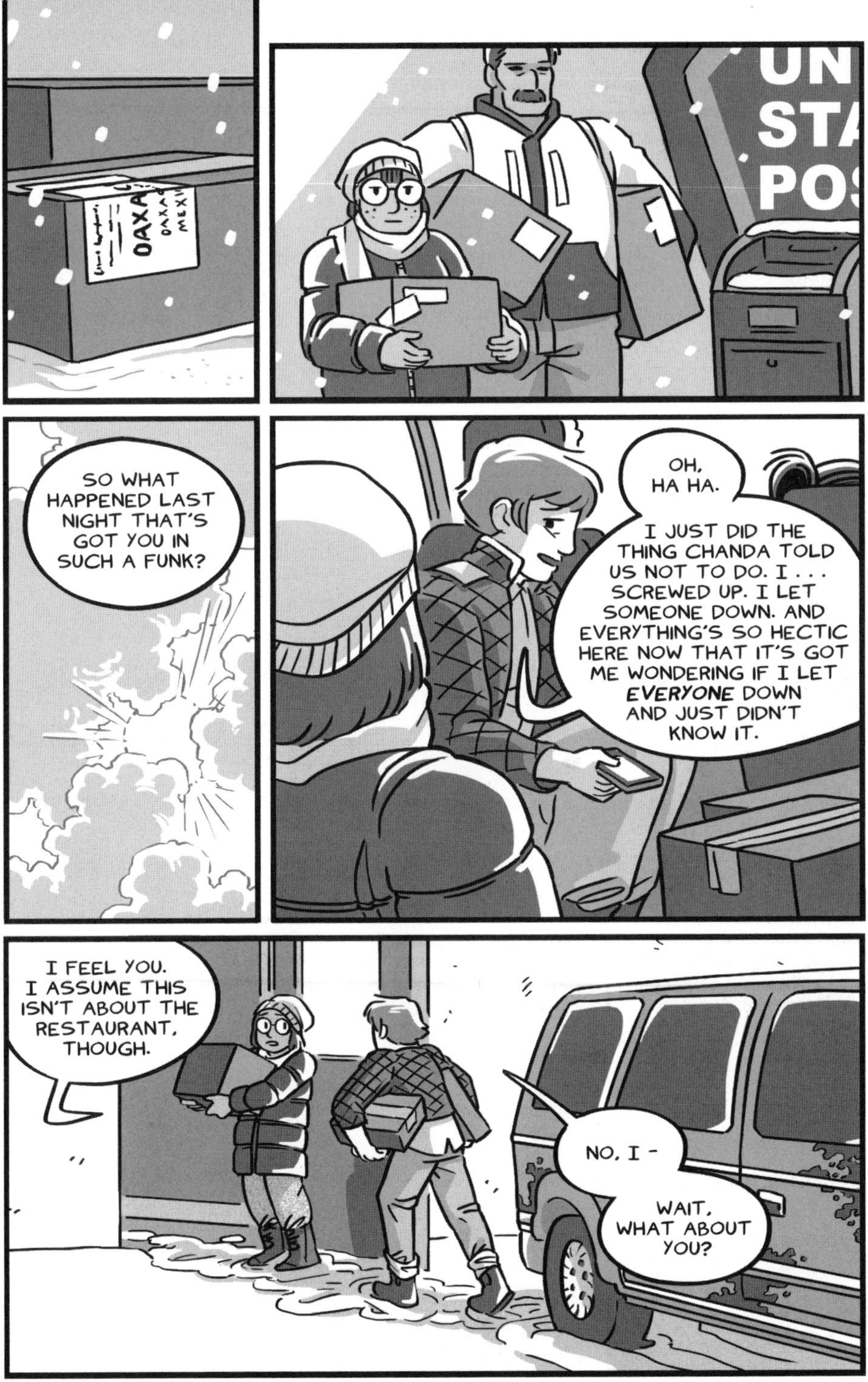
UN
STA
POS
SO WHAT HAPPENED LAST NIGHT THAT'S GOT YOU IN SUCH A FUNK?
OH, HA HA.
I JUST DID THE THING CHANDA TOLD US NOT TO DO. I . . . SCREWED UP. I LET SOMEONE DOWN. AND EVERYTHING'S SO HECTIC HERE NOW THAT IT'S GOT ME WONDERING IF I LET ***EVERYONE*** DOWN AND JUST DIDN'T KNOW IT.
I FEEL YOU. I ASSUME THIS ISN'T ABOUT THE RESTAURANT, THOUGH.
NO, I -
WAIT, WHAT ABOUT YOU?

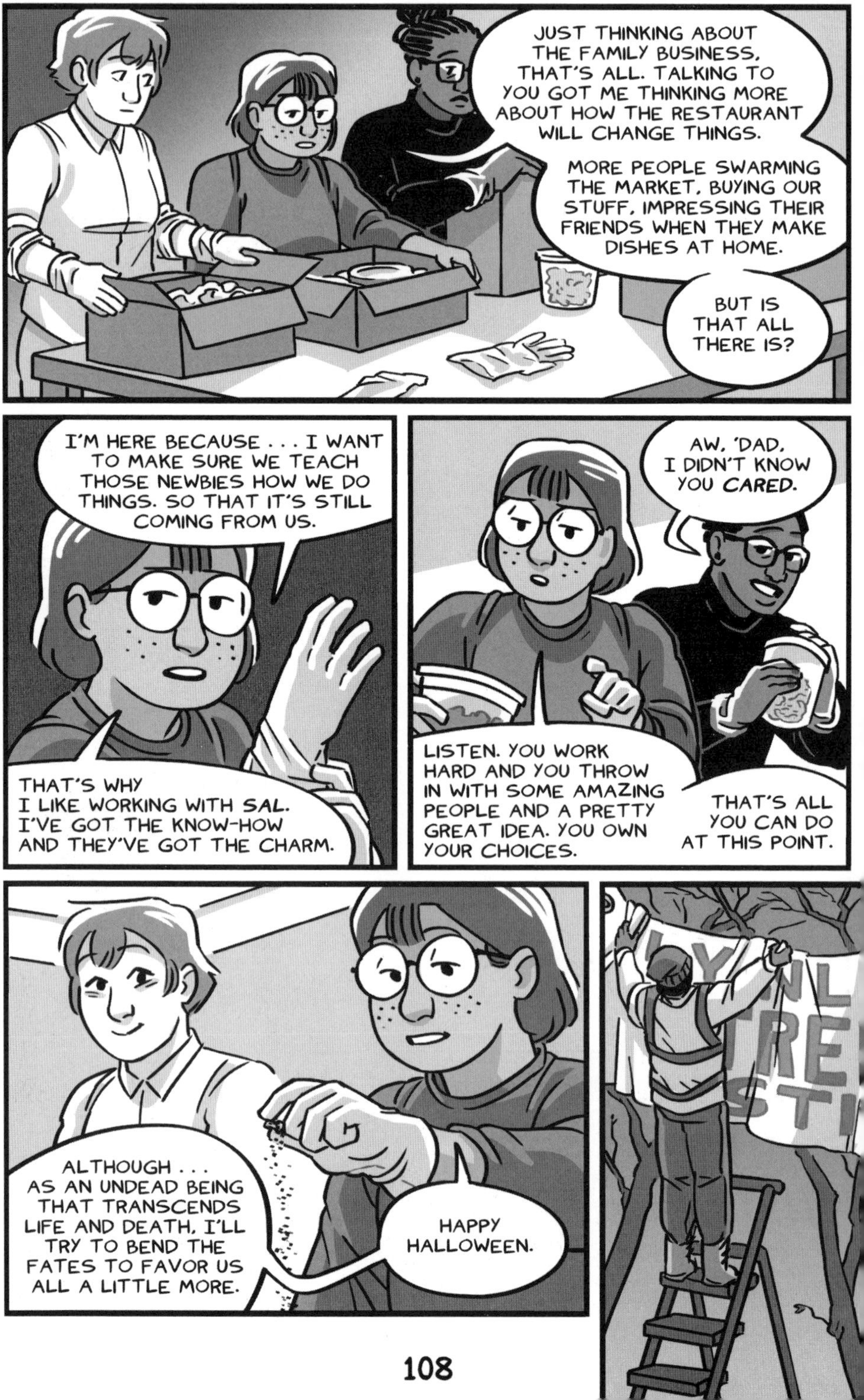
JUST THINKING ABOUT THE FAMILY BUSINESS, THAT'S ALL. TALKING TO YOU GOT ME THINKING MORE ABOUT HOW THE RESTAURANT WILL CHANGE THINGS.
MORE PEOPLE SWARMING THE MARKET, BUYING OUR STUFF, IMPRESSING THEIR FRIENDS WHEN THEY MAKE DISHES AT HOME.
BUT IS THAT ALL THERE IS?
I'M HERE BECAUSE . . . I WANT TO MAKE SURE WE TEACH THOSE NEWBIES HOW WE DO THINGS. SO THAT IT'S STILL COMING FROM US.
THAT'S WHY I LIKE WORKING WITH **SAL**. I'VE GOT THE KNOW-HOW AND THEY'VE GOT THE CHARM.
AW, 'DAD, I DIDN'T KNOW YOU **CARED**.
LISTEN. YOU WORK HARD AND YOU THROW IN WITH SOME AMAZING PEOPLE AND A PRETTY GREAT IDEA. YOU OWN YOUR CHOICES.
THAT'S ALL YOU CAN DO AT THIS POINT.
ALTHOUGH . . . AS AN UNDEAD BEING THAT TRANSCENDS LIFE AND DEATH, I'LL TRY TO BEND THE FATES TO FAVOR US ALL A LITTLE MORE.
HAPPY HALLOWEEN.

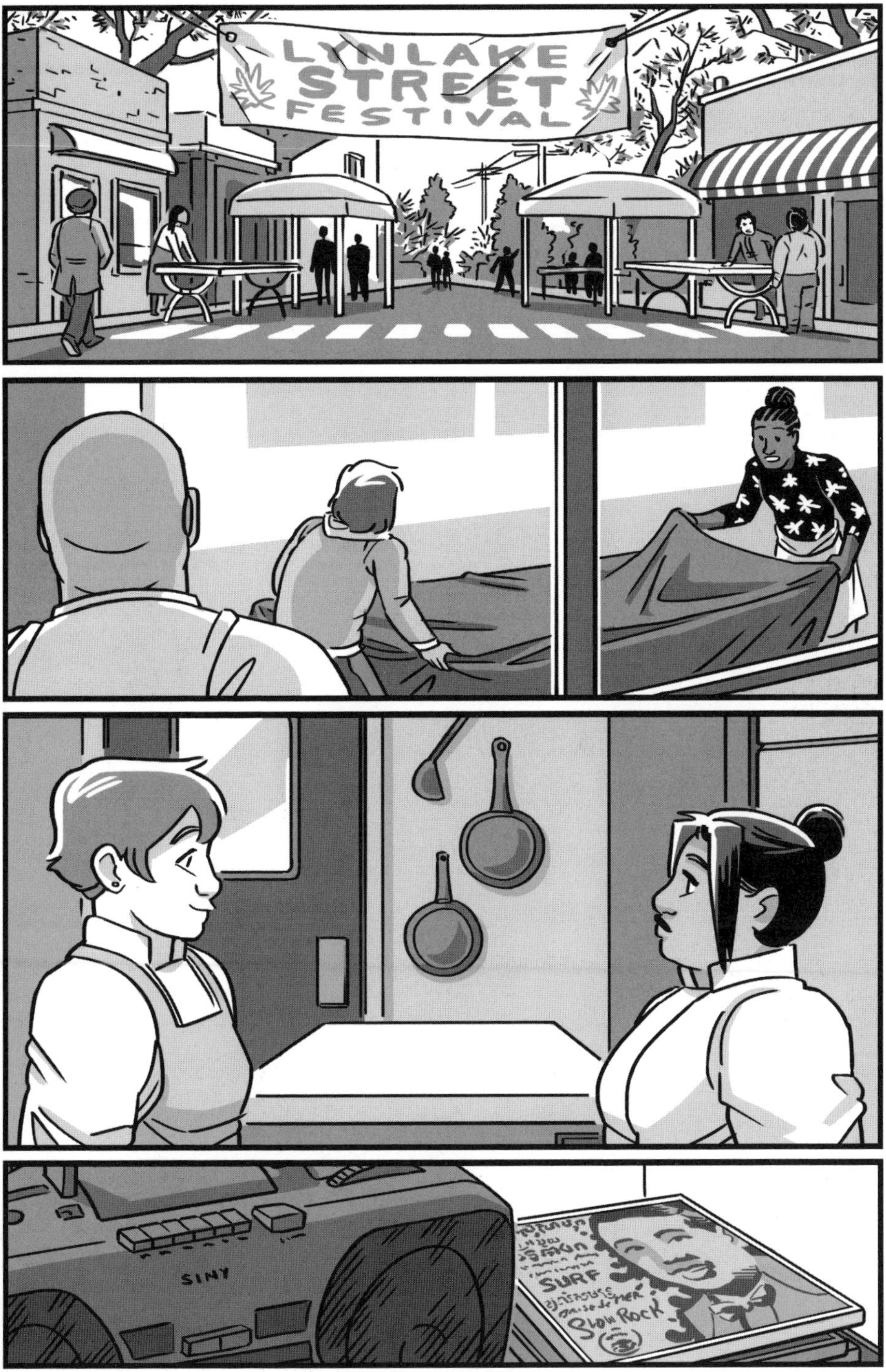
LYNLAKE STREET FESTIVAL
SINY
SURF
SLOW ROCK

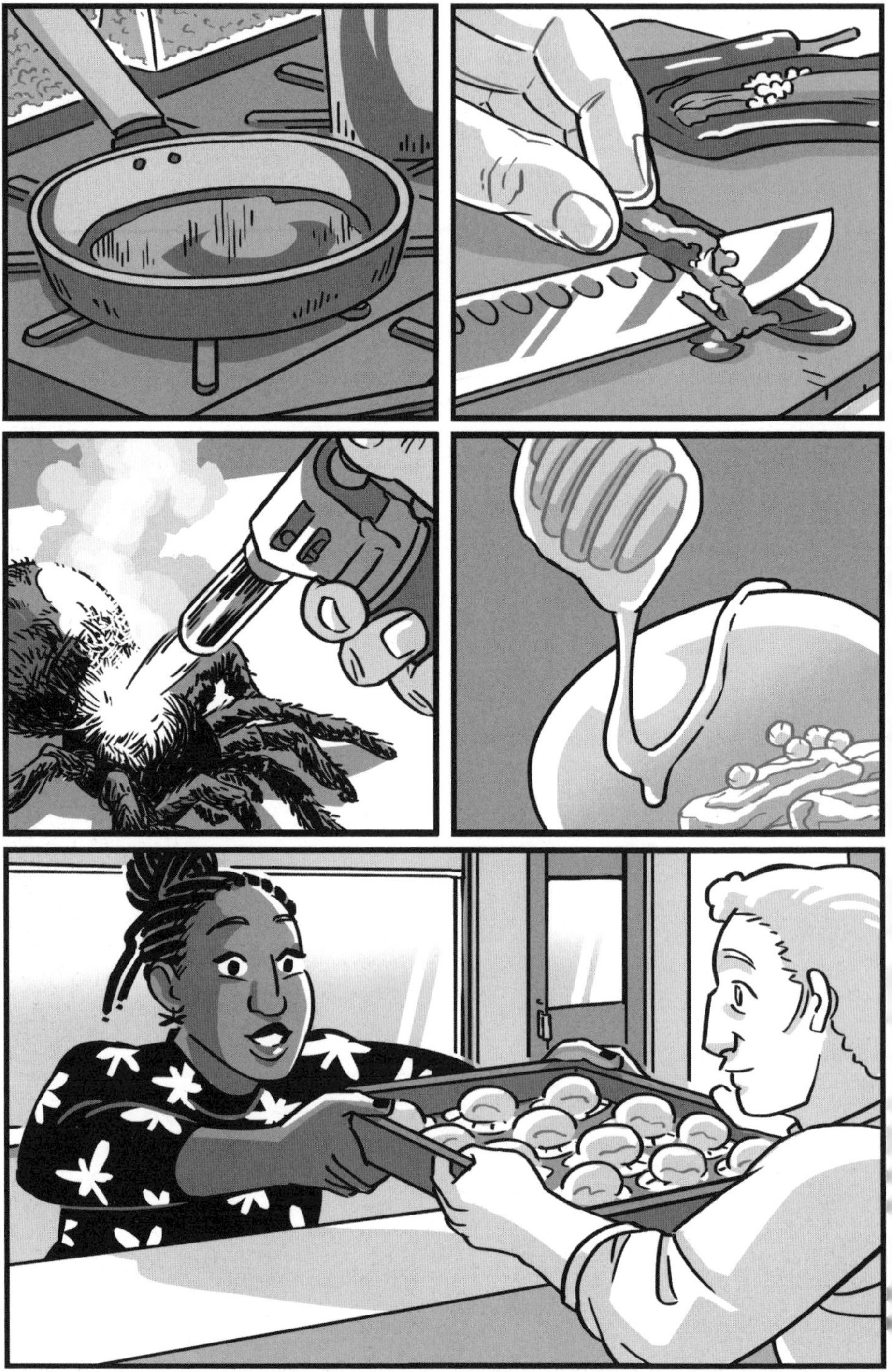

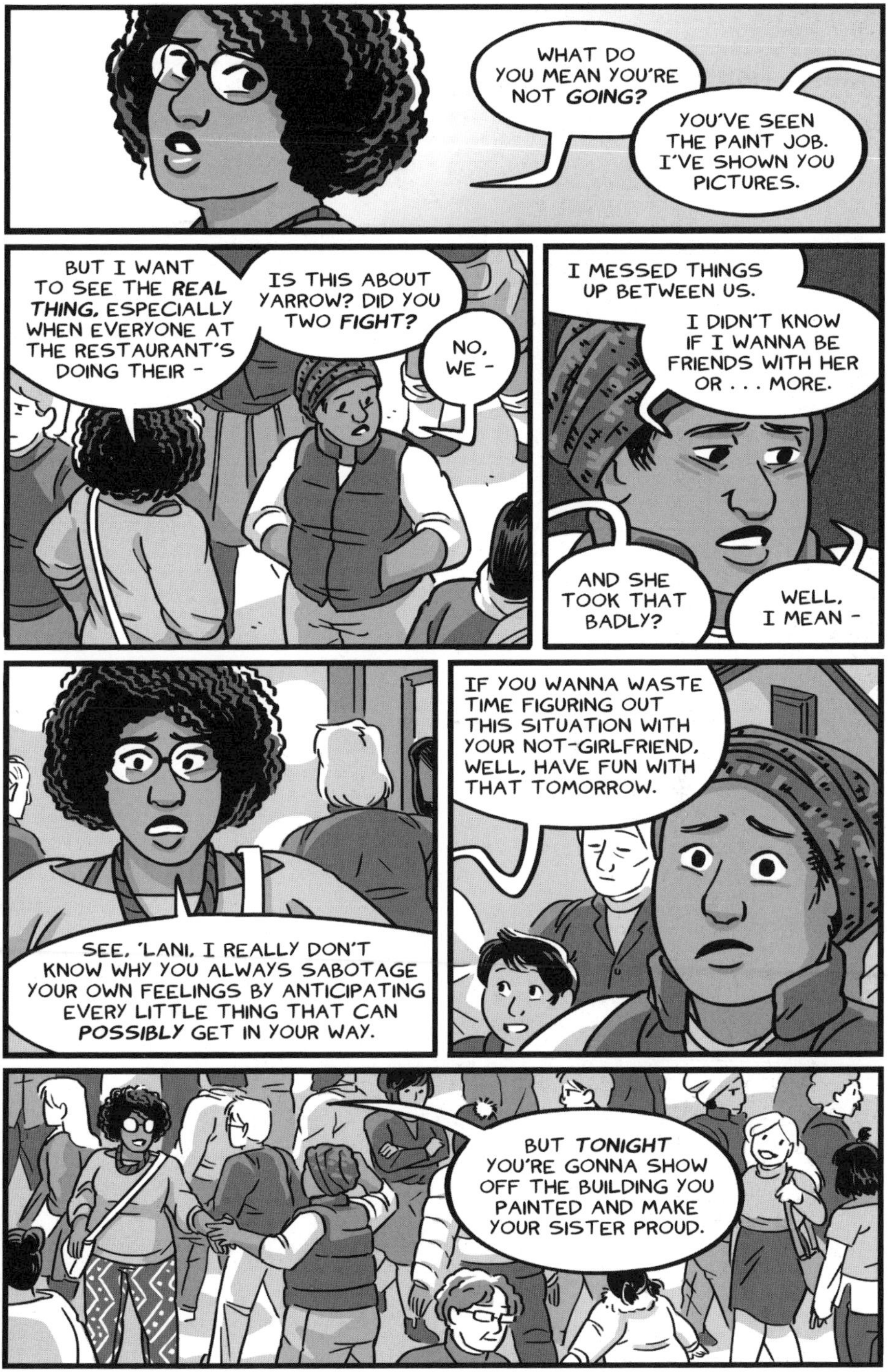

WHAT DO YOU MEAN YOU'RE NOT *GOING?*
YOU'VE SEEN THE PAINT JOB. I'VE SHOWN YOU PICTURES.
BUT I WANT TO SEE THE *REAL THING,* ESPECIALLY WHEN EVERYONE AT THE RESTAURANT'S DOING THEIR -
IS THIS ABOUT YARROW? DID YOU TWO *FIGHT?*
NO, WE -
I MESSED THINGS UP BETWEEN US.
I DIDN'T KNOW IF I WANNA BE FRIENDS WITH HER OR . . . MORE.
AND SHE TOOK THAT BADLY?
WELL, I MEAN -
SEE, 'LANI, I REALLY DON'T KNOW WHY YOU ALWAYS SABOTAGE YOUR OWN FEELINGS BY ANTICIPATING EVERY LITTLE THING THAT CAN *POSSIBLY* GET IN YOUR WAY.
IF YOU WANNA WASTE TIME FIGURING OUT THIS SITUATION WITH YOUR NOT-GIRLFRIEND, WELL, HAVE FUN WITH THAT TOMORROW.
BUT *TONIGHT* YOU'RE GONNA SHOW OFF THE BUILDING YOU PAINTED AND MAKE YOUR SISTER PROUD.

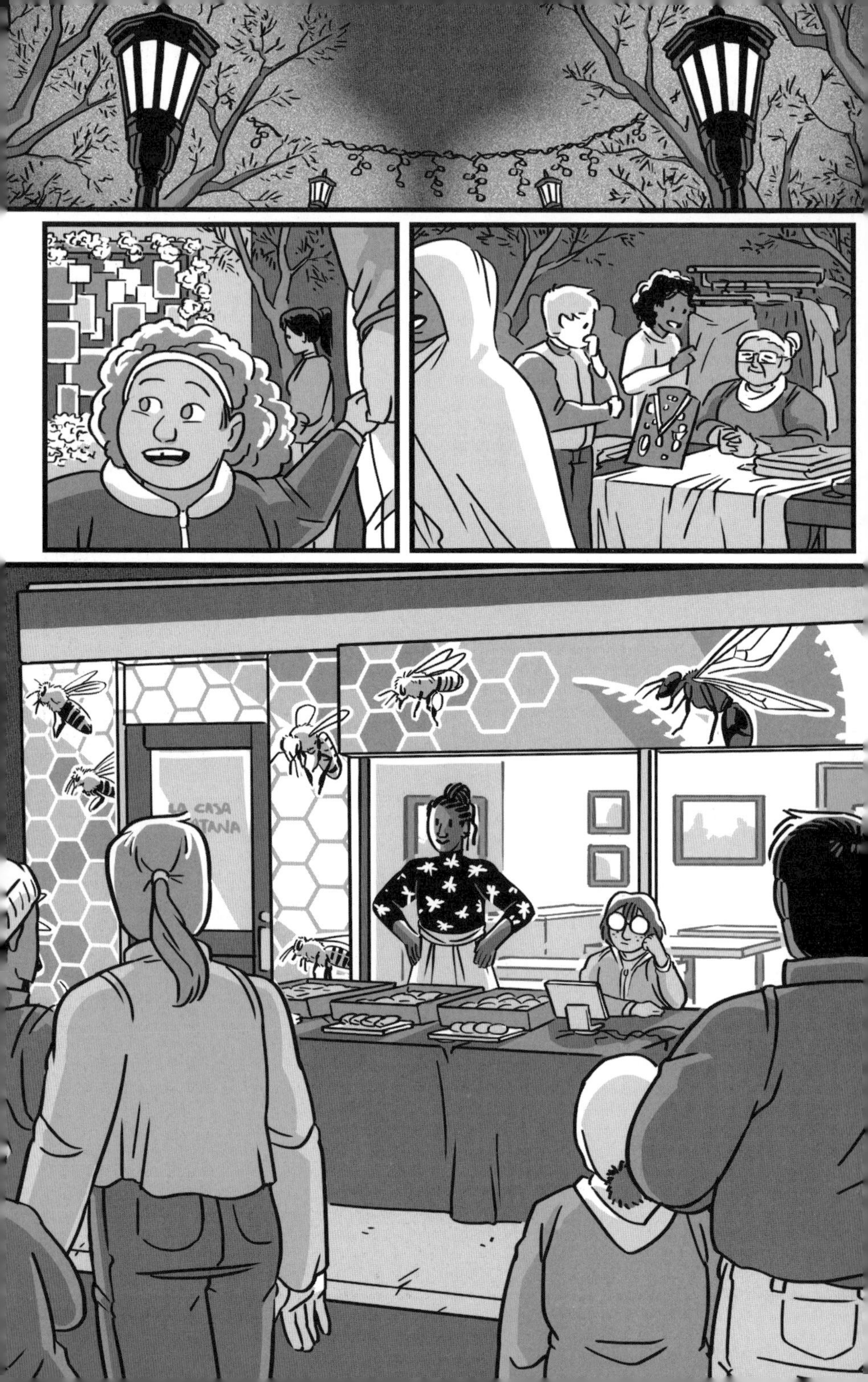
LA CASA

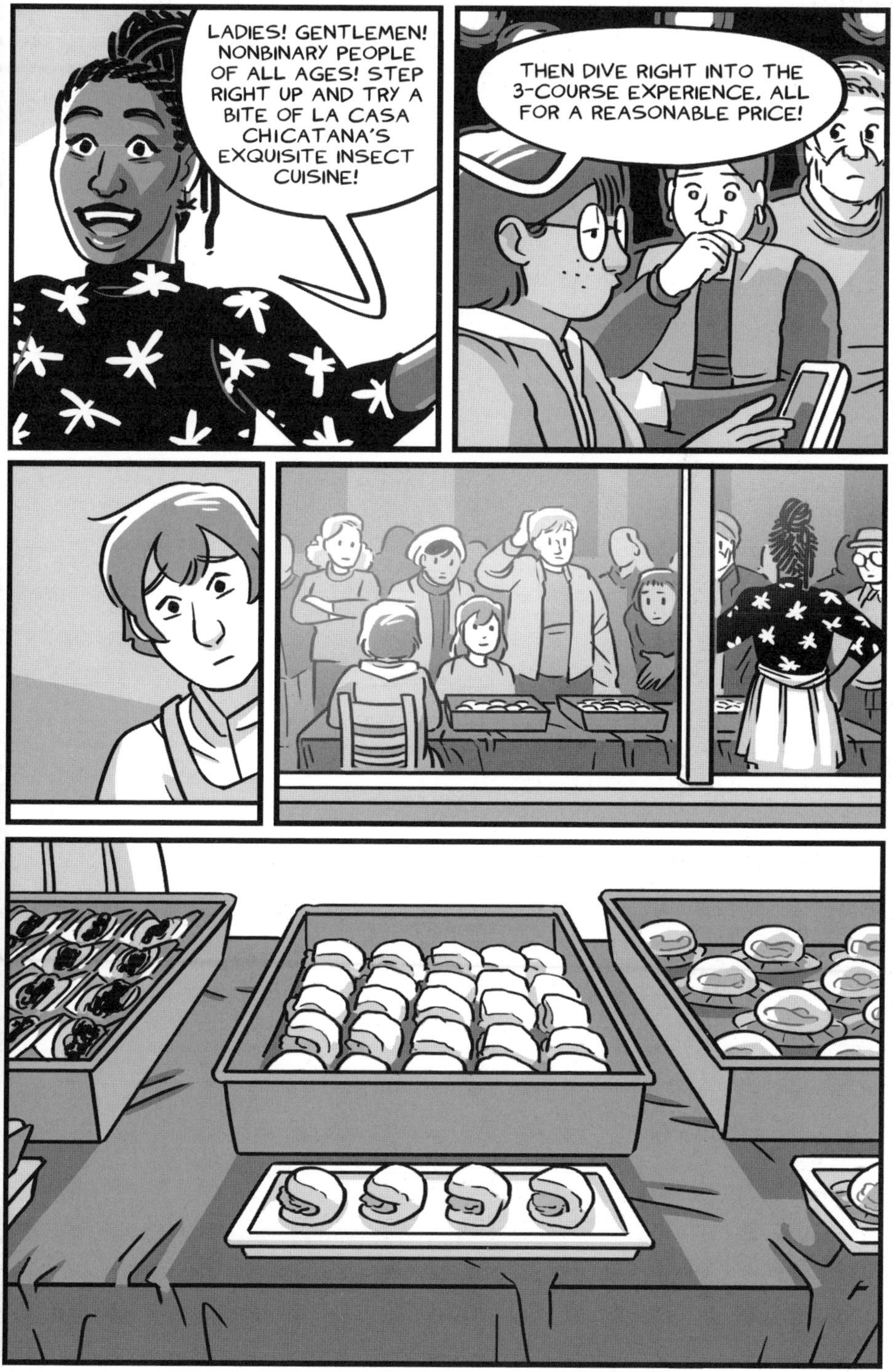
LADIES! GENTLEMEN! NONBINARY PEOPLE OF ALL AGES! STEP RIGHT UP AND TRY A BITE OF LA CASA CHICATANA'S EXQUISITE INSECT CUISINE!
THEN DIVE RIGHT INTO THE 3-COURSE EXPERIENCE, ALL FOR A REASONABLE PRICE!

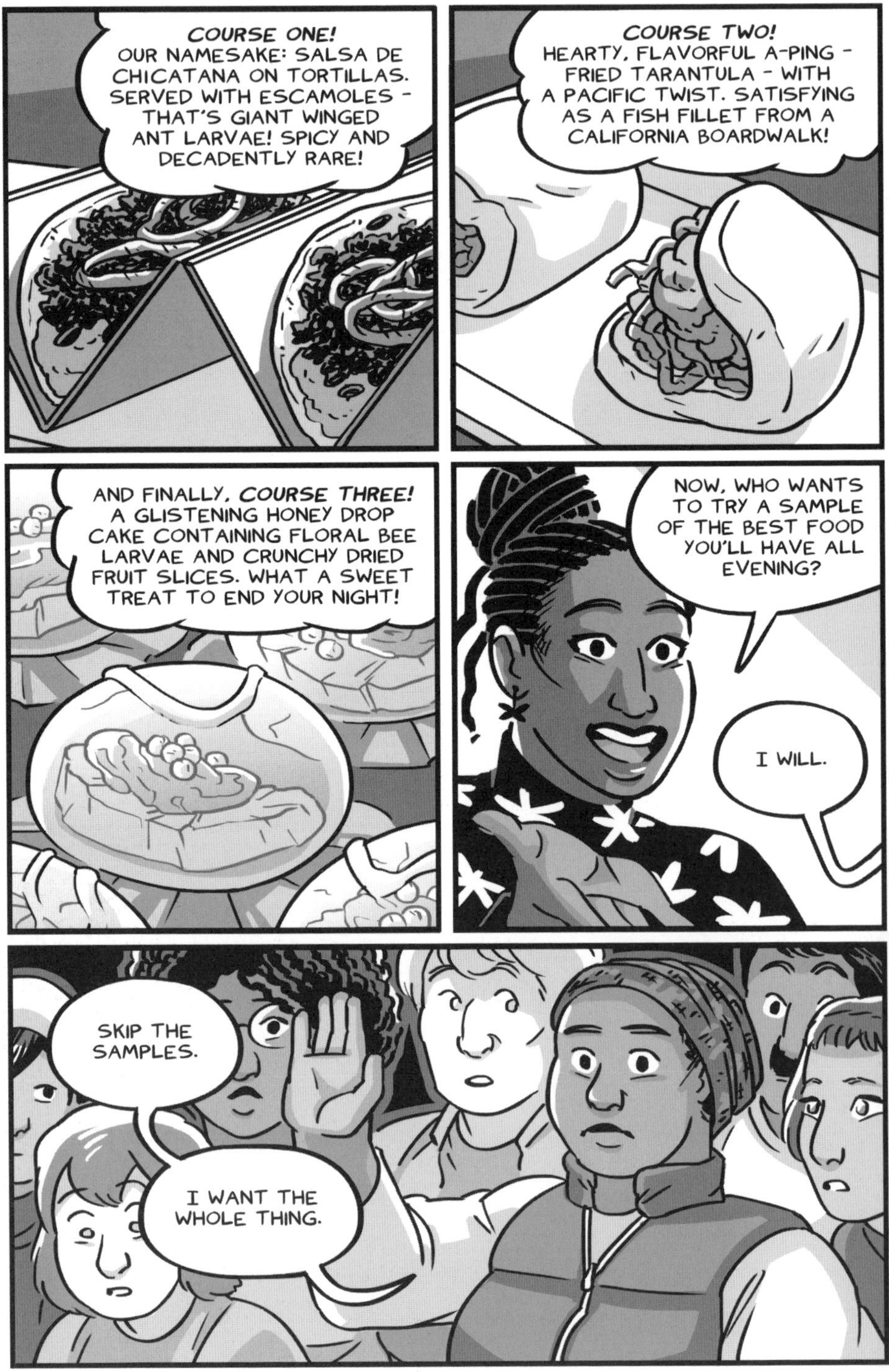
COURSE ONE!
OUR NAMESAKE: SALSA DE CHICATANA ON TORTILLAS. SERVED WITH ESCAMOLES - THAT'S GIANT WINGED ANT LARVAE! SPICY AND DECADENTLY RARE!
COURSE TWO!
HEARTY, FLAVORFUL A-PING - FRIED TARANTULA - WITH A PACIFIC TWIST. SATISFYING AS A FISH FILLET FROM A CALIFORNIA BOARDWALK!
AND FINALLY, COURSE THREE! A GLISTENING HONEY DROP CAKE CONTAINING FLORAL BEE LARVAE AND CRUNCHY DRIED FRUIT SLICES. WHAT A SWEET TREAT TO END YOUR NIGHT!
NOW, WHO WANTS TO TRY A SAMPLE OF THE BEST FOOD YOU'LL HAVE ALL EVENING?
I WILL.
SKIP THE SAMPLES.
I WANT THE WHOLE THING.

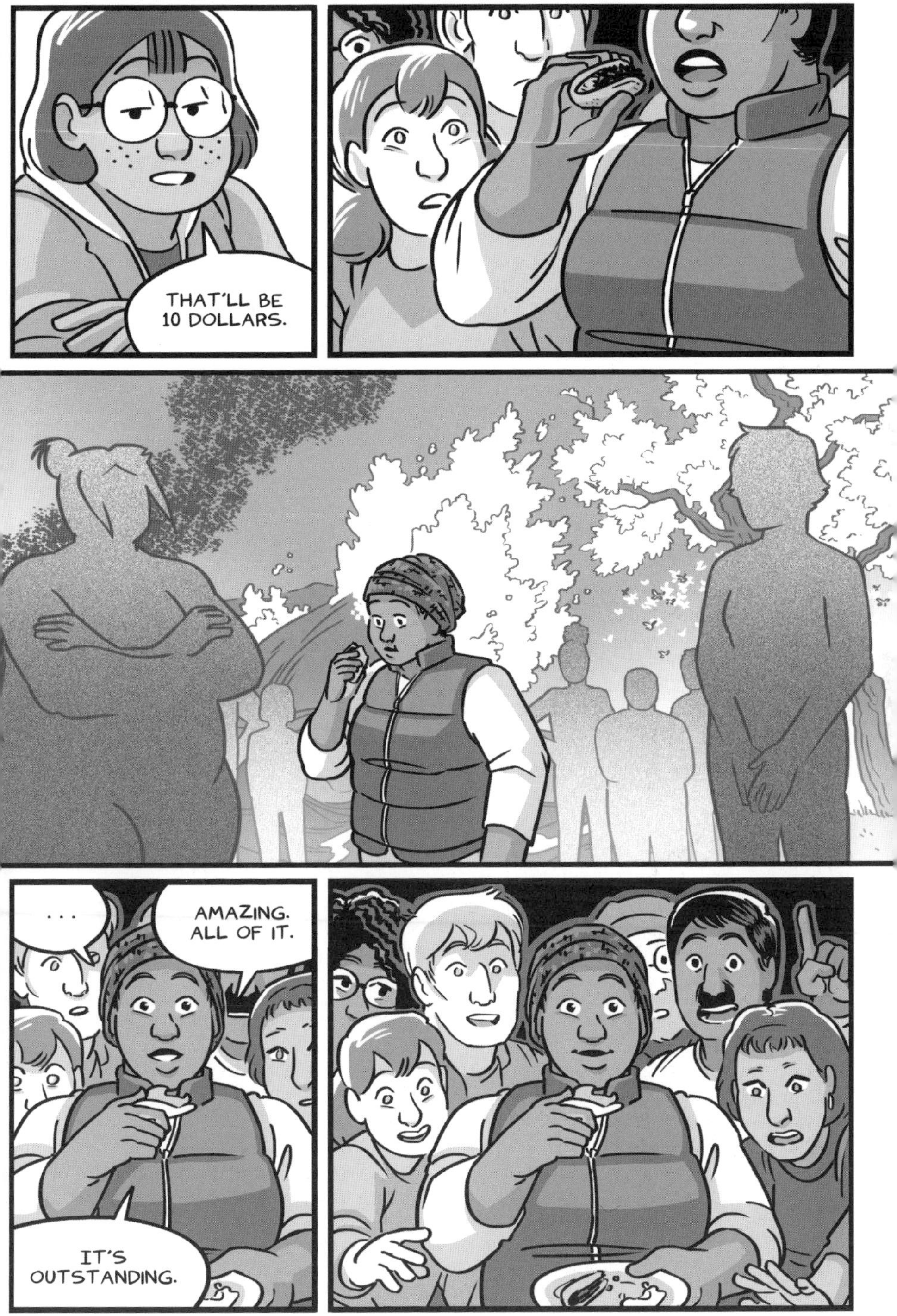
THAT'LL BE 10 DOLLARS.
...
AMAZING. ALL OF IT.
IT'S OUTSTANDING.

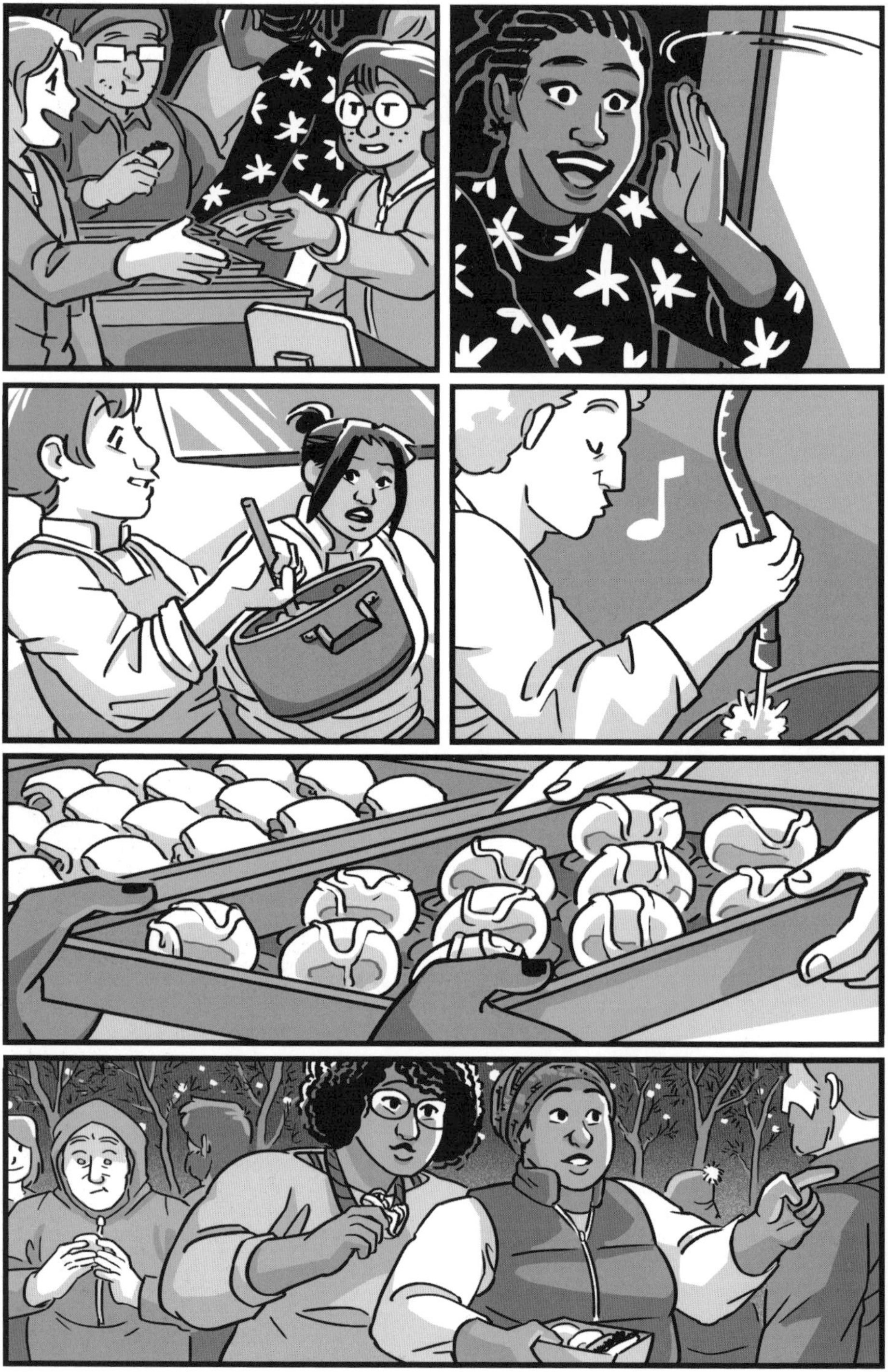

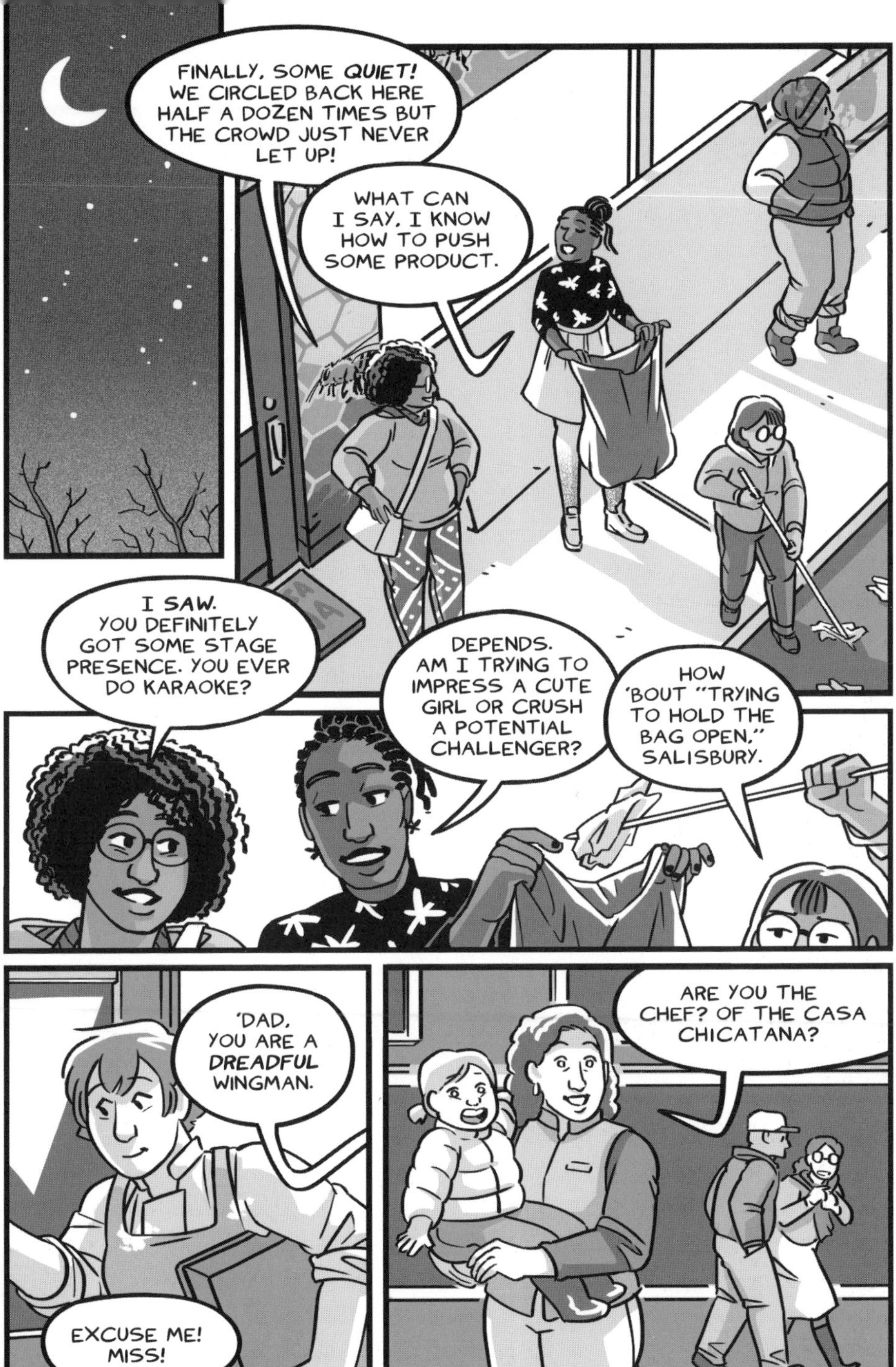
FINALLY, SOME *QUIET!* WE CIRCLED BACK HERE HALF A DOZEN TIMES BUT THE CROWD JUST NEVER LET UP!
WHAT CAN I SAY, I KNOW HOW TO PUSH SOME PRODUCT.
I *SAW.* YOU DEFINITELY GOT SOME STAGE PRESENCE. YOU EVER DO KARAOKE?
DEPENDS. AM I TRYING TO IMPRESS A CUTE GIRL OR CRUSH A POTENTIAL CHALLENGER?
HOW 'BOUT "TRYING TO HOLD THE BAG OPEN," SALISBURY.
'DAD, YOU ARE A *DREADFUL* WINGMAN.
EXCUSE ME! MISS!
ARE YOU THE CHEF? OF THE CASA CHICATANA?

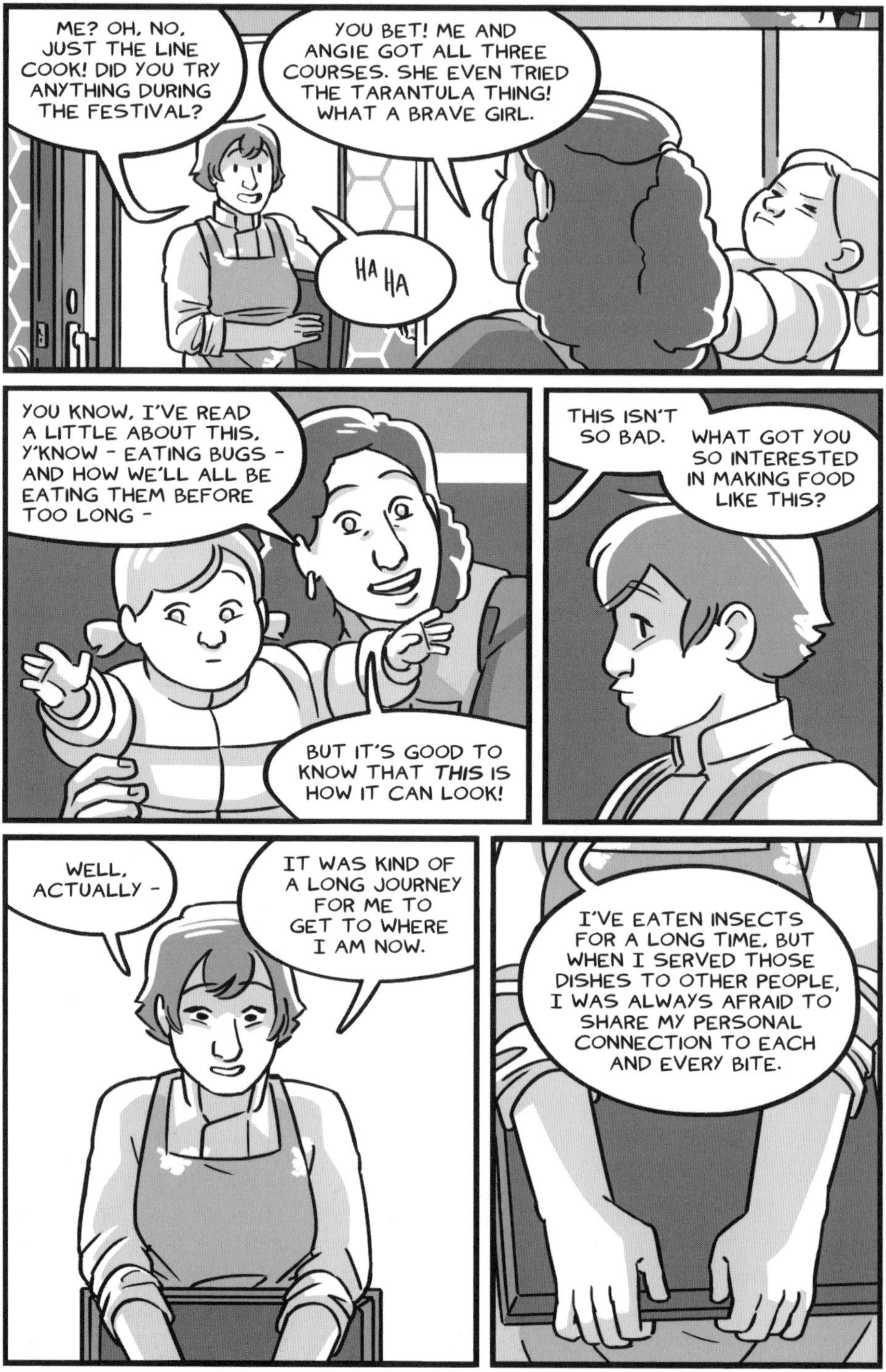
ME? OH, NO, JUST THE LINE COOK! DID YOU TRY ANYTHING DURING THE FESTIVAL?
YOU BET! ME AND ANGIE GOT ALL THREE COURSES. SHE EVEN TRIED THE TARANTULA THING! WHAT A BRAVE GIRL.
HA HA
YOU KNOW, I'VE READ A LITTLE ABOUT THIS, Y'KNOW - EATING BUGS - AND HOW WE'LL ALL BE EATING THEM BEFORE TOO LONG -
BUT IT'S GOOD TO KNOW THAT *THIS* IS HOW IT CAN LOOK!
THIS ISN'T SO BAD.
WHAT GOT YOU SO INTERESTED IN MAKING FOOD LIKE THIS?
WELL, ACTUALLY -
IT WAS KIND OF A LONG JOURNEY FOR ME TO GET TO WHERE I AM NOW.
I'VE EATEN INSECTS FOR A LONG TIME, BUT WHEN I SERVED THOSE DISHES TO OTHER PEOPLE, I WAS ALWAYS AFRAID TO SHARE MY PERSONAL CONNECTION TO EACH AND EVERY BITE.

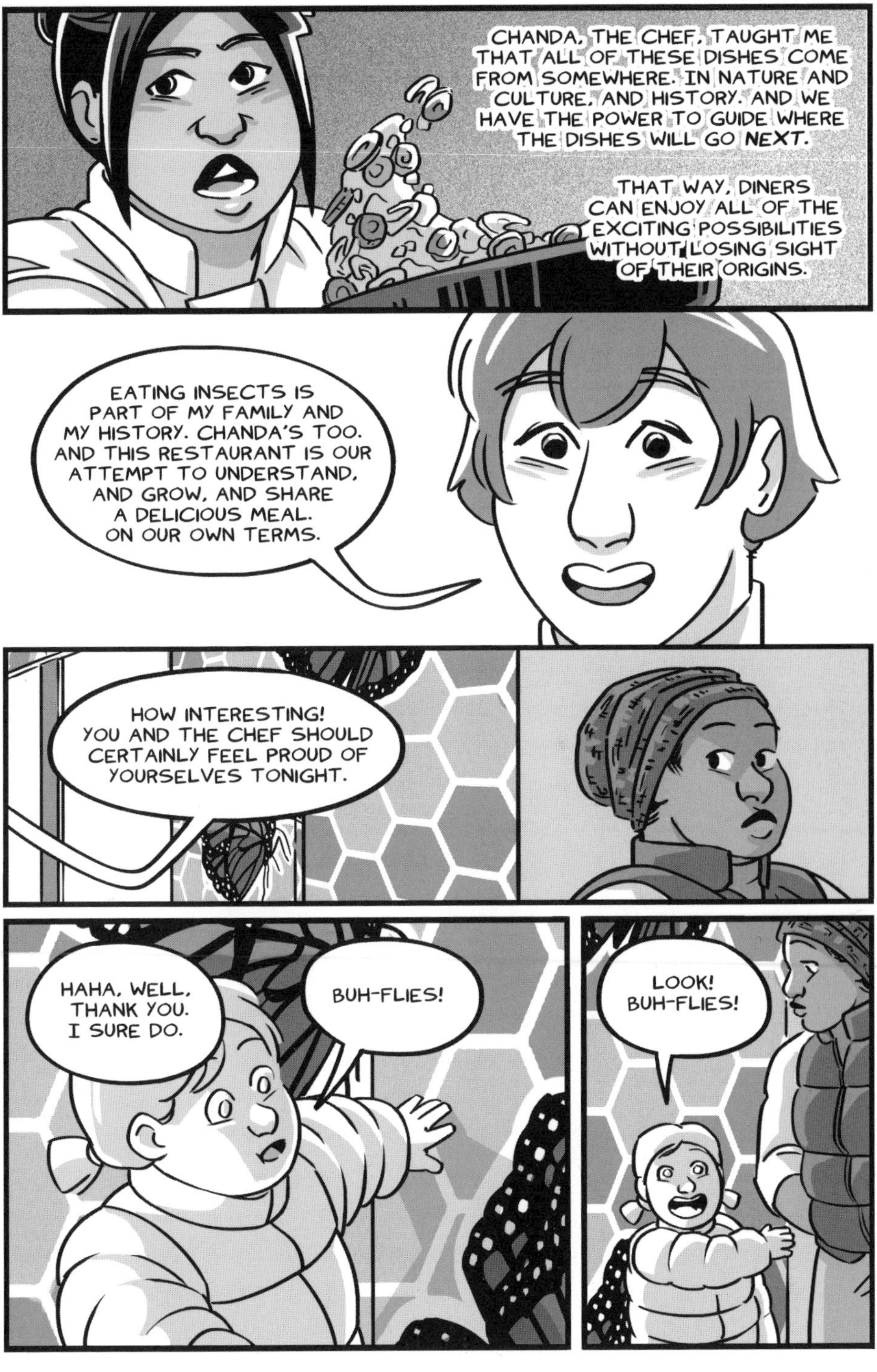
CHANDA, THE CHEF, TAUGHT ME THAT ALL OF THESE DISHES COME FROM SOMEWHERE. IN NATURE AND CULTURE, AND HISTORY. AND WE HAVE THE POWER TO GUIDE WHERE THE DISHES WILL GO **NEXT**.
THAT WAY, DINERS CAN ENJOY ALL OF THE EXCITING POSSIBILITIES WITHOUT LOSING SIGHT OF THEIR ORIGINS.
EATING INSECTS IS PART OF MY FAMILY AND MY HISTORY. CHANDA'S TOO. AND THIS RESTAURANT IS OUR ATTEMPT TO UNDERSTAND, AND GROW, AND SHARE A DELICIOUS MEAL. ON OUR OWN TERMS.
HOW INTERESTING! YOU AND THE CHEF SHOULD CERTAINLY FEEL PROUD OF YOURSELVES TONIGHT.
HAHA, WELL, THANK YOU. I SURE DO.
BUH-FLIES!
LOOK! BUH-FLIES!

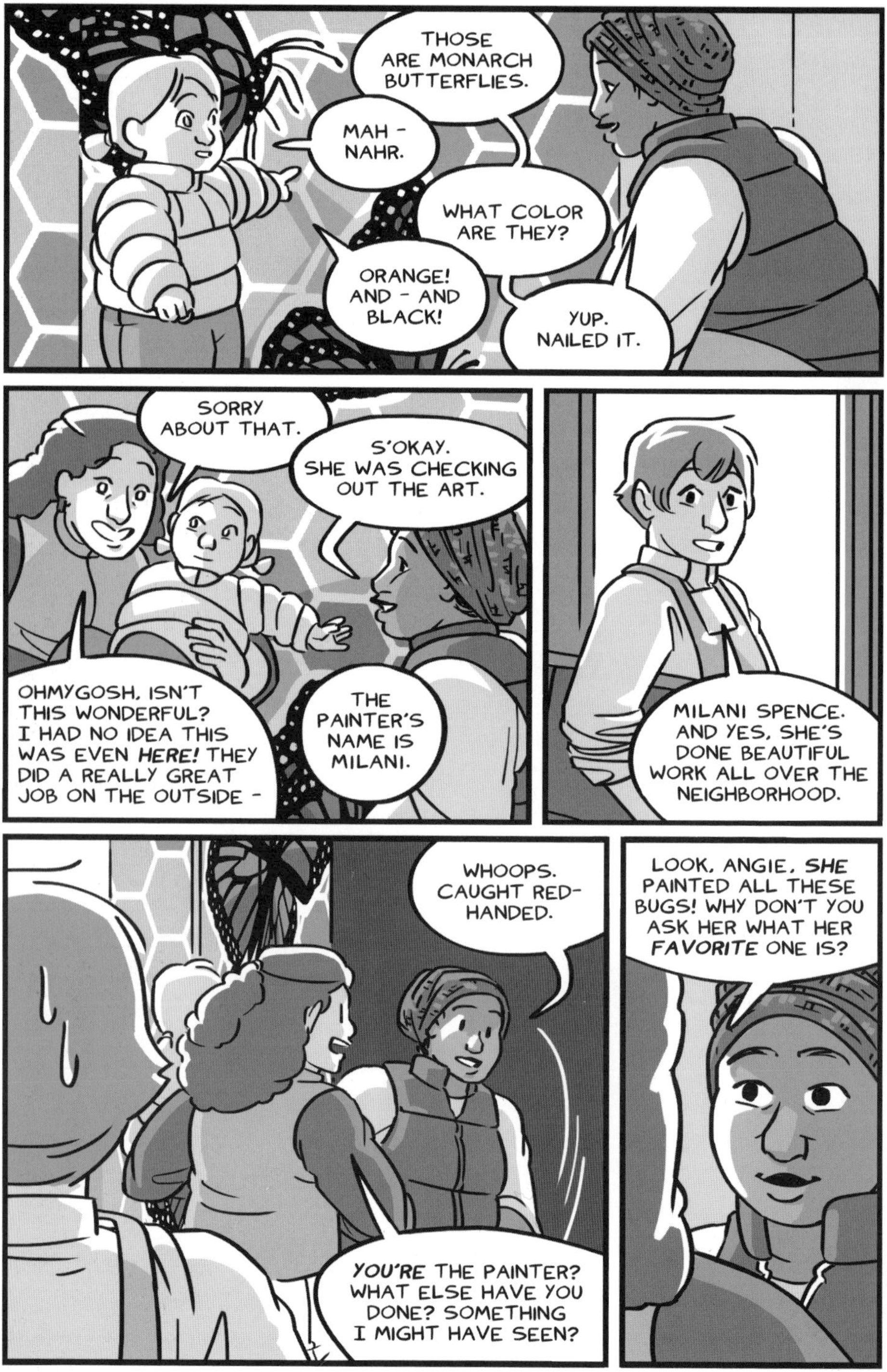
THOSE ARE MONARCH BUTTERFLIES.
MAH - NAHR.
WHAT COLOR ARE THEY?
ORANGE! AND - AND BLACK!
YUP. NAILED IT.
SORRY ABOUT THAT.
S'OKAY. SHE WAS CHECKING OUT THE ART.
OHMYGOSH, ISN'T THIS WONDERFUL? I HAD NO IDEA THIS WAS EVEN *HERE!* THEY DID A REALLY GREAT JOB ON THE OUTSIDE -
THE PAINTER'S NAME IS MILANI.
MILANI SPENCE. AND YES, SHE'S DONE BEAUTIFUL WORK ALL OVER THE NEIGHBORHOOD.
WHOOPS. CAUGHT RED-HANDED.
YOU'RE THE PAINTER? WHAT ELSE HAVE YOU DONE? SOMETHING I MIGHT HAVE SEEN?
LOOK, ANGIE, *SHE* PAINTED ALL THESE BUGS! WHY DON'T YOU ASK HER WHAT HER *FAVORITE* ONE IS?

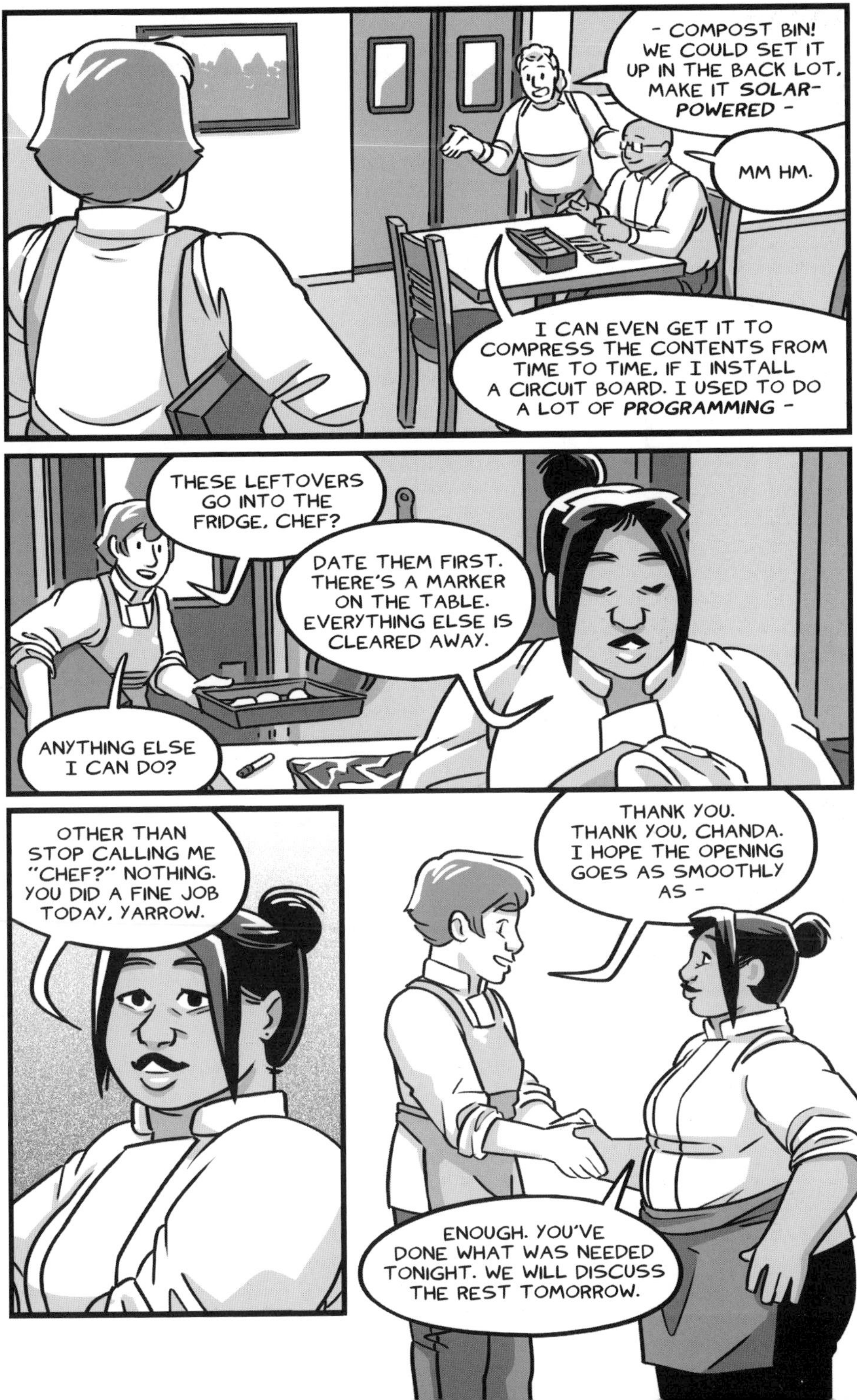
- COMPOST BIN! WE COULD SET IT UP IN THE BACK LOT, MAKE IT **SOLAR-POWERED** -
MM HM.
I CAN EVEN GET IT TO COMPRESS THE CONTENTS FROM TIME TO TIME, IF I INSTALL A CIRCUIT BOARD. I USED TO DO A LOT OF **PROGRAMMING** -
THESE LEFTOVERS GO INTO THE FRIDGE, CHEF?
DATE THEM FIRST. THERE'S A MARKER ON THE TABLE. EVERYTHING ELSE IS CLEARED AWAY.
ANYTHING ELSE I CAN DO?
OTHER THAN STOP CALLING ME "CHEF?" NOTHING. YOU DID A FINE JOB TODAY, YARROW.
THANK YOU. THANK YOU, CHANDA. I HOPE THE OPENING GOES AS SMOOTHLY AS -
ENOUGH. YOU'VE DONE WHAT WAS NEEDED TONIGHT. WE WILL DISCUSS THE REST TOMORROW.

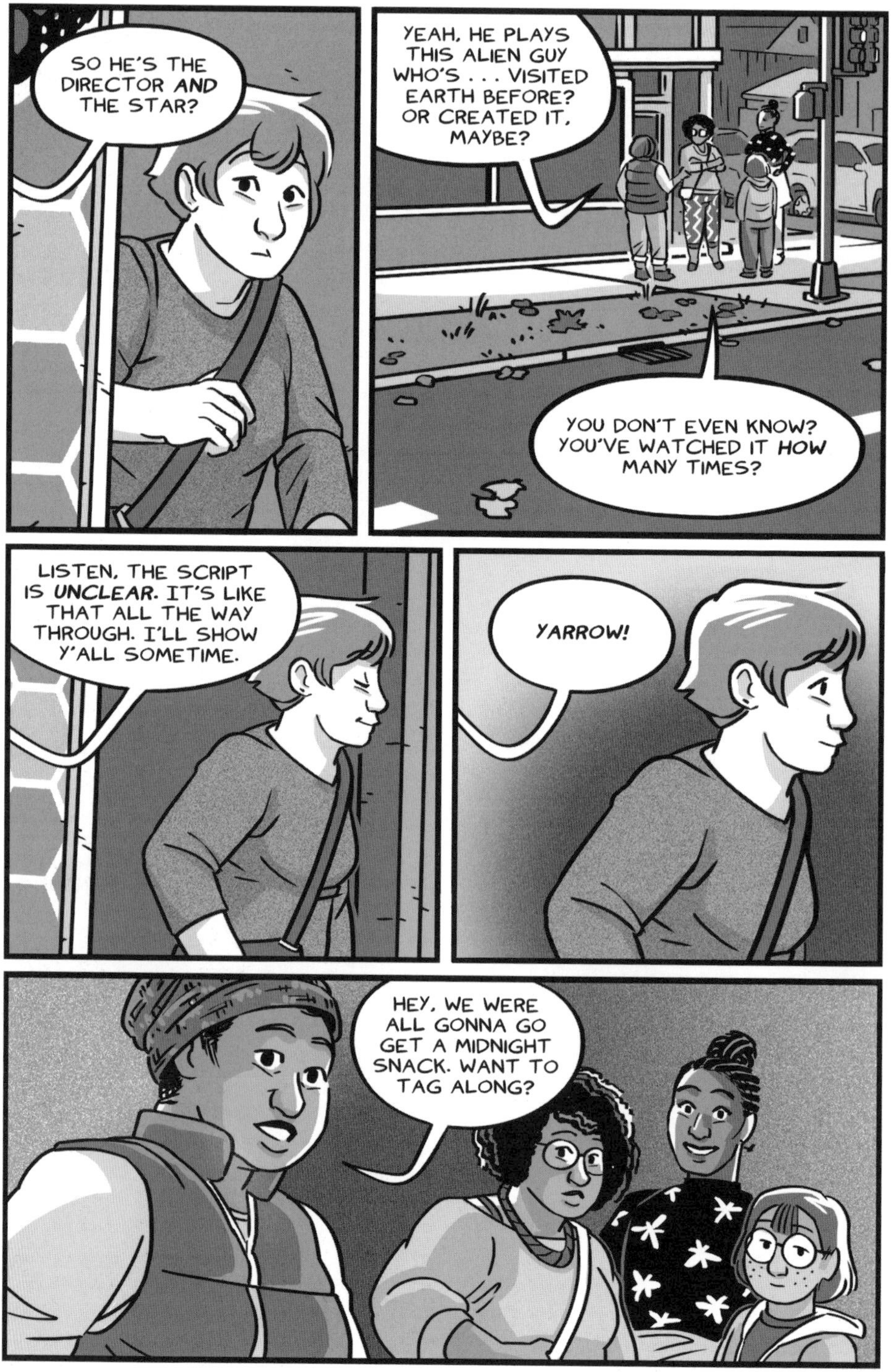
SO HE'S THE DIRECTOR AND THE STAR?
YEAH, HE PLAYS THIS ALIEN GUY WHO'S . . . VISITED EARTH BEFORE? OR CREATED IT, MAYBE?
YOU DON'T EVEN KNOW? YOU'VE WATCHED IT HOW MANY TIMES?
LISTEN, THE SCRIPT IS UNCLEAR. IT'S LIKE THAT ALL THE WAY THROUGH. I'LL SHOW Y'ALL SOMETIME.
YARROW!
HEY, WE WERE ALL GONNA GO GET A MIDNIGHT SNACK. WANT TO TAG ALONG?

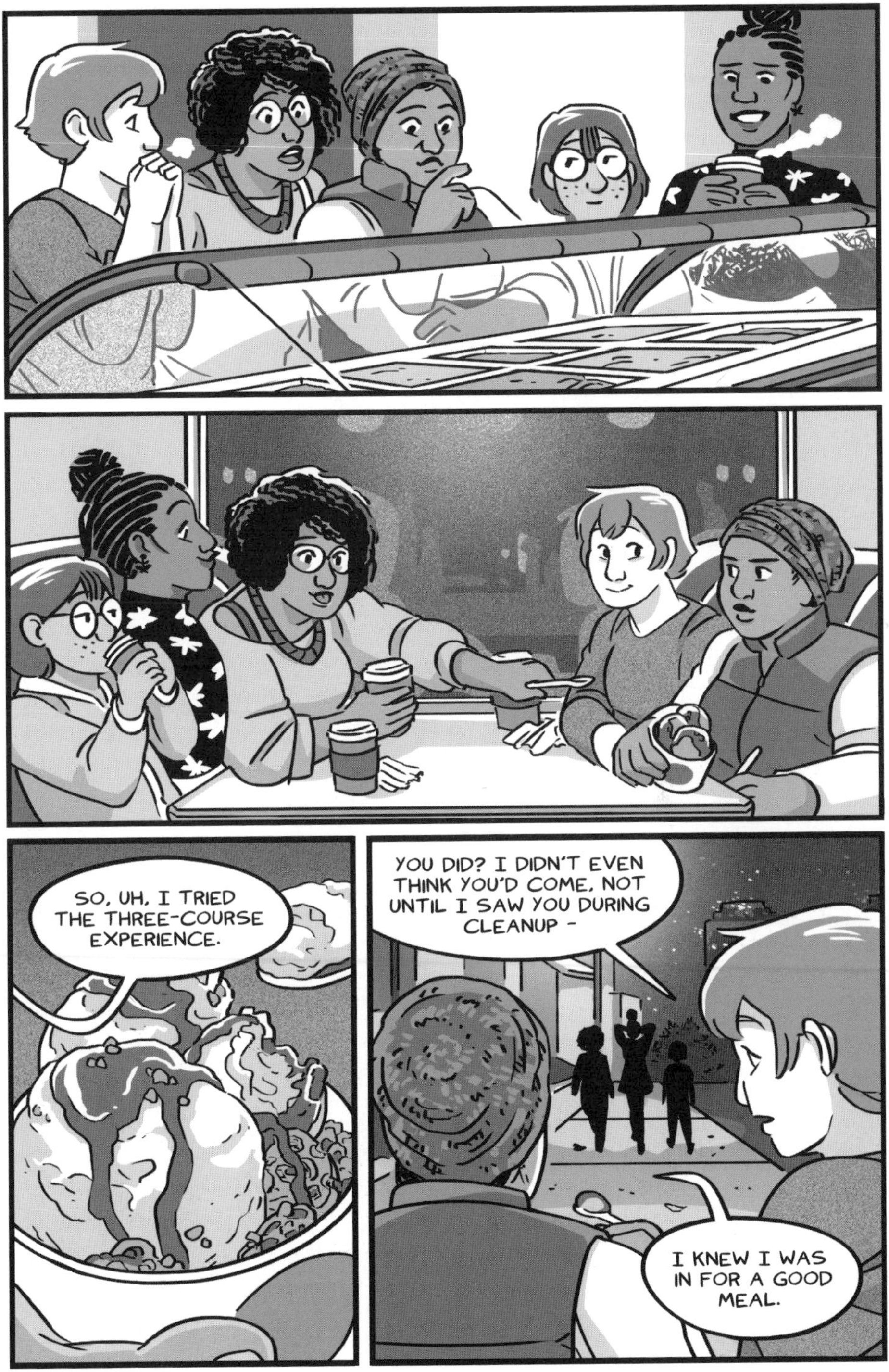
SO, UH, I TRIED THE THREE-COURSE EXPERIENCE.
YOU DID? I DIDN'T EVEN THINK YOU'D COME, NOT UNTIL I SAW YOU DURING CLEANUP -
I KNEW I WAS IN FOR A GOOD MEAL.

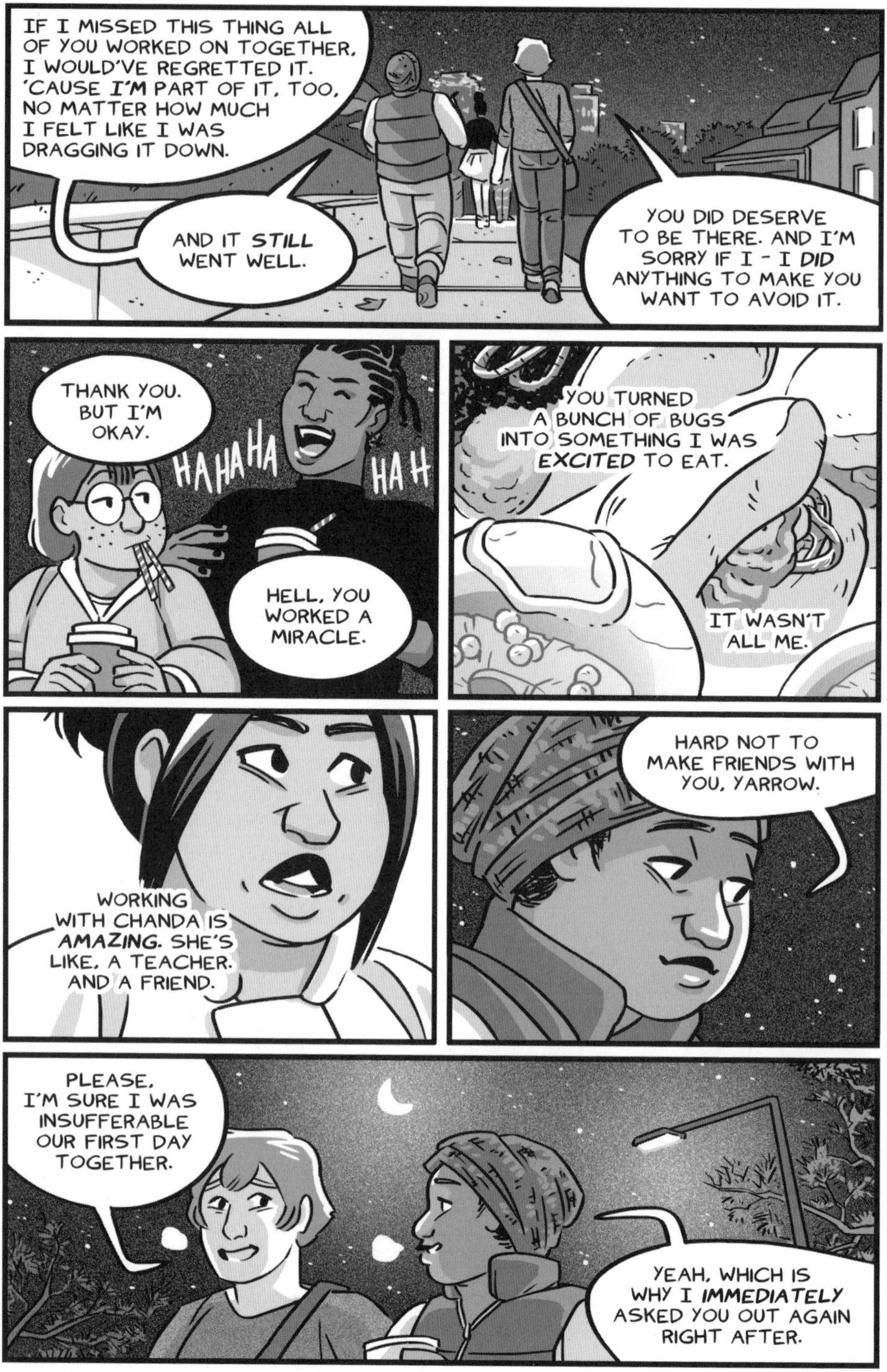
IF I MISSED THIS THING ALL OF YOU WORKED ON TOGETHER, I WOULD'VE REGRETTED IT. 'CAUSE **I'M** PART OF IT, TOO, NO MATTER HOW MUCH I FELT LIKE I WAS DRAGGING IT DOWN.
AND IT **STILL** WENT WELL.
YOU DID DESERVE TO BE THERE. AND I'M SORRY IF I - I **DID** ANYTHING TO MAKE YOU WANT TO AVOID IT.
THANK YOU. BUT I'M OKAY.
HAHAHA
HAH
HELL, YOU WORKED A MIRACLE.
YOU TURNED A BUNCH OF BUGS INTO SOMETHING I WAS **EXCITED** TO EAT.
IT WASN'T ALL ME.
WORKING WITH CHANDA IS **AMAZING**. SHE'S LIKE, A TEACHER. AND A FRIEND.
HARD NOT TO MAKE FRIENDS WITH YOU, YARROW.
PLEASE, I'M SURE I WAS INSUFFERABLE OUR FIRST DAY TOGETHER.
YEAH, WHICH IS WHY I **IMMEDIATELY** ASKED YOU OUT AGAIN RIGHT AFTER.

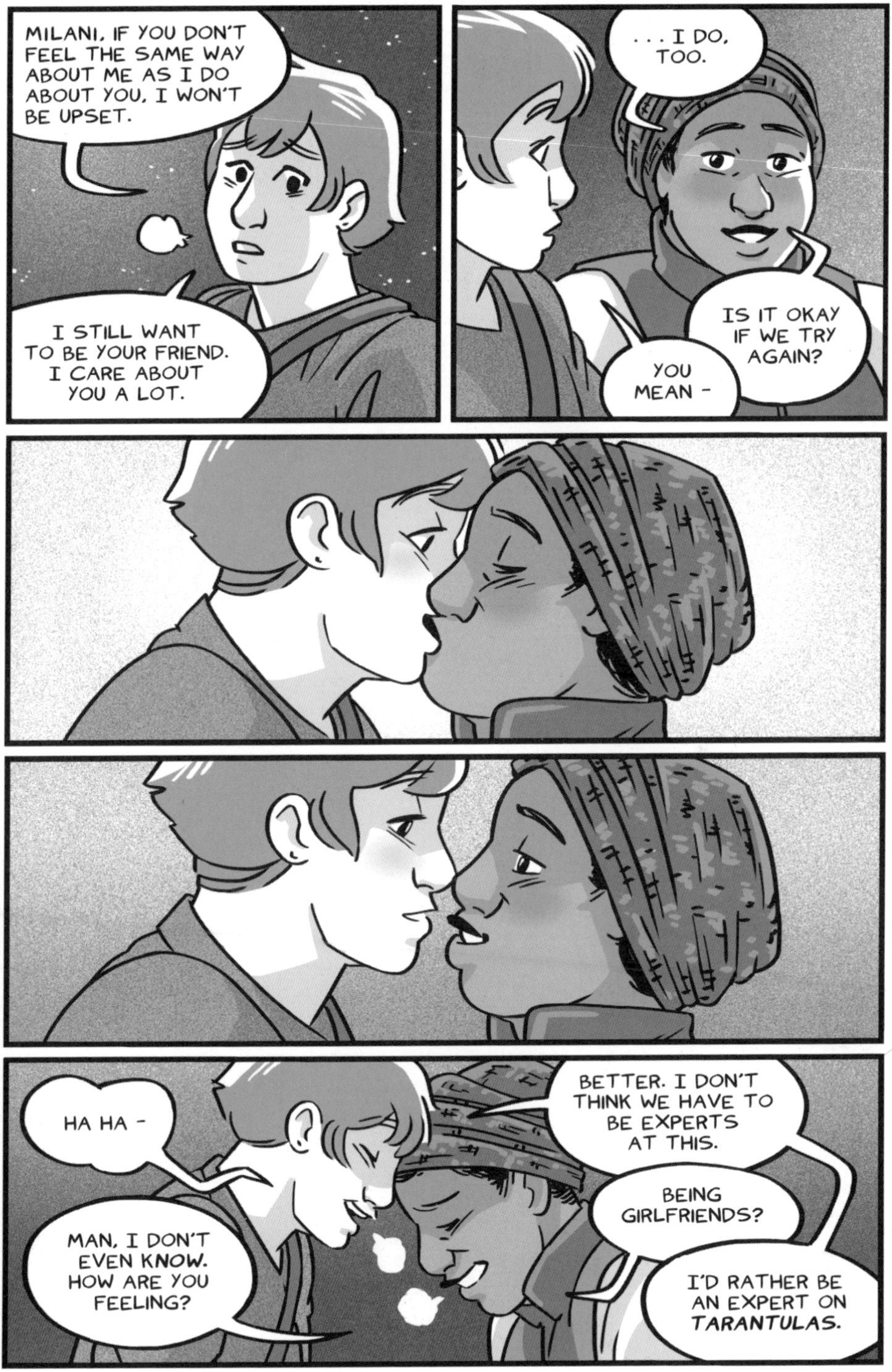
MILANI, IF YOU DON'T FEEL THE SAME WAY ABOUT ME AS I DO ABOUT YOU, I WON'T BE UPSET.
I STILL WANT TO BE YOUR FRIEND. I CARE ABOUT YOU A LOT.
. . . I DO, TOO.
YOU MEAN -
IS IT OKAY IF WE TRY AGAIN?
HA HA -
MAN, I DON'T EVEN KNOW. HOW ARE YOU FEELING?
BETTER. I DON'T THINK WE HAVE TO BE EXPERTS AT THIS.
BEING GIRLFRIENDS?
I'D RATHER BE AN EXPERT ON *TARANTULAS.*

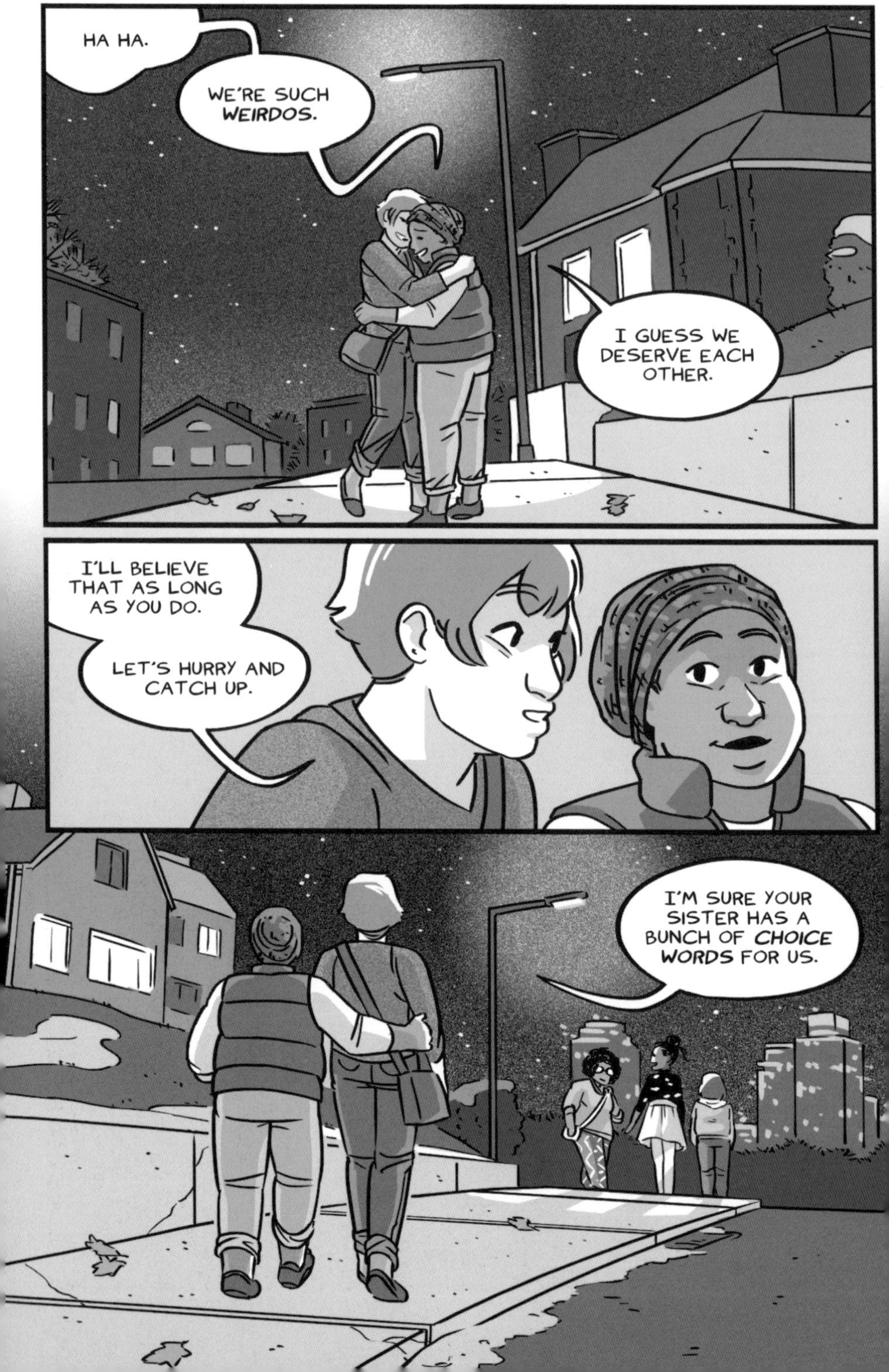
HA HA.
WE'RE SUCH WEIRDOS.
I GUESS WE DESERVE EACH OTHER.
I'LL BELIEVE THAT AS LONG AS YOU DO.
LET'S HURRY AND CATCH UP.
I'M SURE YOUR SISTER HAS A BUNCH OF CHOICE WORDS FOR US.

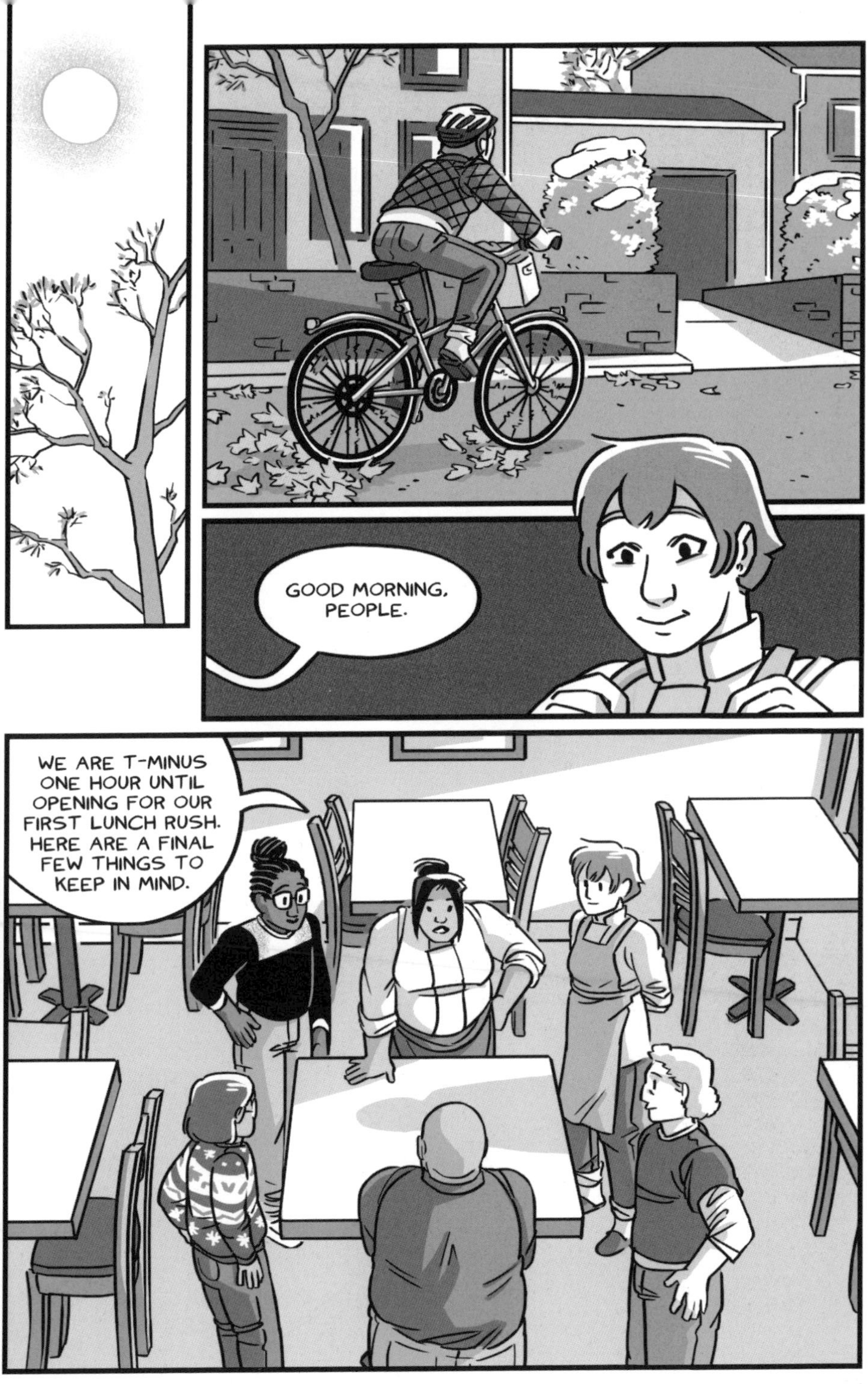
GOOD MORNING, PEOPLE.
WE ARE T-MINUS ONE HOUR UNTIL OPENING FOR OUR FIRST LUNCH RUSH. HERE ARE A FINAL FEW THINGS TO KEEP IN MIND.

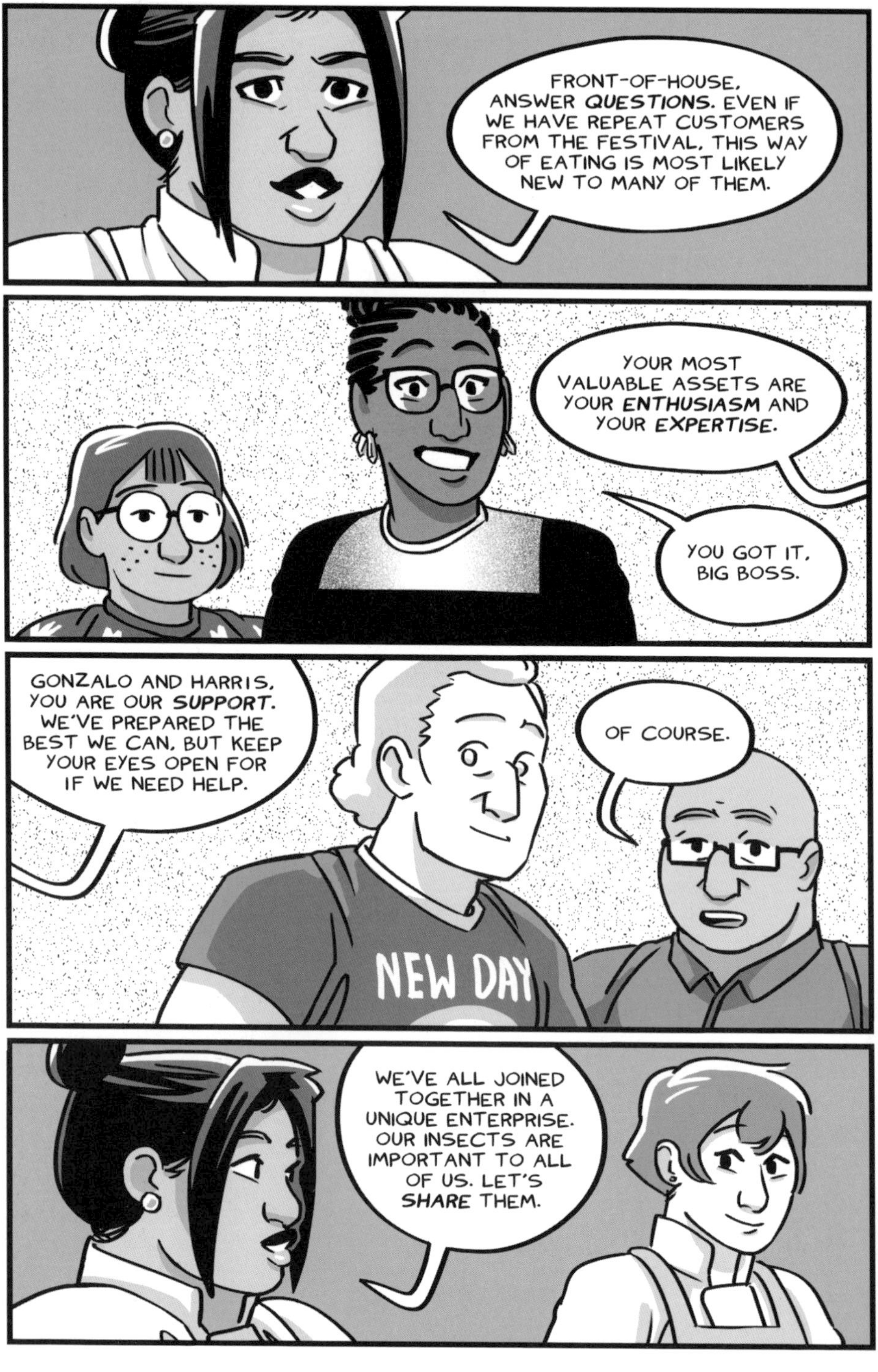
FRONT-OF-HOUSE, ANSWER QUESTIONS. EVEN IF WE HAVE REPEAT CUSTOMERS FROM THE FESTIVAL, THIS WAY OF EATING IS MOST LIKELY NEW TO MANY OF THEM.
YOUR MOST VALUABLE ASSETS ARE YOUR ENTHUSIASM AND YOUR EXPERTISE.
YOU GOT IT, BIG BOSS.
GONZALO AND HARRIS, YOU ARE OUR SUPPORT. WE'VE PREPARED THE BEST WE CAN, BUT KEEP YOUR EYES OPEN FOR IF WE NEED HELP.
OF COURSE.
NEW DAY
WE'VE ALL JOINED TOGETHER IN A UNIQUE ENTERPRISE. OUR INSECTS ARE IMPORTANT TO ALL OF US. LET'S SHARE THEM.

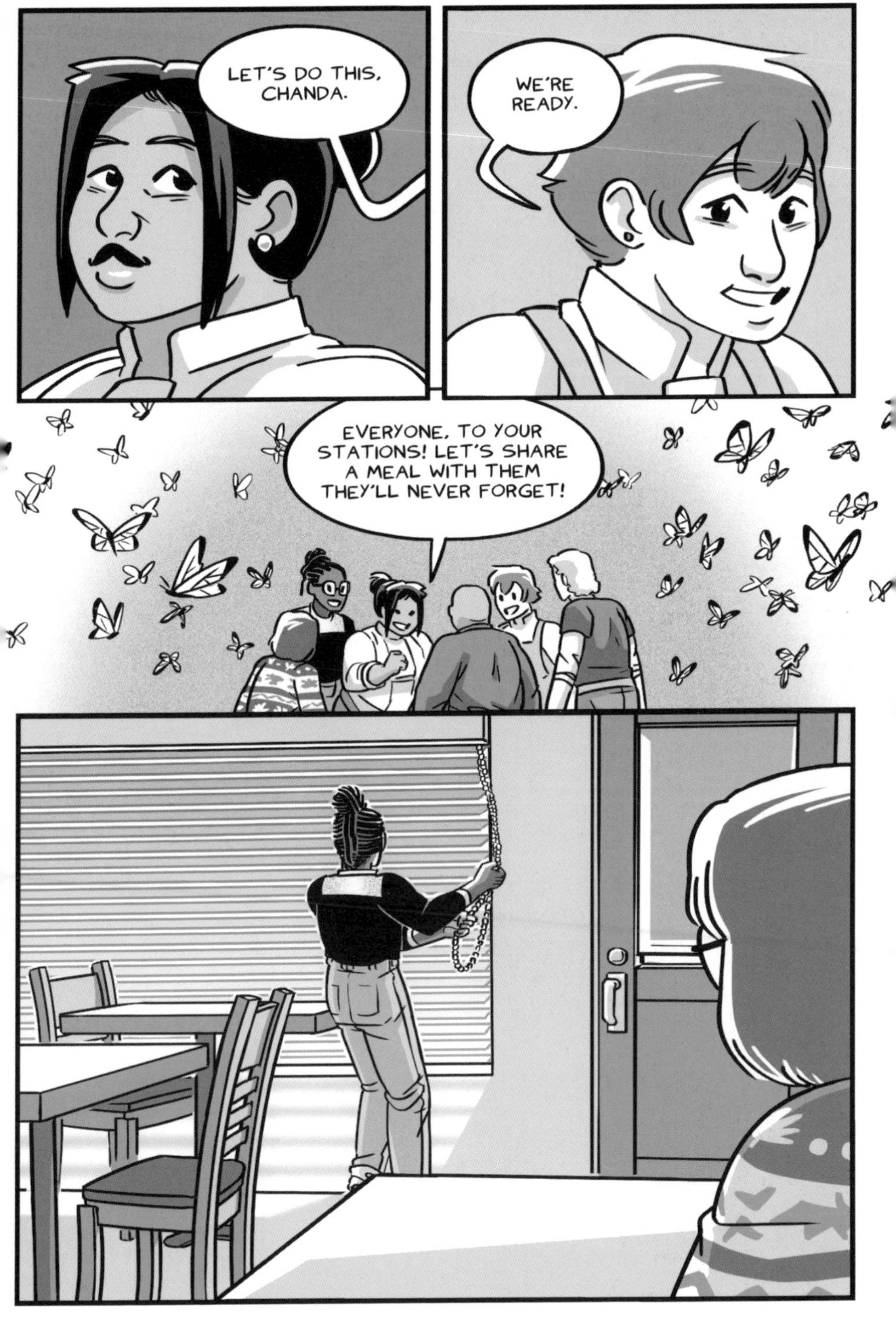
LET'S DO THIS, CHANDA.
WE'RE READY.
EVERYONE, TO YOUR STATIONS! LET'S SHARE A MEAL WITH THEM THEY'LL NEVER FORGET!

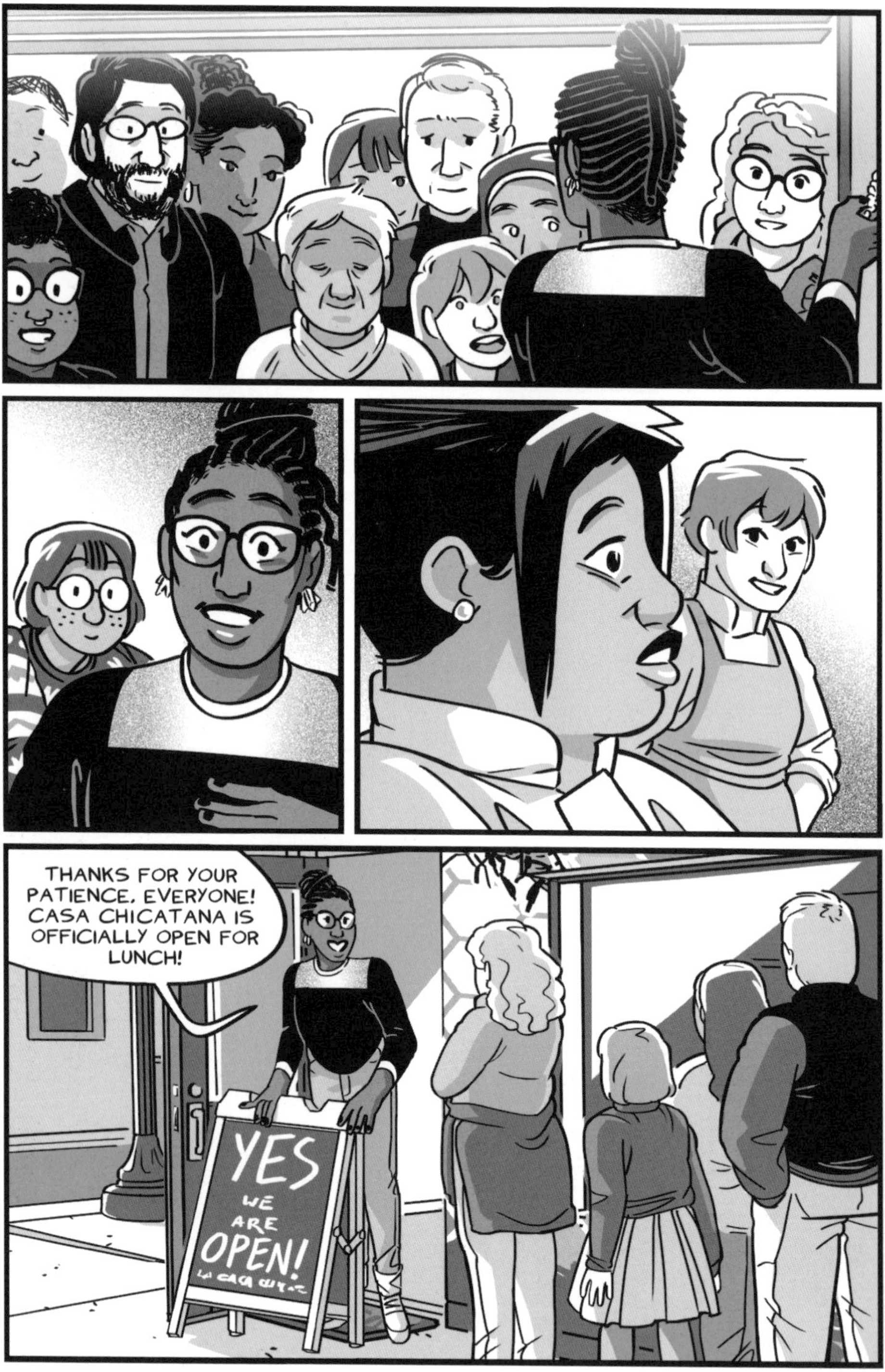
THANKS FOR YOUR PATIENCE, EVERYONE! CASA CHICATANA IS OFFICIALLY OPEN FOR LUNCH!
YES WE ARE OPEN!

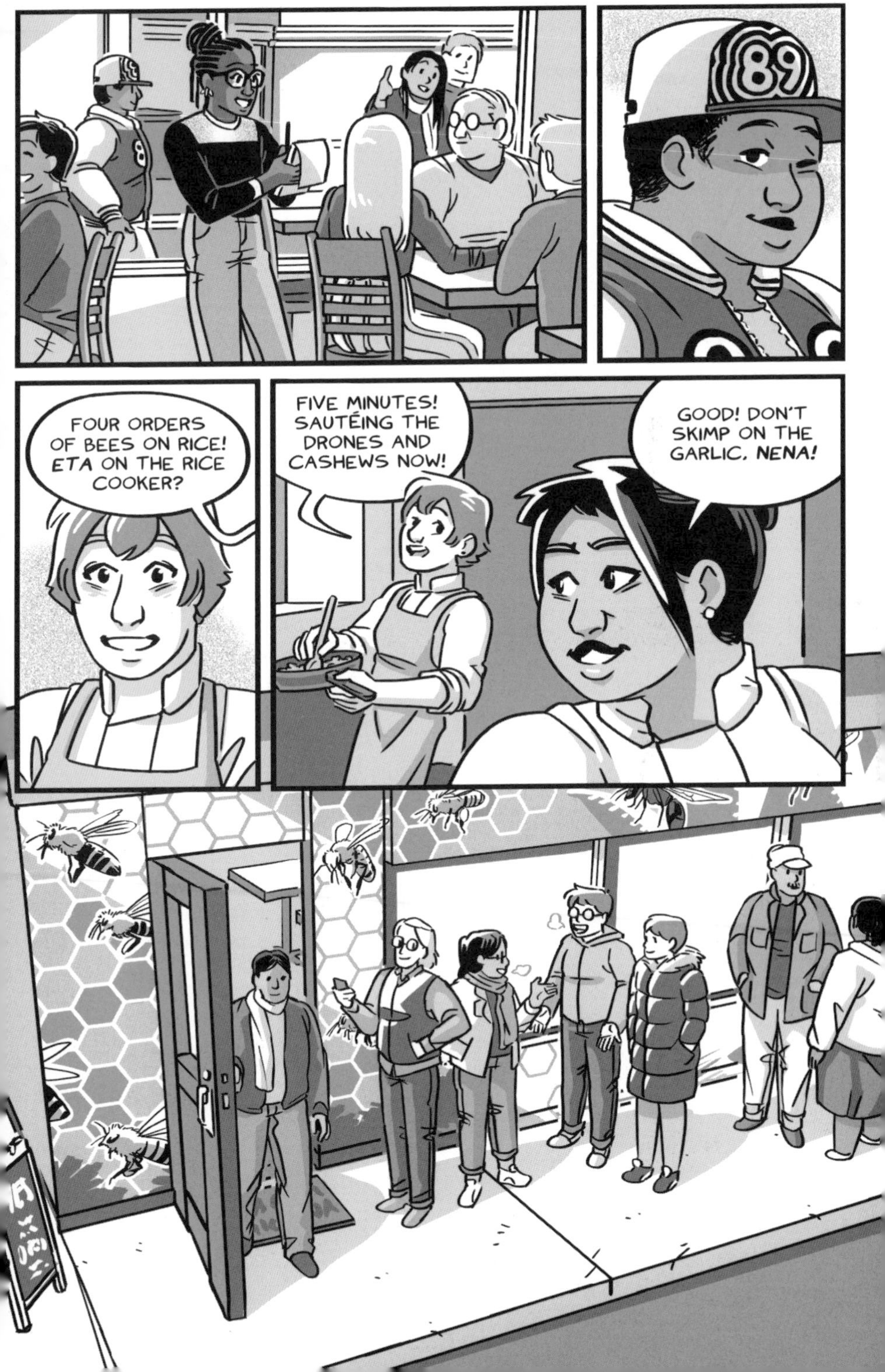
89
FOUR ORDERS OF BEES ON RICE! ETA ON THE RICE COOKER?
FIVE MINUTES! SAUTÉING THE DRONES AND CASHEWS NOW!
GOOD! DON'T SKIMP ON THE GARLIC, **NENA!**

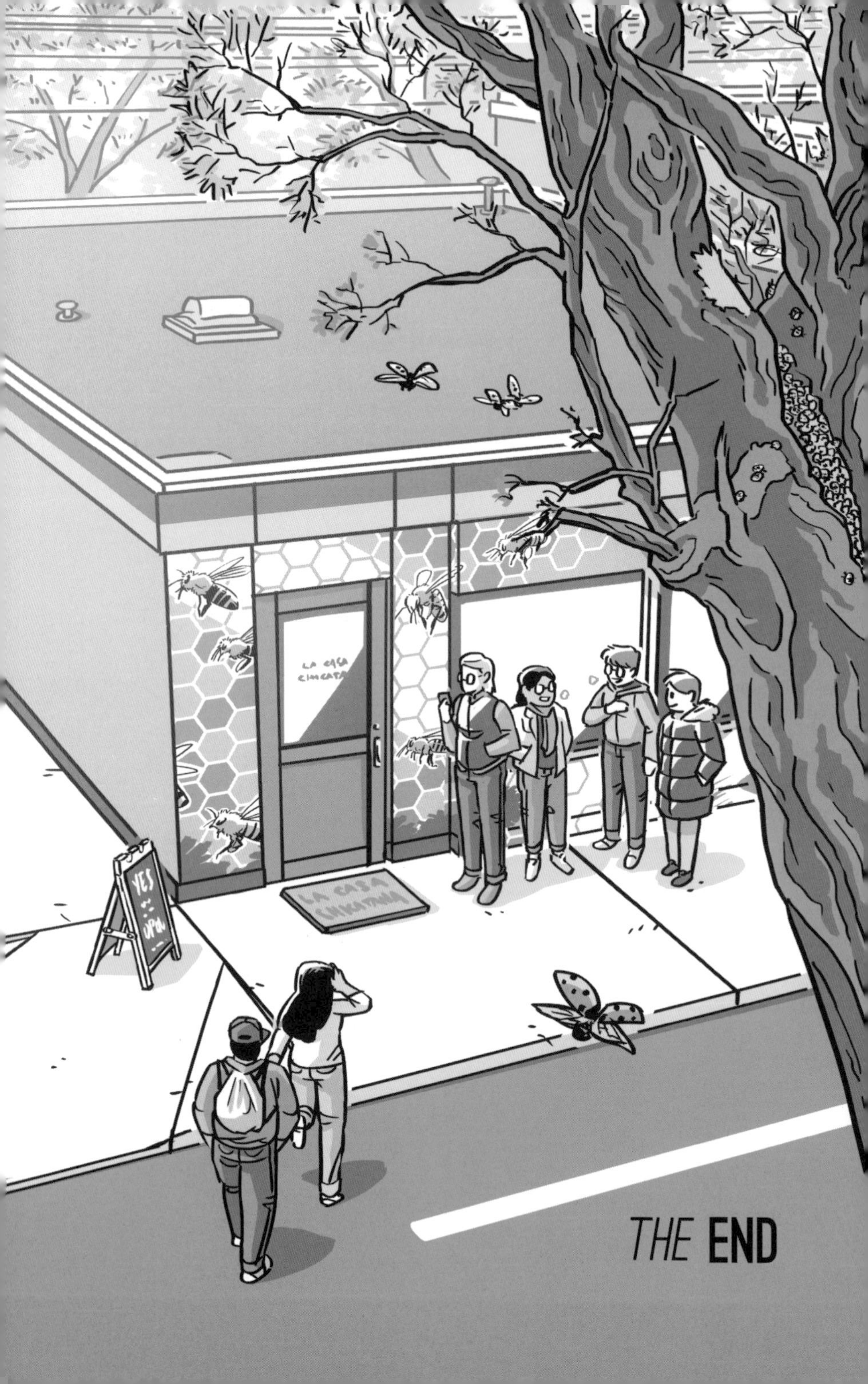
LA CASA CHICATANA
YES OPEN
THE END

HOW CAN I DESCRIBE THE TASTE OF CHICATANAS?

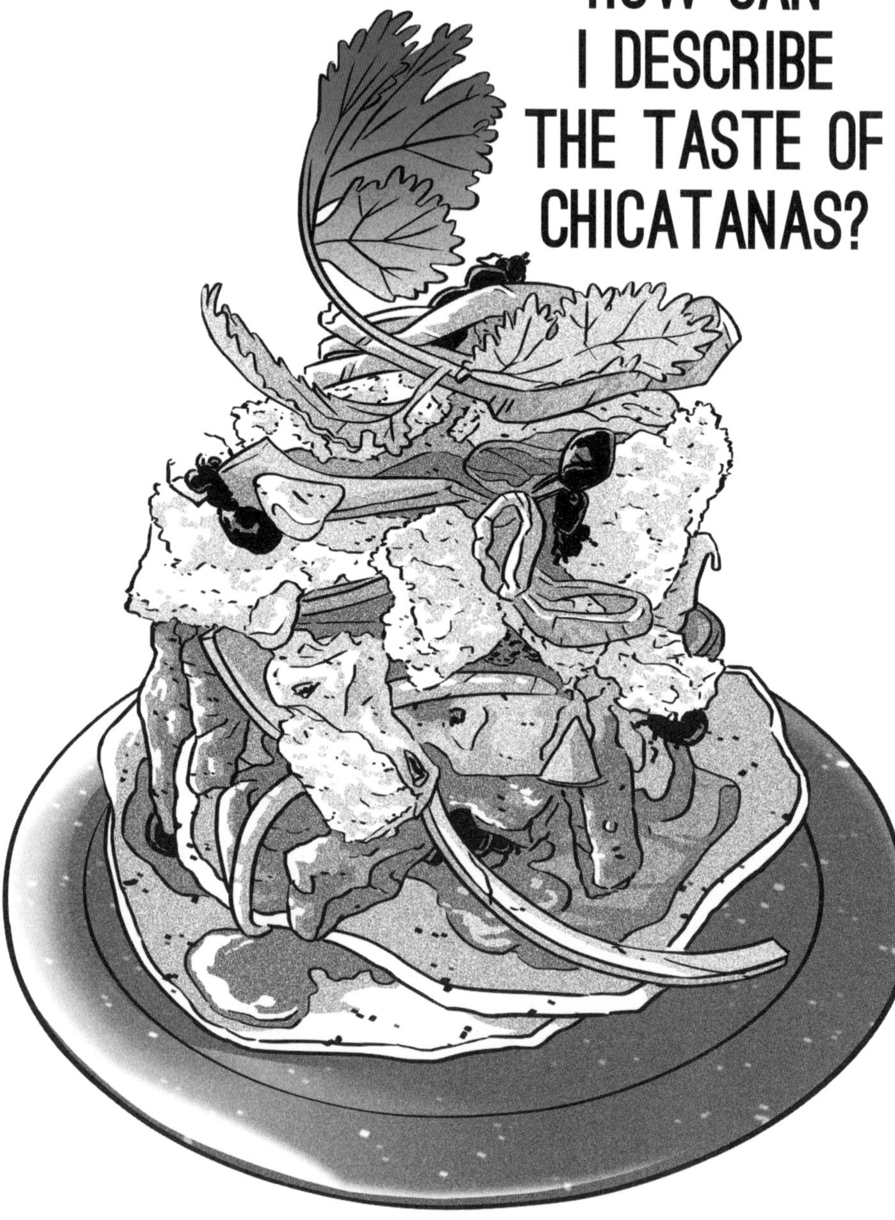

AN ESSAY BY SOLEIL HO

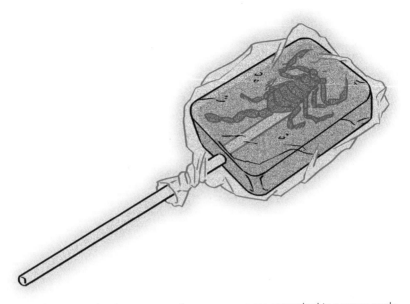

My first taste of insect — that I was aware of, anyway — came entombed in a green apple lollipop that I got during a museum field trip. The tiny brown dune scorpion inside had its claws stretched outward, looking almost as if it had been caught in the middle of doing the wave. It's just like a crab, my teacher told me. I took my first tentative licks on the way out to the parking lot while silently wishing I'd gotten the freeze-dried astronaut ice cream instead. I didn't want to lose face to my classmates who grinned and stared, wide-eyed. When I pushed past the green apple sourness and arrived at the scorpion after what felt like hours, I took a small bite of claw. Bitter. Mealy. *Buggy.* I frowned and quietly slipped the rest out of the bus window. For a long time, I associated insect cuisine with that experience at the museum: kind of a freak show.

Today, fans of insect cuisine in the United States can munch on mealworm protein shakes, sour cream and onion crickets, and chocolate-covered ants, mainly sold in high-end natural food stores or online retailers. In 2013, the United Nations' Food and Agriculture Organization (FAO) released *Edible insects: future prospects for food and feed security*, a paper whose findings on insects' nutritional benefits, environmental impact, and potential for addressing impending worldwide food shortages are now cited frequently by Western insect cuisine evangelists and entrepreneurs. Insects, many say, are the future of food, and there's a vast sum of money being invested in turning that possibility into a reality. But for whom? Many of the vendors are Silicon Valley-esque startups selling their cricket flour in sleek, minimalist packaging from websites packed full of statistics on feed-to-yield ratios and photos of smiling white people. Adding fuel to the flames is a recent Research and Markets report that has projected that the insect agriculture business will generate more than a billion US dollars in revenue by 2022. The future is coming, and fast.

But as I read and talked to people more about this version of the future, my mind kept going back to that lollipop. Reducing insect cuisine to a spectacle, to a reaction to climate change or industrialized food production, erases the fact that it's been a meaningful part of many cultures throughout the world. In fact, it's more likely that the people who *don't* eat insects — mainly those in Western Europe and countries in the Anglosphere like the United States —

are the weirdos. So when we talk about insects being the "future" of food, we're also talking about other people's past and present: it's only the future for us because we chose to ignore and belittle what was right in front of us all along.

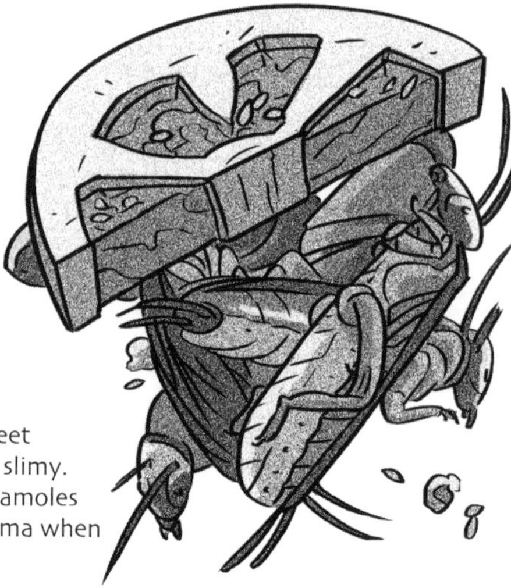

"Growing up in the Philippines, eating bugs was just a normal thing," chef Yana Gilbuena told me. Her family eats kamaru, also known as rice field crickets, simmered in soy and vinegar: "They just tasted like any other adobo!" They also enjoy tamilok, or shipworm, a rare ingredient only available after the local mangroves flood. "The worms have almost a sweet note; they're slimy, but the good, oyster kind of slimy. So when I was in Mexico, the chapulines and escamoles didn't faze me." She paused. "Why is there a stigma when eating insects is so wonderful?"

In an interview with the Nordic Food Lab, Mexican chef Enrique Olvera remarked, "Insects are often only the ones we don't eat — when they are delicious, we instead say they are 'delicacies.'" So what are we actually talking about when we discuss "insect cuisine"? Insects, the members of the taxonomic class Insecta, represent between six to thirty million unique species. To further complicate matters, we often include centipedes, spiders, and scorpions in these discussions: they're technically not insects, though they do hang out in the same phylum, Arthropoda, along with their crustacean cousins. To people who eat insects and the insect-adjacent, saying that they, well, eat "insects" is as strange as saying that one eats "animals." Like, sure, but which ones are you talking about? Just like anyone else, people who eat chapulines, hissing cockroaches, tarantulas, and water scorpions make strong mental distinctions between what's edible and what's not.

When asked if she thought crawfish were bugs, my friend Laura McKnight, a Louisiana native, had to mull it over a bit. "They're definitely kind of insect-*like*. I know sometimes we call them 'mudbugs,' but I really don't think of them that way." She still remembers the reactions her Texan cousins had to their first crawfish boil: "They were too grossed out to eat the crawfish! I wasn't offended, but I thought, 'Wow, that's really strange.' But I guess it's like, some people don't like chocolate, and some people don't like crawfish." It must have been quite a shock to the cousins to see their relatives — people they thought they *knew* — gorging on plastic trays of the "bugs," ripping their bodies in half, and wiggling fingers capped with the decapitated heads. What tends to put a lot of people off from crawfish is the head thing: even Laura stays away from them, though she loves the rest of it. But part of the appeal of eating crawfish lies in sucking on the head after you sever it from its tail, tasting the way the boil's aromatics and spices mingle with the richness of the animal's hepatopancreas, which many mistake as the "brains": also known euphemistically as "crawfish butter."

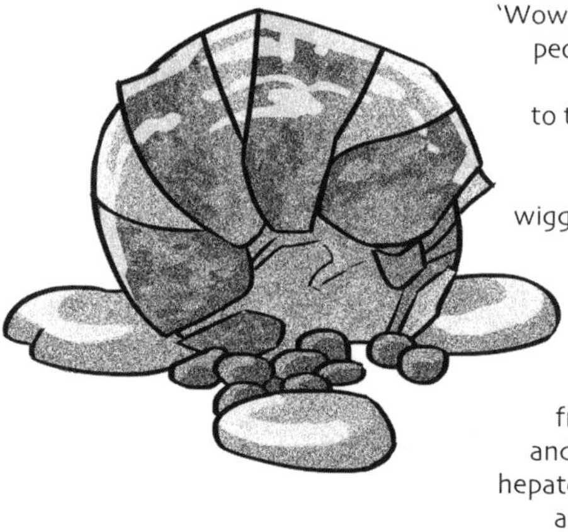

By contrast, that sense of viscerality doesn't really exist in fine dining: a lobster dish that I had at a Michelin-starred restaurant came simply with the tail, poached in butter and curled elegantly over a mound of English peas. It looked less like an animal and more like a piece of glazed ceramic. "In American restaurant culture, we're all about eating without seeing," Karla Calderon, the producer of the Brooklyn Bugs Festival, told me over the phone. "We don't want to see it. Seeing everything full-on, as we do with insects, bugs people out. Like what is chicken breast? It's a literal blob of meat." It's harder to maintain that level of distance with insects, though it does seem like the rush to create and sell bug products without the "bugginess" comes from the same psychological sense of repulsion as Westerners' preference for plastic-wrapped animal parts.

During a dinner that took place at the Brooklyn Bugs Festival, chef/event director Joseph Yoon served a dish of cellophane noodles and vegetables topped with a whole intact water scorpion, which diners were encouraged to fillet themselves. In the age of mechanically separated chicken, isn't it more subversive, more honest to look what you're eating in the eyes? You don't have to butcher bee larvae: just put the entire body in your mouth and feel it burst between your teeth.

I recently went to a small tostadería where I ate a tostada piled high with marinated raw tuna, pickled onions, and fried pork skin, all garnished with toasted chicatanas as well as a chile mayonnaise blended with the ants. The chef, named Adrian Avila, came over before I ordered to show me a sample of the half-inch-long insects, which were clumped together inside of a tiny blue mug. He got them directly from his family in El Tule, Jalisco: they set up bus tubs of water in the town square during the two days in July when chicatanas come out of their nests. The ants, attracted by the light reflected in the water, drown themselves en masse, after which Avila's friends and family gather them up and freeze them so they can enjoy them for the rest of the year. Before the advent of freezer technology, he told me, they would bury them in containers as deep underground as possible, similarly to how Korean people would traditionally store kimchi.

But how can I describe the taste of chicatanas? It was like the sound of dead leaves crunching underfoot, the smell of an over-fried tortilla chip, and the sensation of eating unseasoned popcorn all rolled into a single bite. When eaten in combination with the other ingredients on the plate, they added a subtle earthiness to the dish that made me think of the smell of a freshly doused campfire. It was a singular, exceptional taste that I had never encountered before, and I think a major part of the experience was viewing the ants in their wholeness and knowing exactly what they meant.

Over a dinner of chapuline tacos at El Arrayán in downtown Puerto Vallarta, I asked Carmen Porras, who owns the restaurant with her wife, Claudia Victoria, what made them want to serve grasshoppers. This was early on in the course of my research into insect cuisine, and my head was already swimming with numbers pertaining to insects' food and water imprints and nutritional profiles. She thought for a while and laughed. "Well… they're delicious, aren't they?" I nodded silently, threw more salsa on my tacos, and kept eating.

MEALWORM CURRY

TOASTY AND COMFORTABLE

2 cups rice
1 tbsp butter
1/2 tsp ginger, peeled & grated
1/2 tsp turmeric powder
1/4 tsp ground coriander
1/4 tsp cardamon
1/4 tsp cayenne pepper
1/2 sliced onion
1 medium zucchini
2 carrots
1 sweet potato
1 tomato
1 cup coconut milk
1 cup water
salt and pepper to taste
1 tbsp mealworms, fresh or frozen

HERE'S MY FIRST RECIPE! YOU CAN REPLACE THE BUGS WITH ANY PROTEIN, REALLY, BUT THIS IS A GOOD PLACE TO TALK ABOUT RAISING, STORING, AND PREPARING THE MEALWORMS THEMSELVES!

-YARROW

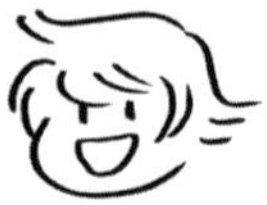

COOK INSECTS LIKE YOU WOULD OTHER MEATS! IT'S ALWAYS SAFEST TO TOAST, BAKE, OR SAUTÉE RAW ANIMAL PROTEIN, EVEN FROM ANIMALS YOU RAISE YOURSELF!

1. Prepare rice in a pot or rice cooker. Preheat oven to 350 degrees F. In medium sized pot on medium-high heat, melt butter and sauté ginger, garlic, and spices until it smells nutty and fragrant.

2. Slice and dice onion, zucchini, carrots, sweet potato, and tomato. Add the onion and potato to the pot, cook until half-tender, then add carrots, zucchini, and tomato.

3. Add coconut milk and water to the pot, reducing heat to medium-low for 6 to 8 minutes until vegetables are tender. Add salt or pepper as desired.

4. Spread parchment paper on a baking sheet and spread out mealworms. Toast in the oven for 5 minutes, keeping an eye on them so they don't burn. Remove and let cool.

5. Ladle curry onto rice and sprinkle mealworms on top.

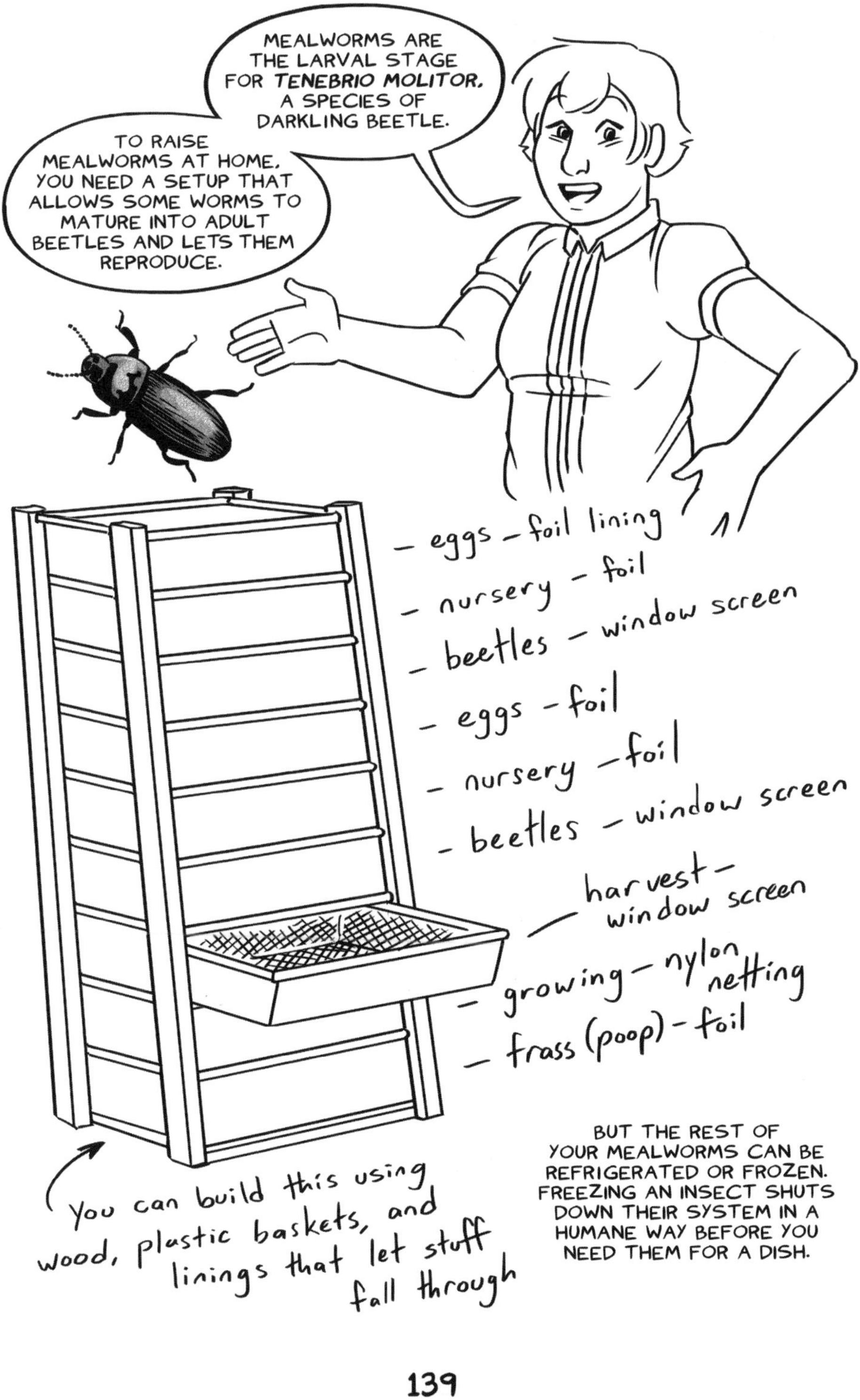
MEALWORMS ARE THE LARVAL STAGE FOR *TENEBRIO MOLITOR*, A SPECIES OF DARKLING BEETLE.
TO RAISE MEALWORMS AT HOME, YOU NEED A SETUP THAT ALLOWS SOME WORMS TO MATURE INTO ADULT BEETLES AND LETS THEM REPRODUCE.
eggs – foil lining
nursery – foil
beetles – window screen
eggs – foil
nursery – foil
beetles – window screen
harvest – window screen
growing – nylon netting
frass (poop) – foil
You can build this using wood, plastic baskets, and linings that let stuff fall through
BUT THE REST OF YOUR MEALWORMS CAN BE REFRIGERATED OR FROZEN. FREEZING AN INSECT SHUTS DOWN THEIR SYSTEM IN A HUMANE WAY BEFORE YOU NEED THEM FOR A DISH.

TACOS DE CHAPULINES

FLAVORFUL AND FILLING

1 onion
1 tomato
2 cloves garlic
1 serrano chile
1/4 cup olive oil
9 ounces of grasshoppers, fresh or frozen
fresh cilantro, chopped, to taste
1 avocado
1/4 cup lime juice
salt, to taste
optional: a splash of tequila (GROWN FOLKS ONLY)
4 corn tortillas

DID YARROW WRITE THIS? GO WILD WITH THE GARLIC. YOU CAN NEVER HAVE ENOUGH GARLIC.

-SOLEDAD

1. Peel and chop the onion. Cut the tomato into cubes and mince the garlic. Slice the serrano chile in half, remove the seeds, and finely chop the remainder. Wear gloves while preparing the chile, or you'll feel the heat on your hand long after cooking's over.

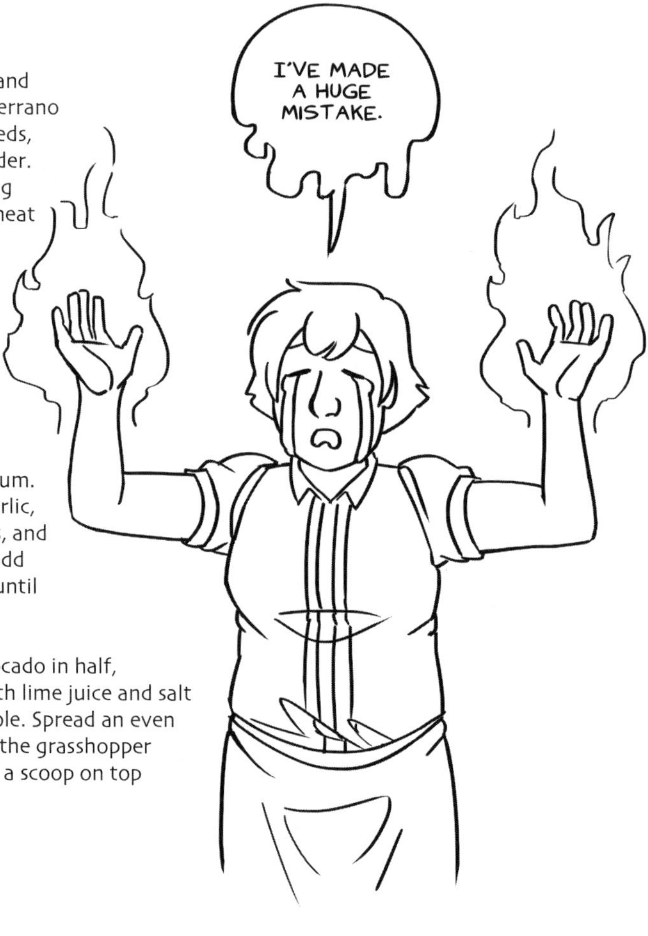
I'VE MADE A HUGE MISTAKE.

2. In a pan, heat oil to medium. Add the onion, then the garlic, tomato, chile, grasshoppers, and cilantro. If you're using it, add tequila here as well. Sauté until onions are golden brown.

3. Meanwhile, chop the avocado in half, remove the pit, and mix with lime juice and salt to make a smooth guacamole. Spread an even layer on the tortillas. Once the grasshopper mix is done cooking, dollop a scoop on top of the guacamole.

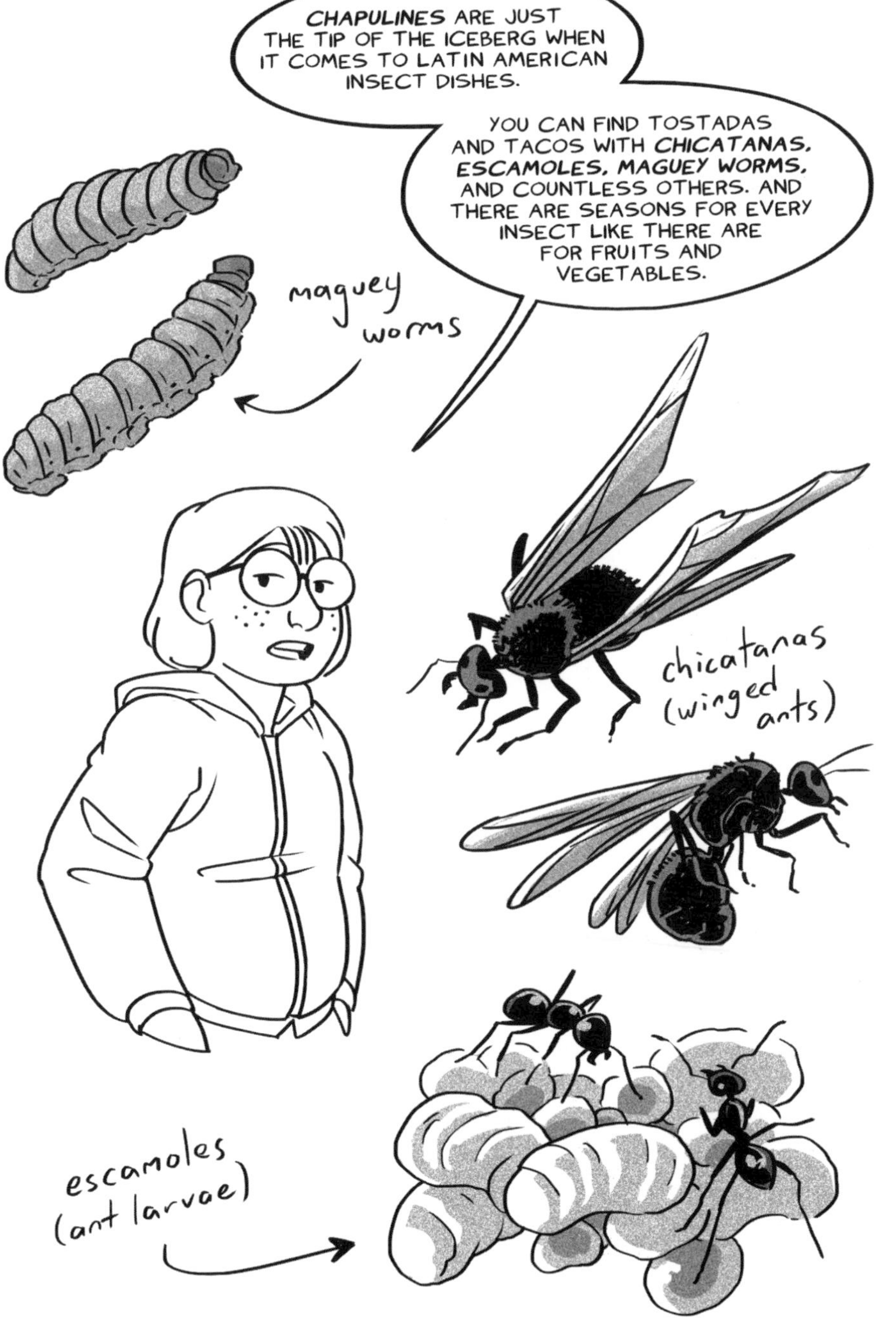
CHAPULINES ARE JUST THE TIP OF THE ICEBERG WHEN IT COMES TO LATIN AMERICAN INSECT DISHES.
YOU CAN FIND TOSTADAS AND TACOS WITH CHICATANAS, ESCAMOLES, MAGUEY WORMS, AND COUNTLESS OTHERS. AND THERE ARE SEASONS FOR EVERY INSECT LIKE THERE ARE FOR FRUITS AND VEGETABLES.
maguey worms
chicatanas (winged ants)
escamoles (ant larvae)

PAN-FRIED TARANTULA ROLL
SMOKEY AND SEAFOODY

FILLING

4 Texas brown or Chilean rose tarantulas, frozen and thawed.
1 cup all-purpose flour
1 cup panko bread crumbs
3 eggs
1 tsp salt
1 tsp black pepper
1/2 tsp cayenne
1 cup vegetable oil

BUNS

3 cups all-purpose flour
1 1/2 tsp yeast
2 tbsp sugar
1 tbsp vegetable oil
1 cup hot water

THESE SPIDERS,
APHONOPELMA HENTZI AND
GRAMMOSTOLA ROSEA,
ARE NEW WORLD TARANTULAS.
THERE ARE SIGNIFICANT
DIFFERENCES IN THEIR BEHAVIOR
AND APPEARANCE FROM THE
OLD WORLD TARANTULAS
USED IN TRADITIONAL
CAMBODIAN A-PING.

— *Chanda*

FILLING

1. With a sharp knife, cut off the tarantula's abdomens, remove the fangs from the head the best you can, and discard. The abdomen's contents are more of an acquired taste, so if you're just starting to experiment with recipes, try it without first. Singe off the body hairs using a lighter or crème brûlée torch.

2. Combine the flour and spices in one pan, beat the eggs in a second pan, and pour the panko crumbs into a third pan.

3. Dredge the tarantulas one at a time in the flour mixture, then the egg, then coat with the panko. Let them rest for at least 10 minutes so the breading sets.

4. Meanwhile, heat the vegetable oil medium-high in a frying pan. Once hot, use tongs or a spatula to carefully add the tarantulas, frying for no more than 30 seconds on each side. Remove with a slotted spoon and lay on a plate lined with paper towels.

BUNS

1. Mix the flour, yeast, sugar, oil, and hot water in a bowl until it becomes dough. Knead the dough on a clean surface for about 8 to 10 minutes. Let rise in a bowl covered with a towel until it doubles in size (about 1 hour).

2. Roll the enlarged dough and divide into 10 equal pieces, rolling each piece into a ball. Let these rest for 10 more minutes, then flatten each ball into a 5 inch circle.

3. Gently fold the circles in half, and let rise again for 15 minutes, letting them sit on small squares of parchment paper. Place the buns in a steamer and steam for 8 minutes.

Stuff the buns with the tarantula pieces as well as any other desired toppings, like chopped green onions or pickled vegetables.

THAI ZEBRA TARANTULA
(Cyriopagopus albostriatus)

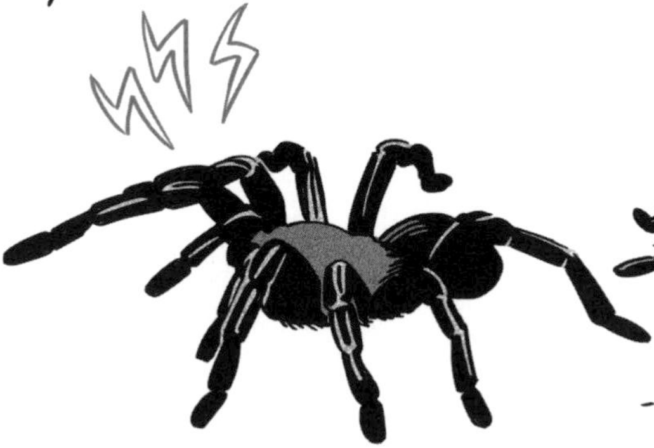

- found in Cambodia, Thailand, and Myanmar
- no urticating (stinging) hairs
- very skittish, will bite to defend itself

TEXAS BROWN TARANTULA
(Aphonopelma hentzi)

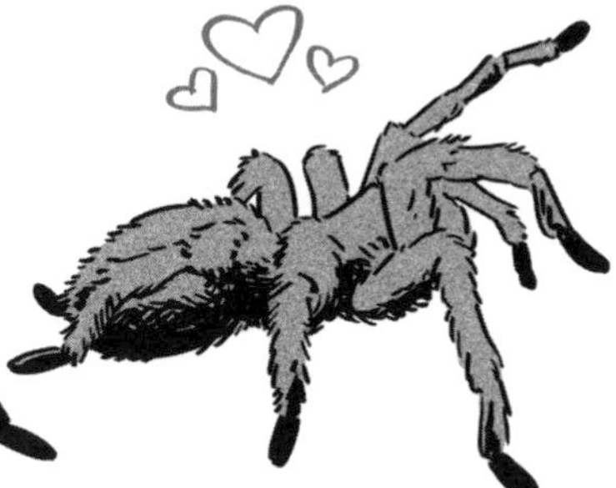

- found in southern United States
- urticating hairs used as defense
- docile, common pet species

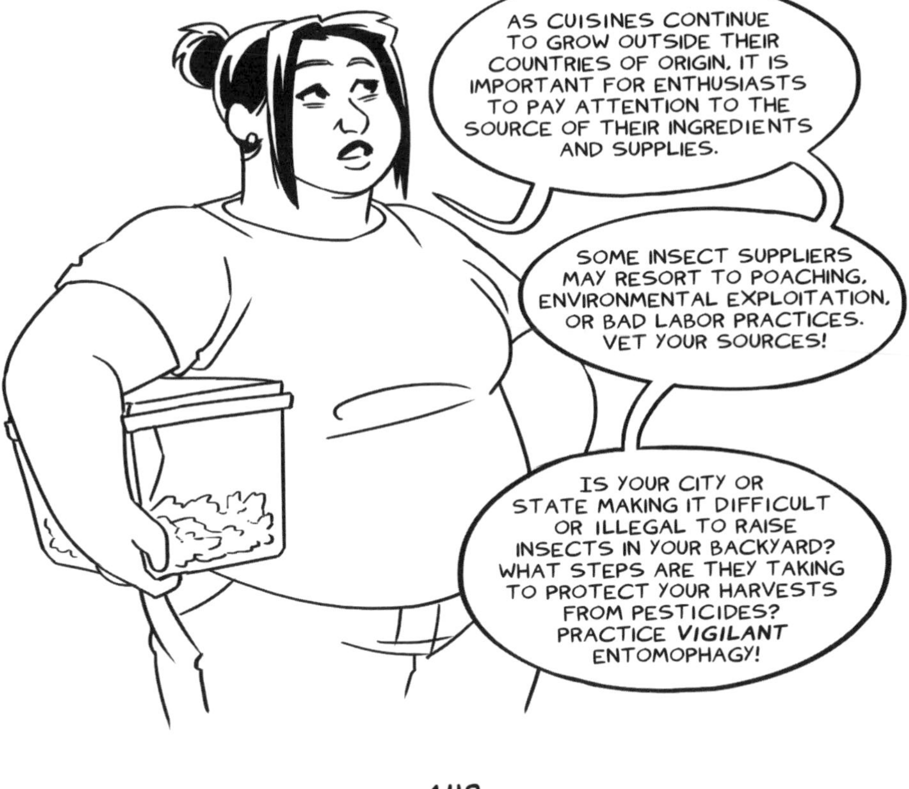
AS CUISINES CONTINUE TO GROW OUTSIDE THEIR COUNTRIES OF ORIGIN, IT IS IMPORTANT FOR ENTHUSIASTS TO PAY ATTENTION TO THE SOURCE OF THEIR INGREDIENTS AND SUPPLIES.
SOME INSECT SUPPLIERS MAY RESORT TO POACHING, ENVIRONMENTAL EXPLOITATION, OR BAD LABOR PRACTICES. VET YOUR SOURCES!
IS YOUR CITY OR STATE MAKING IT DIFFICULT OR ILLEGAL TO RAISE INSECTS IN YOUR BACKYARD? WHAT STEPS ARE THEY TAKING TO PROTECT YOUR HARVESTS FROM PESTICIDES? PRACTICE **VIGILANT** ENTOMOPHAGY!

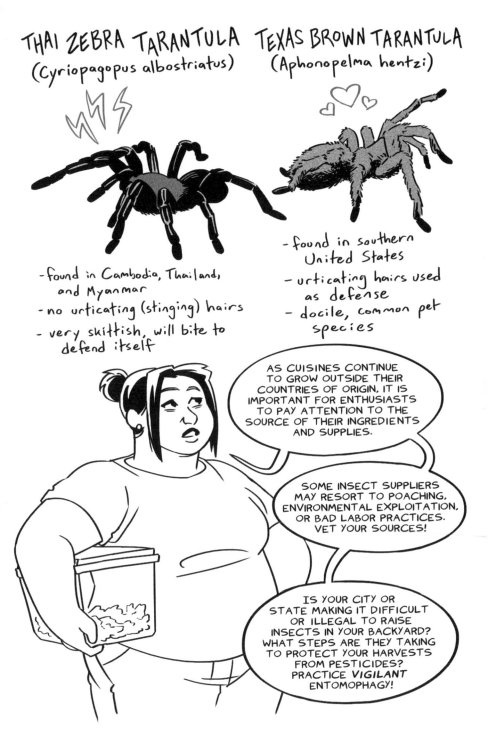

BEE LARVAE HONEY DROPS

SWEET AND FRUITY

FILLING
12 - 18 drone bee larvae, frozen and thawed
1 tsp butter
1 tsp sugar
fruit slices, in season
optional: edible flowers like pansies or violets

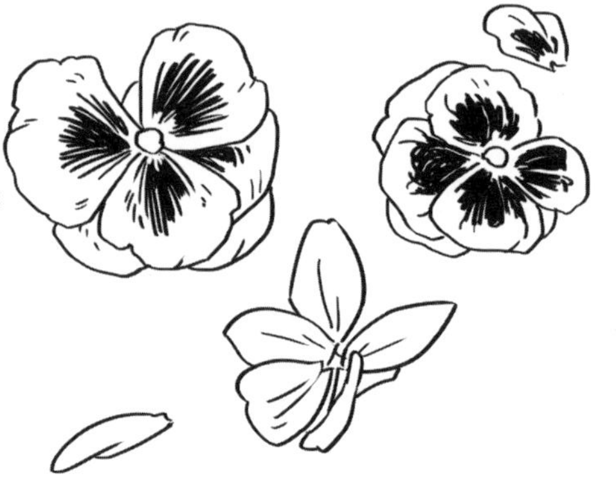

DROPS
4 cups water
4 tsp sugar
3 tsp agar agar
yellow and red food coloring
honey or kuromitsu (brown sugar syrup)
optional: kinako (roasted soybean powder)

A VEGETARIAN SUBSTITUTE FOR GELATIN

I LOVE THIS RECIPE! IT'S INSPIRED BY A JAPANESE TREAT CALLED ***MIZU SHINGEN MOCHI,*** AKA "WATER DROP CAKE." THIS USES THE SAME INGREDIENTS YOU FIND IN THE TRADITIONAL DESSERT, BUT ADDS FRUIT AND LARVAE.

♡ Sat

FILLING

1. Melt the butter in a skillet on medium heat and add the larvae.

2. Add sugar a pinch at a time and sautée until the larvae start to brown and become firmer, approximately 10 minutes. Remove skillet from heat and set larvae aside on a small plate.

DROPS

1. Pour agar and sugar into a small pot. Pour water in 2 to 3 parts and whisk gently until there are no clumps of sugar or agar powder. Bring to a boil and simmer for 2 to 3 minutes while gently mixing.

2. Remove from heat and add the food coloring. To get the mixture golden yellow with this amount, I recommend 1 to 2 drops of yellow to half a drop of red, which you can get by dipping a toothpick or fork tine into the red container.

3. Pour mixture into round molds. Some people use round ice cube molds you can find among bartending supplies - I used flexible silicone cups meant for poaching eggs!

4. Move the molds to the fridge and let set for at least 1 hour. Add the bee larvae and/or flowers before they set, but not too early or they may sink to the bottom of the mold.

5. Remove and serve with the seasonal fruit, honey/kuromitsu, and kinako if you'd like. Eat as soon as possible! The drops will start melting at room temperature after 30 to 45 minutes!

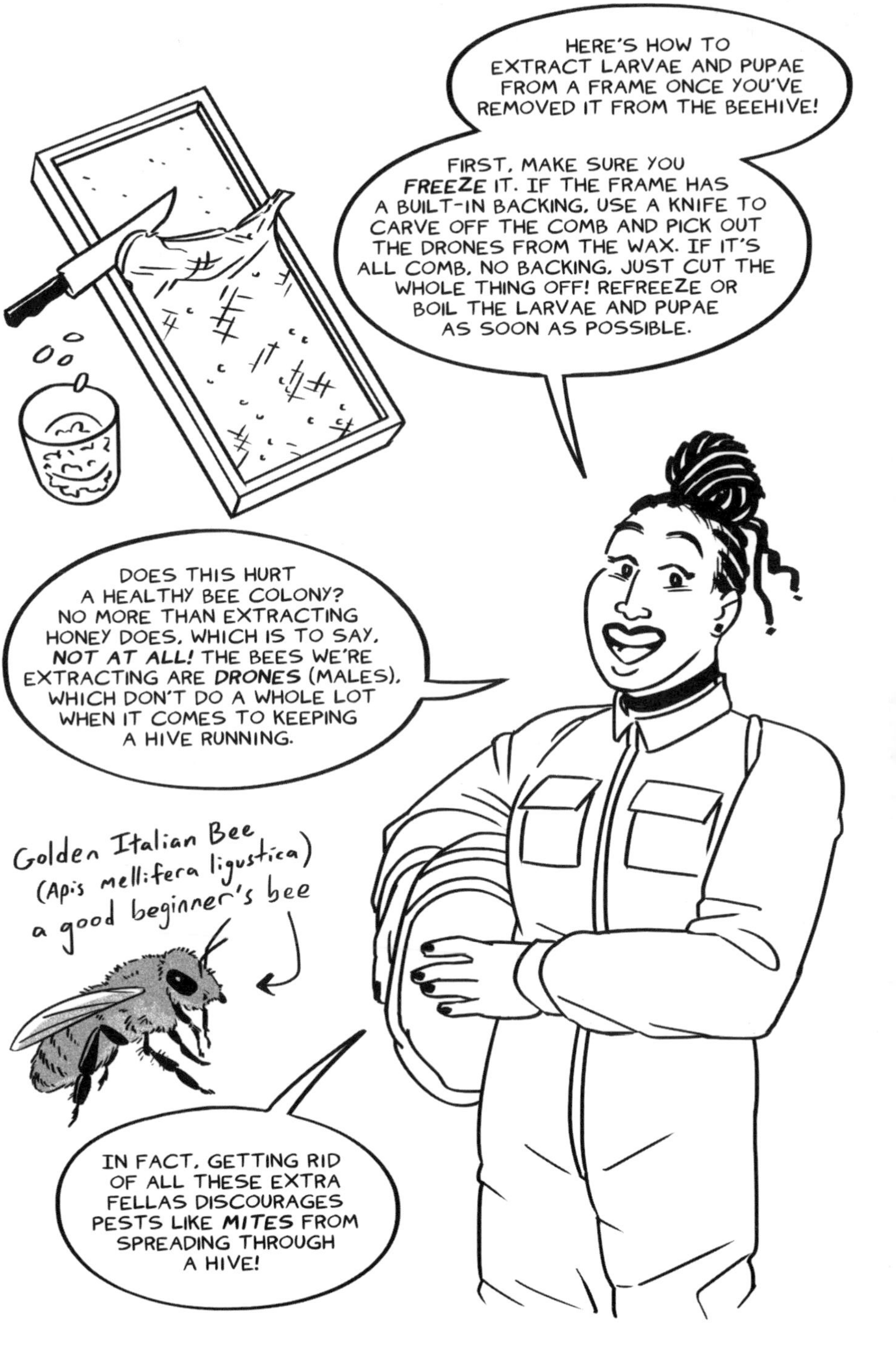
HERE'S HOW TO EXTRACT LARVAE AND PUPAE FROM A FRAME ONCE YOU'VE REMOVED IT FROM THE BEEHIVE!
FIRST, MAKE SURE YOU **FREEZE** IT. IF THE FRAME HAS A BUILT-IN BACKING, USE A KNIFE TO CARVE OFF THE COMB AND PICK OUT THE DRONES FROM THE WAX. IF IT'S ALL COMB, NO BACKING, JUST CUT THE WHOLE THING OFF! REFREEZE OR BOIL THE LARVAE AND PUPAE AS SOON AS POSSIBLE.
DOES THIS HURT A HEALTHY BEE COLONY? NO MORE THAN EXTRACTING HONEY DOES, WHICH IS TO SAY, **NOT AT ALL!** THE BEES WE'RE EXTRACTING ARE **DRONES** (MALES), WHICH DON'T DO A WHOLE LOT WHEN IT COMES TO KEEPING A HIVE RUNNING.
Golden Italian Bee (Apis mellifera ligustica) a good beginner's bee
IN FACT, GETTING RID OF ALL THESE EXTRA FELLAS DISCOURAGES PESTS LIKE **MITES** FROM SPREADING THROUGH A HIVE!

RECIPE NOTES

MAKE THEM YOUR OWN

ACKNOWLEDGEMENTS

FROM BLUE

Thank you to
Kiku Hughes
Wendy Xu
Vanessa Sovanika Na
Chelsea Thomas
Brandon Hinman
Narin Sun
Hanna Kivimäki
Yuya Koike & Brent Millis
Glitch

Suggested books include
Edible by Daniella Martin, 2014
Tacopedia by Déborah Holtz & Juan Carlos Mena, 2015
The Drops of God by Tadashi Agi & Shu Okimoto, 2004
Wakakozake by Chie Shinkyu, 2011

FROM SOLEIL

Thank you to
Karla Calderon
Yana Gilbuena
Jenny Dorsey
Daniela Alexia García
Adrian Avila
Paloma Cupul
Laura McKnight

Suggested books include
Decolonize Your Diet by Luz Calvo & Catrióna Rueda Esquibel, 2015
On Eating Insects by Nordic Food Lab, Joshua Evans, Roberto Flore
& Michael Born Frøst, 2017
The Eat-a-Bug Cookbook by David George Gordon, 2013

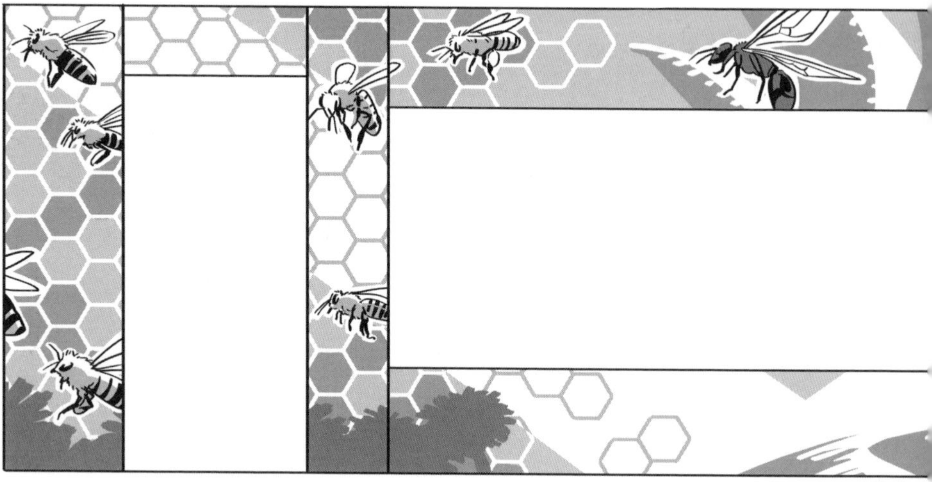

SKETCHES & ART

Pages 148-149:
reference models for La Casa Chicatana's mural and clothing models for six of the main characters.
Pages 150-151:
a fashion sketch, the 3D SketchUp model I created for La Casa Chicatana, and Milani's watercolor in full.

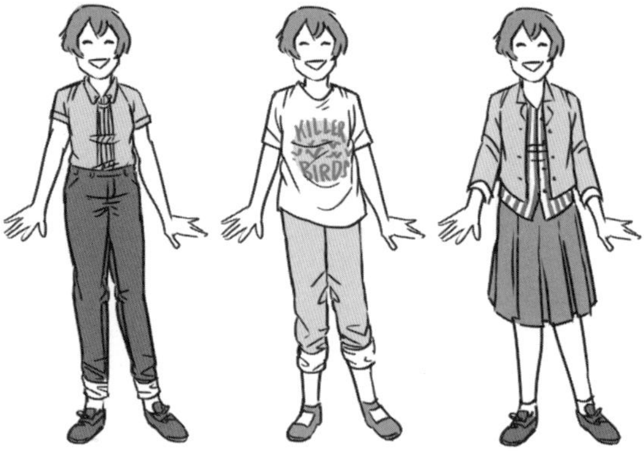
KILLER
BIRDS

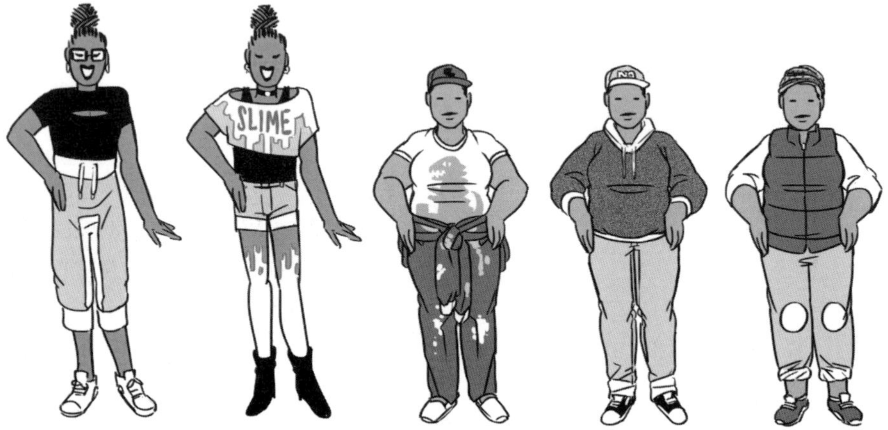
SLIME

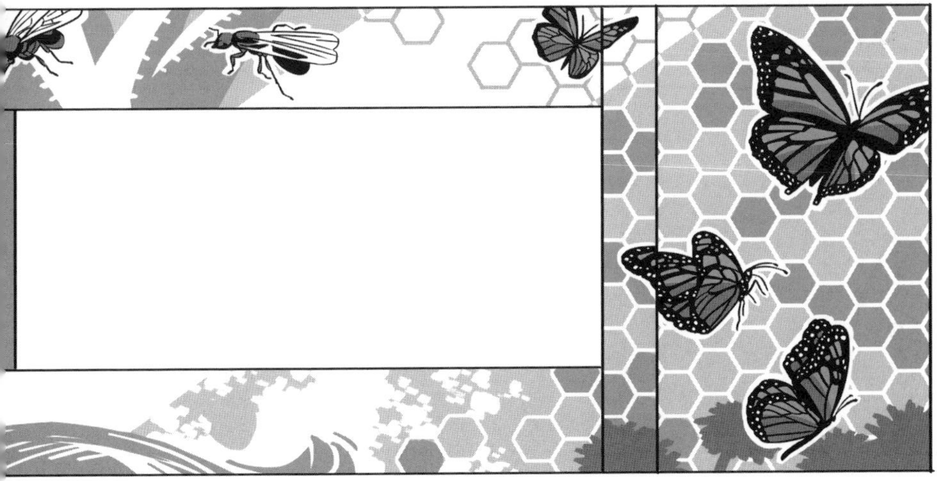

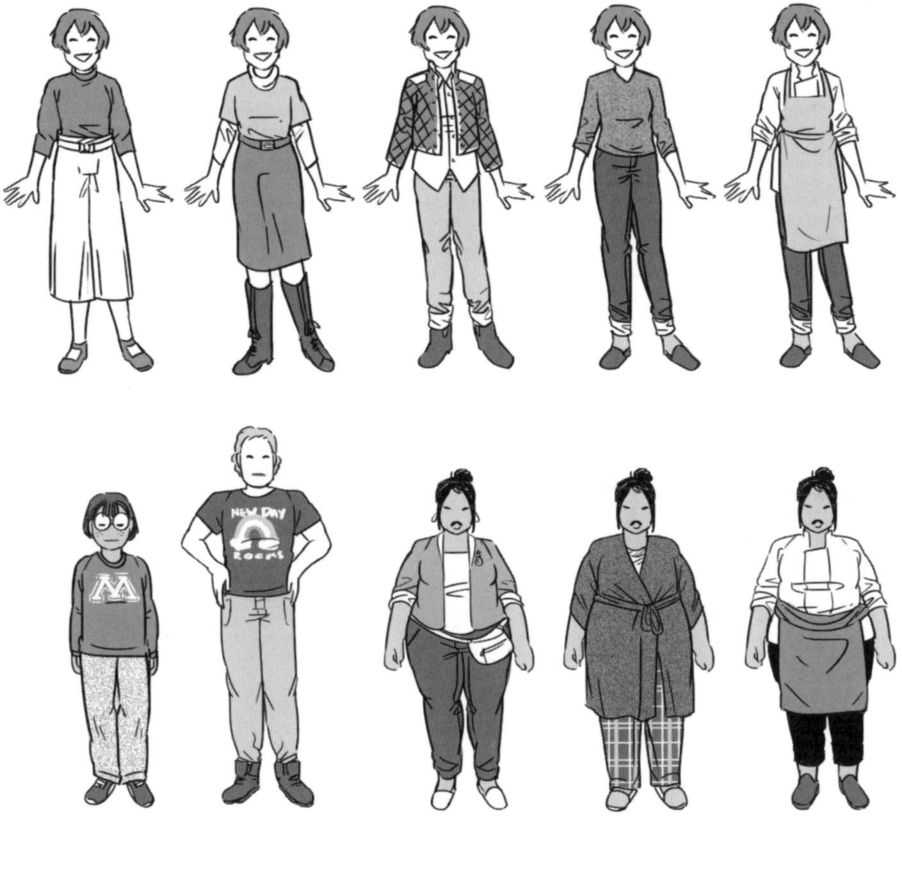
NEW DAY
ROCKS

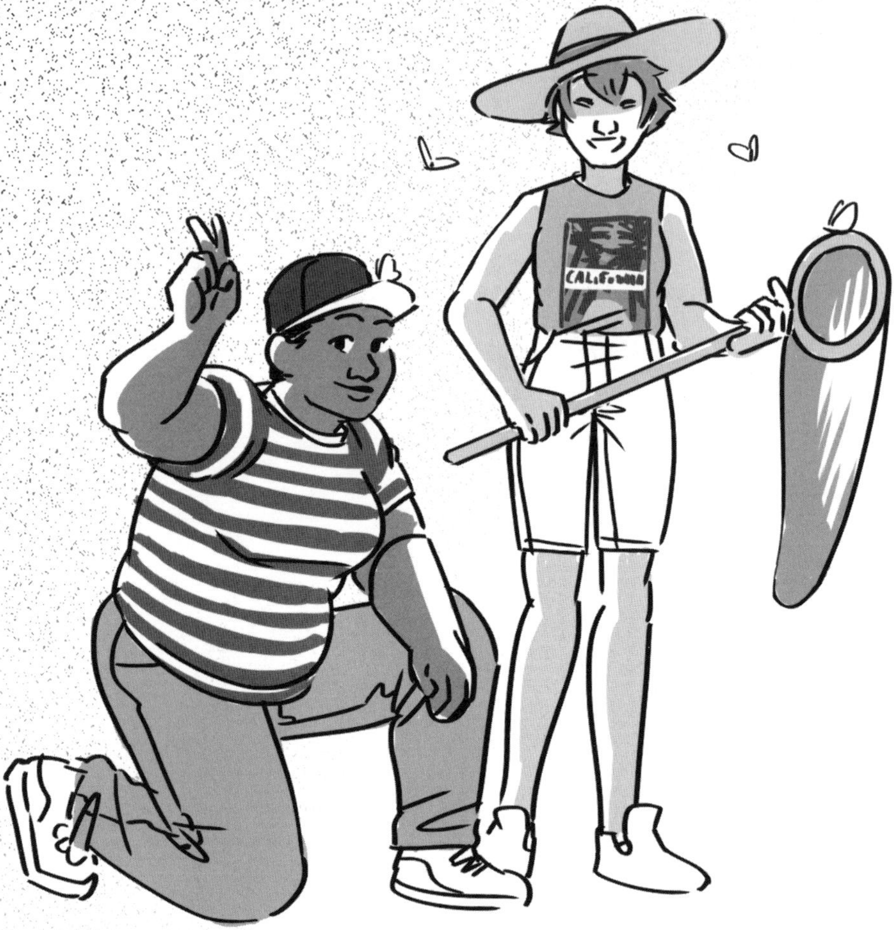

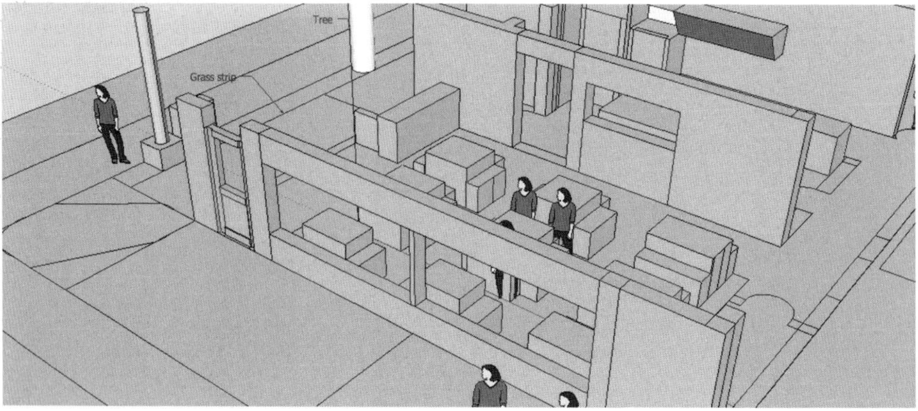
Tree
Grass strip

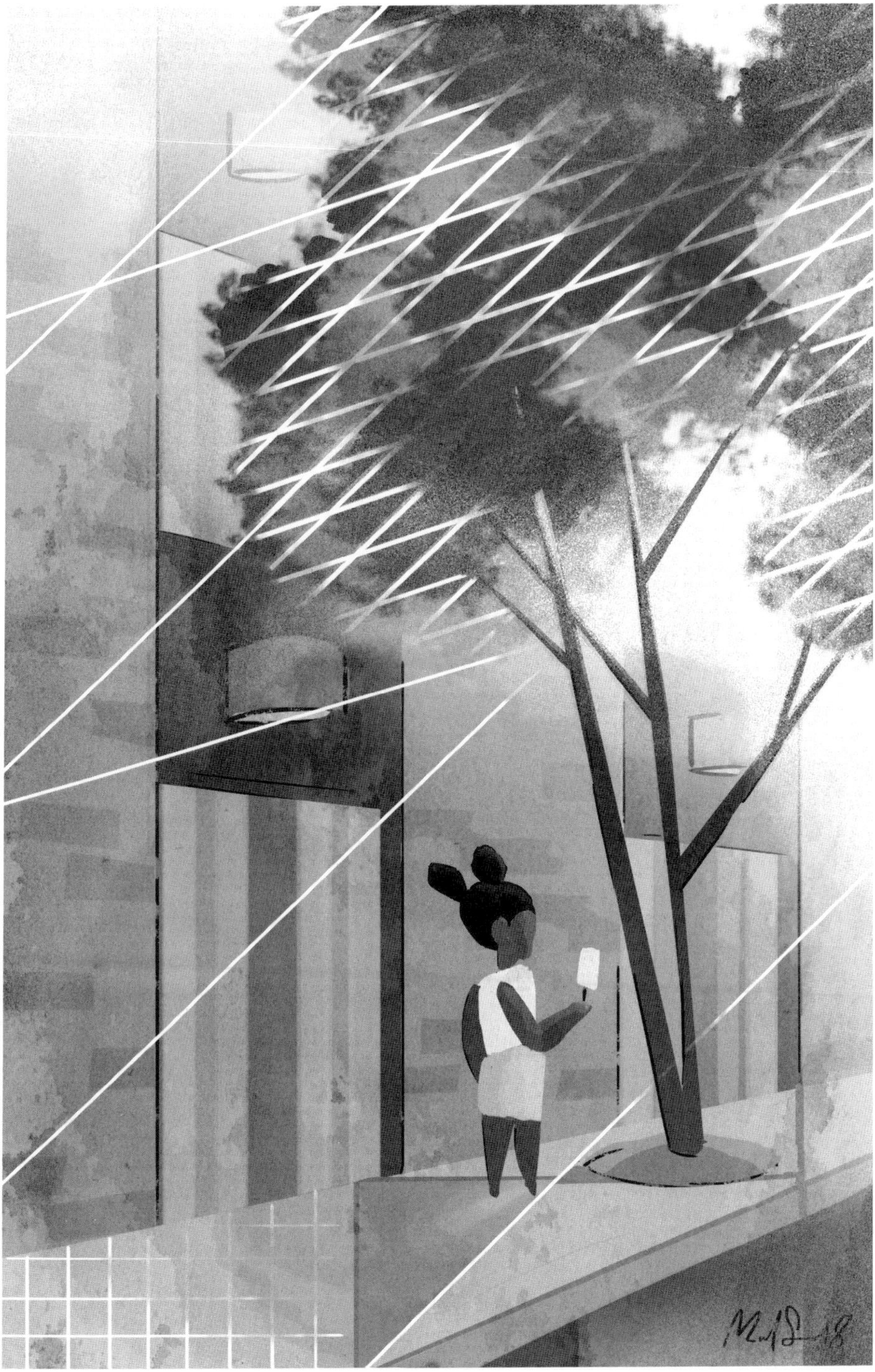

ABOUT THE AUTHORS

BLUE DELLIQUANTI

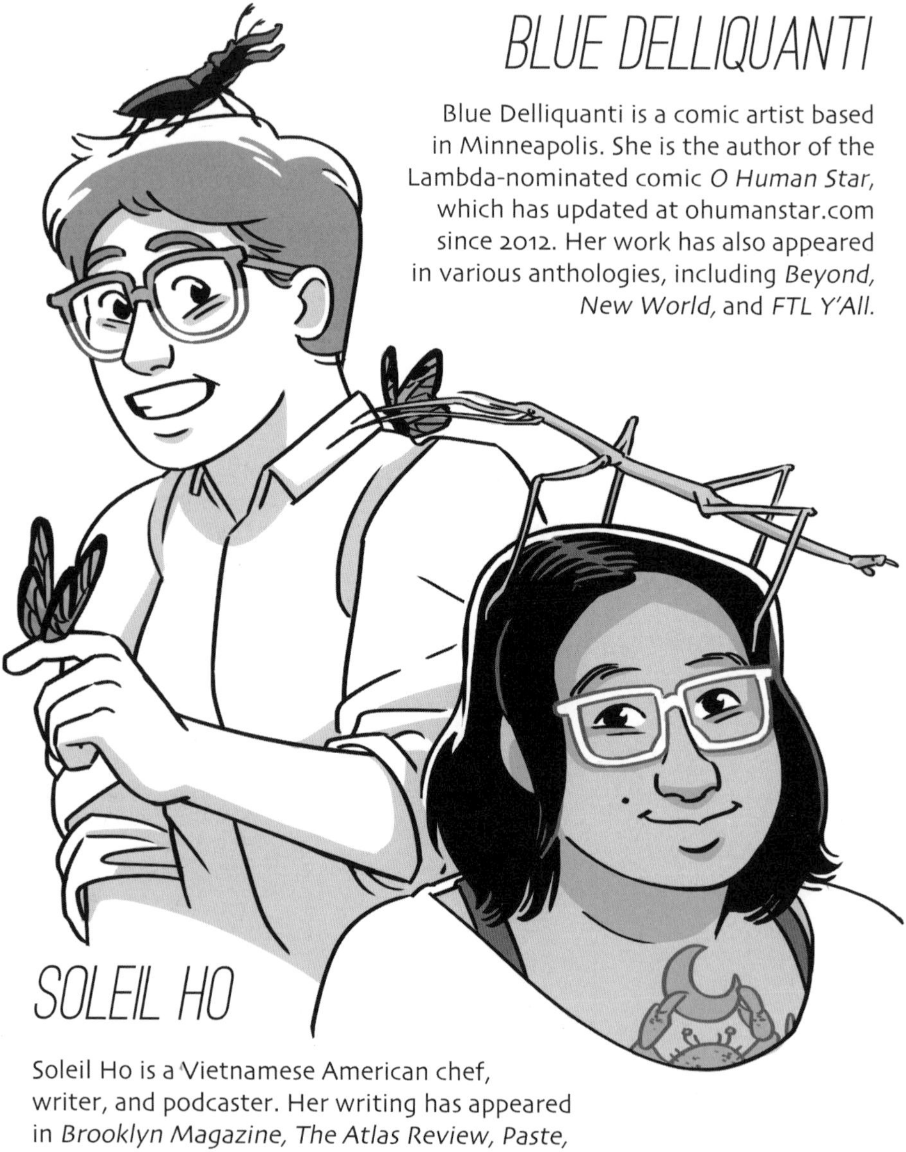

Blue Delliquanti is a comic artist based in Minneapolis. She is the author of the Lambda-nominated comic *O Human Star*, which has updated at ohumanstar.com since 2012. Her work has also appeared in various anthologies, including *Beyond*, *New World*, and *FTL Y'All*.

SOLEIL HO

Soleil Ho is a Vietnamese American chef, writer, and podcaster. Her writing has appeared in *Brooklyn Magazine*, *The Atlas Review*, *Paste*, *On She Goes*, *Edible Manhattan*, *TASTE*, and *Bitch*. She hosts two podcasts: *Bitch Media*'s revered Popaganda podcast and Racist Sandwich, an award-nominated podcast on food and intersectional politics.